GENETICS OF CRIMINAL AND ANTISOCIAL BEHAVIOUR

The Ciba Foundation is an international scientific and educational charity (Registered Charity No. 313574). It was established in 1947 by the Swiss chemical and pharmaceutical company of CIBA Limited—now Ciba-Geigy Limited. The Foundation operates independently in London under English trust law.

The Ciba Foundation exists to promote international cooperation in biological, medical and chemical research. It organizes about eight international multidisciplinary symposia each year on topics that seem ready for discussion by a small group of research workers. The papers and discussions are published in the Ciba Foundation symposium series. The Foundation also holds many shorter meetings (not published), organized by the Foundation itself or by outside scientific organizations. The staff always welcome suggestions for future meetings.

The Foundation's house at 41 Portland Place, London W1N 4BN, provides facilities for meetings of all kinds. Its Media Resource Service supplies information to journalists on all scientific and technological topics. The library, open five days a week to any graduate in science or medicine, also provides information on scientific meetings throughout the world and answers general enquiries on biomedical and chemical subjects. Scientists from any part of the world may stay in the house during working visits to London.

Ciba Foundation Symposium 194

GENETICS OF CRIMINAL AND ANTISOCIAL BEHAVIOUR

1996

JOHN WILEY & SONS

Chichester · New York · Brisbane · Toronto · Singapore

© Ciba Foundation 1996

Published in 1996 by John Wiley & Sons Ltd
Baffins Lane, Chichester
West Sussex PO19 1UD, England

Telephone: National 01243 779777
International (+44) 1243 779777

Reprinted June 1996, October 1996

Other Wiley Editorial Offices

John Wiley & Sons, Inc., 605 Third Avenue,
New York, NY 10158-0012, USA

Jacaranda Wiley Ltd, 33 Park Road, Milton,
Queensland 4064, Australia

John Wiley & Sons (Canada) Ltd, 22 Worcester Road,
Rexdale, Ontario M9W 1L1, Canada

John Wiley & Sons (SEA) Pte Ltd, 37 Jalan Pemimpin #05-04,
Block B, Union Industrial Building, Singapore 2057

Suggested series entry for library catalogues:
Ciba Foundation Symposia

Ciba Foundation Symposium 194
viii+283 pages, 15 figures, 15 tables

Library of Congress Cataloging-in-Publication Data

Genetics of criminal and antisocial behaviour.
        p.   cm.—(Ciba foundation symposium ; 194)
      Based on the Symposium on Genetics of Criminal and Antisocial
Behaviour, held at the Ciba Foundation, London, Feb. 14–16, 1995.
      Editors: Gregory R. Bock and Jamie A. Goode.
      Includes bibliographical references and indexes.
      ISBN 0 471 95719 4 (alk. paper)
      1. Criminal behavior—Genetic aspects—Congresses.   2. Antisocial
personality disorders—Genetic aspects—Congresses.   3. Behavioral
genetics—Congresses.   I. Bock, Gregory.   II. Goode, Jamie.
III. Symposium on Genetics of Criminal and Antisocial Behaviour
(1995 : Ciba Foundation)   IV. Series.
      [DNLM: 1. Genetics, Behavioral—congresses.   2. Crime—congresses.
3. Social Behavior Disorders—genetics—congresses.   W3 C161F v.
194 1995 / QH 457 G3284 1995]
HV6047.G46   1995
364.2′4—dc20
DNLM/DLC
for Library of Congress   95-31427
                                                                              CIP

British Library Cataloguing in Publication Data

A catalogue record for this book is available from the British Library

ISBN 0 471 95719 4

Typeset in 10/12pt Times by Dobbie Typesetting Ltd, Tavistock, Devon
Printed and bound in Great Britain by Biddles Ltd, Guildford and King's Lynn
This book is printed on acid-free paper responsibly manufactured from sustainable forestation, for
which at least two trees are planted for each one used for paper production.

Contents

v

Participants

R. Bartlett Nuffield Council on Bioethics, The Nuffield Foundation, 28 Bedford Square, London WC1B 3EG, UK

T. J. Bouchard Jr Minnesota Center for Twin & Adoption Research, Department of Psychology, University of Minnesota, Elliott Hall, 75 East River Road, Minneapolis, MN 55455-0344, USA

M. Bohman Högbergsgatan 40A, S-11826 Stockholm, Sweden

H. G. Brunner Department of Human Genetics, University Hospital, Nijmegen, Geert Grooteplein 20, PO Box 9101, 6500 HB Nijmegen, The Netherlands

R. B. Cairns University of North Carolina, Chapel Hill, 521 S. Greensboro Street, Suite 203, CB# 8115, Sheryl-Mar Building, Chapel Hill, NC 27599, USA

G. Carey Institute of Behavioral Genetics, University of Colorado, Campus Box 447, Boulder, CO 80309-0447, USA

M. Carlier URA 1294 CNRS, Génétique Neurogénétique et Comportement, UFR Biom dicale, Université Paris V, 45 rue des Saints-Pères, 75270 Paris Cedex 06, France

M. Daly Department of Psychology, McMaster University, Hamilton, Ontario, Canada L85 4K1

D. Denno Law School, Fordham University, 140 West 62nd Street, New York, NY 10023, USA

J. Glover New College, Oxford OX1 3BN, UK

D. Goldman Laboratory of Neurogenetics, NIAAA/National Institutes of Health, 12501 Washington Avenue, Room 2, Rockville, MD 20852, USA

I. Gottesman   Department of Psychology, University of Virginia, Charlottesville, VA 22903, USA

A. Heath   Department of Psychiatry, Washington University School of Medicine, 4940 Children's Place, St Louis, MO 63110, USA

R. A. Hinde   St John's College, Cambridge CB2 1TP, UK

M. J. Lyons   Psychiatry Service 116A, Brockton VAMC, 940 Belmont Street, Brockton, MA 02401, USA

S. C. Maxson   Department of Psychology, University of Connecticut, Storrs, CT 06269, USA

S. A. Mednick   Center for Longitudinal Research, University of Southern California, Social Science Research Institute, Denney Research Building, Rm 128, Los Angeles, CA 90089-1111, USA

R. Plomin   Social, Genetic and Developmental Psychiatry Research Centre, Institute of Psychiatry, De Crespigny Park, London SE5 8AF, UK

D. C. Rowe   Division of Family Studies, FCR Room 210, The University of Arizona, Tucson, AZ 85721, USA

Sir Michael Rutter *(Chairman)*   Department of Child Psychiatry, Institute of Psychiatry, De Crespigny Park, London SE5 8AF, UK

J. L. Silberg   Department of Human Genetics,Virginia Commonwealth University, POB 3, MCV Station, Richmond, VA 23298, USA

W. Slutske *(Ciba Foundation Bursar)*   Department of Psychiatry, Washington University School of Medicine, 4940 Children's Place, St Louis, MO 63110, USA

P. Taylor   Department of Forensic Psychiatry, Institute of Psychiatry, De Crespigny Park, London SE5 8AF, UK

M. Virkkunen   Department of Psychiatry, University of Helsinki, Lapinlahdentie, SF-00180 Helsinki, Finland

I. Waldman   Department of Psychology, Emory University, Atlanta, GA 30322, USA

Introduction: concepts of antisocial behaviour, of cause, and of genetic influences

Sir Michael Rutter

MRC Child Psychiatry, Institute of Psychiatry, De Crespigny Park, Denmark Hill, London SE5 8AF, UK

Despite a vast theoretical and research literature on crime (see e.g. Rutter & Giller 1983) and on childhood disorders of conduct (see e.g. Robins 1991), surprisingly little is known on the role of genetic factors in their causation. Indeed, most criminologists have not considered them worthy of serious attention. Thus, genetics does not even appear in the index of Gottfredson & Hirschi's (1990) book *A general theory of crime.* Nevertheless, there is now a growing body of empirical evidence on the contribution of genetic factors to individual differences in antisocial behaviour (see Carey 1994, DiLalla & Gottesman 1989, Goldsmith & Gottesman 1995 for excellent reviews of the research data and their meaning). In this symposium, we shall be examining some of the newer evidence on this potentially very important topic and, in so doing, we will have to consider some of the crucial ethical, legal and clinical implications that stem from those findings. As we discuss these issues, there are several sets of considerations that need to be borne in mind; these concern concepts of antisocial behaviour, of the different types of causation, and of the measurement and possible modes of operation of genetic influences.

Concepts of antisocial disorder

It is necessary to begin with the basic question of what is this 'thing' termed 'crime and antisocial behaviour' that might involve the operation of genetic factors? Therein lies our first problem. To begin with, it is apparent that we cannot equate breaking the law with disorder or psychopathology (Richters & Cicchetti 1993). Thus, at least some forms of civil disobedience represent highly principled, carefully considered acts designed to change either the law or prevailing practice. The suffragette movement in the early part of this century and the civil protests about racial segregation in the USA during the 1960s both represent examples of this kind. There are also behaviours that are outside the law but yet entirely

1

acceptable within subgroups of society. The occasional recreational taking of cannabis would be an example of that kind in some cultural groups. In addition, there are behaviours that are illegal only because they occur below a legally defined age limit, as is the case with consumption of alcohol. In that connection, we need to note the differences within and between countries in what is the age at which the drinking of alcohol is legal. Also, of course, there are behaviours (the use of drugs and alcohol again provide an example) that are legal in some countries but forbidden by law in others.

However, even if we restrict the concept of antisocial behaviour to that which is socially disapproved in virtually all societies, we shall have to recognize that we are referring to a behavioural tendency shown by all human beings to some degree. Many surveys have shown that, at some time, almost all boys commit acts that fall outside the law and which could have led to prosecution if they had been caught (Rutter & Giller 1983). For example, in Farrington's (1995) longitudinal study of inner-city London males, 96% admitted committing at least one of 10 common offences (including theft, violence, vandalism and drug-taking). Of course, many *do* get caught and over a quarter of males in inner-city areas appear in the official crime statistics. Are we dealing simply with individual differences in a universally present tendency? Perhaps. In many respects, mildly antisocial behaviour has a pattern of correlates and consequences that is similar to that shown by severe antisocial behaviour, although of course the associations are weaker. For example, that seems to be the case with respect to the progression from conduct disturbance to substance abuse (Robins & McEvoy 1990) and possibly to antisocial personality disorder (Robins et al 1991). There is no clear-cut threshold below which minor degrees of antisocial behaviour carry no risk for later disorder of some kind. That negative finding, however, needs to be treated with considerable caution in view of the measurement limitations in the relevant studies.

Does the lack of a demonstrated threshold mean that it is inappropriate or invalid to consider severe degrees of antisocial behaviour as a disorder of some kind if the behaviour is accompanied by manifest harmful social malfunction (Richters & Cicchetti 1993)? Clearly not; the fact that a maladaptive behaviour functions as a continuously distributed dimension is in no way incompatible with the concept of disorder (Plomin et al 1991). Indeed, that is the situation with many multifactorial medical conditions such as diabetes, coronary artery disease and epilepsy. We should note, too, that the same applies to the risk factors for disorder. Thus, for example, variations in cholesterol levels well within the supposedly normal range show an association with the risk of coronary artery disease. Still, if that is the situation, we do have to consider when to regard a constellation of behaviours as a disorder, and to examine possible mechanisms involved in the transition to disorder—the psychiatric parallel, if you like, of the transition from benign to malignant hypertension.

In that connection, the developmental data on antisocial behaviour and conduct disorder are relevant (Lahey & Loeber 1994, Le Blanc & Loeber 1993, Loeber & Hay 1994). Longitudinal data show that oppositional/defiant and disruptive behaviour during the preschool years is predictive of delinquency during adolescence (Farrington 1995, Tremblay et al 1994, White et al 1990). The finding is important in its implication that the roots of antisocial behaviour may lie in a broad behavioural propensity rather than in any predisposition to commit illegal acts as such. The suggestion is that oppositional/defiant disorders may constitute a precursor of conduct disorder rather than a separate diagnostic entity. However, if that is so, there is the need to account for the fact that many children with an oppositional/defiant disorder do *not* progress to a conduct disorder.

It could be just a function of severity. Certainly, it is clear that antisocial behaviour varies greatly in severity and that this variation is associated with chronicity. For example, in the Stattin & Magnusson (1991) longitudinal study, although over a third of males committed criminal offences, the 5% who were chronic offenders accounted for two-fifths of all registered convictions. Much the same applies in other studies (Farrington & West 1993). Moreover, it is evident that the various risk factors associated with crime apply much more strongly to this recidivist group than to one-time offenders.

But is antisocial behaviour a homogeneous entity differing only in degree? Probably not. Several distinctions have been drawn in the literature. First, it has been found that pervasive early-onset hyperactivity/inattention not only carries a much increased risk of later antisocial behaviour, but also is predictive of antisocial behaviour that persists into adult life (Farrington et al 1990). Although that finding is well replicated, two important areas of uncertainty remain. On the one hand, it is unclear whether the risk derives from the presence of a qualitatively distinct hyperkinetic disorder, or from a continuously distributed behavioural trait, or both. On the other hand, in so far as the risk should be conceptualized as a trait, there is a lack of agreement on whether it should be viewed as representing hyperactivity/inattention, or impulsivity, or sensation-seeking, or lack of behavioural control. Theoretical considerations, and to some extent empirical evidence, link the trait with biological neurotransmitter systems (McBurnett 1992).

However, this is not the only trait associated with an increased risk for antisocial behaviour. Low anxiety, reward dependence, aggression and psychopathy have all been implicated (Goldsmith & Gottesman 1995, McBurnett 1992, Tremblay et all 1994). There is overlap between these various dimensions and it is not yet clear whether they represent independent risk factors or rather different facets of a personality composite or constellation in which the different dimensions carry little risk when they occur outside that cluster. The latter certainly remains an important possibility to consider, moreover one with implications for data analysis (Magnusson et al 1993, Magnusson & Bergman 1990).

A second distinction concerns age of onset. Several investigators have proposed that early-onset antisocial behaviour needs to be differentiated from adolescent-onset delinquency (Lahey & Loeber 1994, Moffitt 1993a, Patterson 1995). The suggestion is that the early-onset variety is more likely to be associated with aggression, poor peer relationships and neuropsychological impairment, as well as with greater family psychopathology and maladaptive patterns of interaction. It is also accompanied by a much stronger likelihood of persistence into adult life. By contrast, adolescence-limited antisocial behaviour is seen, at least by some investigators, as a normative response representing a seeking of adult privileges and a rebellion against adult control. There is reasonably good evidence that adolescent-onset delinquency is less pathological (in both a statistical sense and a weaker association with individual and family risk factors) and has a better long-term prognosis. What is much less certain, however, is whether the distinction reflects severity or a qualitative difference.

Other differentiations within the field of antisocial behaviour have concerned aggressive versus non-aggressive varieties, socialized versus unsocialized patterns and presence or absence of associated emotional disturbance (Rutter & Giller 1983). Although each has some weak empirical support, none is as well validated as those based on hyperactivity or on age of onset.

Correlates of antisocial behaviour

The next set of findings to be kept in mind as we discuss possible genetic influences concerns the correlates of antisocial behaviour. The behavioural associations have already been mentioned but three other domains need to be added. First, it is well established that antisocial behaviour is much more common in males, although the explanation for the sex difference is much less clear. We should note, too, that the sex ratio for crime halved in the UK over the 1960s and 1970s and differs by ethnic group (Rutter 1980, Robins et al 1991). Second, parental criminality, family discord, weak family relationships, ineffective discipline and supervision, and a deviant peer group are all well-established risk factors (Patterson 1995, Rutter 1985). It is quite possible that, to some extent, these may reflect both genetic influences (Plomin 1994) and child effects (Anderson et al 1986, Engfer et al 1994) but there is quite strong circumstantial evidence that they also represent environmental mediation. Third, neuropsychological impairment is a risk factor for antisocial behaviour (Moffitt 1993b). It has been argued that the evidence suggests frontal lobe dysfunction. Two findings, however, cast doubt on the centrality of the postulated rule of biologically based cognitive impairment: (1) Goodman et al (1995) have shown that the risks for psychopathology apply to variations in IQ

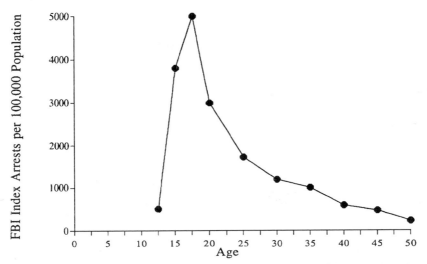

FIG. 1. Age-specific arrests for the United States Federal Bureau of Investigation's (FBI) index offences in 1980. (Index offences include homicide, forcible rape, robbery, aggravated assault, burglary, larceny and auto theft.) Data taken from Blumstein et al (1988); adapted with permission from Moffit (1993a).

across the whole of the range and not just at the lower end; and (2) Maughan et al (1995) found that although reading difficulties were strongly associated with antisocial behaviour in childhood, the association did not persist into adult life. The issue remains open.

Onset, persistence and desistance of antisocial behaviour

Another feature regarding antisocial behaviour that demands our attention concerns its onset, persistence and desistance. The factors involved are not necessarily the same as those that apply to individual differences in propensity. As we have seen, the roots of the most serious and persistent forms of antisocial behaviour lie in early childhood. Nevertheless, we have still to account for the fact that there is a massive rapid rise in delinquent acts during adolescence, and an equally striking but more gradual fall during early adult life (see Fig. 1). The strong continuity in individual differences in antisocial behaviour has led many commentators to assume that we are necessarily dealing with an intrinsic, relatively fixed trait, but this ignores the marked change in level with increasing age. Three findings are important in this connection. First, the continuity into adult life concerns a pervasive pattern of social malfunction and not just criminality (Quinton et al 1993). Second, conduct disorder in childhood carries a much increased risk of stresses and adversities in adult life (Rutter et al 1995). People shape and select their environments as well as respond to them. Third, the degree to which antisocial behaviour persists is much influenced by environmental circumstances, albeit ones that the individuals have done much to bring about themselves. Thus, as Sampson & Laub (1993) showed, a stable marriage and steady employment are protective against, and alcoholism a risk factor for, continuations in crime. The strong implication is that we will need to pay attention to person–environment, and therefore possibly gene–environment, correlations.

The last point concerns possible person–environment interactions. The empirical evidence on their operation is strikingly thin but there is some suggestion that they may be relevant. For example, Farrington (1993) found that parental criminality was a risk factor for delinquency in the offspring only if it was combined with low social status. Similarly, early separation from a parent was a risk factor for boys from average- or high-income families but a protective factor for those from low-income families. Some adoptee study findings also suggest that environmental hazards may carry a greater risk for antisocial behaviour in individuals born to a criminal parent (Cadoret 1985). Vorria's (1991) study of children reared in residential institutions in Greece similarly showed that the psychopathological risks were least evident in the children who had been orphaned or admitted for financial reasons rather than parenting breakdown. Whether their relative resilience reflected a lesser genetic risk or less adverse experiences in infancy is not known.

In summary, the findings on antisocial behaviour indicate that we need to consider its likely heterogeneity, the nature of the individual behavioural risk factors, the reasons for the sex difference in rate of antisocial behaviour, the probability of indirect chain effects in its persistence and desistence, the role of gene–environment correlations, and the possible operation of gene–environment interactions.

Concepts of cause

The next conceptual question that needs addressing is what we mean by 'cause' (Rutter 1994). Most people tend to assume that it must refer to individual differences—in this instance, why 'X' is criminal and 'Y' is not. It is crucial to recognize that this is only one of several quite different causal concepts, and that the causal factors involved in each are not necessarily the same. For example, the past 50 years has seen a massive rise in crime in most western countries (Rutter & Smith 1995). Figure 2 shows the rise as it has occurred in the UK. Clearly, that sudden rise is most unlikely to be due to genetic factors directly, if only because the genetic pool cannot change quickly enough to account for a rise of that speed and degree. Note too, however, that despite popular views to the contrary, the rise does not parallel changes in income

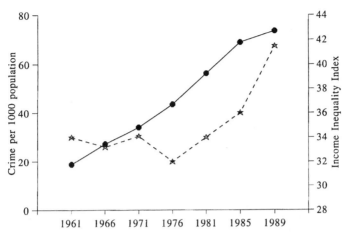

FIG. 2. Crime (filled circles) and income inequality (stars) in UK, 1961–1989. The income inequality index is provided by the Gini coefficient for income distribution. This has a value of zero if each individual has the same income (i.e. complete equality) and a value of 100% if a single person has all the income in the locality and others none (i.e. complete inequality). Data taken from Farrington (1992), Joseph Rowntree Foundation (1995).

inequality. Neither does it parallel the rise in unemployment. The explanation has yet to be established.

Equally, genetic factors are most unlikely to account for the fact that the murder rate in young people today is over 10 times higher in the USA than in the UK. Probably, national differences in the availability of guns plays a role in that contrast. Similarly, we need to be very cautious generalizing from the causes operating within ethnic groups to those accounting for differences between such groups. For example, the American Epidemiological Catchment Area study showed that black men were far more likely than whites to land up in prison but there was no difference in the rate of antisocial personality disorder (Robins et al 1991). The sex ratio for antisocial personality disorders was also substantially lower in blacks than whites (Robins et al 1991). Note that these ethnic differences exist despite the fact that the correlates of antisocial behaviour *within* each ethnic group appear very similar.

Comparable caveats need to be applied to explanations for the sex difference in antisocial behaviour. Although it is very likely to have biological roots, there is still a need to account for the marked variations over time and between ethnic groups in sex ratio.

A further causal question concerns the factors involved in delinquent behaviour being manifest in one situation or circumstance but not in another one (Clarke 1985). Elements of opportunity play a major role in that connection.

Or, again, we may wish to ask why antisocial behaviour tends to fall off markedly during early adult life. Are the factors involved in that reduction the reverse of those leading to the earlier rise in crime, or are they different? Most of the research strategies to be considered in the papers that follow do not address these causal questions. In some instances, they could do so (e.g. the changes with age). In other instances, quite different research tools are needed (as with the secular trend in crime). In our discussions, we will need to remember that, for the most part, it is only the causal question of individual difference that is being examined and, in our overall conceptualization, the other, equally important causal questions must not get overlooked.

Concepts of genetic effects

The next conceptual issue concerns the nature of possible genetic influences on antisocial behaviour. As Goldsmith & Gottesman (1995) have emphasized, they will be probabilistic and not deterministic. Moreover, the interest has to lie in the mechanisms by which they operate and not in the quantification of heritability as such (although that is a necessary step in the study of causal processes). The genetic study of antisocial behaviour should have practical benefits just because, if undertaken in the right way, the findings will aid our understanding of causal processes. That is crucial for the development of effective means of prevention or alleviation. In that connection, of course, we should recognize that genetic research designs are as crucial for the testing of hypotheses about environmental risk mechanisms as for the study of genetic factors.

Before we examine the new evidence in the papers to be given later in this symposium, it may be useful to look back briefly at the research literature, as reviewed by Carey (1994) and by Goldsmith & Gottesman (1995), to see whether there are any lessons to be learned. I suggest that there are four main conclusions. First, although the findings suggest a significant (but far from overwhelming) genetic effect on individual differences in the propensity to engage in antisocial behaviour, the effects appear to vary by both age group and measures used. Thus, the old twin studies (of somewhat variable quality) suggest a stronger genetic component in adult crime than juvenile delinquency (see Fig. 3). It may be relevant, however, that the base rate for juvenile crime is much higher. In addition, it is likely that the heritability of behavioural traits or disorders associated with crime are greater than that of crime itself. In so far as that is the case, the implication is that the genetic effects on crime may well be mediated through these traits or disorders. The Swedish adoptee data also suggest that some of the genetic effects may operate through alcoholism.

The second point is that there is a need to consider jointly the findings from research using different genetic strategies. Conclusions are always more solidly based when all strategies give comparable answers (Rutter et al 1990). Twin

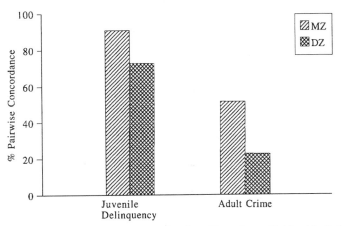

FIG. 3. Twin data for juvenile and adult crime (data from Goldsmith & Gottesman 1995). MZ, monozygotic; DZ, dizygotic twin pairs.

and adoptee data agree in showing a modest to moderate genetic effect. O'Connor et al's (1995) findings from the blended family design pioneered by Hetherington et al (1994) are also consistent (see Fig. 4). Note the falling genetic cascade from the 0.81 correlation for monozygotic (MZ) twin pairs to 0.27 for unrelated siblings living together in the same stepfamily. The last figure incidentally provides a reflection of the shared environmental effect.

The third point, however, is that the genetic data are full of as yet unexplained contradictions. Thus, why is the dizygotic (DZ) twin correlation here (as in other twin studies) higher than that for full sibs? Why in the Danish twin sample is the cross-sex correlation (0.23) lower than both the female and male same-sex correlations in DZ pairs (0.46 and 0.47, respectively) (Goldsmith & Gottesman 1995)? Why do the Danish adoptee data suggest a heritability about half that suggested by the Danish twin data (Carey 1994)? Why, in both sexes, is the rate of criminality in Danish MZ twins somewhat higher than same-sex DZ twins and substantially higher than opposite-sex DZ twins (Carey 1994)? These discrepancies point to the likely importance of both imitation or collusion effects and also assortative mating (which is substantial for serious antisocial disorder—Quinton et al 1993). Why was the rate of criminality in Swedish adoptees the same as that in the general population, whereas it was raised in Danish adoptees? The finding that the rate of criminality in Swedish adopting parents was zero, whereas it was average in Danish adopting parents suggests that a better than average rearing environment may serve to counter genetic risk (regarding level of crime, although not necessarily regarding individual differences) (Carey 1994).

The fourth conclusion is that the evidence is consistent in pointing to the operation of environmental risk mechanisms, both shared and non-shared,

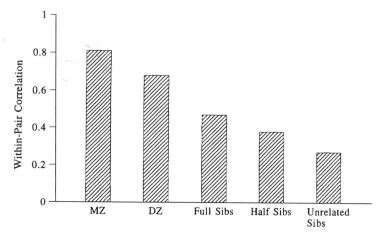

FIG. 4. Within-pair correlations by genetic relatedness. (Reproduced with permission from O'Connor et al 1995.)

although much less conclusive in the identification of the most important environmentally mediated risk variables.

Many people are sceptical about claims that genetic research on antisocial behaviour could be useful because it is so implausible that there could be a gene for 'crime'. Indeed, that *is* implausible, but therein lies one of the main uses of genetic research. Does the genetic risk operate through an effect on hyperactivity/inattention, or on impulsivity, or on physiological reactivity, rather than aggression (Raine & Venables 1992)? Or does the effect lie in neuropsychological or cognitive dysfunction (Moffitt 1993b)? Moreover, we need to go on to ask whether these possibly genetically influenced temperamental traits or behavioural predispositions operate directly and independently, or through an effect that requires combination with some environmental risk mechanism (such as parental hostility or neglect, or deviant role models, or lack of supervision). Do genetic factors operate through an effect on susceptibility to environmental hazards? Person–environment interactions are widespread in biology and medicine (Rutter & Pickles 1991)—do they operate here? In answering that question it is necessary that we bear in mind that the adoptee design, that is in many ways best suited to detect such interactions, provides a misleading measure of the proportion of population variance to gene–environment interactions (because adoptee families provide less overlap between genetic and environmental risks than occurs in the population at large). The interplay between nature and nurture also involves person–environment correlations; people shape and select their environments as well as responding differentially to the environments they encounter (Rutter et al 1995). Do children with personal characteristics associated with an increased risk of antisocial behaviour behave in ways that elicit negative reactions from other people?

Chromosomal studies have been important in taking forward the investigation of possible risk mechanisms. At one time, XYY individuals were thought to show extreme aggressive antisocial tendencies. General population longitudinal studies have shown that the early studies of prison samples greatly exaggerated the risks; nevertheless, there is an increased risk of conduct problems, perhaps especially associated with hyperactivity (Ratcliffe 1994). One question to be addressed now is why the behavioural correlates of this chromosomal abnormality are as varied as they have been found to be? Of course, such variability is extremely common even with Mendelian single-gene disorders (Simonoff et al 1995), but its existence serves to remind us that the elucidation of causal mechanisms must include an understanding of the routes from gene, to gene product, to behaviour.

In that connection, molecular genetic studies have a huge potential because the genetic factor can be studied directly and not merely inferred in 'black box' fashion. Of course, several cautions are necessary. Replication of findings in an independent laboratory on a different sample is as essential here as in the rest of science—as the unfortunate history of premature claims with respect to schizophrenia and manic-depressive disorder reminds us. Genetic heterogeneity must be anticipated, as in the rest of medicine and, furthermore, we must expect in most cases to find several genes each having a small effect as part of multifactorial liability and not one major gene operating in Mendelian fashion. Such small effects may well account for little of the overall population variance but their potential importance lies in the power to shed light on causal processes and not in their predictive strength in the population as a whole.

Implications of genetic factors

This search for genetic factors is not without its risks—clinical, ethical and legal—and it will be important that society acts in ways that capitalize on the positive potentials and minimize the dangers. The general public is not used to thinking in probabilistic terms and especially not so when the absolute risks are low, although increased relative to the general population. There are real dangers of discriminatory labelling, as the history of chromosome studies and sickle-cell screening in the USA shows us. Also, there may be clinical problems involved in people finding out about their own genetic risks, as research with single-gene disorders has demonstrated. These risks are greater when there is no effective intervention that can follow identification of the genetic risk and greater still when the lack of remedy is combined with low predictive power and negative public attitudes to the trait in question (as is the case with antisocial behaviour). As the Nuffield Council on Bioethics (1993) noted, the potential for eugenic misuse of genetic testing will increase as a result of the ability to test for genetic factors in multifactorial disorders.

These caveats should not deter us from undertaking the necessary research but they should guide us in *how* we proceed and in *how* we interpret and communicate our findings. Moreover, they present considerable challenges to genetic counselling services; these will have to adapt and develop to respond to the new issues involved in the identification of specific observable genetic risk factors for multifactorial disorders. It would be unrealistic to expect this symposium to solve all these problems but there should be plenty to keep us engaged over the next few days and I do anticipate some clarification of the issues by the time we finish.

References

Anderson KE, Lytton H, Romney DM 1986 Mothers' interactions with normal and conduct-disordered boys: who affects whom? Dev Psychol 22:604–609

Blumstein A, Cohen J, Farrington DP 1988 Criminal career research: its value for criminology. Criminology 26:57–74

Cadoret RJ 1985 Genes, environment and their interaction in the development of psychopathology. In: Sakai T, Tsuboi T (eds) Genetic aspects of human behaviour. Igaku-Shoin, Tokyo, p 165–175

Carey G 1994 Genetics and violence. In: Reiss AJ, Miczek KA, Roth JA (eds) Understanding and preventing violence: biobehavioral influences, vol 2. National Academy, Washington, DC, p 21–58

Clarke RVG 1985 Jack Tizard memorial lecture: delinquency, environment and intervention. J Child Psychol Psychiatry Allied Discip 26:505–523

DiLalla LF, Gottesman II 1989 Heterogeneity of causes for delinquency and criminality: lifespan perspectives. Dev Psychopathol 1:339–349

Engfer A, Walper S, Rutter M 1994 Individual characteristics as a force in development. In: Rutter M, Hay D (eds) Development through life: a handbook for clinicians. Blackwell Scientific, Oxford, p 79–111

Farrington DP 1992 Trends in English juvenile delinquency and their explanation. Int J Comp Appl Criminal Justice 16:151–163

Farrington DP 1993 Interactions between individual and contextual factors in the development of offending. In: Silbereisen R, Todt E (eds) Adolescence in context. Springer-Verlag, New York, p 366–389

Farrington DP 1995 The challenge of teenage antisocial behavior. In: Rutter M (ed) Psychosocial disturbances in young people: challenges for prevention. Cambridge University Press, New York, p 83–130

Farrington DP, West DJ 1993 Criminal, penal and life histories of chronic offenders: risk and protective factors and early identification. Crim Behav Ment Health 3:492–523

Farrington DP, Loeber R, Van Kammen WB 1990 Long-term criminal outcomes of hyperactivity–impulsivity–attention deficit and conduct problems in childhood. In: Robins LN, Rutter M (eds) Straight and devious pathways from childhood to adulthood. Cambridge University Press, Cambridge, p 62–81

Goldsmith HH, Gottesman II 1995 Heritable variability and variable heritability in developmental psychopathology. In: Lenzenweger MF, Haugaard JJ (eds) Frontiers of developmental psychopathology. Oxford University Press, New York

Goodman R, Simonoff E, Stevenson J 1995 The impact of child IQ, parent IQ and sibling IQ on child behavioural deviance scores. J Child Psychol Psychiatry Allied Discip 36:409–425

Gottfredson MR, Hirschi T 1990 A general theory of crime. Stanford University Press, Stanford, CA

Hetherington EM, Reiss D, Plomin R (eds) 1994 Separate social worlds of siblings: impact of nonshared environment on development. Lawrence Erlbaum, Hillsdale, NJ

Joseph Rowntree Foundation 1995 The enquiry into income and wealth. Joseph Rowntree Foundation, York

Lahey BB, Loeber R 1994 Framework for a developmental model of oppositional defiant disorder and conduct disorder. In: Routh DK (ed) Disruptive behavior disorders in childhood. Plenum Press, New York, p 139–180

Le Blanc M, Loeber R 1993 Precursors, causes and the development of criminal offending. In: Hay DF, Angold A (eds) Precursors and causes in development and psychopathology. Wiley, Chichester, p 233–263

Loeber R, Hay DF 1994 Developmental approaches to aggression and conduct problems. In: Rutter M, Hay DF (eds) Development through life: a handbook for clinicians. Blackwell Scientific, Oxford, p 488–516

Magnusson D, Bergman LR 1990 A pattern approach to the study of pathways from childhood to adulthood. In: Robins LN, Rutter M (eds) Straight and devious pathways from childhood to adulthood. Cambridge University Press, Cambridge, p 101–115

Magnusson D, af Klinteberg B, Stattin H 1993 Autonomic activity/reactivity, behavior, and crime in a longitudinal perspective. In: McCord J (ed) Facts, frameworks, and forecasts. Transaction, New Brunswick, NJ, p 287–318

Maughan B, Pickles A, Rutter M, Hagell A, Yule W 1995 Reading problems and antisocial behaviour: developmental trends in comorbidity. J Child Psychol Psychiatry Allied Discip, in press

McBurnett K 1992 Psychobiological approaches to personality and their applications to child psychopathology. In: Lahey BB, Kazdin AE (eds) Advances in clinical child psychology, vol. 14. Plenum Press, New York, p 107–164

Moffitt TE 1993a Adolescence-limited and life course-persistent antisocial behavior: a developmental taxonomy. Psychol Rev 100:674–701

Moffitt TE 1993b The neuropsychology of conduct disorder. Dev Psychopathol 5: 135–151

Nuffield Council on Bioethics 1993 Genetic screening ethical issues. Nuffield Council on Bioethics, London

O'Connor TG, McGuire S, Reiss D, Hetherington EM, Plomin R 1995 Co-occurrence of depressive symptoms and antisocial behavior in adolescence: a common genetic liability, submitted

Patterson GR 1995 Some characteristics of a developmental theory for early onset delinquency. In: Lenzenweger MF, Haugaard JJ (eds) Frontiers of developmental psychopathology. Oxford University Press, New York

Plomin R 1994 Genetics and experience: the developmental interplay between nature and nurture. Sage, Newbury Park, CA

Plomin R, Rende R, Rutter M 1991 Quantitative genetics and developmental psychopathology. In: Cicchetti D, Toth SL (eds) Internalizing and externalizing expressions of dysfunction. Lawrence Erlbaum, Hillsdale, NJ, p 155–202

Quinton D, Pickles AR, Maughan B, Rutter M 1993 Partners, peers and pathways: assortative pairing and continuities in conduct disorder. Dev Psychopathol 5:763–783

Raine A, Venables PH 1992 Antisocial behaviour: evolution, genetics, neuropsychology, and psychophysiology. In: Gale A, Eysenck MW (eds) Handbook of individual differences: biological perspectives. Wiley, Chichester, p 287–321

Ratcliffe SG 1994 The psychological and psychiatric consequences of sex chromosomal abnormalities in children based on population studies. In: Poustka F (ed) Basic approaches to genetic and molecular biological developmental psychiatry. Quintessenz, Berlin, p 99–122

Richters JE, Cicchetti D 1993 Mark Twain meets DSM-III-R: conduct disorder, development, and concept of harmful dysfunction. Dev Psychopathol 5:5–29

Robins LN 1991 Conduct disorder. J Child Psychol Psychiatry Allied Discip 32:193–212

Robins LN, McEvoy L 1990 Conduct problems as predictors of substance abuse. In: Robins LN, Rutter M (eds) Straight and devious pathways from childhood to adulthood. Cambridge University Press, Cambridge, p 182–204

Robins LN, Tipp J, Przybeck T 1991 Antisocial personality. In: Robins LN, Regier DA (eds) Psychiatric disorders in America: the epidemiologic catchment area study. Free Press, New York, p 258–290

Rutter M 1980 Changing youth in a changing society: patterns of adolescent development and disorder. Harvard University Press, Cambridge, MA

Rutter M 1985 Family and school influences on behavioural development. J Child Psychol Psychiatry Allied Discip 26:349–368

Rutter M 1994 Beyond longitudinal data: causes, consequences, changes, and continuity. J Consult Clin Psychol 62:928–940

Rutter M, Giller H 1983 Juvenile delinquency: trends and perspectives. Penguin, Harmondsworth

Rutter M, Pickles A 1991 Person–environment interactions: concepts, mechanisms, and implications for data analysis. In: Wachs TD, Plomin R (eds) Conceptualization and measurement of organism–environment interaction. American Psychological Association, Washington, DC, p 105–141

Rutter M, Smith DJ 1995 Psychosocial disorders in young people: time trends and their causes. Wiley, Chichester

Rutter M, Bolton P, Harrington R, Le Couteur A, Macdonald H, Simonoff E 1990 Genetic factors in child psychiatric disorders. I. A review of research strategies. J Child Psychol Psychiatry Allied Discip 31:3–37

Rutter M, Champion L, Quinton D, Maughan B, Pickles A 1995 Origins of individual differences in environmental risk exposure. In: Moen P, Elder G, Luscher K (eds) Perspectives on the ecology of human development. Cornell University Press, Ithaca, NY, in press

Sampson RJ, Laub JH 1993 Crime in the making: pathways and turning points through life. Harvard University Press, Cambridge, MA

Simonoff E, Bolton P, Rutter M 1995 Genetic perspectives on mental retardation. In: Burack J, Hodapp E, Zigler E (eds) Handbook of mental retardation and development. Cambridge University Press, New York, in press

Stattin H, Magnusson D 1991 Stability and change in criminal behaviour up to age 30. Br J Criminol 31:327–346

Tremblay RE, Pihl RO, Vitaro F, Dobkin PL 1994 Predicting early onset of male antisocial behavior from preschool behavior. Arch Gen Psychiatry 51:732–739

Vorria P 1991 Children growing up in Greek institutions: their behaviour and relationships at school and in the institution. PhD thesis, University of London, London, UK

White JL, Moffitt TE, Earls F, Robins L, Silva PA 1990 How early can we tell? Predictors of childhood conduct disorder and adolescent delinquency. Criminology 28:507–533

DISCUSSION

Hinde: We must not lose sight of the diachronic factor. All your definitions of antisocial behaviour are defined against cultural norms. It is important to remember that these cultural norms are *determined* by peoples' behaviour as well as *determining* peoples' behaviour, and that they change with time and differ between cultures.

Secondly, you implied that the general behavioural propensities that may underlie antisocial behaviours are undesirable. This may not be the case. In young men, the graph of antisocial behaviour appears to follow the curve of risk-taking. These behavioural propensities may be the same as those that make, for example, good explorers or fighter pilots: in these contexts they may be desirable.

Rutter: That is an important point. There is all too frequently an assumption that risk factors must be in themselves abnormal and should therefore be eliminated: this is not the case.

Denno: I was interested in your point about sex differences and differences within ethnic groups. Some studies show that black females have a higher rate of violence than white males (Kruttschnitt 1994, Baskin et al 1993, Bowker 1978, Chilton & Datesman 1987, Hill & Crawford 1990, Laub & McDermott 1985).

Rutter: Yes, the sex ratio is much lower in black groups in both the USA and the UK. But, at least in the UK, within Asian groups the sex ratio is much higher (Rutter & Giller 1983).

Denno: I was curious about that finding in relation to the sex-ratio difference in spatial intelligence. Some research suggests that there's an inverse sex ratio in terms of spatial intelligence among minorities versus whites. Minority females score higher on tests of spatial IQ than minority males, whereas this is reversed among white males and females.

Rowe: One of the questions that has interested me is whether the causes of individual differences within males and females are the same as the causes of the mean sex differences. There are a couple of things that suggest they overlap. One is that a correlation exists between opposite-sex siblings, although it's not as great as that between the same-sex siblings. Another is that the different traits relating to antisocial behaviour that load most highly on a liability towards criminality also produce a large mean sex difference.

Our study indicates that the mean sex differences reflect the individual differences very well (Rowe et al 1995). We can take a variable, and on the basis of its association with delinquency within a sex (with no mean information at all), we can decide how big a sex difference we will find on it later.

Early prenatal hormonal influences may masculinize or feminize the brain to some degree, creating sex differences, and also creating variation within a sex. So there are possible biological theories for why one finds some overlap. The relationship between mean differences and individual differences is a very interesting question—one that is almost never addressed in criminological theory. Criminologists note the sex difference and they note the individual differences, and they can't imagine that the two are in any way related.

Rutter: I'm sure, as you say, that they overlap. However, there is the additional problem of explaining the changes over time in sex ratio. Since World War II, the male:female ratio for crime has halved (Rutter & Giller 1983). The explanation for this secular trend is not likely to be the same as that for the male excess that has been consistent over time, in spite of variations in the size of excess.

Rowe: The secular trends have to be given some kind of environmental explanation outside of this, unless we are exposed to antihormone agents in our environment, as some radical environmentalists have suggested. I doubt that this is a factor here.

Rutter: That is not quite as ridiculous a suggestion as it sounds. It is very striking that over the past 50 years there has been a progressive reduction in male sperm counts. This has been explained in terms of environmental oestrogens. Of course, whether that would lead to a change in the sex ratio for crime is another matter.

Heath: You spoke about the possibility of a continuum of antisocial behaviours and then argued for the importance of focusing on disorder in the medical model sense. I'm not clear why you made that jump. After all, if there is a continuum of antisocial behaviour, then we have much more power to detect risk factors if we are just using binary data. Why are you thinking in those terms?

Rutter: Because the fact that a trait functions as a dimension in many respects does not mean that risk factors will be the same throughout the dimension. Clearly, they will not be so if the causal influences are different for part of the dimension that is made up of a qualitatively different set of categorical disorders. IQ and mental retardation provide a striking example. IQ functions as a dimension throughout the whole of its range with respect to the prediction of scholastic attainment or social functioning. Despite that, the causal risk factors for severe retardations (such as Down's syndrome) are quite different from those for variations in IQ within the normal range, and markedly disparate even from those for mild retardation. Thus, the finding that antisocial behaviour in childhood functions as a dimension with respect to the prediction to drug misuse or adult crime does not mean that there will not be categories of antisocial behaviour in childhood that differ from the remainder in cause.

The second reason for focusing on categories as well as (not instead of) dimensions is that it may be necessary to ask a separate question about the risk factors involved in the transition to overt disorder. Once more, a medical example illustrates the point. Thus, increases in blood pressure throughout the range are associated with an increase in mortality. Nevertheless, the transition from benign to malignant hypertension totally changes the pathology and outcome. At that point different causal factors come into play. We need to consider the possibility that that might apply to antisocial disorder. Thus, in some respects, transient minor delinquent behaviour in adolescence seems to be on the same dimension as severely handicapping antisocial personality disorder that begins in early childhood and persists into adult life. But does the latter involve causal mechanisms that do not apply to the former? It is important that our analyses presuppose neither a positive nor a negative answer to that question. The use of techniques that bring extra statistical power is appropriate but it should not be at the price of preventing the investigation of possible categorical distinctions.

Goldman: The discrepancies that you pointed out in the twin data are interesting because they are the sorts of results that raise questions and provide rationales for investigators to continue to do twin studies, to learn more about mechanisms. However, it should be pointed out that there is an alternative explanation for some of the discrepancies between studies: random variation in the correlations. It would be interesting and potentially important to see the confidence intervals for the correlations and the heritabilities.

Heath: With Dr Wendy Slutske, I have recently carried out this exercise, reviewing the alcoholism literature. We have been estimating the heritabilities and the 95% confidence limits (Heath et al 1995). It is quite a frightening procedure! The confidence limits for twin data, in particular, are highly asymmetric. The upper band is fairly well known, but for many studies the lower band can be 10–20%. One can review the literature using point estimates and as soon as one looks at how imprecise those estimates are, one realizes that probably they're all estimates of the same value.

Rutter: I am sure that is an important point. It is crucial to explore explanations for different findings in different studies if the variations are truly valid. But, by the same token, it would be foolish to look for substantive reasons for differences that reflect nothing more than measurement error or chance sampling variations.

Bouchard: Let me elaborate on this. I have spent a lot of time doing industrial organizational psychology, where they have looked at the correlation of mental abilities with job performance. For many years, it was believed that success in different jobs was only predictable from different abilities. It literally took hundreds of studies, combined into meta-analyses, before it became clear that there was a general factor that predicted success equally well across almost all jobs. Three to four small twin studies don't provide much information at all.

Gottesman: It's always intimidating to have to contend with the standard error of heritabilities—this is a good reason for us to avoid relying on them. If we go back to the safe and sound practice of reporting correlation coefficients of the type that we've calculated here, then I can answer all of your questions. Overall, if you are looking at the pool of seven twin studies of adult criminality already in the literature (Gottesman & Goldsmith 1994), the standard error on the MZ concordance rate of 91% is only 3.3%, and the standard error on the DZ concordance rate of 73% is 2.4%. If you look at the Danish twin study (Cloninger & Gottesman 1987, Gottesman & Goldsmith 1994) (which is the only large study of criminality *per se* in twins) and shift away from heritability, the tetrachoric correlation for the liability to crime in male MZ twins is 0.74 (SEM ±0.07). Between the male–male DZ twins the tetrachoric correlation is 0.47 (±0.06). The standard errors for the other sexes and the opposite-sex pairs are of the same order of magnitude (see Table 1, p 135).

Heath: Let me argue against that. Suppose we're interested in estimating how much of the variation we can explain by shared environmental effects. The standard errors on your correlations won't give you that information. If you use the standard errors of your variance component estimates, you are assuming a symmetric sampling distribution. But because of the strong negative correlation in twin data between the additive genetic and the shared environmental variance component estimates, you don't have a symmetric sampling distribution. For example, if we say we're looking at a binary trait with a prevalence in the population of 10% and a heritability of around 60%, the 95% confidence limits for that point estimate of 60% could be something like 68% for the upper band and as low as 20% for the lower band. Instead of using standard errors or pooled correlations, you should fit models to the full set of data and then look at the distribution of your estimates. It's important that we don't get carried away into believing that we know precisely what in fact is very imprecise.

Mednick: It might also be beneficial to consider what factors contribute to the definition of the dependent variable. I worked with Karl O. Christiansen in the Danish twin study to which Irving Gottesman referred. We have to remember that we are dealing with a measure of the dependent variable several steps removed from the actual behaviour. This adds 'noise'.

Waldman: Two important points have emerged in this discussion that are not unrelated. These two points correspond to the substantive and methodological components of the distinction between dimensions and types. The first point relates to Andrew Heath's question about the distinction between studying a continuum and studying disorder. In future studies it will be important to use statistical methods that allow us to test whether antisocial behaviour or related characteristics (e.g. psychopathy) are continuous or typological, and to examine whether extreme antisocial behaviour represents simply a greater level of severity, or whether there are some additional causal factors that result in some individuals showing disordered levels of antisocial behaviour. It would be interesting to look at whether the heterogeneity in twin study estimates of genetic and environmental influences on antisocial behaviour are due simply to severity differences across studies.

Taylor: If anything is going to come of this area of work, it is essential to have a better definition of the characteristics of the social activities of interest. No amount of sophistication in the genetics and the statistics is going to help if some of us are talking about antisocial behaviour and some of us are talking about crime, without defining either further. Both are heterogeneous concepts—they overlap but they are not at all the same thing. Further, crime varies considerably between societies and over time, being only that which is contrary to any law of any given society at any given time. Even the very few areas where the categories are broken down more precisely serve to illustrate how heterogeneous these concepts are. For example, everybody gets very excited about unlawful homicide figures, because homicide is considered to be a relatively homogeneous kind of crime; it is not. It is also an unusual crime, because it is not a particularly recidivist sort of crime. Only a tiny minority of people repeat it. Further, we have curious habits, well illustrated by homicide, with regard to how we apply criminal statistics. Neither in the USA nor the UK, for example, are figures for death by dangerous drunk driving included in the official, national statistics within the category of unlawful homicide. They are added separately, elsewhere in the listing. Research should depend on reliable and valid behavioural descriptions, not legal artefacts.

Carey: It is absolutely crucial that this type of research be done: there are, however, very good reasons why, largely, it hasn't been. This is because it's almost impossible to do with many of the data that are available. In our own twin study, for example, in which we are looking at symptoms of antisocial personalty disorder, we really wanted to examine differences in violent symptoms versus property crimes. We ran into an immediate base rate problem: thankfully, violence is rare.

In addition to analysing the big samples that we have, where we may be able to subdivide categories, in future studies we need to pay much more attention to looking at phenotypes, rather than just lumping things together as antisocial behaviour or crime. That's not going to get us very far.

References

Baskin D, Sommers I, Fagan J 1993 The political economy of female violent street crime. Fordham Urban Law J 20:401–477

Bowker LH 1978 The incidence of female crime and delinquency—a comparison of official and self-report studies. Int J Women's Stud 1:178–192

Chilton R, Datesman SK 1987 Gender, race and crime: an analysis of urban arrest trends, 1960–1980. Gender & Society 1:152–171

Cloninger CR, Gottesman II 1987 Genetic and environmental factors in antisocial behavior disorders. In: Mednick SA, Moffitt TE, Stack SA (eds). The causes of crime: new biological approaches. Cambridge University Press, New York, p 92–109

Gottesman II, Goldsmith HH 1994 Developmental psychopathology of antisocial behavior: inserting genes into its ontogenesis and epigenesis. In: Nelson CA (ed) Threats to optimal development: integrating biological, psychological and social risk factors. Lawrence Erlbaum, Hillsdale, NJ, p 69–104

Heath AC, Slutske WS, Madden PAF 1995 Gender differences in the genetic contribution to alcoholism risk and to alcohol consumption patterns. In: Wilsnack RW, Wilsnack SC (eds) Gender and alcohol. Rutgers University Press, Rutgers, NJ, in press

Hill GD, Crawford EM 1990 Women, race and crime. Criminology 28:601–623

Kruttschnitt C 1994 Gender and interpersonal violence. In: Reiss AJ, Roth JA (eds) Understanding and preventing violence, vol 3: Social influences. National Academy Press, Washington, DC, p 293–376

Laub JH, McDermott MJ 1985 An analysis of serious crime by young black women. Criminology 23:81–98

Rowe DC, Vazsonyi AT, Flannery DJ 1995 Sex differences in crime: do means and within sex variation have similar causes? J Res Crime & Delinquency 32:84–100

Rutter M, Giller H 1983 Juvenile delinquency: trends and perspectives. Penguin, Harmondsworth, Middlesex

Issues in the search for candidate genes in mice as potential animal models of human aggression

Stephen C. Maxson

Department of Psychology, Biobehavioral Sciences Graduate Degree Program, The University of Connecticut, Storrs, CT 06269-4154, USA

Abstract. Conceptual and methodological issues in the search for candidate genes for mouse aggression and for the development of animal models of human aggression are considered. First, the focus is on genetic and then behavioural aspects of the search for candidate genes in mice. For the genetic aspect, two approaches are presented. In mice, these are chromosome mapping of polymorphic genes and evaluation of gene (polymorphic or monomorphic) function using knockout mutants. For the behavioural aspect, several parameters, including the type of aggression, measure of aggression, test situation and opponent type can have effects on the obtained genetics. This is illustrated for the offence type of attack behaviour in mice. The current combination of sophisticated genetic and behavioural analyses will result in time in the identification of many of the genes with effects on variation and development of one or more types of murine aggression. Since mouse and humans have many homologous genes mapped to homologous chromosome regions, it is conceivable that individual genes identified for one or more types of mouse aggression may be developed as animal models for human aggression. Genetic, physiological and behavioural limitations and uses of such models are discussed.

1996 Genetics of criminal and antisocial behaviour. Wiley, Chichester (Ciba Foundation Symposium 194) p 21–35

For a long time, there have been three goals in research on the genetics of any behaviour. These are to determine whether the behaviour is heritable, to map or identify the genes for the behaviour, and to determine the mechanisms for effects of genes on the behaviour (Hall 1953). For mammalian aggression, these issues have been primarily studied in mice. Research on the first issue began about 50 years ago, and there has accumulated much evidence that variation in one or more types of aggression in mice is heritable (Maxson 1981). Advances in molecular genetics have now made it possible to identify genes with effects on complex traits, such as a type of aggressive behaviour (Maxson 1992a).

In this paper, conceptual and methodological issues in research on gene mapping and gene function of complex traits are considered and illustrated. The genes for mouse aggression that will be identified by these approaches are a function of behavioural parameters. Conceptual and methodological issues in research on social behaviour are also considered. Such a combination of sophisticated genetic and behavioural analysis will result in time in the identification of many of the genes with effects on variation and development of one or more types of murine aggression. Since mouse and humans have many homologous genes mapped to homologous chromosome regions, it is conceivable that individual genes identified for one or more types of mouse aggression may be developed as animal models for human aggression. Genetic, physiological and behavioural limitations and uses of such models are discussed. Such animal models are relevant to this Ciba Foundation symposium to the extent that criminal and antisocial behaviour in humans are a function of one or more types of aggression, or that there are parallel conceptual and methodological issues in genetic analysis of social behaviour in mice and humans.

Genetics and complex traits

A feature of complex traits, such as behaviour, is that both genetic and environmental factors contribute to individual development and variation. Until recently, this fact made it difficult to identify genes with effects on mouse behaviour, including any type of aggression. Progress in molecular genetics has changed that. Polymorphic genes for a complex trait can be identified by mapping them to regions of a chromosome. Monomorphic genes for a complex trait can be identified by *in vivo* effects of mutated genes. About one-third of the genes in any species are polymorphic. Since both polymorphic and monomorphic genes have a role in phenotypic development, the identification of both is essential to an understanding of the genetics of a specific trait, such as a type of aggression.

Gene mapping

Gene mapping has two features. First, the gene is located to a chromosome. The mouse has 20 pairs of these. Second, its position in relation to other genes on the chromosome is determined. For complex traits, these genes are sometimes referred to as quantitative trait loci (QTLs).

Two approaches currently exist for mapping QTLs. One of these is association analysis (Plomin & McClearn 1993). The other is linkage analysis (Lander & Botstein 1989). The success of each depends in the mouse on the high density of DNA (Dietrich et al 1994) and other markers (O'Brien et al 1988) mapped to its chromosomes. There are advantages and disadvantages to each approach. Association analysis does not make any assumptions about the number of QTLs or about the heritability of the trait. But it does not identify the exact chromosomal position of the QTL with regard to an associated marker, and real versus spurious associations must be checked in a second genetic analysis. So far, this has been the approach most used for mapping QTLs with effects on mouse behaviour, especially in regard to drugs of abuse (Crabbe et al 1994). In contrast, linkage analysis uses models based on assumptions about the number of genes, their interactions and trait heritability. If the model is in error, the mapped QTLs might be invalid. However, linkage analysis can specify the location of the QTL relative to other genes on a chromosome. Because spurious linkages are unlikely, they need not be confirmed, but should be, by another genetic analysis. This approach to mapping QTLs in mice has been used for hypertension, diabetes and epilepsy susceptibility in rodents (Ghosh & Todd 1991).

As far as I know, there are now only two groups attempting to map QTLs for a type of mouse aggression (offence). These are Pierre Roubertoux's in Paris and mine in Storrs. The genetic systems being used are different. Roubertoux is using the F2 of two inbred strains (CBA/H and NZB) divergent in many of their genes. Many of the polymorphic genes for a few measures of offence may be detected by this. My group is using the recombinant inbred strain (RIs) set, BXD/Ty. Because the parental strains for the BXD/Ty RIs are less divergent genetically than the parental strains for Roubertoux's F2s, it may be that fewer polymorphic QTLs will be detected in my study than in Roubertoux's. However, the RIs approach has the advantage that data are cumulative. For example, variants in the gene for the dopamine D2 receptor are known and mapped in the BXD/Ty RIs (Smith et al 1992). This information can be used to determine from my behavioural data and the existing D2 receptor data whether or not the gene for the D2 receptor is involved in some measures of a type of murine aggression.

Mutagenesis

If a gene exists in two alleles, its *in vivo* function can be determined by comparing effects on each homozygous pair of alleles on a trait (Maxson 1992a). For monomorphic genes, two alleles can be established by mutating the known allele via *in vitro* gene targeting and by breeding mice that differ only in homozygotes for normal and knockout mutant alleles. Gene targeting can produce mutant mice for any cloned and sequenced gene. Using reverse genetics, the DNA of genes of the receptors of many neurotransmitters has been cloned and sequenced, and the role of neurotransmitters in rodent aggression has been extensively and intensively investigated by pharmacological manipulations. Strains of mice differing in alleles of the gene for a neurotransmitter receptor would be of value in determining the role of that receptor in one or more types of murine aggression and in its interaction with pharmacological variables. There is one study on the aggressive behaviour of mice with normal and knockout alleles for neurotransmitter receptors.

Serotonin (5-hydroxytryptamine; 5-HT) has been implicated in the offensive attack by resident male mice against intruder male mice, and pharmacological data suggest a role of the $5\text{-HT}_{1A/B}$ receptor types in this kind of mouse aggression (Rodgers 1991). Knockout mutants were made for the 5-HT_{1B} receptor gene (Saudou et al 1994). They are missing the gene for this 5-HT receptor. Ligands specific for this 5-HT receptor were used to show its absence in the brains of the knockout mutants. Also, there are no hyperlocomotor or anxiogenic effects of 5-HT_{1B} drugs in the knockout mutants as there are in normal mice. The homozygous knockout mice do not display any gross abnormalities and appear to be normal in development, breeding, and eating or other gross behaviours. They also appear normal in tests for exploration and 'anxiety' but they show reduced activity. In aggression tests, resident mice homozyous for 5-HT_{1B} knockout alleles attacked intruders with twice the intensity as that of resident mice homozygous for normal 5-HT_{1B} alleles.

There are at least three genetic issues to be considered in the use of knockout mutants. First, there are maternal effects on behaviour. Thus, the cytoplasm, mitochondria and maternal (uterine and postnatal) environments must be the same for the homozygous normal and knockout mice. This can be achieved by breeding heterozygous males and females. Second, effects of some knockouts on behaviour may be missed because they occur on some genetic backgrounds but not others. Thus, positive but not negative findings are meaningful. Third, genes identified by this method can be mapped and homologies between mouse and human shown. The gene for the 5-HT_{1B} receptor of mice is on their chromosome 9 and that of its human homologue, $5\text{-HT}_{1D\beta}$ is on chromosome 6.

Behavioural parameters

Aggression is not a single behavioural category. There are many types of aggression. Four types of murine aggression are, for example, offence, defence, infanticide and predation (as described in Maxson 1992b). The obtained genetics will, among other things, depend on the category of aggression under study. For example, the polymorphic or monomorphic genes involved in offence may not be the same as in defence (Maxson et al 1982).

Other behavioural parameters can also affect the obtained genetics. Elsewhere, I have reviewed possible effects of test, behavioural and life history parameters on the obtained genetics for offence attack in mice (Maxson 1992a). Here, I will focus on two effects of two behavioural parameters on the obtained genetics for offence. These are behavioural measurement and type of opponent.

Behavioural measurement

The aspects of offence that are observed, measured, recorded and analysed can influence the finding of a genetic analysis (Benton 1981). For example, Popova & Kulikov (1986) showed that the percentage of mice attacking at least once had a different mode of inheritance than the number of attacks or the accumulated attack time. Also, there are effects of the mouse Y chromosome on mean number of attacks but not an attack latency (Carlier & Roubertoux 1986), and there are effects of the mouse Y chromosome on measures of the motor components of offence but not on measures of tail rattling (reviewed in Maxson 1992a).

The above implies that composite scores for offence or single measures of offence provide insufficient information for a thorough genetic analysis of offence in mice. At the very least, there should be data on the latency, frequency and duration of each motor component. These are chase, upright offence posture, sideways offence posture and bite–kick attack (Maxson 1992a). Such data can best be obtained by videotaping the dyadic encounters in a test of offence, and then using a computer program for data analysis. This can provide information not only on latency, frequency and duration of each component, but also on sequence of behavioural elements, on the temporal patterning of episodes of offence versus non-offence behaviours, and on total time allocated to different categories of behaviour (Miczek et al 1993a). I know of only two groups currently using this approach to investigate the genetics of offence. These are mine in Storrs and Hahn's in Wayne, NJ.

Type of opponent

Strain or genetic differences in offence often depend on the genotype not only of the experimental mouse, but also of the opponent mouse. For example, when mice of the one genotype encountered mice of the same genotype (homogeneous set test), the mean number of fights/animal per week was higher for males of the BALB/c than the C57BL/6 strain. In comparison, when mice of each genotype encountered mice of a single genotype (standard opponent test), the mean number of fights was higher for males of C57BL/6 than the BALB/c strain (Eleftheriou et al 1974). Also, there are effects of the non-recombining part of the mouse Y chromosome on offence in homogeneous set tests but not in tests with some strains as standard opponent (Maxson et al 1989, Guillot et al 1995). Also, opponent mice differing in major histocompatibility complex haplotypes give different genetic results for offence from those of the same set of inbred strains (Maxson 1992c).

Recent speculations on the causes of escalation in animal fights (Archer & Huntingford 1994) may have implications for the findings that the obtained genetics for offence depends on the genotype of the opponent. Escalation in animal, and perhaps human, fights appears to be due to assessment of the resource holding power (RHP) of the other conspecific and on the value of the resource to each contestant. There is a single study on this in mice (Parmigiani et al 1989). The results of this study are in agreement with game theory models. Fighting tends to escalate and last longer when the mice had similar RHP and the resource has common value. Also, fighting success increases as a function of resource value. Perhaps, genetic analysis of offence should include not only its motivational and motor aspects but also risk assessment and RHP aspects. Some work in this direction is being done by Hahn & Schanz (1995) on passive versus interactive opponents in tests of offence. Also, research on chemosignals and aggression in mice would be relevant (Novikov 1993). For mice, chemosignals are a rich source of information on another individual's identity, history and abilities.

Animal models of human aggression

Individual genes will eventually be identified for one or more type of mouse aggression, and the role of each gene in the development and expression of these murine social behaviours will be understood from its DNA sequence, to its protein structure, to its cellular and temporal expression, to its physiological function, to its behavioural consequences. Identification of genes for other neural, behavioural, or complex traits in mice has led to the development of animal models for parallel human traits. These include myotonic dystrophy, diabetes and obesity. Such models provide insight into the role of genetic, environmental and life-history variables in trait development, physiology or pathology. In part, these models are based on DNA and linkage homologies for mouse and human genes (Nadeau 1989).

There is a recent specific example of this for a behaviour and its consequences—overeating and obesity. Five genes have been implicated in weight control of mice (Friedman et al 1991). One of these is the obesity (*Ob*) gene on mouse chromosome 6. This gene codes for a protein or factor that is secreted from fat cells into the bloodstream. It may contain a 'stop eating' signal for the hypothalamus. *Ob* mice do not produce this signal. The mouse gene was cloned and sequenced. The DNA sequence of this gene in mouse was used to identify the homologous gene in humans, which may be on human chromosome 7 and which may play a role in regulating human appetite. However, there are limits to such animal models. These occur at the genic, physiological and behavioural levels. These will be considered in turn for the development of animal models for human aggression.

At the genic level, mice and humans have homologous genes coding for homologous proteins, and these have homologous functions at some but not all biological levels. For example, mice and humans have a homologous gene, sex determining region on the Y (*Sry*) chromosome, coding for the testis determining factor (Goodfellow & Lovell-Badge 1993). The part of this gene required for testis determination in mice and humans is very homologous. Other regions are not. In mice, one of these regions has many CAG repeats. This region of the gene may be involved in sex reversals and in offence in mice (Maxson 1995). Since such repeats do not exist in this region of the homologous human gene, this region of the human gene may not have any effect on sex reversal or aggression. Thus, homologous genes may not always have homologous functions. Consequently, as part of the development of animal models of human aggression, the DNA sequence should be determined for both mouse and human homologues of mouse genes with effects on a type of mouse aggression.

At the physiological level, different neural processes may regulate apparently similar behaviours. For example, different neurotransmitter systems appear to be involved in the predatory behaviour of rodents and carnivores. This conclusion is based on pharmacological studies of predation in rodents and carnivores (Miczek et al 1993b). Similarly, it may be that testosterone (Benton 1992) or 5-HT (Miczek et al 1993b) act differently in rodent and in human offensive aggression. Such differences at the physiological level may be due to: (1) different biochemical pathways; (2) different developmental pathways; and (3) different life histories and lifespans of mice and humans (Erickson 1989). Thus, the physiological pathway for a gene's effect on a type of mouse aggression must be fully understood and similarities and differences between mice and humans in this physiological pathway should be identified as part of the process of developing it as an animal model of human aggression.

An animal behaviour will always be, at best, both similar and different in comparison with that of humans. For this reason, Scott (1984, 1989) suggests that no animal species can serve as an exact model for any type of human aggression. Consequently, he proposed that information should be accumulated on the various kinds of aggression in a wide range of species. Scott has carried out part of this program by considering the advantages and disadvantages of dogs (Scott 1984) and mice (Scott 1989) as potential animal models for some aspects of human aggression.

Blanchard & Blanchard (1989) have taken a similar approach in their research program on animals models of aggression. This is a two-part strategy. The first is to describe, examine and analyse in detail aggressive behaviour in the context of a species' ecology and evolution. The second is a systematic comparison of the human behaviour with the animal model to determine the extent of point-by-point correspondence. They have done this for two types of aggression—offence and defence—in rats and humans as well as to some degree for other mammalian species. They have cogently argued that across species (including humans): (1) offence and defence motor patterns differ; (2) defensive attack is more likely to be seriously injurious than offensive attack; and (3) offence and defence serve different functions. They suggest that defence serves the function of self-protection from injury by others and that offence serves the function of obtaining and retaining survival and reproductive resources. Furthermore, it has been proposed that each is a motivational system with potential neural homologies across species.

Most genetic research on mouse attack behaviour has been on offensive aggression of males. When genes are identified for this behaviour and when the mechanism of their effects are understood, these may be developed as animal models for comparable aspects of human offence. These are more likely to be for motivational than sensory or motor aspects of offence. But assessment of risk and RHP may also be part of such animal models. For the development of animal models at this level, there must be a careful point-by-point comparison of the mouse and human behaviours.

Conclusion

Critical evaluation of each of the following aspects will be important in the development of animal models for any type of human aggression, which are based on identification of individual genes for one or more types of mouse aggression. First, the obtained genetics must be scrutinized. What is the evidence and how good is it for this or that gene to be involved in a type of mouse aggression? Second, information on the behaviour should be detailed and complete. This requires video recording of encounters, and their computer analysis. Third, the mechanism for effect of the gene on aggression must be analysed from the DNA sequence to the behaviour and it must be related to the role of contextual and life history variables in behavioural development and expression. Fourth, the points of similarity and dissimilarity for the effects of this gene on a type of mouse and human aggression must be determined. Thus, animal models of human aggression can be developed from genes identified for a type of mouse aggression, but this requires careful and critical attention to each of these issues. Animal models of human aggression will contribute to our understanding of it by providing exact information of the interrelation of biological and environmental variables in the development, expression and escalation of a type of aggression.

References

Archer J, Huntingford F 1994 Game theory models and escalation of animal fights. In: Potegal M, Knutson JF (eds) The dynamics of aggression: biological and social processes in dyads and groups. Lawrence Erlbaum, Hilsdale, NJ, p 3–31

Benton D 1981 The measurement of aggression in the laboratory. In: Brain PF, Benton D (eds) The biology of aggression. Sijthoff & Noordhoff, Rockville, MD, p 487–502

Benton D 1992 Hormones and human aggression. In: Björkqvist K, Niemelä P (eds) Of mice and women: aspects of female aggression. Academic Press, New York, p 37–48

Blanchard DC, Blanchard RJ 1989 Experimental animal models of aggression: what do they say about human behavior? In: Archer J, Browne K (eds) Human aggression: a naturalistic approach. Routledge, New York, p 94–121

Carlier M, Roubertoux P 1986 Difference between CBA/H and NZB mice in intermale aggression. In: Medioni J, Vaysse G (eds) Genetic approaches to behaviour. Privat (International Ethological Congress) IEC, Toulouse, p 47–57

Crabbe JC, Belknap JK, Buck KJ 1994 Genetic animal models of alcohol and drug abuse. Science 264:1715–1723

Dietrich WF, Miller JC, Steel RG et al 1994 A genetic map of the mouse with 4,006 simple sequence length polymorphisms. Nat Genet 7:220–225

Eleftheriou BE, Bailey DW, Denenberg VH 1974 Genetic analysis of fighting behavior in mice. Physiol & Behav 13:773–777

Erickson RP 1989 Why isn't a mouse more like a man? Trends Genet 5:1–3

Friedman JM, Leibel RL, Bahary N 1991 Molecular mapping of obesity genes. Mamm Genet 1:130–144

Ghosh S, Todd JA 1991 Genetic analysis of multifactorial disease: lessons from type-1 diabetes. In: Davies KE, Tilghman SM (eds) Genes and phenotypes. Cold Spring Harbor Laboratory, Plainview, NY, p 79–104

Goodfellow PH, Lovell-Badge R 1993 SRY and sex determination in mammals. Annu Rev Genet 27:71–92

Guillot P-V, Carlier M, Maxson SC, Roubertoux PL 1995 Intermale aggression tested in two different procedures, using four inbred strains of mice and their reciprocal congenics: Y chromosomal implications. Behav Genet 25:357–360

Hahn ME, Schanz N 1995 Issues in the genetics of social behavior: revisited. Behav Genet, in press

Lander ES, Botstein D 1989 Mendelian factors underlying quantitative traits using RFLP linkage maps. Genetics 121:185–199

Maxson SC 1981 The genetics of aggression in vertebrates. In: Brain PF, Benton D (eds) The biology of aggression. Sijthoff & Noordhoff, Rockville, MD, p 69–104

Maxson SC 1992a Methodological issues in genetic analyses of an agonistic behavior (offense) in male mice. In: Goldowitz D, Wahlsten D, Wimer RE (eds) Techniques for the genetic analysis of brain and behavior: focus on the mouse. Elsevier Science, New York, p 349–373

Maxson SC 1992b Potential genetic models of aggression and violence in males. In: Driscoll P (ed) Genetically defined animal models of neurobehavioral dysfunctions. Birkhäuser, Boston, MA, p 174–188

Maxson SC 1992c MHC genes, chemosignals, and genetic analyses of murine social behaviors. In: Doty RL, Müller-Schwarze S (eds) Chemical signals in vertebrates. VI. Plenum, New York, p 197–204

Maxson SC 1995 Searching for candidate genes with effects on an agonistic behavior, offense, in male mice. Behav Genet, in press

Maxson SC, Platt T, Shrenker P, Trattner A 1982 The influence of the Y chromosome of Rb/1Bg mice on agonistic behaviors. Aggressive Behav 8:285–291

Maxson SC, Didier-Erickson A, Ogawa S 1989 The Y chromosome, social signals, and offense in mice. Behav Neural Biol 52:251–259

Miczek KA, Weerts EM, DeBold JF 1993a Alcohol, benzodiazepine–GABA$_A$ receptor complex and aggression: ethological analysis of individual differences in rodents and primates. J Stud Alcohol S11:170–179

Miczek KA, Haney M, Tidey J, Vivian J, Weerts E 1993b Neurochemistry and pharmacotherapeutic management of aggression and violence. In: Reiss AJ, Miczek

KA, Roths JA (eds) Understanding and preventing violence, vol 2: Biobehavioral influences. National Academy, Washington, DC, p 245–514

Nadeau JH 1989 Maps of linkage and synteny homologies between mouse and man. Trends Genet 5:82–86

Novikov SN 1993 The genetics of pheremonally mediated intermale aggression in mice: current status and prospect of the model. Behav Genet 23:505–508

O'Brien SJ, Seuanex HN, Womack JE 1988 Mammalian genome organization: an evolutionary view. Annu Rev Genet 22:323–351

Parmigiani S, Brain PF, Palanza P 1989 Ethoexperimental analysis of different forms of intraspecific aggression in house mice (*Mus musculus*). In: Blanchard RJ, Brain PF, Blanchard DC, Parmigiani S (eds) Ethoexperimental approaches to the study of behavior. Kluwer Academic, Boston, MA, p 418–431

Plomin R, McClearn GE 1993 Quantitative trait loci (QTL) analysis and alcohol-related behaviors. Behav Genet 23:197–211

Popova NK, Kulikov AV 1986 Genetic analysis of 'spontaneous' intermale aggression in mice. Aggressive Behav 12:425–431

Rodgers RJ 1991 Effects of benzodiazepine and 5-HT receptor ligands on aggression and defense in animals. In: Rodgers RJ, Cooper SJ (eds) 5-HT$_{1A}$ agonists, 5-HT$_3$ antagonists and benzodiazepenes: their comparative behavioral pharmacology. Wiley, New York, p 195–231

Saudou F, Amara DA, Dierich A et al 1994 Enhanced aggressive behavior in mice lacking 5-HT$_{1B}$ receptor. Science 265:1875–1878

Scott JP 1984 The dog as a model for human aggression. In: Flannelly KJ, Blanchard RJ, Blanchard DC (eds) Biological perspectives on aggression. A. R. Liss, New York, p 95–103

Scott JP 1989 The evolution of social systems. Gordon & Breach, New York

Smith DL, Julian A, Erwin BG et al 1992 Dopamine D$_2$ receptor RFLP in BXD RIs and assignment to chromosome 9. Mouse Genome 90:439–440

Tolman EC 1924 The inheritance of maze learning in rats. J Comp Psychol 42:58–63

DISCUSSION

Carey: Is there a human polymorphism for the 5-HT$_{1B}$ receptor gene that Saudou et al (1994) knocked out?

Maxson: I don't know, but there is a human equivalent (5-HT$_{1D\beta}$).

Goldman: We've screened more than 300 impulsive Finnish alcoholics, many with very low CSF 5-hydroxyindoleacetic acid levels, using the single-strand conformational polymorphism method to identify mutations in the 5-HT$_{1D\beta}$ coding sequence. We did not observe an amino acid substitution that could alter the function of the 5-HT$_{1D\beta}$ receptor, although a synonymous substitution was detected (Lappalainen et al 1995). Also, Peter Propping's group recently reported a rare amino acid substitution in the 5-HT$_{1D\beta}$ receptor (Nothen et al 1994).

Hinde: In discussing the identification of mouse genes for aggression, you mentioned the discrepancy between measures. Should you not also investigate many other behaviours as well, to see whether latency might not just be a general characteristic that affects a whole range of behaviours other than aggression?

Maxson: Yes; that's why I prefer analysing mouse aggression by videotaping, because by doing this you can study the other behaviours.

Rowe: Are there many genes that have been identified on the mouse Y chromosome?

Maxson: Recent literature on both the mouse and human Y chromosome suggested that there may be as many as 300–400 genes on it (Affara & Lau 1994). Among others, the mouse Y has *Sry*, *Zfy-1*, *Ube-1Y* and *SmcY*.

Goldman: One of the strengths of these mouse studies was that it was possible to arrange crosses between genetically homogeneous strains and to perform reciprocal crosses. When you did this, you found evidence for an aggressivity gene on the Y chromosome. Could you also interpret the results from the reciprocal crosses as indicating that a genetically imprinted gene was involved in the behaviour? This would again point you to a narrower set of the total complement of genes, namely the genes that are differentially imprinted.

Maxson: I don't think so, because among the crosses were a DBA1 female by a BL/10 male, and a DBA1 female by a BL/10 male carrying a DBA1 Y chromosome. If there had been imprinting, we would have obtained the same results for both crosses, and we didn't.

Virkkunen: I find it difficult to see the clear connections between animal (especially rat and mouse) and human studies concerning aggression. In these studies we speak, for instance, about offensive, defensive, predatory and isolation-induced aggression. It is difficult to envisage the equivalent human behaviours in each case and whether the equivalents even exist. Human impulsive violence, especially, is very strongly connected with alcohol abuse.

Concerning the study you mentioned on the 5-HT$_{1B}$ receptor knockout mice, how important do you think this receptor is in animal aggression?

Maxson: Unfortunately, what I reported is all I know about this. The 5-HT$_{1B}$ knockout mice show twice the level of aggressiveness. I don't know what twice the level of aggressiveness means in terms of the behaviours I was describing.

Goldman: I think the importance of a finding like that made by Saudou and colleagues (1994) is not that it shows what *is* happening in the human; it shows what *could* happen if 5-HT$_{1D\beta}$ function were to be knocked out, for example by a stop codon mutation.

Maxson: You will not necessarily find the same variants in humans as in mice. One reason for using the knockout approach is that it is possible to investigate monomorphic as well as polymorphic genes of the mouse, and look at their functions. Results from such studies can also be suggestive of what could happen in humans.

Brunner: I would like to emphasize the limitations of animal models. For instance, there are mouse models for both variants of Waardenburg syndrome. For type I, mice lacking the *Pax-3* gene have normal hearing, whereas this causes deafness in humans. There's also a high incidence of neural tube defects in mice with this condition, whereas these are much rarer in human patients. Mutations in the homology of the Waardenburg gene type II give mice micropthalmia, and they don't do this in humans. The mouse model for myotonic dystrophy involves cardiac symptoms and cerebral ventricular dilatation, which are minor symptoms in humans, and none of the classic symptoms of myotonic dystrophy. So far, there has been no identical animal model for any human condition.

Maxson: I don't think that we'll ever be able to find any with complete identity at all biological levels. What we have to look for are those pieces that may be similar.

Carlier: Animal models such as mice provide us with the opportunity to disentangle some mechanisms with techniques that cannot be used in humans. For example, we spoke earlier about the possible implications of the Y chromosome on aggression. In mice, three teams working on different populations have demonstrated the implications of possession of a Y chromosome in attack behaviour against conspecific males (Maxson et al 1979, Roubertoux et al 1994, van Oortmerssen & Sluyter 1994). Moreover the gene(s) involved are not on the same region of the Y chromosomes in these three populations. For example, Maxson's group found Y correlate(s) located on the specific part of the Y, and Roubertoux & Carlier's group found these on the pairing region of this chromosome. In our research, the candidate gene is either the steroid sulphatase gene (*Sts*) or a different gene close to *Sts*. Recently, Hervé Degrelle and Séphane Mortaud found that the steroid sulphatase is expressed in the brain (personal communication). Note that the *Sts* locus is located on the specific part of the X chromosome in humans. Moreover, in the experimental models used by all three teams, the Y chromosome effect interacts with the genetic background. This is very important: it means that it is not possible accurately to predict the behaviour of an individual solely on the basis of the knowledge that this individual bears a given gene. The picture is even more complicated because of the involvement of the maternal environments (pre- and postnatal—see Fig. 1 [*Carlier*]). Under such conditions any attempt to extrapolate to humans is risky.

Plomin: One other point that needs to be made about animal models is that we don't have to argue for isomorphism at the phenotypic level—we can make comparisons at the fundamental level of DNA. That is, we do not need to argue that aggressive behaviour in mouse and man is the same. Instead, we can use a mouse model—and the experimental power offered by mouse genetics— to identify genes or at least chromosomal regions that affect aggressive behaviour in mice. Then we can use these as candidate genes in studies of human aggression. For example, we have extended the RIs approach to single-gene mapping to the case of QTLs in which multiple genes are involved in complex, quantitatively distributed traits (Plomin & McClearn 1993). The RIs

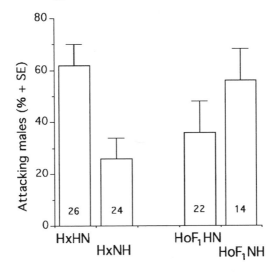

FIG. 1. (*Carlier*) Interaction between genotype and maternal environment (from Carlier et al 1991). The number of subjects is indicated in the columns. The subjects are male mice observed at adulthood in an aggression test. They were born from crosses of inbred strains of laboratory mice (CBA/H, abbreviated H; BZB/B1N, abbreviated N). HxHN males were born to an H mother crossed with an HN father. HxNH males were born to an H mother crossed with an NH father. The two groups share the same genotype except for the Y chromosome (whose origin is either H or N) and the same maternal environments (pre- and postnatal from H). The two other groups also share the same genotype except for the Y chromosome. However, they were born to and reared by F1 females grafted with H ovaries ('o' indicates the operation: for more details on such an experimental design see Carlier et al 1992). This design allows one to test for the effect of change in the maternal environments (pre- and postnatal) on males differing only in the Y chromosome. Here the interaction is significant ($P < 0.05$): in an H maternal environment, males bearing the Y chromosome from the N strain attack more frequently than males bearing the Y chromosome from the H strain. The reverse is observed when the mother has another genotype (here a hybrid genotype obtained by the cross of the two parental strains H and N).

QTL approach and other experimental genetic approaches have revolutionized genetic studies of behaviour in mice (Crabbe et al 1994). The pay-off of this work lies in nominating candidate chromosomal regions and genes for human genetic studies. Such candidates are sorely needed in human genetic research. In the outbred human species, it is difficult to conduct systematic searches of the genome, but it is quite straightforward to test nominated regions and genes.

Cairns: When we think about models of animal behaviour, it's a special folly to hop from one phenotype in a species to what is seemingly a similar phenotype in a rather distant species. A broader issue is that we should embed the behaviour in an understanding of that organism's adaptation. That is, we should aim to understand the network of relationships that exist in that species under the conditions that it is adapted to in terms of its evolutionary and developmental history. If we use polythetic criteria as opposed to monothetic criteria, we're going to have a more complete and more accurate story at the end.

If we're going to talk about animal models and generalization, we should have a logical and systematic way to approach the development of patterns of behaviour, as opposed to looking at single characteristics and hoping that somehow a homologue will be identified.

Bouchard: If you want to look at the natural behaviour of the organism that has been shaped by evolution that's fine, but you can't look at it in all these inbred animals. They are unrepresentative of the species. In inbred animals, the organization of the genome is broken up. If you want naturalness and adaptation you have to use wild-type animals; if you want to be able to control the genetic background and the breeding history you have to use inbred animals.

Hinde: But naturalness isn't the whole point here; the main issue is the need for psychological analysis before you can specify genes for aggression in any species. You need to know the relationships between the different types of behaviour in that species, never mind whether they are natural or not.

Goldman: The point that Tom Bouchard has raised is being addressed: people are not only studying a wide variety of strains, they are also beginning to study wild strains, such as *Mus spretus*, *Mus castaneus* and *Mus molossimus*, to verify their conclusions. However, this type of work is not yet well reflected in the literature.

Bouchard: It adds another layer to the analysis.

Goldman: Particular behaviours, for example nest-building behaviours, may be lost in inbred strains. But, on the other hand, if a behaviour is present you can probably study its genetics in the inbred strain.

Maxson: The motor patterns in the aggressive behaviours I described are the same in wild mice as in our inbred mice. In fact, the motor patterns are the same across all the rodents. So it really doesn't matter in these cases whether you are looking at laboratory or wild animals.

Carlier: I agree with Stephen Maxson. van Oortmerssen & Sluyter (1994) are working on selected lines of wild house mice. They obtained results comparable to those obtained on inbred strains, although the genetic pool of the populations used was quite different.

Daly: I have a question about the inference of possible Y chromosome effects from the reciprocal crosses. Couldn't reciprocal cross differences sometimes mean that autosomal genes from the paternal line acting in the maternal-line uterine environment are producing different effects than in their own strain's uterine environment? I surmise that other ways of checking that these are really Y chromosome effects are then brought to bear, but I was wondering: when people get a hint in these reciprocal crosses that there might be a Y chromosome effect, do you carry that Y chromosome down through several generations of matings with the maternal strain to see if it's really the Y?

Maxson: That's basically what's done. We make congenic strains for the Y chromosome, and compare strains that differ only in a specific part of the Y. In these cases, we get the same kinds of differences for reciprocal F1s and for Y congenic strain pairs.

Daly: Does one typically find that if you have something that shows a reciprocal-cross difference, it will turn out to be borne on the Y chromosome?

Maxson: There are three studies that showed aggression differences for reciprocal F1s. These are mine in Storrs, and those in France and The Netherlands. Y congenic and other crosses have been used to show that the reciprocal F1 differences in the Storrs and The Netherlands studies involve the specific part of the Y and in the French and Dutch studies involve the pairing region of the Y.

References

Affara NA, Lau Y-FC 1994 Report on the first international workshop on human Y chromosome mapping. Cytogenet Cell Genet 67:359–402

Carlier M, Roubertoux PL, Pastoret C 1991 The Y chromosome effect on intermale aggression in mice depends on the maternal environment. Genetics 129:231–236

Carlier M, Nosten-Bertrand M, Michard-Vanhee Ch 1992 The separation of genetic from maternal effects. In: Goldowitz D, Wahlsten D, Wimer RE (eds) Techniques for the genetic analysis of brain and behaviour: focus on the mouse. Elsevier, Amsterdam, p 111–126

Crabbe JC, Belknap JK, Buck KJ 1994 Genetic animal models of alcohol and drug abuse. Science 264:1715–1723

Lappalainen J, Dean M, Charbonneau L, Virkkunen M, Linnoila M, Goldman D 1995 Mapping of the 5-HT1Dβ autoreceptor gene on chromosome 6 and direct analysis for sequence variants. Am J Med Genet 60:157–161

Maxson S, Ginsburg BE, Trattner A 1979 Interaction of Y-chromosomal and autosomal gene(s) in the development of intermale aggression in mice. Behav Genet 9:219–226

Nothen MM, Erdmann J, Shimron-Abaranell D, Propping P 1994 Identification of genetic variation in the human serotonin 1D beta receptor gene. Biochem Biophys Res Commun 205:1194–1200

Plomin R, Daniels D 1987 Why are children in the same family so different from each other? Behavioral & Brain Sci 10:1–16

Roubertoux PL, Carlier M, Degrelle H, Haas Dupertuis MC, Phillips J, Moutier R 1994 Co-segregation of intermale aggression with the pseudoautosomal region of the Y chromosome in mice. Genetics 135:225–230

Saudou F, Amara DA, Dierich A et al 1994 Enhanced aggressive behavior in mice lacking 5-HT$_{1B}$ receptor. Science 265:1875–1878

van Oortmerssen GA, Sluyter F 1994 Studies on wild house mice. V. Aggression in lines selected for attack latency and their Y-chromosomal congenics. Behav Genet 24:73–78

General discussion I

Rowe: I just wanted to comment on the phenotypes that we're looking at. There is a large literature in criminology that concerns whether delinquent behaviours are specialized or generalized. For instance, 'specialization' would describe someone who commits burglaries without threatening people, and never commits assaults or robberies, whereas a 'generalization' view is that these acts are substitutable. The criminological literature comes out pretty strongly on the side of generalization—that there is not, for instance, an aggressive type of individual. Rather, aggression is a less frequent behaviour that occurs among people who display many other kinds of antisocial behaviour. It's also a lifestyle: there are elements of it that are not illegal, but antisocial individuals tend to have a higher frequency of, say, tattooing or wearing nose and lip rings (but that's probably just my prejudice showing at the surface!). It's a broader thing than just specific violations of a criminal code. In terms of the close cultural relativity, although these risk-taking behaviours may have positive aspects, I don't think you will find a society where they're regarded positively. One thing we know from evolutionary psychology is that social reciprocity is a basic underlying human process for behaviour—relationships are expected to involve repayments of favours done toward others. Antisocial behaviour, at the elemental level, always violates that law of repaying. Sometimes they do direct harm and sometimes they do harm indirectly by not following through social obligations.

Rutter: I agree that the evidence does favour generality. However, one has to be cautious about using crime statistics, because a majority of crimes of violence involve people who are convicted because they are *associated* with crimes and violence (such as by serving as a look-out or driver) rather than actually having committed violent acts themselves. This confuses things.

Mednick: I would like to comment on the question of 'cafeteria-style' crime versus specialization. What you get out depends on what you put in. There have been many studies that are difficult to interpret because their samples were too small and they didn't follow samples long enough to detect specialization. One of the better studies was done by Marvin Wolfgang, but his definition of specialization was unusual (Wolfgang et al 1972). For example, if an individual committed a violent crime, he defined the individual as specializing if the *very next* crime they committed was a violent crime. We have examined specialization in a cohort (32 000 men) followed to age 26, and found that using a different criterion you do observe specialization (Brennan et al 1990). If one person commits a violent crime for his first offence, and another commits a property crime, what is the probability that either of these men would subsequently commit a violent crime? It's significantly higher for the individual who first committed a violent crime. I believe that this is a more reasonable definition of specialization. We are not claiming that the person only commits violent crimes; people who commit violent crimes commit a lot of crimes, including property crimes. It's also true that many commit a large number of property crimes and never commit a violent crime.

Hinde: I take issue with the argument that just because reciprocity is a cultural norm in all human societies, the propensities that underlie antisocial behaviour are never advantageous and have never have been selected for. A major problem in understanding human behaviour is this balance between positive reciprocity and cooperation on the one hand, and assertiveness, aggressiveness and all these other 'nasties' on the other.

Rowe: I didn't say they were never advantageous. In fact, I think there are circumstances when the 'nasties' are advantageous. From the point of view of an organized society, I think you would be hard pressed to find a society that would encourage you to cheat on your neighbour, lie to your wife, and not fulfil your obligations. However, there may be both financial and reproductive pay-offs for individuals who engage in such antisocial behaviours.

Heath: The fact that people who commit property crimes keep committing property crimes and that people who commit violent crimes have an increased probability of committing further violent crimes, isn't necessarily supportive of a specificity hypothesis. In the same way, if you compare people who pass easy IQ tests but not difficult ones with people who pass difficult ones, you see exactly the same phenomenon, but it's not inconsistent with the generalized model. There are other things that you can look at in the data which might support specificity, but that particular result doesn't contradict the generalized model.

Rutter: In short, the validation of any classificatory distinction necessarily relies on showing that the categories or traits differ in their correlates with some feature outside the behaviours that define the traits (Cantwell & Rutter 1994).

Gottesman: There's an empirical example that relates to some of these questions. During the time that I was working with Sarnoff Mednick (Mednick & Christiansen 1977) on the adoption and twin studies, prostitution and pornography were decriminalized in Denmark. When this happened, we thought that we would lose a lot of subjects that had been hits under the old system. It turned out that we lost some, but many of these people had, in the meantime, committed other offences that got them back on the books.

Denno: My own research also sheds some light on whether criminal activity is general or specific. I developed a model with numerous biological and sociological variables in order to predict two different measures of crime: (1) number of offences committed in the age range 7–18; and (2) the seriousness of those offences, using a crime seriousness index. The crime seriousness index reflected the total of assigned numerical weights to different components of a juvenile's offence, such as level of injury. The weights were developed from a national survey of a representative sample of individuals in the USA concerning their weighting of crime severity. The seriousness score allowed a more precise representation of offence seriousness relative to that reflected in number of offences and also provided a method of summarizing, in one score, the severity of an offender's juvenile record throughout adolescence (see Wolfgang et al 1985).

I found that my model's results with male offenders were pretty much the same, regardless of whether I used number of offences or seriousness of offences as my dependent measure. Among females, however, the dependent variables did make a difference. Females who had a high seriousness score were a much more dangerous bunch than those females who committed a large number of offences. It appeared that there were some females who engaged in a relatively large number of petty crimes, such as shoplifting, and would not do anything more than that. This was less the case with males.

Cairns: One of the findings I have been surprised by in animal behaviour studies—our own included—has been how general genetic mechanisms can bring about very specific phenotypic outcomes. Aggressive behaviour is a social act, and common sense suggests that it would be a difficult activity to fine-tune through general genetic and neurobiological mechanisms. In fact, aggressive behaviour is fine-tuned to situations, to sex and to age.

On a separate issue, I would like to emphasize that not all genes contributing to antisocial behaviour are carried on the Y chromosome. One of the problems in these studies has been that investigators have failed to look at sex-appropriate conditions for assessment. Kathy Hood (at Penn State) and I have published on this issue, showing that the heritability of aggressive or attack behaviour is autosomal, at least in the lines that we have created (Hood & Cairns 1988, 1989, Cairns et al 1990). You don't see it expressed unless you test the females in female-appropriate attack conditions, i.e. post partum. The females who attack in post partum have brothers who attack in territorial situations. We should know the behaviour systems, and it requires assessment across the broader spectrum of adaptation before we can come to definitive conclusion on whether or not a given behaviour is linked to a specific biological or genetic substrate.

Waldman: It is probably fairly obvious to most people in this group that it's pretty important in the generalization/specificity debate to distinguish between the observed phenotype and liability. With that in mind, it would be interesting to know to what extent violent crimes simply reflect a higher threshold on the same liability continuum as other crimes, and to what extent they reflect a different liability altogether.

Plomin: Inbred mice offer an interesting opportunity to examine shared and non-shared environmental effects. Shared and non-shared environment refers to experiences that make children in the same family similar and different, respectively (Plomin & Daniels 1987). Mice within an inbred strain are genetically identical, which means that all observed differences within a strain of inbred mice can be attributed to environmental effects. Between-litter differences estimate shared environment and within-litter effects are due to non-shared environment. For example, for aggressive behaviour in mice, it would be interesting to know whether shared environmental effects become less influential as mice leave their litters and make their own way in the world.

Carlier: Within-litter differences may be due to the intrauterine position phenomenon. I am referring to the 'morphological, physiological and behavioural differences among animals within a sex which are related to intrauterine placement next to fetuses of the same or opposite sex. The various effects are thought to be mediated through differences in levels of steroid hormones to which fetuses are exposed *in utero*' (Bulman-Fleming & Wahlsten 1991, p 397). Moreover, consequences of crowding or differences in placement in the uterine horn have also been found. Of special interest in this context is vom Saal's (1984) work. He found that females situated in the uterine horn between two males displayed a higher level of aggressive behaviour at adulthood than females between two females. The intrauterine position phenomenon is rarely reported in humans. A masculinization of the auditory system of adult women having male co-twins was recently found and interpreted as a prenatal masculinization related to the presence of the male co-twin (McFadden 1993).

Plomin: What you describe is a genotype-by-environment interaction. That is, the maternal effect differs as a function of genotype. Genotype–environment interactions are interactions in the statistical sense of a conditional relationship—the effect of an environmental factor depends on genotype (or, conversely, the effect of a genotype depends on the environment). Although such interactions are interesting and likely to be important, what I was referring to were 'main effects' of the environment. Maternal effects could, for example, be a source of shared environment regardless of genotype. Although a realization of the importance of non-shared environment has swept through the field of human development during the past decade, non-shared environment has scarcely been considered in animal research, even though, as I have said, inbred strains provide a powerful approach to disentangling shared and non-shared environment. Behavioural differences within inbred strains of mice are very impressive and can only be due to non-genetic factors. Moreover, many of these differences are within litter, suggesting the importance of non-shared environment. That is, genetically identical members of an inbred strain, brought up in the same litter and in the same cage, are remarkably different. In human research, aggressive behaviour and conduct disorder in childhood and adolescence is an exception to the rule that most environmental influence is of the non-shared environment (Plomin 1994).

It would be interesting if it turned out that aggressive behaviour in mice also showed shared environmental influence, at least in the early years.

Carlier: It is known that female rodents are able to discriminate among pups that differ not only by genotype, but also by size or sex (Carlier 1986). For example, the mother's licking behaviour differs according to the sex of the pups. Mothers are also able to recognize wounded pups, and take more care of them.

Cairns: Celia Moore at the University of Massachusetts has studied the differential maternal treatment of males and females (Moore 1992). Essentially, she finds that males provide different chemicals in the urine, leading to differential attraction. In mice, there is also differential access to suckling as a function of the size and activity level of the neonates.

If you look at animals at adolescence, and you put them in a coercive environment where there is a high incidence of within-group fighting, there are very powerful shared environment effects regardless of genetic background.

Plomin: I would like to return to the issue that juvenile delinquency and conduct disorder in adolescence appears to be the exception to the rule that environmental influence is largely of the non-shared variety. That is, whatever the salient environmental factors may be, they make two children growing up in the same family as different as children growing up in different families. Juvenile delinquency is a striking exception to this rule and this is an important example of the usefulness of genetic research for investigating environmental factors. For example, both monozygotic and dizygotic twins are highly similar for juvenile delinquency. The absence of much difference between monozygotic and dizygotic correlations or concordances suggests that genetics has little to do with it, and the high similarity for both types of twins suggests the importance of shared environmental factors. Is it still generally accepted that shared environmental factors are paramount for juvenile delinquency? What about the suggestion that this might be an artefact—the idea that twins, for example, might be partners in crime? Is anyone addressing this issue?

Lyons: Joanne Meyer (from the Medical College of Virginia) and I looked at the individual antisocial criteria in the Vietnam Era Veteran Twin data collected by Ming Tsuang at Harvard. We fitted models that included sibling interaction. Adding sibling interaction to the model with additive genetic, shared environmental and unique environmental effects did not provide a better fit to the data for any of the criteria.

Rowe: The partners in crime is part and parcel of the shared environmental effect for criminal behaviour (Rowe & Gulley 1992, Carey 1992). Greg Carey did a re-analysis of the Mednick twin series, showing that heritability estimates fall for those twin studies when you include the sibling effect. But it's quite clear that identical and fraternal twins and non-twin brothers, for example, cooperate in crime. So there's a direct mutual influence of non-criminal siblings on one another and criminal siblings on one another. West &

Farrington identified 411 boys aged 8–10 in South London in 1961–62. Prospective study continues, material up to age 32 having been reported so far (West 1969, 1982, West & Farrington 1973, 1977, Farrington & West 1990). I took David Farrington's (D. C. Rowe & D. F. Farrington, unpublished results) families that all have three brothers, and I asked the question: how many of these families have no convicted brothers, exactly one convicted brother, exactly two convicted brothers and exactly three convicted brothers? If you look at the overall proportion of convicted men in these families and derive the binomial distribution, then more families than you would expect had three convicted brothers, and more than you would expect had zero convicted brothers. This suggests that if you are in either a conforming or non-conforming sibship, social influence is reinforced; hence, the strange distribution. This distribution departs from any known genetic model.

Taylor: Within a subgroup defined as vulnerable, Farrington & West (1993) showed an interesting difference between the recidivist offenders and their siblings and peers who did not offend. To qualify as vulnerable, boys had to have at least three of the following adverse factors at age 8–10: low family income, large family size, a convicted parent, low non-verbal IQ and poor parental child-rearing behaviour. Both the recidivists and the non-offenders proved to be asocial, but in very different ways. This was to do with their capacity for social interaction. In one sense, this was contrary to what might be expected: not withstanding their early identification as troublesome (they were more likely to be rated as frequent liars, lacking in concentration, restless, frequent truants and precociously sexually experienced), the group who became recidivist offenders had a better capacity for social interaction. Those who were not offending at all were solitary, living in squalor, unmarried, in conflict with their family, in debt and of low social status. Personal traits seem to have been important. Is there a clue here to genetic mediation—children with social disadvantage as a relative constant but with very different criminal propensities? The issue ceases to be whether there is a genetics of crime (which I argued earlier was impossible anyway because of the nature of crime), but becomes one of whether there is genetically determined behaviour (for example, to do with activity levels) that may account for growth from a certain kind of environment and perhaps predispose to crime.

Rowe: This is not exactly relevant to the model I just described. It's true that Farrington & West's non-offenders are not an appealing group. Some of the non-offenders were very shy, socially disabled people.

Carey: This discussion that we're having serves to highlight one of the data sets that we urgently need—that is, some type of longitudinal study that's going to work its way through adolescence and go on to adulthood. Those type of data are sorely needed.

Rowe: There's a new adoption data set that Matt McGue (unpublished results) has developed. He has almost 300 pairs of unrelated kids raised together, and they're not similar on any personality traits; but they're quite similar on whether they drink or smoke. They're a bit alike for antisocial behaviour—that was the other significant correlation. This agrees with the fact that unrelated kids reared together do resemble one another on antisocial, externalizing traits.

Mednick: On this question of shared environment, in the Danish Adoption Study, where we have 14 427 adoptions, we have a few cases where the families have put more than one child up for adoption. These children were not aware of each other and were usually adopted into very different environments. If one is placed in Copenhagen, for example, the next one will tend to be placed in Jutland, in the countryside. We find that as the degree of genetic relationship increases from zero to half siblings to full siblings, there is an increasing degree of concordance for having been convicted of a criminal offence.

Waldman: To go back to the issue of shared environment and sibling interaction, although it's true that sibling interaction hasn't yet been studied all that much in behaviour genetics, it seems to account for just some of the shared environment, not all of it. This still leaves room for looking at the effects of specific environmental variables.

Rowe: I'm sceptical—I think it is mainly the neighbourhood and the contemporaneous environment that's acting on these kids in their teenage years. I don't think it's something that has a long childhood history to it, nor do I believe it's something that's transmitted from parent to child, but it's difficult to tease these things apart.

Rutter: Are you saying that the shared effect begins to operate only in adolescence?

Rowe: Yes, it comes mainly in adolescence—it's not coming from early childhood. It is an immediate effect of siblings' local environmental circumstances; the availability of peers and siblings with particular inclinations. I think there's a lot of horizontal transmission through networks of adolescent kids.

Rutter: Surely a lot will depend on whether you're considering delinquent acts, where this may well apply, as opposed to individual differences in liability to a broader range of antisocial behaviours or conduct disturbance. For example, in our study comparing rates of disorder in 10-year-olds in the Isle of Wight with those from inner London, where the rate was twice as high in London, the main difference between the two areas lay in early-onset disorders, not in those beginning in adolescence (Rutter 1979/80). Moreover, the area differences were largely explicable in terms of the higher rates of family discord, disruption and other psychosocial problems in inner London.

Rowe: But you don't know whether these effects are coming through the family genetically or environmentally. Parents are not randomly assigned to the two regions. They may differ genetically as well as in the nurture they provide. Hence, genetic effects in families could raise the incidence of early-onset disorders in children on the Isle of Wight. And you don't have unrelated parent–child pairs in the two areas.

Mednick: Very often, what happens with families is that after they adopt a child, they then have a natural child, or they adopt another child. Thus, there are two children in the family, raised together from infancy, who are genetically unrelated. In these cases, we find that the rate of concordance for adult criminal law convictions is exactly the same as the concordance for two people chosen randomly who are genetically unrelated and are *not* raised together.

Goldman: But these comparisons may predominantly involve adoptees and non-adoptees raised in the same family. If these tend to be genetically different groups, the environmental concordance could have been masked.

Mednick: We can confine the analysis to cases where there are two adoptions in the same family.

Goldman: In the scenario you have just outlined, the effect of shared environment should be captured, so the issue would be whether the unrelated sib pairs were predominantly natural–adopted or adopted–adopted.

References

Brennan P, Mednick SA, John R 1990 Specialization in violence: evidence for a criminal subgroup. Criminology 27:437–453

Bulman-Fleming B, Wahlsten D 1991 The effects of intrauterine position on the degree of corpus callosum deficiency in two substrains of BALB/c mice. Dev Psychobiol 24:395–412

Cairns RB, Gariépy JL, Hood KE 1990 Development, microevolution, and social behavior. Psychol Rev 97:49–65

Cantwell DP, Rutter M 1994 Classification: conceptual issues and substantive findings. In: Rutter M, Taylor E, Hersov L (eds) Child and adolescent psychiatry: modern approaches. Blackwell Scientific, Oxford, p 3–21

Carey G 1992 Twin imitation for antisocial behavior: implications for genetic and family research. J Abnorm Psychol 101:18–25

Carlier M 1986 Les conduites d'adoption chez la souris: leur impact en analyse génétique. In: Desor D, Krafft B (eds) Les comportements parentaux. CNRS Comportements, Paris, p 115–122

Farrington DP, West DJ 1990 The Cambridge study in delinquent development: a long-term follow-up of 411 London males. In: Kerner H-J, Kaiser G (eds) Kriminalität: personlichkeit, lebensgechichte und verhalten. Springer-Verlag, Berlin, p 115–138

Farrington DP, West DJ 1993 Criminal, penal and life histories of chronic offenders: risk and protective factors and early identification. Crim Behav & Ment Health 3:492–523

Hood KE, Cairns RB 1988 A developmental genetics analysis of aggressive behavior in mice. II. Cross-sex inheritance. Behav Genet 18:605–619

Hood KE, Cairns RB 1989 A developmental genetics analysis of aggressive behaviour in mice. IV. Genotype–environment interaction. Aggressive Behav 15:361–380

McFadden D 1993 A masculinizing effect on the auditory systems of human females having male co-twins. Proc Natl Acad Sci USA 90:1900–1904

Mednick SA, Christiansen KO 1977 Biosocial bases of criminal behavior. Gardner Press, New York

Moore CL 1992 The role of maternal stimulation in the development of sexual behavior and its neural basis. Ann N Y Acad Sci 662:160–177

Plomin R 1994 Emanuel Miller memorial lecture 1993: Genetic research and identification of environmental influences. J Child Psychol Psychiatry Allied Discip 35:817–834

Plomin R, Daniels D 1987 Why are children in the same family so different from each other? Behav Brain Sci 10:1–16

Rowe DC, Gulley BL 1992 Sibling effects on substance use and delinquency. Criminology 30:217–233

Rutter M (ed) 1979/80 Changing youth in a changing society: patterns of adolescent development and disorder. Nuffield Provincial Hospitals Trust, London (1979), Harvard University Press, Cambridge, MA (1980)

vom Saal FS 1984 The intrauterine position phenomenon: effects on physiology, aggressive behaviour and population dynamics in house mice. In: Flennelly KJ, Blanchard RJ, Blanchard DC (eds) Progress in clinical and biological research, vol 169. Biological perspectives on aggression. Alan Liss, New York, p 135-179

West DJ 1969 Present conduct and future delinquency. Heinemann, London

West DJ 1982 Delinquency: its roots, careers and prospects. Heinemann, London

West DJ, Farrington DP 1973 Who becomes delinquent? Heinemann, London

West DJ, Farrington DP 1977 The delinquent way of life. Heinemann, London

Wolfgang ME, Figlio RM, Sellin T 1972 Delinquency in a birth cohort. University of Chicago Press, Chicago, IL

Wolfgang ME, Figlio RM, Tracy P, Singer S 1985 The national survey of crime severity. US Government Printing Office, Washington, DC

Aggression from a developmental perspective: genes, environments and interactions

Robert B. Cairns

Center for Developmental Science, University of North Carolina, 521 South Greensboro Street, Chapel Hill, NC 27599-8115, USA

Abstract. Genetic influences on the social behaviours of non-human mammals are ubiquitous, powerful and readily detected. But demonstrations that social behaviours are influenced by genes constitute only part of the story. Developmental findings have helped complete the picture. Specifically, these studies show that: (1) genetic effects for aggressive behaviours are highly malleable over the course of development; (2) genetic influences on aggressive behaviour are more dynamic, easily achieved and open to rapid manipulation than has been recognized in current models of social evolution and behavioural genetics; (3) developmental timing has a significant impact upon the nature of the genetic effects observed in aggressive behaviours. These empirical results are consistent with the view that social behaviours are among the first features to be influenced by genetic selection and by environmental experience. Social actions have distinctive properties in adaptation because they organize the space between the organism and the environment and promote rapid, selective and novel accommodations. The modern integrative view of the development of individual-in-context brings attention to the correlation between constraints within and external to individuals. This paper reviews findings on how these processes become integrated over time in individuals and species, and their implications for the nurture of nature.

1996 Genetics of criminal and antisocial behaviour. Wiley, Chichester (Ciba Foundation Symposium 194) p 45–60

Investigations of the nature and nurture of aggressive behaviours have been handicapped by the paucity of integrated research programmes. Piecemeal studies of genetics, rearing experiences, hormones and learning have yielded a number of intriguing outcomes (see Cairns 1979). But to account for the behaviour of whole organisms—whether humans or animals—the pieces must be fitted together. In order to clarify the contributions of genetic factors to aggressive and antisocial behaviours, it seems important to begin with a careful analysis of the behavioural phenomena to be explained, so the effects of biological factors can be understood in the context of interactional and environmental influences.

This strategy follows from Anastasi's point (1958) that, in studies of nature and nurture, the question should be 'how?' instead of 'how much?' (See also Bronfenbrenner & Ceci's [1994] recent extension of this line of reasoning to the development of intelligence in humans.) Accordingly, a primary aim of this chapter is to examine how studies of non-human mammals can be useful in clarifying the integration of genetic, neurobiological, social and environmental factors in the development of aggressive behaviours.

The role of animal models

Many students of personality and social development have assumed—erroneously, I believe—that social actions of humans are so complex that no animal model can be informative. As a corollary, it has been feared that any valid generalizations derived from animals will be so general as to be self-evident and vacuous, or so narrow that they could not be applied beyond the particular species investigated. In either case, as the reasoning goes, animal work can be dismissed because of its slender relevance for distinctively human processes.

This conclusion speaks to the logic of comparative behavioural analyses, and the criteria by which cross-species generalizations may be established. Unfortunately, any brief discussion of the problems of generalization on aggression across species is akin to taking a stroll through a semantic jungle (see Bandura 1973). And it may be unnecessary at this juncture. A developmental orientation to social behaviour does not permit one to lift a genetic or behavioural element out of context in judging whether or not a homology exists. Rather, the 'polythetic' strategy of development requires multiple dimensions of similarity in the behaviour system, its functions and its ontogeny prior to generalizing across species (Cairns 1979).

According to this view, the first goal of research should be to understand the multiple factors that regulate aggressive behaviours in a given species. Regardless of eventual cross-specific generalizations, it should be a significant advance to determine how aggressive behaviours, biology and environments are integrated in a given form, whether human or non-human. Once the within-species patterns of development are systematically described, research may then focus on commonalities and differences observed in ontogenies across species.

Accordingly, studies of non-human mammals offer non-trivial opportunities for systematic analysis. Specifically:

(1) Because of the relatively short period from conception to maturity in some species, studies on non-human species permit the manipulation of experiences over the life course, the tracking of effects in social behaviour

over generations, and the comparison of the ontogenies of successive generations.

(2) Through selective breeding and other procedures of genetic regulation, it is possible to manipulate heritable characteristics that are potentially related to aggressive and defensive behaviours.

(3) Aspects of the environment that are presumably relevant can be manipulated—early rearing, conditions of housing, characteristics of partner, length and timing of assessments—and thereby it is possible to identify precisely how the index social actions are influenced.

(4) Investigations of interconnections among biological and environmental manipulations can be conducted. Such research is critical to understanding precisely how biological and social–ecological factors become linked in social behaviours, and how the biology of organisms is influenced by their environments and social interactions.

(5) Similarities among mammals in brain architecture, along with similarities in neurobiological and endocrinological functions and processes, promote the comparative analysis of the neurotransmitters and the identification of their primary sites of activity relevant to aggressive behaviours.

Genetic influences on aggressive behaviours of mice

Several years ago, I described a developmental model of mouse aggression (Cairns 1973). This work was taken up after I had spent years in the study of human aggression in children and adolescents. Although the results from the human work were informative, they were piecemeal. It became clear that the social learning model I employed had simply failed to address some basic issues of aggressive behaviour. Detailed longitudinal studies of organisms from birth to maturity were required to determine when, how, where and why attacks occurred, and the role that learning played in the process. It was necessary for these studies also to have included experimental manipulations in order to determine the necessary and sufficient conditions for the emergence, maintenance and change of aggressive patterns.

In the course of subsequent experimental work with mice, we were able to plot the developmental course of the behaviour, the conditions that elicited attacks and the points in the organization of the behaviour where learning played a role. For example, it was a surprise to learn that male mice reared alone from weaning to early maturity show a strong tendency to attack other male conspecifics on their first exposure to the other animal. No specific learning or modelling experiences were required, a finding that presents obvious complications for social learning interpretations. A detailed analysis of this 'innate' response indicates a reasonable developmental explanation. Previously isolated male mice show heightened arousal when confronted with novel male conspecifics, and the interactive feedback brings about rapid escalation in the intensity of the actions and counteractions. The escalation sets the stage for heightened arousal in both animals, but previously isolated males are most affected, presumably due to psychobiological conditions induced by their rearing conditions. Once initial attacks occur, recurrence is jointly dependent upon the psychobiological states of the animals and the outcomes of preceding attacks. As it turns out, nature and nurture are intertwined. *Aggressive acts in mice are not learned but, once in the repertoire, they are highly learnable.* The factors required for the establishment of the behaviour can be different from those required for its maintenance and generalization.

Further investigation confirmed that a credible model of aggressive behaviour was within our grasp for at least one species. Moreover, it soon became clear that the model would be incomplete if it did not systematically address the roles of genetic, neurobiological and endocrine influences on aggressive behaviour. Empirical studies completed with students and colleagues over the past 20 years have helped complete the picture (e.g. Cairns et al 1983, 1990, Gariépy et al 1995).

Three findings of this work on the genetic contributions to aggressive behaviour should be noted. First, the effects of genetic background on aggressive behaviour are robust and ubiquitous. Second, the effects of selective breeding can be produced with remarkable ease and speed, typically within one to four generations in studies of mice. This is part of a broader picture which indicates that time and timing are crucial to understanding the relations between genetic manipulations, aggressive behaviours and development. Third, the effects of genetic background inevitably interact with experiences and other social and organismic events. These detailed studies of behaviour have permitted researchers to provide a preliminary account of the neuro-biological and endocrinological mediators for experience and genetic manipulations. Such interactions, described systematically, are required to account for observed variance in aggressive behaviour.

The resultant model can be depicted in three different ways: by a set of summary propositions, by a schematic diagram, or by a tabulation of findings. I will cover each in turn.

Propositions on genetic and experiential
contributions to the development of aggression

Aggressive social behaviours play a unique role in the biological organization and environmental adaptations of mice. The story of how aggressive acts are bound to biology and context provides an elegant illustration of how nature and nurture are interwoven over development (Cairns 1973, 1993, Cairns et al 1990).

The following generalizations have been derived from those observations:

(1) Social interactions, including aggressive behaviours, play a key role in modifying the biological organization of individuals and in the structuring of their physical and social environments.

Simply stated, social interactions serve two distinct functions in organismic and contextual adaptation. First, they provide for rapid and/or reversible accommodations. It would not make survival sense for individuals to fight and attack regardless of their opposition or likelihood of being injured. Accordingly, actions must be constantly coordinated with the relationship, the context, and momentary effectiveness of the behaviour. There is considerable evidence from the microanalysis of behavioural exchanges that these monitoring processes occur (e.g. Cairns et al 1985). Second, social interactions occur in the space between organisms and their environments, and they affect both. Hence aggression cannot be reduced to the biology of either participant, or to the context. It is an illusion to view aggressive behaviour as a static phenotype or the outcome of the internal processes (genetic or otherwise) of a single organism.

(2) Nature and nurture are not static or immutable determinants of aggressive behaviours. To the contrary, they are fused at each stage of ontogeny with maturational, neurobiological, endocrine, social learning and interactional processes.

Interaction between context and these processes is the norm, not the exception. Conservation in aggressive behaviour is supported by correlated constraints, both internal and external to the individual. The biological states of the individual tend to be brought into line with the aggressive behaviour, and vice versa. The result is that behaviour organization tends to be continuous and conservative over time, despite the fluidity and change that is inevitable in development.

(3) Single variables rarely act alone or in isolation in the support of aggressive patterns.

The 'package of variables' can include biological characteristics such as the increases in testosterone among males following successful attacks, or it could refer to social network variables such as the propensity to attack that occurs among animals that are maintained together in a coercive context. Such combinations of variables provide a basis for stability and predictability through their interconnectedness. Mutual alignment of behaviour and biology arises as a consequence of the bidirectional relations among these levels.

(4) In ontogeny, correlated constraints promote the identification of configurations of aggressive development, and a limited number of behavioural pathways can be described in each species.

This proposition suggests the solution of the problem that confronts any systems analysis of social behaviour. One fear is that social systems are so complicated that they seem beyond the limits of contemporary science. This proposition holds that the identification of a network of relationships serves to

Individuals

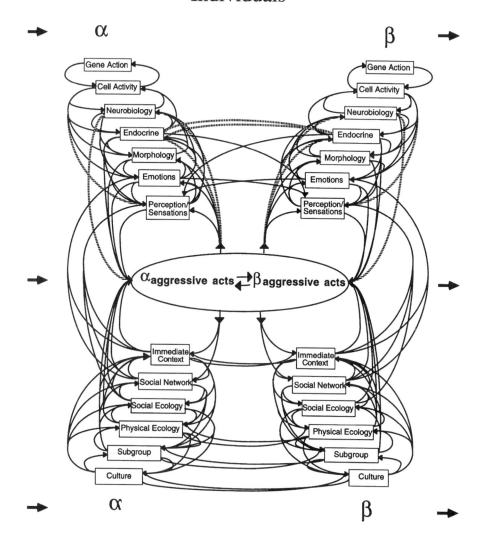

FIG. 1. Schematic to describe two interacting individuals (α and β) in terms of the system of relationships which have been observed within each organism and within each environment. The solid lines represent relationships between levels that have been firmly established in empirical studies of aggressive behaviour in mice (see Table 1), and the dotted lines represent relationships observed in some investigations. The arrows represent time and directionality of the relationships.

simplify the analysis rather than render it more complicated. The correlated constraints place limits on the pathways that are possible, and thereby reduce the directions in which development can occur. Once these developmental pathways are reliably identified, the relevant parameters can be manipulated and their effects observed upon changes in individual trajectories.

To illustrate, the manipulation of rearing conditions demonstrated that learning and training are *not* required to establish aggressive behaviours in mice. Rather, isolation rearing is sufficient to produce aggressive animals in most species. This is possible because isolation mimics the conditions of dominance, since the dominance of isolated creatures is never challenged. Once the behaviour occurs, however, learning and experience in a specific context play a major role in maintaining and accelerating attacks.

At a more speculative level, Fuller (1967) and others (Cairns et al 1990) have observed that the aspects of aggressive behaviour that are most modifiable by variation in experience may also be particularly sensitive to genetic variation. Although most properties of social systems are closed to rapid ontogenetic and microevolutionary change, some key elements remain open to change through variations in developmental timing (de Beer 1958). We have previously shown that heterochronies can provide the first stage for cross-generational changes in trajectories of aggressive behaviours (Cairns 1993).

These considerations of timing and adaptation are consistent with the general proposition that social behaviours, including aggressive interactions, constitute a leading edge of biological change (Bateson 1991, Cairns 1986). Once interactions prove effective, they create the scaffolding for further changes in neurobiology, morphology and physiology in ontogeny. They can also create conditions that influence genetic selection and transmission across generations (Bateson 1991, Cairns et al 1990). The upshot is that aggression and other social actions are among the first features to be influenced by selection pressures, not the last.

A schematic model of aggressive behaviours in mice

A second way to summarize the model is through a schematic diagram. Figure 1 represents a model of aggressive behaviour that has evolved from studies of mice. The model depicts three classes of events: those within organisms, those in the environment and those in the behavioural interactions. Although only two animals are shown (α and β), they represent processes that can occur in triads and larger groups.

The upper section depicts the contributions of organisms, including the several levels of genetic, neurobiological, physiological, morphological, motor reactivity and perceptual phenomena within the individual. The lines connecting certain levels simply represent the feedback loops that have been identified with varying levels of completeness. The internal states of one

organism can affect the internal states of the other via chemical messages and visual communication in ways that are functionally similar to internal feedback loops (i.e. pheromones). This diagram is the heuristic representation of a process to emphasize that levels of analysis related to behaviour have internal relations that are related to actions, but they have an organization and coherence that extend beyond behaviours.

The lower section represents environments, including the several levels of contextual, social networks, specific ecology, general ecology, strain and species-typical environments outside the individual. The lines connecting certain levels also represent the feedback loops that have been identified across levels of the environment. As in the upper diagram, α and β identify two organisms whose environments are distinctive or shared. Again, environments related to behaviour have internal relations that are related to actions but they have an organization and coherence that extend beyond behavioural phenomena.

The middle section of the schema depicts social actions. The placement illustrates that social actions occupy the space between organisms and environments, with distinctive properties that extend beyond both. In empirical analyses, they cannot be reduced to the organismic characteristics of either the individuals or their environments. The larger arrows within the action underscore the strong relationships between the social behaviours of α and β, whereby one guides and constrains the other. The focus of the figure is upon the unique properties of social interaction. Indeed, the primary determinants of aggressive behaviour are proximal, and they are represented in the bidirectional arrows of the carry-over effects of prior actions (autocorrelations) and in the dyadic interchange (interactive correlations).

The connecting lines across levels are based upon experimental data from studies of various strains of mice. Social interactions are viewed as ongoing, dynamic processes, more akin to biological metabolism than to biological structure. Time and sequence are implicated by the arrows within and outside of the social interchange. Over time, interactions, organisms and environments change, each with distinctive intervals and schedules. In ontogeny, the events that are required to initiate a feedback loop are not necessarily the same as those required to maintain it.

Three other assumptions should be emphasized:

(1) aggressive behaviours involve two or more individuals, and their determinants cannot be reduced to the conditions of either organism or to either environment;

(2) behavioural interchanges are by nature dynamic and their explanation requires attention to time and sequence; it is a mistake to view actions as a static phenotype. Social actions, including aggressive behaviours, serve distinctive functions in adaptation that take place in the space between the environmental and organismic events;

(3) correlated constraints operate between and across organismic, behavioural and contextual levels. The network of correlated constraints, taken together, help create and reinforce pathways which limit the range of possible actions.

The connections across organisms indicate that mechanisms exist to condition or otherwise synchronize the biologies of both individuals in ways that facilitate or bias social interchanges. The synchrony of behaviours is not wholly dependent upon overt actions. Moreover, the most powerful regulations of the behaviour of one organism involve the immediate behaviour of the other. Aggression begets aggression, all things being equal. The interchange requires immediate behavioural adjustments in both individuals, and these adjustments help determine the further course of the interaction.

Interchanges affect the internal conditions of both organisms and their environments. As the diagram indicates, more direct linkages can be drawn to internal levels than to external ones. The upshot is that interchanges organize the biology of individuals and bring them into synchrony with ongoing behaviour and future exchanges. For example, in male mice, winning a bout results in increased levels of some hormones (i.e. testosterone) and decreased levels of others (i.e. corticosterone).

Linkages between genetics, environments and aggressive behaviours

A third way to summarize the model is to construct a table of relevant empirical findings. Studies which plot the network of relationships between internal and external sources of variance are required if the nature–nurture controversy is to be resolved. On this score, a reasonable amount of evidence from studies on the aggressive behaviours in mice is now available. Taken together, the data provide support for empirical linkages within and across the domains of biology (O), the interactions (I) and environments (E).

It should be noted that two general classes of linkages are represented in Fig. 1. Class I consists of horizontal linkages between individuals (i.e. from the biology of α to the biology of β, from the actions of α to the actions of β, and from the environment of α to the environment of β). Class II consists of vertical linkages across levels and domains. These include environmental levels (E) to organismic (O) and interactional (I) levels; I to O and E; and O to I and E.

Table 1 provides examples from the empirical literature on each of the pathway types. Nine types of linkages have been identified in studies of the aggressive behaviour of mice. These include linkages that occur within and across different levels (e.g. genetic, neurotransmitters, endocrine, social network, social ecology, interactional). The table is not exhaustive; it is intended merely to illustrate the kinds of empirical findings that have given rise

TABLE 1   Class I and class II linkages from studies of aggression in mice (*Mus musculus*)

Linkage type	Phenomena	Sample references
Class I linkages (horizontal i.e. between individuals)		
$I_\alpha \to I_\beta$	Actions: aggression begets aggression in the short term (interactional correlation $\geqslant 0.70$–0.90) and inhibition and defeat in the long term	Cairns et al 1985, Lagerspetz & Sandnabba 1982
$O_\alpha \to O_\beta$	Biological states: pheromones in the arousal of sex/dimunition of attack; stress-induced odours	Sandnabba 1985
$E_\alpha \to E_\beta$	Environmental influences: status hierarchies in social groups; similarity in living conditions	Mackintosh 1981
Class II linkages (vertical)		
$E \to O$	Context→organism: changes in ecology (e.g. familiar to unfamiliar, dark to light) affect biology of organisms	Brain et al 1989, Cairns 1973
$E \to I$	Context→interaction: effects of territoriality on the likelihood to attack or to retreat	Mackintosh 1981
$I \to O$	Interaction→organism: effects of prior interaction on internal conditions, including testosterone and neurotransmitters	Gariépy et al 1995, Lagerspetz & Lagerspetz 1975
$I \to E$	Interaction→context: effects of prior experience on limits of territory among individuals	Crowcroft 1966
$O \to I$	Organism→interaction: effects of genetic selection on the likelihood to fight or to escape	Lagerspetz 1964, Cairns et al 1990, Hood & Cairns 1988, 1989
$O \to E$	Organism→context: effects of genetic selection on movement in territory and response to ambient stimuli	van Oortmerssen & Bakker 1981, Fuller 1967

I, interactional; O, organismic; E, environmental levels. Linkages are described between individuals α and β.

to the linkages described in Fig. 1 (see reviews in Brain et al 1989, Cairns et al 1990).

In brief, interactive behaviours are determined in an organismic system where feedback loops exist among behaviours and outcomes. Rather than render the scientific task implausible, each link serves to reduce degrees of freedom and constrain the possible ways the system can develop and function.

In this regard, recognition of the complexity of the relationships should help identify the underlying simplicity and parsimony of the interactional processes. As each fresh connection is established, it becomes easier to bring order out of a chaotic interactional–biological–ecological system.

Concluding comments

The recent study of aggressive interactions and how they develop has begun to yield a coherent account of these behaviours in at least one mammalian species. In the light of these findings, there is a special folly in recent attempts to identify the 'gene' for aggressive behaviours, whether by the methods of molecular genetics or by pedigree analysis. The problem is that genetic influences that have been identified and plotted over ontogeny constitute but one source of influence on aggressive interactions. The behaviours themselves are necessarily plastic and dynamic over time and space. Genetic influences, like physiological, hormonal, social network and experiential influences, are modified during the course of ontogeny. When integrated over ontogeny and over generations, these investigations point to collaborating rather than competing processes across levels of analysis.

It would be misguided, however, to generalize from mice to monkeys to humans. Each mammalian species must be investigated in its own right. For example, I omitted from Fig. 1 the distinctively human processes of language, planning and expectations. When included, they add another level of organization that cannot be overlooked in any systematic approach to aggressive behaviour in humans. None the less, an animal model of genetic, developmental and social ecological effects demonstrates that a science is within reach, and that it is possible to plot the pathways of influence within and across domains. It underscores that nothing can substitute for the detailed analysis of the concrete phenomena during development. The model also provides an answer to the 'developmental paradox' of why there are reasonable levels of aggressive behaviour continuity through ontogeny, despite the inevitability of age-related changes.

The task of formulating an integrated cognitive–behavioural–developmental model of aggressive behaviour in humans is a formidable challenge. But it is a challenge that must be met. If there is a single lesson to be gained from this examination of animal behaviour models, it is that attempts to leap directly from genes to phenotypes of aggression are doomed to fail. Explicit recognition of the interdependence in the levels of analysis of aggressive actions is a necessary step towards understanding their elegant organization and simplicity.

Acknowledgement

This research was supported by NIH grant P50 MH 52429.

References

Anastasi A 1958 Heredity, environment, and the question 'How?' Psychol Rev 65: 197–208

Bandura A 1973 Aggression: a social learning analysis. Prentice-Hall, Englewood Cliffs, NJ

Bateson PPG 1991 The development and integration of behaviour: essays in honour of Robert Hinde. Cambridge University Press, Cambridge

Brain PF, Mainardi D, Parmigiani S 1989 (eds) House mouse aggression: a model for understanding the evolution of social behaviour. Harwood Academic, Chur

Bronfenbrenner U, Ceci SJ 1994 Nature–nurture reconceptualized in developmental perspective: a biosocial model. Psychol Rev 101:568–586

Cairns RB 1973 Fighting and punishment from a developmental perspective. Nebr Symp Motiv Pap 20:59–124

Cairns RB 1979 Social development: the origins and plasticity of interchanges. W. H. Freeman, San Francisco, CA

Cairns RB 1986 An evolutionary and developmental perspective on aggressive patterns. In: Zahn-Waxler C, Mark Cummings E, Iannotti R (eds) Altruism and aggression: biological and social origins. Cambridge University Press, Cambridge, p 58–87

Cairns RB 1993 Belated but bedazzling: timing and genetic influence in social development. In: Turkewitz G, Devenny DA (eds) Developmental time and timing. Lawrence Erlbaum, Hillsdale, NJ, p 61–84

Cairns RB, Hood KE, Midlam J 1985 On fighting in mice: is there a sensitive period for isolation effects? Anim Behav 33:166–180

Cairns RB, Gariépy J-L, Hood KE 1990 Development, microevolution, and social behavior. Psychol Rev 97:49–65

Crowcroft P 1966 Mice all over. Dufour Editions, Chester Springs, PA

de Beer G 1958 Embryos and ancestors, edn 3. Oxford University Press, London

Fuller JL 1967 Experiential deprivation and later behavior. Science 158:1645–1652

Gariépy J-L, Lewis MH, Cairns RB 1995 Genes, neurobiololgy, and aggression: time frames and functions of social behaviors in adaptation. In: Stoff DM, Cairns RB (eds) Aggression and violence: neurobiological, biosocial and genetic perspectives. Lawrence Erlbaum, Hillsdale, NJ, in press

Hood KE, Cairns RB 1988 A developmental-genetic analysis of aggressive behavior in mice. II. Cross-sex inheritance. Behav Genet 18:605–619

Hood KE, Cairns RB 1989 A developmental-genetic analysis of aggressive behavior in mice. IV. Genotype–environment interaction. Aggressive Behav 15:361–380

Lagerspetz KMJ 1964 Studies on the aggressive behavior of mice. Ann Acad Sci Fenn Ser B 131:1–131

Lagerspetz KMJ, Lagerspetz KYH 1975 The expression of the genes of aggressiveness in mice: the effect of androgen on aggression and sexual behavior in females. Aggressive Behav 1:291–296

Lagerspetz KMJ, Sandnabba K 1982 The decline of aggressiveness in male mice during group caging as determined by punishment delivered by cage mates. Aggressive Behav 8:319–334

Mackintosh JH 1981 Behaviour of the house mouse. Symp Zool Soc Lond 47:337–365

Sandnabba NK 1985 Differences in the capacity of male odours to affect investigatory behaviour and different urinary marking patterns in two strains of mice, selectively bred for high and low aggressiveness. Behav Processes 11:257–267

van Oortmerssen GA, Bakker TCM 1981 Artificial selection for short and long attack latencies in wild *Mus musculus domesticus*. Behav Genet 11:115–126

DISCUSSION

Goldman: From your selection study, what is your estimate for the number of genes that are involved in aggressive behaviour in mice?

Cairns: That is difficult to say, but it is now clear that the effect we're producing is autosomal. There are a number of reasons why we are fairly sure the genes involved aren't on the Y chromosome. One key piece of evidence has been that we find parallel differences in aggression among females of these lines when they are tested in female-appropriate conditions (Hood & Cairns 1988, 1989). Thanks to my neurobiological collaborators, Mark Lewis and Louis Gariépy, we've been able to identify neurotransmitter loci in the D1 and D2 dopamine receptors. So as far as our effects are concerned, we've been able to move to the neurobiological level and to plot where some of the activity is. We have reviewed the neurobiological and endocrinological evidence in a recent paper (Gariépy et al 1995).

Goldman: It's exciting that you're already finding differences in some neurotransmitter systems. From the selection response, it looked like the genetic architecture might be one where there are not that many genes involved. There was a fairly rapid response over three to four generations.

Carey: The rapidity of the selection is really a function of the heritability, not necessarily the number of genes involved. That is in terms of the differentiation between the highs and lows in a few generations. The extent to which it plateaus may be a function of the number of genes involved.

Rowe: Did you use albino mice in these studies?

Cairns: Yes, they are ICR albinos, although we've experimented with a whole range of mice, including C57BL/6 and DBA strains, in the past. Interestingly, Kirsti Lagerspetz and her research group in Finland have obtained strikingly similar results. Their mice looked quite like ours, but they came from an entirely different line (e.g. Lagerspetz 1964, Lagerspetz & Lagerspetz 1975).

Carey: Doesn't the albino locus produce neurological abnormalities?

Cairns: The obvious defect is that albino mice can't see very well. We have run control studies to identify differences in the sensory systems of the selected and non-selected lines—as far as we can tell, there are very few morphological differences (Cairns 1973). For example, within-line variation in birth weight and weight at maturity is far greater than the between-line variation.

Gottesman: In the selection part of your work, did you allow brother–sister mating?

Cairns: We followed the Falconer guidelines: we originally used 12 unrelated breeding pairs, and we avoided brother/sister mating. This strategy was used in developing and maintaining the ICR lines. So far, it has been successful: we have two separate sets of lines that are now in their 30th generations, at Chapel Hill and Penn State.

Maxson: Is this selection based on the resident intruder test?

Cairns: Not really. Selection in each generation was based on the latency and frequency of attacks that occur between males when they are assessed at 45 days of age with an unfamiliar partner in a neutral compartment (Cairns 1973, Cairns et al 1990). The mice are weaned and reared alone from Day 21. When we first began in the 1960s we found a lot of suspicions in this literature, and we initially believed them because they seemed to make so much sense. We thought that in order to make the mice aggressive, they had to be trained to fight with preliminary bouts. But this turned out to be completely wrong. If anything, our attempts to train them to fight calmed the mice down. We found, however, that it is important to try to mimic, in the test circumstances, the characteristics of the ecology in which they have been reared. So our neutral test compartments were similar in space and substrate to the home compartments.

Maxson: I have a conceptual question. Genes exist in individuals, genes are expressed in individuals, genes are mapped through individual differences: how can you reconcile that to your statement that 'aggression cannot be reduced to the biology of either participant, or to the context'?

Cairns: That is the central question, and I'm very pleased that you raised it. The idea is simply that we're talking about an interactional phenomenon. My colleague, Gilbert Gottlieb, plots behaviour as a hierarchical relationship in the individual, where you have feedback effects at each of several levels, from behaviour, to society, down to the genome.

But Gottlieb describes a monadic or individual analysis, not a dyadic or social one. That is why I included Fig. 1 in my paper. Think about it, in a social analysis, where you have biological events occurring simultaneously in both creatures at all levels of analysis. The fact is that the actions of these individuals must be synchronized with events within and external to them. The behaviours that we're trying to explain, whether we call them antisocial behaviours or aggressive behaviours, are occurring in the interactions between two individuals, and they reflect the biologies and environments of both. Indeed, the most potent predictor of one individual's actions is the preceding act of his partner. Social behaviour has very distinct properties that cannot be wholly reduced to the biology of either participant in the interchange.

Maxson: The reason I brought this up is because it raises a problem for me: in my experiments, when you change the opponent, it often changes the level of aggression. This raises a question of how you can map genes for this behaviour.

Cairns: We did a relevant experiment several years ago. We did a kind of 'milieu therapy', where we took all of the partners of aggressive animals and tested them with increasing doses of chlorpromazine. We thus had highly aggressive individuals, but their partners showed decreasing levels of reaction to their actions. The results were striking. We were able to directly control our subjects' behaviour by the levels of reactivity of their partners. This illustrates that we ought to be careful about reducing aggressive behaviour patterns to the genetics or biology of either animal, as opposed to interactional dynamics and context.

Maxson: But, as geneticists, we also have to think of some way to map genes for this interaction.

Cairns: Work that's been done in our and other laboratories indicates that there are some good neurobiological candidates for events that can bias the interactional system and bring about changes in the quality of that interaction. However, they are changing the quality of the interaction, not controlling it.

Hinde: I don't see the problem. In mapping genes, you are looking at the difference between one individual and another individual. The supposition is that the interaction is taking place with a constant partner—the fact that the interaction depends on both doesn't affect the differences between the individuals.

Maxson: I think you're right. If you take one particular standard opponent, you can go ahead and map the genes for aggression towards that standard opponent. I'm referring to a standard opponent in the usual sense—for example, it doesn't initiate attacks or fight back.

Bouchard: Part of the problem is that one tends to think of all these interactions as terribly important; I don't think they are. They are highly dependent on the use of peculiar and abnormal animals. Natural selection averages over many of these factors. Any genes that we're selecting for have pleiotropic effects, so nature is never just picking a single gene for a particular effect.

Cairns: Of all mammals, mice seem to be among the winners in the long-term competition for survival, as Brain et al (1989) have argued. They can exist in a tremendous range of habitats, including the laboratory. These are not abnormal animals. We've made comparisons with wild-type animals and, although the levels of aggression may differ, the phenomena themselves are replicated.

We are often daunted by the apparent complexity of moving between sophisticated accounts of behaviour and biology. The evidence now suggests that looking at the complexity is the first step towards establishing its simplicity and coherence. That is a point that I hoped would emerge from my chapter. Because of the restricted pathways that are available for actions and because of the limitations that the behaviour places upon neurobiology, we're going to be in a much better position to do the gene search that Dr Goldman has indicated.

References

Brain PF, Mainardi D, Parmigiani S (eds) 1989 House mouse aggression: a model for understanding the evolution of social behaviour. Harwood Academic, Chur

Cairns RB 1973 Fighting and punishment from a developmental perspective. Nebraska Symp Motiv Pap 20:59–124

Cairns RB, Gariépy JL, Hood KE 1990 Development, microevolution, and social behavior. Psychol Rev 97:49–65

Gariépy J-L, Lewis MH, Cairns RB 1995 Genes, neurobiology, and aggression: time frames and functions of social behaviors in adaptation. In: Stoff DM, Cairns RB (eds) Aggression and violence: neurobiological, biosocial and genetic perspectives. Lawrence Erlbaum, Hillsdale, NJ, in press

Hood KE, Cairns RB 1988 A developmental genetics analysis of aggressive behavior in mice. II. Cross-sex inheritance. Behav Genet 18:605–619

Hood KE, Cairns RB 1989 A developmental genetics analysis of aggressive behaviour in mice. IV. Genotype–environment interaction. Aggressive Behavior 15:361–380

Lagerspertz KMJ 1964 Studies on the aggressive behavior of mice. Ann Acad Sci Fen Ser B 131:1–131

Lagerspertz KMJ, Lagerspertz KYH 1975 The expression of the genes of aggressiveness in mice: the effect of androgen on aggression and sexual behavior in females. Aggressive Behav 1:291–296

A twin study of self-reported criminal behaviour

Michael J. Lyons

Psychiatry Service 116A, Brockton VAMC, 940 Belmont Street, Brockton, MA 02401, Psychology Department, Boston University, 64 Cummington Street, Boston, MA 02215 and Harvard Institute of Psychiatric Epidemiology and Genetics, Harvard Medical School, Boston, MA 02115, USA

Abstract. Twin studies can be used to investigate the contributions of genetic factors, the common or shared environment, and the unique or non-shared environment to individual differences in a measurable characteristic. This paper reports the results of preliminary analyses of self-reported data on arrests and criminal behaviour from the Vietnam Era Veteran Twin Registry. The subjects for the study were 3226 male twin pairs in which both members served in the military during the Vietnam era. There were significant influences from both genetic factors and the common environment on early arrests. Genetic factors, but not the common environment, significantly influenced whether subjects were ever arrested after age 15, whether subjects were arrested more than once after age 15, and later criminal behaviour. The common environment, but not genetic factors, significantly influenced early criminal behaviour. The environment shared by the twins has an important influence on criminality while the twins are in that environment, but the shared environmental influence does not persist after the individual has left that environment. Genes are likely to influence the occurrence of criminal behaviour in a probabalistic manner by contributing to individual dispositions that make a given individual more or less likely to behave in a criminal manner.

1996 Genetics of criminal and antisocial behaviour. Wiley, Chichester (Ciba Foundation Symposium 194) p 61–75

The existence of twins presents an opportunity to explore the relative contributions of genetic influences, the common or shared environment, and the unique or non-shared environment to differences observed among individuals in some measurable outcome. The logic of the twin study is straightforward. There are two reasons why monozygotic (MZ) twins resemble one another—they share 100% of their genes and 100% of their common environment. There are two reasons why dizygotic (DZ) twins resemble one another—they share 50% of their genes and 100% of their common environment. To the extent that the similarity observed in MZ pairs is greater than that in DZ pairs, genetic influences are implicated. The extent to

61

which twins resemble each other above and beyond the influence of genes reflects the influence of the common or shared environment. Differences between MZ twins reflect the influence of non-shared environmental factors (as well as reflecting errors in measurement of the outcome).

Twin studies of delinquency and adult criminality have been thoroughly reviewed by Gottesman and his colleagues (DiLalla & Gottesman 1989, LaBuda et al 1993, McGuffin & Gottesman 1985), most recently by Gottesman & Goldsmith (1994). They concluded that studies that identified twin pairs on the basis of delinquency found high concordance rates for both MZ and DZ twins, supporting an important role for the common environment, but not for genetic factors. However, they pointed out that Rowe (1983), using self-report in a population-based sample (an approach similar to the present study), found evidence for both genetic and common environmental influences. Gottesman & Goldsmith (1994) found considerably more evidence for the heritability of adult criminality, in contrast to delinquency. The results reported here are preliminary results from the Harvard Twin Study.

Study

Subjects

Subjects were drawn from the Vietnam Era Veteran Twin Registry. The Registry was compiled from computerized military records and includes men who were born between 1939 and 1957 and served in the US military during the Vietnam War (May 1965 to August 1967). Details about the creation of the Registry have been published elsewhere (Eisen et al 1987). Zygosity was determined using questions on twin resemblance and blood group typing information from military records. This approach to zygosity determination yields 95% accuracy (Eisen et al 1989). Eligibility for inclusion in the present study was based on participation in at least one of three previous attempts to contact the twins. There were 10 300 eligible individuals (5150 pairs). Forty-seven eligible individuals were incapacitated or deceased, and 8039 (78.4%) were successfully interviewed. There were 3226 pairs in which both members provided information required for the analyses reported here (pair-wise response rate 62.6%). Approximately 55% of the respondents were MZ; the proportion of MZ twins is higher than in the general population because there are no opposite-sex dizygotic pairs in the Registry.

The average age of respondents at the time of the interview was 44.6 years (SD 2.8 years) with a range of 36–55 years. Respondents were 90.4% non-Hispanic white, 4.9% African-American, 2.7% Hispanic, 1.3% Native American/Alaskan Native, and 0.7% 'other'. The proportion of non-Hispanic white respondents is somewhat higher than their proportion among all Vietnam-era veterans because they had a higher response rate than other groups. Among respondents, 38.6% were college graduates and 33.3% were high school graduates.

Definition of outcome variables

The variables used in the present study were selected from items in the Diagnostic Interview Schedule (DIS; Robins et al 1981), which was administered by telephone to members of the Registry. The DIS contains items that are required for making DSM-III and DSM-III-R diagnoses of antisocial personality disorder (Diagnostic and Statistical Manual; American Psychiatric Association 1980). For this study, items were not selected to yield a DSM diagnosis; rather, they were selected to reflect criminality. The outcome variables were defined as follows:

Early Arrest—'Were you ever arrested as a juvenile or sent to juvenile court?' This outcome was scored one or zero.

Later Ever Arrested—'Have you ever been arrested since you were 15 years old for anything other than traffic tickets?' This outcome was scored one or zero.

Later Multiple Arrests—'Have you been arrested more than once since you were 15 years old?' This outcome was scored one or zero.

Felony Conviction—'Have you ever been convicted of a felony?' This outcome was scored one or zero.

Early Criminal Behaviour—'When you were a child, did you more than once swipe things from stores or from other children or steal from your parents or from someone else?'; 'Before you were 15, did you ever intentionally damage someone's car or do anything else to destroy or severely damage someone else's property?'; 'Before you were 15, did you intentionally start any fires?' Each item was scored one or zero, and the three items were totalled to yield a score from zero to three.

Later Criminal Behaviour—'Since you were 15, have you stolen anything or robbed or threatened anyone?'; 'At age 15 or after, did you intentionally start any fires or try to destroy something that belonged to someone else?'; 'Have you ever been paid for having sex with someone?'; 'Have you ever made money finding customers for male or female prostitutes?'; 'Have you ever made money illegally by buying or selling stolen goods, selling drugs, or being part of a gambling or betting operation?' Each item was scored one or zero and the five items were totalled to yield a score from zero to five.

Statistical analyses

The first step in data analysis is to quantify the degree of similarity between members of twin pairs for each outcome. The degree of association for dichotomous outcomes (early arrest, later ever arrested, later multiple arrests, and felony conviction) is quantified by the tetrachoric correlation (Neale &

Cardon 1992). The degree of association for ordinal outcomes (early criminal behaviour and later criminal behaviour) is quantified using the polychoric correlation (Neale & Cardon 1992). Cross-twin same-trait correlations are calculated separately for MZ and DZ pairs. These correlations indicate the degree to which members of MZ and DZ pairs resemble one another.

The next step in data analysis is to determine whether the degree of resemblance between members of twin pairs differs as a function of zygosity. Hypotheses are tested using an adaptation of the Mantel–Haenszel procedure and logistic regression for analysis of twin data described by Ramakrishnan et al (1992). Three independent tests are performed to evaluate the probability of familial clustering, genetic influence and shared environmental effects.

Results

Table 1 contains the frequency distribution of scores on each of the criminal behaviour variables. The four arrest variables are dichotomous. Scores for later criminal behaviour range from 0 to 4; scores of 4 were combined with scores of 3 for the purposes of computing the twin polychoric correlations. The prevalence rates of early arrest (8.2%) and later multiple arrests (6.6%) are quite similar. Compared with early arrest and multiple later arrests, ever being arrested after age 15 (16.2%) was considerably more prevalent and being convicted of a felony (2.5%) was considerably less prevalent. Approximately 66% of subjects had no early criminal behaviour compared with approximately 84% with no later criminal behaviour.

Table 2 contains the within-twin or phenotypic correlations for arrest and criminal behaviour variables. These correlations reflect the association between two outcomes for the same individual; for example, the correlation between an individual's early criminal behaviour and the same individual's early arrests.

TABLE 1   Distribution of scores on the arrest and criminality variables

Variable	Scores				
	0	1	2	3	4
Early arrest	91.8%	8.2%	-	-	-
Later ever arrested	83.8%	16.2%	-	-	-
Later multiple arrests	93.4%	6.6%	-	-	-
Felony	97.5%	2.5%	-	-	-
Early criminal behaviour	66.2%	27.9%	5.1%	0.8%	-
Later criminal behaviour	83.7%	10.7%	3.9%	1.0%	0.7%

TABLE 2 Phenotypic correlations among the arrest and criminality variables

Variable	Later criminal behaviour	Early arrests	Multiple later arrest
Early criminal behaviour	0.43	0.43	0.26
Later criminal behaviour	-	0.41	0.51
Early arrests	-	-	0.50

Table 3 contains the cross-twin same-trait correlations for the arrest and criminality variables. The table also includes the proportion of variance in each outcome that is attributable to additive genetic effects (h^2), the common or shared environment (c^2), and the unique or non-shared environment (e^2). There were significant influences from both genetic factors and the common environment on early arrests. Genetic factors, but not the common environment, significantly influenced whether subjects were ever arrested after age 15, whether subjects were arrested more than once after age 15, and later criminal behaviour. The common environment, but not genetic factors, significantly influenced early criminal behaviour. The influence of genetic factors and the common environment on being convicted of a felony was not significant. Less than 3% of subjects reported being convicted of a felony, resulting in low statistical power for testing the significance of genetic and common environmental influences.

Discussion

The highest cross-twin correlations were obtained for early arrests. Twins resemble each other more for this outcome than for any other. Approximately

TABLE 3 Twin correlations for arrest and criminality variables and proportions of variance attributable to additive genetics (h^2), shared environment (c^2) and unique environment (e^2)

Variable	r_{mz}	r_{dz}	h^2	c^2	e^2
Early arrest	0.73	0.53	0.39**	0.34*	0.27
Later ever arrested	0.45	0.30	0.30*	0.15	0.55
Later multiple arrests	0.47	0.28	0.39*	0.08	0.53
Felony	0.59	0.40	0.38	0.21	0.41
Early criminal behaviour	0.42	0.37	0.11	0.32***	0.58
Later criminal behaviour	0.47	0.32	0.30*	0.17	0.53

$*P < 0.05$; $**P < 0.01$; $***P < 0.001$; r, correlation coefficient; mz, monozygotic twins; dz, dizygotic twins.

three-quarters of the variance in this outcome is familial, that is, due to genes and the shared environment. Of the three other later arrest variables, it is probably best to compare early arrest with later multiple arrests because their similar prevalence rates indicate that they reflect experiences that are similarly deviant. The heritability of later multiple arrests is the same as that for early arrests. However, in contrast to early arrest, there is no significant influence of the common environment on later multiple arrests.

The common environment contributes significantly to both variables from the earlier age period. None of the five variables from the later age period have a significant contribution from the family environment. This does not seem simply to reflect increased unreliability in the reporting of childhood experiences, because the e^2 parameter, which reflects measurement error, does not differ substantially for most 'early' versus 'later' variables. These results suggest that the environment shared by the twins has an important influence on criminality while the twins are in that environment. The fact that none of the later variables demonstrates a significant influence from the common environment shared by the twins while they were growing up suggests that the influence of the common environment on criminality does not persist after the individual has left that environment.

For the purposes of studies such as the one described here, the common environment is defined as those aspects of the environment to which both members of a twin pair are exposed equally. In the vast majority of cases, both members of twin pairs grow up in the same neighbourhood and attend the same school. Another potentially important aspect of the common environment is family structure (e.g. two-parent versus one-parent arrangements, number of siblings). This also includes parental characteristics, such as disciplinary style, occupations and educational levels, time spent away from the family, substance use and abuse, and criminal behaviour. To assert that the common environment does not influence adult criminality does not necessarily imply that characteristics of the family cannot do so. It is still possible that features of family life to which twins may not be exposed equally, such as physical or sexual abuse, may influence adult criminality. Also, extreme but infrequently occurring characteristics of the shared environment might influence criminality but be difficult to detect. However, the results reported here are not consistent with a strong influence of shared family, school or neighbourhood characteristics on later criminality.

A comparison of early arrest with early criminal behaviour indicates that they are both influenced by the common environment to a very similar degree, but early criminal behaviour does not demonstrate a significant heritability as does early arrest. The phenotypic correlation in Table 2 indicates a moderate association between early criminal behaviour and arrests. The failure of these variables to be associated more strongly may reflect the limited nature of the definition of early criminal behaviour. The present study was constrained to define early criminal behaviour using items that are included in the DIS. The three items that were available provided a narrow view of the illegal activities in which a young person may engage. However, the influence of the common environment on early criminal behaviour is of the same magnitude as the influence of the common environment on early arrests. The difference in the heritability of the two outcomes raises questions about how the included criminal behaviours differ from being arrested. One possible mechanism may be 'getting caught'. That is, the current results suggest that carrying out illegal behaviours may be less influenced by genes than being apprehended for the behaviours. It is possible that genetically influenced characteristics, such as intelligence and impulsivity, may play a greater role in being arrested than in actually carrying out juvenile criminal behaviours. This must be interpreted cautiously because the discrepancy between early arrests and criminal behaviour may reflect the fact that many subjects may have been arrested for acts, e.g. selling drugs or assault, that are not included in our definition of criminal behaviours. The pattern for later criminal behaviour and later arrests is dissimilar to that for early criminal behaviour and early arrests; neither later arrests nor later criminal behaviour are significantly influenced by the common environment, but both are significantly heritable.

In concordance with the results reported here, McGuffin & Gottesman (1985) concluded from their review that the common environment more strongly influences delinquency, and genetic factors more strongly influence adult criminality. The pattern of later criminal behaviour being more highly heritable than early criminal behaviour is similar to the pattern reported for cognitive abilities by a number of investigators (McGue 1993).

Obviously, there is not a gene for being arrested or for stealing. Genes do not influence criminal behaviour (or any other type of behaviour, for that matter) in an invariant, one-to-one manner. Genes are likely to influence the occurrence of criminal behaviour in a probabilistic manner by contributing to dispositions that make a given individual more or less likely to behave in a criminal manner. Genetic influences on personality characteristics, such as risk taking (Krueger et al 1994), probably play a role in mediating the relationship. As mentioned above, genetic influences on intelligence might mediate the association between genetic factors and being arrested. In adulthood, intelligence might also be related to criminal behaviour by influencing the individual's options for making a living. It is quite likely that there are many independent pathways by which genes influence the probability that an individual will behave in a criminal manner and how likely he or she is to be apprehended. Two individuals who are arrested, even for committing the same crime, may be reflecting very different determinants. Although the present results demonstrate that genetic factors exert an important influence on criminal behaviour, these results also demonstrate that environmental factors, especially those that are not shared by both members of twin pairs, exert a very powerful influence on criminality.

There are advantages and disadvantages to the present sample. The fact that the sample was drawn from a population-based registry, rather than from an incarcerated or treated sample, allows the estimation of the relative contributions of genes and environmental influences and enhances our ability to generalize the results. Unfortunately, the Registry does not include women and the results described here may not be applicable to women. The Registry only includes men who served in the military and may have excluded some individuals whose early criminal behaviour disqualified them from service. The preliminary analyses presented here do not assess the potential roles of twin imitation or reciprocal influence (Rowe & Gulley 1992). Carey (1992) reported that the greater imitation within MZ compared with DZ pairs may inflate estimates of heritability. Gottesman & Goldsmith (1994) suggested, however, that findings from adoption studies and twins reared apart indicate that differential imitation cannot account for all of the observed heritability. Another potential limitation is exclusive reliance on self-reports of arrests and criminal behaviour. Social desirability may reduce reports of criminal behaviour but, because it is unlikely to differ by zygosity, it is unlikely to threaten the basic conclusions of this study. Results reported here are preliminary; future analyses will use multivariate approaches and assess for twin-imitation effects.

Research addressing the causes of criminal behaviour raises important, complex and socially sensitive issues. It is important to recognize what the results presented here do and do not tell us. These results indicate that genetic factors contribute significantly to observed individual differences in the probability of being arrested before and after age 15, and to individual differences in criminal behaviour after age 15. The environment shared by twins contributes significantly to individual differences in criminal behaviour and being arrested before age 15. The reasons that people differ in their criminal behaviour (at least as measured by the items in this study) before age 15 do not include genetic influences. The reasons that people differ in their criminal behaviour and probability of being arrested after age 15 do not include features of the environment that are shared by members of a twin pair. The data presented here address the sources of individual differences; these data do not address the sources of any group differences that may exist. It is important to remember that individuals within a group may differ from one another primarily because of genetic factors, whereas differences between groups may be primarily environmental in origin. The data presented here also do not address the question, 'Is criminality in our genes?' Criminality *per se* is not a biological characteristic of the individual—it is a social construct. Society designates the types of behaviour that are 'criminal'. Some individuals behave in a way that society classifies as criminal and some do not. The twin method allows the determination of whether behavioural differences between individuals are due, at least in part, to genetic differences. Why criminal behaviour is part of the human behavioural repertoire is a much less tractable question and one that does not lend itself readily to empirical investigation.

Acknowledgements

Supported by a grant (DA04604) from the National Institute on Drug Abuse to Dr Ming T. Tsuang and the Department of Veterans Affairs MRSCSP (Study #992). Investigators: Ming T. Tsuang, MD, PhD; Seth Eisen, MD; Jack Goldberg, PhD; Lindon Eaves, PhD; William R. True, PhD. Scientific Advisory Group: Alan Green, MD; Jerome Jaffe, MD; A. Thomas McLellan, PhD; Lee N. Robbins, PhD; Bruce Rounsaville, MD. Department of Veterans Affairs MRSCSP Central Administration: Chief, Daniel Deykin, MD; Staff Assistant, Ping C. Huang, PhD; Administrative Officer, Janet Gold. Hines VA CSPC Center, Vietnam Era Twin Registry: Director, William G. Henderson, PhD; Epidemiologist, Jack Goldberg, PhD; Registry Coordinator, Mary Ellen Vitek; Programmer, Kenneth Bukowski; Statistical Assistant, Mary Biondic. Human Rights Committee: Eileen Collins, MSN (Chairperson) (past); Mary Ann Emanuele, MD (past); Barbara Harvey (past); Patrick Moran (past); Rev. Ronald Burris; Sheldon Wagner (past); Terry Vering. The author acknowledges the contribution of Mary Ann Ausetts and the interviewers at Temple University. Drs Irving Gottesman and Jag Khalsa also made important contributions to the success of this study. Most importantly, the author thanks the members of the Registry.

References

American Psychiatric Association 1980 The Diagnostic and Statistical Manual, 3rd edn. American Psychiatric Association, Washington, DC

Carey G 1992 Twin imitation for antisocial behavior: implications for genetics and family research. J Abnorm Psychol 101:18–25

DiLalla LF, Gottesman II 1989 Heterogeneity of causes for delinquency and criminality: lifespan perspectives. Dev Psychopathol 1:339–349

Eisen S, True W, Goldberg J, Henderson W, Robinette CD 1987 The Vietnamese Era Twin (VET) registry: method of construction. Acta Genet Med Gemellol 36:61–66

Eisen S, Neuman R, Goldberg J, Rice J, True W 1989 Determining zygosity in the Vietnam Era Twin registry: an approach using questionnaires. Clin Genet 35: 423–432

Gottesman II, Goldsmith HH 1994 Developmental psychopathology of antisocial behavior: inserting genes into its ontogenesis and epigenesis. In: Nelson CA (ed) Threats to optimal development: integrating biological, psychological, and social risk factors. Lawrence Erlbaum, Hillsdale, NJ, p 69–104

Krueger RF, Schmutte PS, Caspi A, Moffitt TE, Campbell K, Silva PA 1994 Personality traits are linked to crime among men and women: evidence from a birth cohort. J Abnorm Psychol 103:328–338

LaBuda MC, Gottesman II, Pauls DL 1993 Usefulness of twin studies for exploring the etiology of childhood and adolescent psychiatric disorder. Am J Med Genet Neuropsychiatr Genet 48:47–59

McGue M 1993 From proteins to cognitions: the behavioral genetics of alcoholism. In: Plomin R, McClearn GE (eds) Nature, nurture and psychology. American Psychological Association, Washington, DC, p 245–268

McGuffin P, Gottesman II 1985 Genetic influences on normal and abnormal development. In: Rutter M, Hersov L (eds) Child and adolescent psychiatry: modern approaches. Blackwell Scientific, Oxford, p 17–33

Neale MC, Cardon LR 1992 Methodology for genetic studies of twins and families. Kluwer Academic, Norwell, MA

Ramakrishnan V, Goldberg J, Henderson WG, Eisen SA, True W, Lyons MJ 1992 Elementary methods for the analysis of dichotomous outcomes in unselected samples of twins. Genet Epidemiol 9:273–287

Robins LN, Helzer JE, Croughan J, Ratcliff KS 1981 National Institute of Mental Health diagnostic interview schedule. Arch Gen Psychiatry 38:381–389

Rowe D 1983 Biometrical genetic models of self-reported delinquent behavior: a twin study. Behav Genet 13:473–489

Rowe DC, Gulley B 1992 Sibling effects on substance use and delinquency. Criminology 30:217–233

DISCUSSION

Heath: You haven't given us a single test statistic to address the question of whether your estimates of genetic variance are significantly heterogeneous. Showing that you've got a significant effect in one group and not in another is not the same as showing that if you estimate a single parameter, that gives you a significantly worse fit. From your model, you must have a likelihood ratio χ^2 which tests what happens if you constrain the heritability to be the same for both early and late criminality.

Lyons: Your point is well taken. The results I presented are univariate results based on the separate examination of early criminality and later criminality. Finding that later criminality is significantly heritable in our data and that early criminality is not, is not the same as demonstrating that they differ significantly from one another. These analyses have not been done yet, but they will be in the near future.

Heath: That is a point worth emphasizing, because in the alcoholism literature chaos has been caused by people assuming that because they couldn't demonstrate a significant effect in women but they could in men, genetic factors were more important in men than women. But if you look at the data from the individual studies, the estimates are not significantly heterogeneous.

Lyons: It is a typical problem. It is not the same to say that one parameter differs from zero and another one doesn't, as to say that they differ significantly from each other.

Daly: I was quite surprised about the self-reported so-called juvenile criminal behaviour. Some of those behaviours sounded pretty innocuous. The questionnaire sounded like a lie test. Surely every boy would own up to at least a couple of those three acts, and yet most didn't. I wonder how people are interpreting these items: was it in a context of making them sound terribly criminal?

Lyons: In some of the DIS sections there are 'skip-out' items. Consequently, some of the other diagnoses may suffer from the fact that people learn that if they say 'yes' to a particular item they will be asked another 20 questions. Fortunately, in this section, each respondent is asked all the questions, although some of them may have been thinking that they get off the hook if they say 'no'. Every approach has its benefits and drawbacks. Obviously, this is different from using arrest records, which have nothing to do with the person's willingness to disclose. However, about 50% of our sample did acknowledge using illegal drugs, so I think they were relatively candid. There is no way we can be certain that they are telling the truth, and that we're not picking up the genetics of lying. But these results fit with the results that Irving Gottesman and colleagues reviewed on contemporaneously assessed juvenile delinquency (Gottesman & Goldsmith 1994, McGuffin & Gottesman 1985). Gottesman's reviews looked at antisocial behaviour during childhood and adolescence in some studies, and antisocial behaviour during adulthood in other studies. In our study, we have adult and juvenile antisocial behaviour assessed in the same individuals. This avoids having to compare results across different studies.

Mednick: You could answer some of these questions by taking a state such as California, which has a fairly good criminal register. I would suggest that you check the self-reports of the California residents in your populations against official records.

Lyons: That's a very good idea.

Daly: Some of the juvenile 'criminal' behaviours weren't criminal at all. For instance, who hasn't swiped something before the age of 15? And yet most people said no to all those items.

Lyons: The wording of some of the items may suggest a rather low threshold for judging a behaviour to be 'antisocial'. However, the relative infrequency of endorsement by our subjects (about two-thirds denied all antisocial symptoms) suggests that the subjects were responding to a threshold that identified relatively infrequent and deviant behaviour.

Virkkunen: How do your results relate to the picture of antisocial personality disorder (APD) in DSM-IV (American Psychiatric Association 1994)? In this, asocial problems (conduct disorder) in adolescence often continue into adulthood, leading to APD.

Lyons: The data that I have been talking about are either individual items or continuous scores obtained by adding individual items together. We have, however, also used a diagnostic approach in which we impose a threshold on the number of items, to come up with a dichotomous classification. We used the DSM-III-R convention of a threshold of three symptoms before age 15 and a threshold of four symptoms after age 15. We used this dichotomous classification to calculate tetrachoric correlations for diagnoses. The results of those analyses are very similar to those I have been describing. We have not yet looked at questions of diagnostic stability—that is, we have not looked at the data in terms of how many subjects are only antisocial as juveniles, how many are only antisocial as adults, and how many are antisocial at both times. We will be looking at these questions in the near future.

Taylor: If these data are from the DIS (Robins et al 1979), it is not possible from these to link antisocial behaviour to APD, because the questions about antisocial behaviour on the DIS are the questions derived from the DSM-III criteria for APD. Ratings on these items are thus, by definition, correlated with APD in DSM-III terms. I share some of the concerns about the triviality of some of the criteria which led to a DSM-III diagnosis of APD. It is important to recall that DSM-IV does not use most of those criteria, for the good reason that the reliability of the individual diagnoses for personality disorder under DSM-III was poor (Bronisch & Mombour 1994), perhaps partly because many of those behaviours occur not uncommonly in the ordinary general population.

Lyons: Actually, the DSM-IV criteria for APD are quite similar to the DSM-III-R criteria.

Taylor: I also have some concerns about the assumption that environment is necessarily the same, even in an ordinary family, for all the sibship. I can come close to believing it for MZ twins, but I think there must be more variance for DZ twins—at one extreme, if they are of different sex it becomes obvious that the environment of each is very different, but even same-sex twins will each have a different experience of the environment, for internal and external reasons, if they are non-identical.

Lyons: The twin method does not assume that the environment is the same for both members of a twin pair (or all members of a sibship). The 'unique environment' refers to aspects of the environment that are not shared by twins. What the twin method does assume is that the environment is not more similar for MZ twins than it is for DZ twins in a way that would inflate the observed resemblance for MZs relative to DZs. Such an inflation would lead to an over-estimation of heritability. When this has been evaluated empirically, the evidence is quite supportive of the 'equal environments' assumption (Kendler et al 1993).

Taylor: Another problem in comparing the juvenile with the adult, apart from obvious social status and responsibility differences, is that there is likely to be a considerable difference in relation to the influence of mental disorder on the criminal figures. Disorder patterns tend to differ between juveniles and adults, and some disorders appear to have a disproportionate effect on offending.

It is possible to argue that this might apparently reinforce the genetic position, but it would reinforce it possibly through the genetics of mental disorder rather than through any direct genetic effect on 'criminality'.

Lyons: I don't believe that there are genes for criminality that we are trying to detect with our approach. I believe that there are likely to be numerous causal pathways that lead to criminal behaviour. Some of these pathways may include genetic vulnerability to mental disorder; the mental disorder may put the individual at risk for behaving criminally. Genetic factors may also influence the likelihood of criminal behaviour through genetic influences on alcohol and drug abuse, and through genetic influences on personality traits such as impulsivity. There may also be other traits—such as a failure of empathy and lack of capacity to experience remorse—that overlap with criminality but are not identical to it. These characteristics could mediate to a great extent the relationship between genes and the likelihood of behaving criminally.

Bouchard: Remember that your population has been screened for health, because they are veterans. Some of the individuals at risk were selected out when the population was recruited into the military.

Rutter: Pamela Taylor, what proportion of a general population sample of offenders do you think would have serious mental disorders in their adult life? Presumably substantially fewer than in a psychiatric clinic or hospital group.

Taylor: It's difficult to say. Schizophrenia is a relatively late-onset disorder. The age of onset tends to be earlier for men, so that many young men who are going to develop the disorder would have done so by age 17 or 18. The military would probably screen out many of these, but those aged 20 or over by the date of onset would almost certainly be missed. Schizophrenia certainly occurs among soldiers. There is a USA literature that has depended on evidence from military samples for research into aspects of schizophrenia and particularly premorbid states. People who were interested, for example, in pre-morbid IQs in schizophrenia did the work by comparing test results obtained on entry to the military with results obtained once the disease was established (e.g. Mason 1956).

Lyons: We have a list of schizophrenics in the sample. It is relatively small—I suspect that we have fewer than 10 schizophrenics who answered the interview.

Goldman: It's more difficult to collect subjects who have alcoholism and antisocial behaviour than it is to collect those who don't have these problems. There are a substantial number of veterans who you weren't able to study. To obtain an affected twin pair is even more difficult. Do you think that this could have led to an underestimation of the pairs that are concordant for the trait?

Lyons: We're working on that right now. Obviously, we can't see how antisocial the people who didn't respond were, but we can take our concordant pairs and compare them with the singleton responders. In fact, the singletons are more antisocial. Mike Neale and his colleagues have published a paper that addresses the effects of non-response (Neale et al 1989). If subjects who are higher on a trait—in this case, how criminal or antisocial they are—are less likely to respond than subjects who are lower on a trait, then MZ and DZ correlations should both be somewhat reduced. This could lead to an underestimation of the influence of the family or shared environment.

Carey: In terms of representativeness, it would seem natural to compare your results with those of the Epidemiological Catchment Area survey. There's such a dramatic overlap between them, so you should have very similar results. Have you done this?

Lyons: The data we have looked at so far have been at the individual item level or at the scale score level. We have not yet determined the overall prevalence rates for diagnoses such as APD.

Denno: I have a question about your juvenile and adult crime categories. Could your adult crime category include people who were juvenile offenders?

Lyons: People who committed adult crimes may also have committed juvenile crimes.

Denno: If that's the case, then the adult crime category could include individuals who had either committed offences as juveniles, or had not. Perhaps it would be more accurate and informative to look at three categories of juvenile and adult criminals: (1) individuals who committed crimes only when they were juveniles but not when they were adults; (2) individuals who committed crimes only when they were adults but not when they were juveniles; and (3) individuals who committed crimes when they were both juveniles and adults.

Lyons: The examination of adult criminal behaviour and juvenile criminal behaviour was carried out separately. In some ways it is like measuring IQ. If you measure IQ at age eight, and then at age 25, you find a much stronger environmental influence at age eight, and a much stronger genetic influence at age 25. We are thinking about antisocial behaviour in a similar kind of way: we see our variables as assessing some underlying vulnerability, not some condition that either you have or you don't. I think of it as liability to criminality. Everybody has some liability to criminality, low or high: we draw a threshold. We don't look at whether someone is a criminal or not, but at what influences the liability to behave in a criminal way.

Mednick: I think Dr Denno is suggesting that you draw a line at age 20–21 and study crimes that have first onset after that age, rather than including individuals as adult criminals who have first onset at age 16.

Lyons: The DIS interview that we used follows the DSM-III-R convention of dividing antisocial behaviours into those that occur prior to age 15 and those that occur after age 15. In the results that I described here, we have used the before and after age 15 distinction. However, many (but not all) of the items in the APD section also provide information about the first time and the last time that a given behaviour was present. It would probably be possible for us to use these onset and recency data to study alternative approaches to defining 'early' and 'later' criminal behaviour.

References

American Psychiatric Association 1994 The diagnostic and statistical manual, 4th edn. American Psychiatric Association, Washington, DC

Bronisch T, Mombour W 1994 Comparison of a diagnostic checklist with a structured interview for the assessment of DSM-III-F and ICD-10 personality disorders. Psychopathology 27:312–320

Gottesman II, Goldsmith HH 1994 Developmental psychopathology of antisocial behaviour: inserting genes into its ontogenesis and epigenesis. In: Nelson CA (ed) Threats to optimal development: integrating biological, psychological, and social risk factors. Lawrence Erlbaum, Hillsdale, NJ, p 69–104

Kendler KS, Neale MC, Kessler RC, Heath AC, Eaves LJ 1993 A test of the equal-environment assumption in twin studies of psychiatric illness. Behav Genet 23:21–28

McGuffin P, Gottesman II 1985 Genetic influences on normal and abnormal development. In: Rutter M, Hershov L (eds) Child and adolescent psychiatry: modern approaches. Blackwell Scientific, Oxford, p 17–33

Mason CF 1956 Pre-illness intelligence of mental hospital patients. J Consulting Psychol 20:297–300

Neale MC, Eaves LJ, Kendler KS, Hewitt JK 1989 Bias in correlations from selected samples of relatives: the effect of soft selection. Behav Genet 19:163–170

Robins LN, Hezler JC, Croughan J, Williams JBW, Spitzer RL 1979 The National Institute of Mental Health diagnostic interview schedule. National Institute of Mental Health, Rockville, MD

Heterogeneity among juvenile antisocial behaviours: findings from the Virginia Twin Study of Adolescent Behavioural Development

Judy Silberg*, Joanne Meyer*, Andrew Pickles†, Emily Simonoff†, Lindon Eaves*, John Hewitt‡, Hermine Maes* and Michael Rutter†

*Department of Human Genetics, Medical College of Virginia, Virginia Commonwealth University, MCV Station, Richmond, VA 23298, USA, †Department of Child and Adolescent Psychiatry, Institute of Psychiatry, De Crespigny Park, London SE5 8AF, UK and ‡Institute for Behavioral Genetics, University of Colorado, Boulder, CO 80309, USA

Abstract. The examination of heterogeneity in antisocial behaviour was accomplished by applying latent class analytic methods to multivariate categorical data on 389 same-sex male twins, aged 11 to 16 from the Virginia Twin Study of Adolescent Behavioural Development (VTSABD). The data included multiple measures of oppositional and conduct disorder, attention deficit disorder, hyperactivity, impulsivity, reading disability and anxiety from mother, teacher, and child report from both questionnaire and interview (child and adult psychiatric assessment; CAPA). A latent four-class model provided a good fit to the data and yielded four phenotypically and aetiologically distinct latent classes: (1) a non-symptomatic class influenced by both additive genetic and shared environmental factors; (2) a hyperactivity–conduct disturbance class accounted for by both additive and non-additive genetic effects; (3) a 'pure' conduct disturbance class with a very strong shared environmental component; and (4) a multisymptomatic class explained entirely by the additive effect of the genes. Further characterization of these four latent classes by age of the child and parental psychiatric history is also shown.

1996 Genetics of criminal and antisocial behaviour. Wiley, Chichester (Ciba Foundation Symposium 194) p 76–92

The suggestion that there could be a genetic component to antisocial behaviour is anathema to many clinicians and social scientists (cf. Blackburn 1993). The objections arise from four main considerations. First, there is scepticism about finding a gene for crime, given that criminal behaviour is defined by societal and cultural mores, and encompasses a large and diverse range of behaviours.

Of course, it is unlikely that there is a single gene for crime *per se*, but genetic factors are likely to play an important role in behaviours, such as aggression or impulsivity, that are associated with or predispose to crime. Second, there is concern about the possible implications of negative labelling of individuals as a result of genetic studies, without any concomitant implications for treatment or prevention of antisocial behaviour. Although this may be true, it is useful to know which behaviours are genetically determined, to elucidate relevant environmental factors and the mechanisms underlying the interplay between genes and environment in the expression of disturbances of conduct. Third, there are 'political' concerns that a focus on hereditary factors in antisocial behaviour will detract from concerns regarding the impact of social disadvantage and family deprivation. This is understandable, but misplaced because, although we know a lot about the correlates of delinquency, we know little about the causal processes involved (Rutter & Giller 1983). For example, parental antisocial behaviour constitutes one of the best predictors of recidivist juvenile delinquency, but it is unclear whether this association is genetically or environmentally mediated. Finally, there is concern about using a single heritability coefficient to characterize a group of behaviours that are quite heterogeneous. At one extreme there are isolated illegal acts that are committed by adolescents at one time or another and are not associated with any significant impairment, and, at the other, there are pervasive antisocial acts that are characteristic of a small minority of individuals, are extreme and persistent, and are associated with general social malfunction. As with the first three concerns, genetic studies can be quite useful in accounting for heterogeneity based upon the demonstration of distinct genetic and/or environmental mechanisms underlying groups of antisocial behaviour. For example, early twin studies have shown a very low genetic component for juvenile delinquency considered as a whole, but a stronger genetic effect on clinically significant conduct disorders (DiLalla & Gottesman 1989). It is the goal of this paper to show how genetically informative data on twins and their parents from the Virginia Twin Study of Adolescent Behavioural Development (VTSABD) can provide unique information that might help resolve the nosological ambiguities that characterize childhood disruptive behaviours, while at the same time help in our understanding of the genetic and environmental mechanisms underlying their expression.

The VTSABD (Eaves et al 1993a, Silberg et al 1995) is an epidemiologically based prospective study designed to show how genetic and environmental factors contribute to the development of the more common forms of psychopathology among children and adolescents. The VTSABD's most important strengths are that it is longitudinal, it is a general epidemiological population sample, it includes data on parents and their twins, and it uses interview and questionnaire data from multiple informants for comparing dimensional and categorical approaches to assessing psychopathology. We used data on male twins, aged 11 to 16, from the first wave of data collection from the VTSABD, to explore heterogeneity in antisocial behaviours by examining the co-occurrence of various forms of disruptive behaviours and the aetiological factors that account for their association.

Antisocial behaviour clearly varies in its severity and degree of persistence (Robins 1991, Rutter & Giller 1983). Whereas many adolescents do engage in antisocial acts at some time or another, there is a small group of offenders who begin offending early, are responsible for a disproportionate amount of criminal activity that is both extreme and recurrent (Farrington et al 1986, Loeber 1982, Patterson 1982), and often progress to a diagnosis of antisocial personality disorder in adulthood. Although there is as yet no general consensus as to how to subclassify antisocial behaviour, it has been proposed that conduct disturbance alone may be aetiologically and developmentally distinct from conduct problems that co-occur within the context of other conditions such as hyperactivity, aggression and anxiety. However, it has not yet been unequivocally demonstrated whether antisocial behaviour and hyperactivity represent independent behavioural domains (i.e. are genuinely co-morbid) or, rather, that they reflect different manifestations of the same underlying behavioural syndrome. The large intercorrelation between conduct problems and hyperactivity reported in numerous epidemiological and clinical studies, using both the same and different informants, do show that (at least on a phenotypic level) the two disorders are related (Fergusson et al 1991, Farrington et al 1990, Silberg et al 1995). Further evidence suggesting that the two may represent the same construct is that a large majority of children with conduct problems also exhibit concomitant symptoms of hyperactivity and inattention (Anderson et al 1987, August & Stewart 1982, Offord et al 1987), and that attention deficit disorder hyperactivity (ADDH) and conduct disorder (CD) are both early developmental precursors of offending in adolescence. In addition, co-occurring hyperactivity with CD is associated with earlier-onset conduct problems (Farrington et al 1990), and the presence of hyperactivity with conduct disturbance symptoms increases the risk for persistent conduct problems into adult life (Farrington et al 1990). Yet factor-analytic studies consistently yield two distinct behavioural dimensions (Fergusson et al 1991). Moreover, development studies show that conduct problems are more prognostic of delinquency in adolescence, and that hyperactivity is more closely associated with learning problems and scholastic underachievement (Farrington et al 1990, Fergusson et al 1993). Also, with regard to background and ancillary variables, hyperactive individuals and their families are likely to exhibit attentional deficits and learning problems, whereas individuals with CD are associated with adverse family backgrounds, characterized by substance abuse and antisocial behaviour (Hinshaw et al 1993).

A similar degree of ambiguity characterizes the relationship between CD and oppositional defiant disorder (Loeber et al 1995). Some investigators argue that the degree of isomorphism between the two disorders is great enough to justify merging them into a single syndrome. The majority of children with a diagnosis of CD also meet criteria for oppositional defiant (OPD) behaviours, or have at an earlier stage of development, supporting OPD disorder as a developmental precursor to the more serious acts that comprise CD; however, not all children with OPD disorder progress to a diagnosis of CD in early adolescence. Though there is a marked phenotypic association between the two disorders, as with ADDH and CD, the nature of their association is yet to be fully understood, but is undoubtedly multifaceted and complex.

The investigation of heterogeneity in antisocial behaviour rests upon delineating diagnostic categories comprised of homogenous patterns of symptoms that are relatively distinct from other groupings (Klein & Riso 1993). For example, investigators have postulated three different classes of individuals having differential associations with other behavioural syndromes; a 'pure' hyperactive group; a 'pure' CD group displaying conduct problems only; and a 'co-morbid' group of individuals who exhibit numerous and severe behaviour problems (including hyperactivity, inattention and OPD disorder, for example), a high level of aggression, an earlier age of onset of problem behaviours, lower verbal intelligence and greater overall social impairment (Moffitt 1990, Hinshaw et al 1993). It has also been suggested that these differentiations in co-occurring conditions can be linked to distinct aetiological factors. The results of a structural equation analysis of the VTSABD data provide confirmatory, though not unequivocal evidence for subtyping these behaviours into 'pure' hyperactivity and a co-morbid syndrome of hyperactivity and conduct disturbance. In this analysis, the overall covariance between conduct problems and hyperactivity could be partitioned into a unique non-additive genetic component for hyperactivity alone, and a separate additive genetic component that influences both hyperactivity and conduct disturbance.

One powerful statistical technique for demonstrating distinct diagnostic groupings of behaviour is latent class analysis, which attempts to account for the pattern of responses by hypothesizing a number of latent classes. This technique provides information on the number of individuals that fall into each latent class and the probability of symptom endorsement given membership in that class, on the basis of the method of maximum likelihood (Eaves et al 1993b). The advantage of the latent class approach is that it is multivariate, enabling us to include a number of co-morbid conditions and data from multiple informants, and making no *a priori* assumptions about linearity. In this analysis, we applied latent class analytic methods to data on conduct disturbance and other putative associated psychiatric conditions in 389 juvenile male twins, aged 11 to 16, from the VTSABD.

TABLE 1 Estimates of latent class frequencies and item endorsement probabilities from phenotypic latent class analysis of co-morbidity in male adolescent twins

| Variable | Latent class | | | |
	I - 72%	II - 14%	III - 8%	IV - 6%
MCAPA-ADDH	0.029	**0.240**	0.000	**0.557**
MSRQ-ADDH	0.000	**0.300**	0.011	**0.349**
TEACH-ADDH	0.000	**0.377**	0.047	**0.227**
READING	0.109	**0.195**	**0.391**	**0.289**
MCAPA-COND	0.022	0.000	0.089	**0.365**
CCAPA-COND	0.013	0.041	**0.373**	**0.292**
MCAPA-OPP	0.024	0.000	0.091	**0.706**
CCAPA-OPP	0.041	0.037	**0.279**	**0.240**
MSRQ-COND	0.004	0.137	0.098	**0.624**
M-OLWEUS	0.012	0.166	**0.408**	**0.503**
C-OLWEUS	0.027	0.074	**0.899**	**0.421**
TEACHER-COND	0.025	**0.288**	0.121	**0.297**
CCAPA-ANX	0.103	0.068	**0.213**	0.161
MSRQ-IMP	0.042	**0.245**	0.000	**0.427**
ABS-DISC	0.056	**0.395**	**0.517**	**0.475**

The estimates of the population frequency of a four-class latent class model and the probability of endorsing any one behaviour given membership in that particular class are shown. For clarification of the latent classes, behaviours having an endorsement $P < 0.2$ are in bold.
MCAPA-ADDH, mother's CAPA ratings of attention deficit disorder hyperactivity; MSRQ-ADDH, mother's Rutter 'A' scale ratings of ADDH; TEACH-ADDH, teacher's Rutter 'B' scale ratings of ADDH; READING, Slosson Oral Reading Test; MCAPA-COND/OPP, mother's CAPA ratings of conduct/oppositional defiant disorder; CCAPA-COND/OPP, child's CAPA ratings of conduct/oppositional defiant disorder; MSRQ-COND, mother's Rutter 'A' scale ratings of conduct disturbance; M-OLWEUS, mother's Olweus Aggression Scale ratings; C-OLWEUS, child's Olweus Aggression Scale ratings; TEACHER-COND, teacher's Conners' scale ratings of conduct disturbance; CCAPA-ANX, child's CAPA rating of Generalized Anxiety Disorder; MSRQ-IMP, mother's Rutter 'A' scale and EASI Temperament Scale ratings of impulsivity; ABS-DISC, composite score of parental absence and Dyadic Adjustment Scale score of marital discord.

Latent class analysis of co-morbidity

We first carried out a conventional latent class analysis to determine whether there are separate classes or categories of male adolescents who show varying degrees of co-occurring conduct and oppositional behaviours, hyperactivity, aggressiveness, reading disability, anxiety and parental disruption, using multiple ratings and informants on the children's behaviour from both questionnaire and interview. In this phenotypic analysis, twins were treated as individuals, and each behaviour was coded categorically as present or absent (1 or 0). Next, we explored the extent to which these classes could be accounted for by genetic and environmental factors, using a latent class analysis which models the association between twins for class membership. The latent class analysis based upon twin resemblance provides estimates of the latent class frequencies for monozygotic (MZ) and dizygotic (DZ) twin pairs, and provides the raw data necessary for modelling the influence of genetic and environmental factors on twin resemblance for each latent class.

The results of the phenotypic latent class analysis of interview (child and adolescent psychiatric assessment; CAPA) and questionnaire (denoted by other than CAPA) ratings from mothers, teachers and children of conduct, attention deficit–hyperactivity, impulsivity, OPD disorder, generalized anxiety, reading disability, and parental absence/marital discord are shown in Table 1.

The four classes can be construed as follows: (1) a class of unaffected individuals, with an estimated population prevalence rate of 72%, having very low endorsement probabilities on all the items; (2) a co-morbid class with an estimated class frequency of 14%, based upon moderately high endorsements of ADDH and conduct problems from both mother and teacher questionnaires, and to a lesser extent reading disability; (3) a class of children with conduct disturbance only (i.e. 8%) with zero probabilities of endorsing ADDH items and who have a high probability of endorsing behaviours on the Olweus aggression scale, self-report ratings of oppositional and CD from the child CAPA, reading disability and to a lesser extent generalized anxiety; and (4) a multisymptomatic co-morbid class consisting of individuals who have a high probability of endorsing nearly all the items.

The results of the phenotypic latent class analysis clearly support the existence of both co-morbid and non-co-morbid categories of antisocial behaviour among boys during adolescence. The uncovering of subtypes of antisocial behaviour with different symptom profiles coincides with previous empirical work on multiple pathways to deviance in adolescence. For example, the second latent class of primarily ADDH symptoms with conduct disturbance from parent and teacher report coincides with the general finding that, by the time of adolescence, the majority of children with ADDH no longer exhibit ADDH-like symptoms alone, but show impairments in other behavioural domains (Klein & Manuzza 1991). The second latent class may represent one possible developmental pathway that begins with hyperactivity in early childhood and results in associated antisocial behaviour during adolescence, in contrast to latent class III that reflects conduct disturbance alone. However, it is only with longitudinal data, soon available from the VTSABD sample, that these findings may be examined within a development context.

To determine the genetic and environmental contributions to membership in each of these four classes, we converted the latent frequencies of MZ and DZ

TABLE 2   Variance components obtained by fitting full univariate structural equation path models to latent class data

Latent class	Additive genes (A)	Shared environment (C)	Dominant genes (D)	Unique environment (E)
Latent class I 'unaffected'	0.45	0.52	-	0.03
Latent class II 'hyperactive–conduct'	0.54	-	0.34	0.12
Latent class III 'pure conduct'	0.01	0.97	-	0.02
Latent class IV 'multisymptomatic'	0.99	0.00	-	0.01

twin pairs within each of the classes to a contingency table, and fitted structural equation models to estimate the influence of additive genetic (A), shared environmental (C) or dominant genetic (D), and unique environmental (E) factors on each class. Because these are frequency estimates, the usual likelihood-ratio χ^2 tests cannot be used to compare submodels and heterogeneity across classes. Hence, Table 2 presents the standardized components of variance from fitting full univariate models to each class.

The results of model fitting show quite different patterns of genetic and environmental influences from one class to another. Whereas both additive genetic and shared environmental factors predominate in explaining membership in the first class (i.e. why some children are non-symptomatic), additive and non-additive genetic effects account for membership in the co-morbid ADDH–CD class, shared environmental factors in the 'pure' CD class, and additive genetic effects alone for the multisymptomatic co-morbid class. The impact of the unique environment—that is, enduring specific environmental effects that make one twin differ from the other—is minimal in all four classes.

These findings are consistent with the phenotypic latent class analysis in demonstrating aetiologically distinct categories of antisocial behaviour. The second latent class, reflecting both hyperactivity and conduct symptoms, is distinguishable from the other classes in showing a strong non-additive genetic constituent factor. L. J. Eaves (personal communication 1995) has shown that the low DZ correlation for ratings of hyperactivity can be explained by parental contrast effects, that is, parents consistently rating their DZ twins as more different than they really are. Hence, the very low DZ correlation in the second latent class may be due to these types of contrast effects, rather than to

TABLE 3   Mean and standard deviation of age within each latent class

Latent class	n	Mean	SD
Unaffected	467	13.23	1.70
Hyperactive–conduct	109	13.23	1.77
Conduct only	61	**14.82**	1.35
Multisymptomatic	41	13.66	1.75

Entry in bold represents a statistically significant assocation ($P < 0.001$).

dominant genetic effects *per se*, a process which is overshadowed by multiple ratings of other conduct symptoms in class IV. The relatively greater influence of shared environmental factors strongly distinguishes the third latent class— 'pure' conduct disturbance—which likely represents the more transient delinquent acts of adolescence. This finding is consistent with separating 'adolescence-limited antisocial behaviour' (Moffitt 1993) with the more severe and intractable forms of delinquency, on the basis of distinct aetiological mechanisms. It has been hypothesized that earlier-onset conduct disturbance is most likely to persist into adult life, is associated with greater social impairment, and may have a stronger genetic component than the more transient adolescence-limited forms of antisocial behaviour. To test whether this second latent class of individuals reflects a later onset of conduct problems, and to further characterize the nature of these latent classes, we compared the age of the child at interview and the psychiatric history of the parents within each of the four classes.

The mean age of individuals for each of the four classes is shown in Table 3. Using an analysis of variance, our prediction that individuals in the second and fourth classes (the co-morbid classes) will be significantly younger than individuals in the more transient conduct disturbance only class is borne out in these data ($P < 0.001$), lending support for the existence of separate categories of antisocial behaviour with possibly different developmental trajectories and underlying aetiologies.

In Table 4, the frequency of parental psychiatric diagnosis of major depression, generalized anxiety disorder, alcoholism, panic disorder, simple phobia and antisocial personality are compared across the four latent classes using χ^2 analysis. These results show that the mother's history of nearly all the major psychiatric diagnoses (except for alcoholism and antisocial personality) significantly differentiates the four classes of children, with the highest frequency of parental psychopathology in the fourth, multisymptomatic class, followed by the hyperactivity–conduct disorder class, then conduct disturbance alone. The father's psychiatric history is not as strong a predictor

TABLE 4 Percentage of parental psychopathology in each latent class

Parental psychopathology	Class I (unaffected)	Class II (hyperactive–conduct)	Class III (conduct)	Class IV (multi-symptomatic)	χ^2	P
Mother						
Major depression	36.76	47.57	42.86	66.67	15.81	0.001
Generalized anxiety	24.66	37.86	39.29	58.97	26.77	0.001
Alcoholism	4.11	1.94	5.36	7.69	2.73	0.435
Panic disorder	12.79	17.86	10.68	33.33	14.14	0.003
Simple phobia	19.86	19.64	21.36	46.15	14.74	0.002
Antisocial personality	1.83	4.92	1.94	2.63	2.46	0.483
Father						
Major depression	25.15	17.65	18.18	25.00	2.22	0.529
Generalized anxiety	10.18	8.82	22.73	8.33	8.98	0.029
Alcoholism	15.57	11.76	12.12	33.33	6.67	0.083
Panic disorder	4.49	0.00	7.58	8.33	3.55	0.314
Simple phobia	10.48	14.71	21.21	25.00	8.89	0.031
Antisocial personality	4.34	3.28	7.77	5.26	2.49	0.477

Entries in bold represent statistically significant associations.

of a son's psychopathology as is the mother's. However, paternal generalized anxiety disorder and phobias are significantly associated with the expression of 'pure' conduct disturbance in this sample of adolescent boys. These findings are consistent with the results of numerous studies in demonstrating a strong association between parental psychopathology and various forms of antisocial behaviour in childhood and adolescence (Jary & Stewart 1985, Lahey et al 1988, Robins 1966). Whereas parental disturbance constitutes a very strong risk factor for these disorders, the mechanisms underlying the elevated risk to children is unknown, although there is some evidence that the mediation is environmental (Rutter 1985). Alternatively, it is possible that the association between parental psychopathology and their offspring's antisocial behaviour is attributable to a heritable third factor. Although these questions cannot be addressed here, the extensive array of genetically informative data emerging from the VTSABD promises to yield the tools required to address some of the most important and exciting questions in the field of child psychiatry, specifically those concerning genetic and environmental influences on antisocial behaviour.

Acknowledgements

This work has been supported (in part) by a Junior Faculty Research Award for Drs Silberg and Meyer from the John D. and Catherine T. MacArthur Foundation Research Network on Psychopathology and Development, and NIMH grants MH45268 and MH48604.

References

Anderson JC, Williams S, McGee R, Silva PA 1987 DSM-III disorders in preadolescent children. Arch Gen Psychiatry 44:69–76

August GJ, Stewart MA 1982 Is there a syndrome of pure hyperactivity? Br J Psychiatry 140:305–311

Blackburn R 1993 The psychology of criminal conduct: theory, research, and practice. Wiley, New York

DiLalla LF, Gottesman I 1989 Heterogeneity of causes for delinquency and criminality: lifespan perspectives. Dev Psychopathol 1:339–349

Eaves LJ, Silberg JL, Hewitt JK et al 1993a Genes personality and psychopathology: a latent class analysis of liability to symptoms of attention deficit hyperactivity disorder in boys. In: Plomin R, McClearn G (eds) Nature, nurture, and psychology. American Psychological Association, Washington, DC, p 285–306

Eaves LJ, Silberg JL, Hewitt JK et al 1993b Analyzing twin resemblance in multi-symptom data: genetic applications of a latent class model for symptoms of conduct disorder in boys. Behav Genet 23:5–19

Farrington D, Ohlin L, Wilson JQ 1986 Understanding and controlling crime. Springer-Verlag, New York

Farrington DP, Loeber R, Van Kammen WB 1990 Long-term criminal outcomes of hyperactivity–impulsivity–attention deficit and conduct problems in childhood. In: Robins LN, Rutter M (eds) Straight and devious pathways from childhood to adulthood. Cambridge University Press, New York, p 62–81

Fergusson DM, Horwood LJ, Lloyd M 1991 Confirmatory factor models of attention deficit and conduct disorder. J Child Psychol Psychiatry Allied Discip 32:257–274

Fergusson DM, Horwood LJ, Lynskey MT 1993 The effects of conduct disorder and attention deficit in middle childhood on offending and scholastic ability at age 13. J Child Psychol Psychiatry Allied Discip 34:899–916

Hinshaw SP, Lahey BB, Hart EL 1993 Issues of taxonomy and comorbidity in the development of conduct disorder. Dev Psychopathol 5:31–49

Jary ML, Stewart MA 1985 Psychiatric disorder in the parents of adopted children with aggressive conduct disorder. Neuropsychobiology 13:7–11

Klein RG, Manuzza S 1991 Long-term outcome of hyperactive children: a review. J Am Acad Child Adolesc Psychiatry 30:383–387

Klein DN, Riso LP 1993 Psychiatric disorders: problems of boundaries and comorbidity. In: Costello CG (ed) Basic issues in psychopathology. Guilford Press, New York, p 19–66

Lahey BB, Piacentini JC, McBurnett K, Stone P, Hartdagen S, Hynd G 1988 Psychopathology in the parents of children with conduct disorder and hyperactivity. J Am Acad Child Adolesc Psychiatry 27:163–170

Loeber R 1982 The stability of antisocial and delinquent child behavior. Child Dev 53:1431–1446

Loeber R, Green SM, Keenan K, Lahey BB 1995 Which boys will fare worse? Early predictors of the onset of conduct disorder in a six-year longitudinal study. J Am Acad Child Adolesc Psychiatry 34:499–509

Moffitt TE 1990 Juvenile delinquency and attention deficit disorder: boys' developmental trajectories from age 3 to 15. Child Dev 61:893–910

Moffitt TE 1993 Adolescence-limited and life course-persistent antisocial behavior: a developmental taxonomy. Psychol Rev 100:674–701

Offord DR, Boyle MH, Szarmari P et al 1987 Ontario Child Health Study. II. Six-month prevalence of disorder and service utilization. Arch Gen Psychiatry 44:832–836

Patterson GR 1982 Coercive family process. Castalia, Eugene, OR

Robins LN 1966 Deviant children grown up. Williams & Wilkins, Baltimore, MD

Robins LN 1991 Conduct disorder. J Child Psychol Psychiatry Allied Discip 32: 193–212

Rutter M 1985 Family and school influences on behavioural development. J Child Psychol Psychiatry Allied Discip 26:349–368

Rutter M, Giller H 1983 Juvenile delinquency: trends and perspectives. Penguin, Harmondsworth

Silberg J, Rutter M, Meyer J et al 1995 Comorbidity among symptoms of hyperactivity and conduct problems in male and female juvenile twins. J Child Psychol Psychiatry Allied Discip, in press

DISCUSSION

Gottesman: Your results are interesting and paradoxical. They seem to contradict those in the Rutter (1966) monograph, in which it seemed that any kind of abnormality in the parents, whether it was somatic or psychiatric, had a bad effect on their offspring. Your multisymptomatic group have a lot of pathology in their mothers, but it's not related in any obvious way to antisocial behaviour. It's as if it has nothing to do with genetics, and the parental environmental atmosphere is generating this antisocial behaviour in the kids.

Silberg: The lack of a specific association between antisocial personality disorder in the mothers and conduct disturbance in their offspring is likely to be due to the low prevalence of parental antisocial personality (ASP) in our sample; as you might expect, the ASP parents are not participating in our study, whether due to a lack of cooperation or absence from the home. However, as you say, it appears to be a generalized effect in that nearly any other kind of maternal psychopathology is predictive of CD in children. This does not necessarily imply that genetic factors are not operating because the transmission is non-specific.

Rowe: Some allowance ought to be made for the reverse direction of causality. Parents care a lot about their children; if your child is getting into trouble with the law and failing at school, that is a big stress on a family. Some elevation of parental psychopathology may be partly their reaction to having a very difficult child.

Silberg: The significant association between fathers' generalized anxiety disorder and children's psychopathology may be an example of this occurring; these fathers are anxious and worried because their adolescent sons are getting into trouble.

Heath: When you showed us the contingency table, was that estimated by pairwise analysis, or based on a casewise analysis, taking the most likely class membership for each pair?

Silberg: The criteria were based upon the highest likelihood for class membership of each individual.

Heath: I know that Lindon Eaves set up his latent class programme so that he could do pairwise analysis and do tests of genetic hypotheses in that framework, by likelihood ratio test. Was there a reason you didn't do this?

Silberg: In Lindon Eaves's original latent class analysis of ADDH (Eaves et al 1993), the phenotype of interest was more homogeneous, permitting the tests of different genetic models. Because membership in each of the four classes in this analysis is due to very different genetic and environmental aetiologies, it is not clear what kind of genetic model you would fit. Rather, you want to allow for different genetic and environmental influences on membership in the different classes.

Heath: One would then have greater confidence in the numbers. But if you are going to proceed with a casewise analysis, it would be much more efficient to use an EM algorithm; if you do this, you have the feasibility of bootstrapping to estimate the confidence intervals around your estimates, so that when we see these high numbers for heritability we could have a better sense of whether a 99% estimate is from a distribution for which the lower boundary of 95% confidence is 50% or 30%, for instance.

Silberg: The standard errors around these estimates are small since the model accounts for error variance when estimating the class frequencies. This is reflected in the near-zero concordances in the off-diagonals of the MZ twins contingency table.

Rowe: When you have your follow-up data, it will be interesting to see whether these children stay in their class membership. The identity and reality of these classes is based on the assumption that they will remain over time in a particular class. If they all switch between classes, a severity model may be more appropriate than a class model.

Mednick: I was interested in the relationship between maternal psychopathology and child crime. If the mothers of the criminals suffer from an elevated rate of antisocial personality, you might have attributed the relationship to genetics. There is a high degree of depression in these mothers. Is there a genetic relationship between depression in the mother and disorders in the children?

Silberg: As previously stated, the weak association between maternal ASP and conduct disturbance is likely to be due to the low rate of ASP. In the results of a genetic analysis of parent–offspring data on conduct disorder (J. Meyer, personal communication) it was found that though small, the association between parental ASP and children's CD was due entirely to genetic factors. The results here suggest an important correlation between mothers' depression and disorders in the children. However, the parent–offspring models that we have previously fitted require the inclusion of the same phenotype in parents and offspring.

Gottesman: If you are hoping that your latent classes of psychopathology in children will be accurate predictors of ASP later on, you're bound to be disappointed just by the contrast between the base rates in the juvenile sample compared with the results in the epidemiological catchment area study (Robins et al 1991). The base rate in the epidemiological catchment area study for male adult ASP is about 7%. However, your latent classes add up to 28%, so your false-positive rate would be very high.

Waldman: Could the multisymptomatic category be conceptualized as general severity or general impairment?

Silberg: Yes, I think that is an important point—the multisymptomatic class is really a more severe form of a generalized liability to behavioural problems. We hope to be able to test this hypothesis in future analyses.

Waldman: I wondered about your characterization of the second class as a co-morbid (hyperactivity–conduct) class. I assume you based this on the Conners' aggression scale?

Silberg: The teacher questionnaire includes a separate hyperactivity factor based upon the Conners' and Rutter 'B' scale. This hyperactivity 'item' has a high probability of being endorsed if an individual is a member of the second co-morbid class. Hence, this class reflects both conduct disturbance *and* attention deficit hyperactivity disorder.

Waldman: I wonder about the validity of using that scale as a marker of aggression or conduct problems, because it doesn't reliably separate out aggression and conduct problems on the one hand from impulsivity and hyperactivity on the other. I wonder whether that second class may be more of a pure impulsivity/hyperactivity class.

Silberg: However, we have also included the mother's Olweus aggression scale, a good measure of conduct disturbance, which has a high endorsement probability in the second class.

Waldman: I'm wondering about the second class being an impulsivity/ hyperactivity class, especially in terms of the variance components that you report for the classes. Given that you find variance due to dominance for the second class, I would find it very surprising if it had something to do with conduct problems, as I am not aware of any previous assertion of the role of genetic dominance for antisocial behaviour. In contrast, a number of past studies have provided at least a suggestion of dominance for inattention, impulsivity and hyperactivity.

Rutter: If you compare the list of behaviours included in each class, in terms of the possibility of a rating bias or sibling contrast effect, it is striking that you have hyperactivity included in both class II and class IV. Yet the very low DZ correlation is found only in class II. Is this a consequence of the hyperactivity measure or is it a function of the class? The point of the question is that what is different about class IV is that it includes many CD items. When CD is considered as a dimension, there is no contrast effect. Is the contrast effect found with class II, but not IV, simply a function of the fact that it is 'driven' more by the hyperactivity than the conduct behavioural items?

Silberg: I expect that the reason we are getting non-additive genetic effects in class II and additive genetic effects in class IV is that the number of conduct disturbance items in class IV is driving up the DZ twin correlation. Class II is comprised of primarily ADDH items by the mothers who may be rating their DZ twins as less similar than the mothers of MZ twins, thereby lowering the DZ twin correlation to less than one-half the MZ correlation.

Heath: From your results, it looks as though you actually have a continuum of classes. Class III is the one exception to this, because of the estimated endorsement probability for the Olweus measure. This is a perfect example of a continuum model explaining most of what's happening, then you've got one or two variables that are behaving differently in class III. My prediction is that if you set up your latent class model to test this, you would have to allow class III to behave differently, but otherwise your data would fit a nice Guttman scale.

Cairns: I'm struck by the similarity of the latent class solution to that which Magnusson and Bergman came up with in their longitudinal work (Magnusson

1988). It's also pretty similar to the one that Beverley Cairns and I have identified using a quite different analytic strategy (Cairns & Cairns 1994).

In cluster analytic solutions, subgroups have been observed which are aggressive but without the multisymptomatic problem group disorder, and still another subgroup was seen whose problems of social rejection appear to be virtually independent of other difficulties. Their prognosis over 10–15 years is remarkably better than that of the multisymptomatic group (Magnusson 1988, Cairns & Cairns 1994).

Looking at your data, I wonder two things. First, the multiproblem group is about the same size as those that have appeared in other studies: one wonders to what extent that group compared with all the rest has some distinctive properties in terms of aetiological background, including genetics. Second, these other studies are duplicated for girls. This comes back to the sex-difference issue that we were talking about earlier. Do you have any information on females?

Silberg: We have conducted a latent class analysis of the females in our sample; with them we find a very similar pattern of results to that in the males.

Cairns: That's not unlike the results of some of the other longitudinal studies.

Silberg: I do want to point out, however, that the model presented here is not the best-fitting model: I selected the four-class model because the higher class models had class frequency estimates that were so small as to be meaningless.

Virkkunen: According to DSM-IV (American Psychiatric Association 1994), between 6 and 16% of male adolescents have CD. But only 3% of adult males develop ASP. Which of your four groups has the poorest prognosis?

Silberg: Classes II and IV probably have equally bad prognoses. I think that the hyperactivity/impulsivity constellation is really deleterious. Do you agree?

Virkkunen: Yes.

Waldman: It might be interesting to redo the latent class analysis, separating the ADDH inattention symptoms on the one hand from the hyperactive and impulsive symptoms on the other, to see whether that helps to define some of the classes more clearly.

Silberg: Because a factor analysis of the CAPA does not yield three independent factors of inattention, impulsivity and motor restlessness, we have not separated these out in the latent class analysis. However, we have included an impulsivity scale based on mothers' ratings of their twins' behaviour for this purpose, and the ADDH scale on the Rutter scales is predominantly a measure of hyperactivity.

Waldman: The other thing to note about prognosis is that the relevant literature suggests that unless ADDH is co-occurring with aggression in childhood, it doesn't necessarily predict later ASP (see Lilienfeld & Waldman 1990). That might be interesting to use as leverage for following up the classes.

Cairns: Have you asked these subjects about their social environment? In other work that has been completed with aggressive adolescents, it has been found that kids with similar profiles tend to hang around together. That is, do you find there's selective affiliation according to the profiles that you've identified?

Silberg: Do you mean that the individuals who comprise class III are socializing with the more disturbed individuals in class II and class IV? If so, these peer effects may be an example of the shared environmental influence on pure conduct disturbance (class III).

Cairns: Yes. This holds not only in general populations, but also in inner city populations—when highly aggressive youths are drawn together, they create gangs and further external support for violence. This suggests that some of the dynamics of interchange then become mapped on in support of these cluster subgroups that you are identifying. If we begin to disaggregate the total population into homogeneous subsets, we might have a handle on how we can plot trajectories towards violent and non-violent outcomes.

Rutter: I'm not quite sure what you're suggesting. Are you arguing that examination of course will throw light on the nature of individual differences? Or are you saying that studying course is a different enterprise but nevertheless one that is of equal importance to the study of individual differences?

Cairns: The heart of the issue is whether or not you disaggregate your samples on the basis of common trajectories. If you do this, operationally, you've created homogeneous subgroups within your population. That would then permit you to track these people over time to see whether or not they follow a common trajectory, and which individuals come off that trajectory. This is not unlike the Rutter & Pickles (1990) paper, where you look at the various choice points in development and then examine whether turning points occur. It's just a more sophisticated way to go about it.

Rutter: You can have major differences in trajectory, which you can call a turning point, that make zero (or near-zero) difference to the individual differences in that population. That is, the *level* of a trait shown by individuals has changed, but without any necessary effect on individual differences with respect to the same trait (see Rutter & Smith 1995). Thus, if children showing antisocial behaviour are followed over time, there is a large reduction in criminal activities in early adult life, but the relative position within the population of individuals who were high on antisocial behaviour at an earlier age remains much the same. Although it's important to study whether particular groups have a different life-course trajectory, the fact that a trajectory changes greatly doesn't necessarily have much impact on individual differences.

Cairns: That's also why it's so important to take a careful look at our measurement strategies. I don't think enough attention has been given to the metric that has been employed. This opens up another set of methodological issues.

Heath: There are also analytic techniques that you can use. For example, you could extend Judy Silberg's two-way table to a four-way table when you do latent class analysis. This would be a natural step to take if you wanted to constrain groups to be stable over time, to test the hypothesis that what identifies a class changes over time but that the class itself is stable.

References

American Psychiatric Association 1994 The diagnostic and statistical manual, 4th edn. American Psychiatric Association. Washington, DC

Cairns RB, Cairns BD 1994 Lifelines and risks: pathways of youth in our time. Cambridge University Press, New York

Eaves LJ, Silberg JL, Hewitt JK et al 1993 Genes, personality and psychopathology: a latent class analysis of liability to symptoms of attention-deficit hyperactivity disorder in twins. In: Plomin R, McClearn GE (eds) Nature, nurture, and psychology. American Psychological Association, Washington, DC, p 285–303

Lilienfeld SO, Waldman ID 1990 The relation between childhood attention-deficit hyperactivity disorder and adult antisocial behavior reexamined: the problem of heterogeneity. Clin Psychol Rev 10:669–725

Magnusson D 1988 Individual differences from an interactional perspective. Lawrence Erlbaum, Hillsdale, NJ

Robins LN, Tipp J, Przybeck T 1991 Antisocial personality. In: Robins LN, Regier (eds) Psychiatric disorders in America. The Free Press, New York, p 258–290

Rutter M 1966 Children of sick parents. Oxford University Press, Oxford

Rutter M, Pickles A 1990 Improving the quality of psychiatric data: classification, cause and course. In: Magnusson D, Bergman LR (eds) Data quality in longitudinal research. Cambridge University Press, Cambridge, p 32–57

Rutter M, Pickles A 1991 Statistical and conceptual models of 'turning points' in developmental processes. In: Magnusson D, Bergman LR, Rudinger G, Törestad B (eds) Problems and methods in longitudinal research: stability and change. Cambridge University Press, Cambridge, p 133–165

Rutter M, Smith D 1995 Psychosocial disorders in young people: time trends and their causes. Wiley, Chichester

General discussion II

Carlier: Over the past few years, several papers have called into question the twin method. For example, Phillips (1993) concluded by saying that the comparison between monozygotic (MZ) and dizygotic (DZ) twins is unreliable. I have been impressed by the research that has been presented at this meeting and my aim is not to imply that these studies are flawed, but to envisage new experimental designs to answer the critics of the twin method.

The comparison between MZ and DZ twins assumes that environmental variations act in a similar way in both types of twins. I have two examples which may illustrate that this is not always true.

The first is the Finnish twin cohort study, where Koskenvuo et al (1992) looked for genetic components in ischaemic heart disease. They estimated heritability at 45%. But, afterwards, they noticed that MZ twins are more similar than DZ co-twins with respect to smoking. I don't know whether the influences leading to smoking are genetic or environmental—they are probably both. But after adjustment with respect to smoking (excluding all MZ and DZ pairs with both co-twins reporting a daily smoking habit exceeding 20 cigarettes per day), the heritability estimate decreased to 29%.

Another variable concerned prenatal factors. We have some results on this. It has been known for a long time (Price 1950) that MZ twins may differ according to the timing of the zygotic division. If the division occurs at an early stage (within 72 h after fertilization), each of the MZ twins will develop its fetal membranes (i.e. chorion and amnion) and they will be classified as dichorionic diamniotic. If the division occurs later (from Day 4 to 7) the two embryos will share the same chorion but have different amnions (monochorionic diamniotic twins). Consequently, it is possible to compare monochorionic MZ twins with dichorionic MZ twins. Of course, all DZ twins are dichorionic. We are not the first to have studied this. For example, Rose et al (1981) tested adult twins using two subtests from the Wechsler Adult Intelligence Scale: vocabulary and block designs. Results showed a chorion effect on the block design but not on vocabulary: in block design, the similarity within the monochorionic MZ twin pairs was greater than within the dichorionic MZ twin pairs. We have also observed a chorion effect on the same test with monochorionic MZ again being more similar than dichorionic MZ (intraclass correlations: monochorionic MZ = 0.84, dichorionic MZ = 0.61; Spitz 1994, Spitz et al 1994). Note that we are talking about a within-pair resemblance; we are not looking for group mean differences. We have used a classical model to estimate heritability by comparing MZ and DZ twins (here r DZ = 0.51). You have to compare dichorionic MZ twins with DZ twins, because they share the same type of placentation (two chorions). Using a classical likelihood-based analysis, the common environment model provided the best fit to the data with common environmental variance accounting for $56 \pm 10\%$ of the total variance. The additive genetic variance was not significant. The comparison of monochorionic MZ and DZ groups told another story. The additive common environment model was the best fit; additive genetic variance accounted for $61 \pm 30\%$ of the variance and the common environment for only $21 \pm 21\%$. I am not suggesting that the chorion effect explains everything, but I think that in twin studies we haven't taken into account all the factors that may contribute to an overestimation of the MZ intraclass correlation.

Gottesman: Doesn't your analysis presume that there are equal base rates of monochorionic and dichorionic MZ twins?

Carlier: No; there are more monochorionic twins.

Gottesman: I think the analysis you did assumed equal weighting for the proportion of monochorionic and dichorionic twins in the general population of identical twins. You selected equal sample sizes for the monochorionic and dichorionic classes, but that will give us a distortion of the effect in an unselected sample of twins of unknown chorionic status.

Carlier: If you want to study dichorionic MZ twins, you are obliged to select them, because there are so few. It was the same in the Rose et al (1981) study.

Gottesman: I would use your argument to argue that we are dealing with underestimates of heritability in all the data in the literature, because nobody bothered to take out the one-third of all MZ pairs who are dichorionic and who may lower the phenotypic similarity.

Carlier: If you don't know the chorionic status, you always have more monochorionic twins through simple probability; about two-thirds of MZ twins are monochorionic. Thus, when we do not know the chorionic status, we overestimate heritability when a chorion effect tends to decrease the within-pair resemblance of dichorionic MZ twins. My aim was just to highlight two recent examples where the heritability coefficient, comparing MZ and DZ twins, changes if you factor in new variables. This is why we should consider redesigning twin studies to take this into account.

Carey: I applaud your suggestion that we pay very close attention to the general problem of intrauterine effects, particularly with this phenotype. Mothers with extreme antisocial behaviour also have high prevalences for substance use, alcohol abuse, poor nutrition and so on. These sorts of things can certainly have an effect on twin data and even some adoption data. This highlights the need for us not to rely on a single method.

Heath: I dispute, for your first example, the interpretation that smoking is an environmental variable. Having analysed some of the published Finnish data, persistent smoking (which presumably is a measure of nicotine dependence) looks as highly heritable as alcoholism. It certainly correlates genetically with measures of conduct problems. I would say that this is another heritable phenotype.

Rutter: It may be, but the well-demonstrated beneficial effects of stopping smoking on the risk of coronary artery disease would suggest that there is an environmental effect here. The origins of a risk factor and its mode of risk mediation have no necessary connection with each other. Thus, individual differences in a liability to smoke may be subject to strong genetic influences but the *effects* of smoking on liability to coronary artery disease are nevertheless environmentally mediated.

The problem that I have with these results is a different one: namely that the way you dealt with smoking is by dropping those cases. That only makes sense if the smoking is working independently of the risk factors in the rest of the group. Doesn't the evidence suggest that this is not so? If that is the case, you are left with an atypical group in which you're estimating heritability.

Carlier: Do you think that it is impossible to estimate heritability of ischaemic heart disease without considering smoking? Why does this bother you?

Rutter: The problem concerns the model proposed; clearly that needs to be biologically plausible. With both your examples, I wonder whether that is so. As I understand it, the effects of smoking are thought to operate through the same risk mechanisms that apply in non-smokers. If that is so, one may suppose that the effects of smoking will vary according to individual differences in the risk factors involved in those mechanisms (coagulation, cholesterol levels, blood pressure, etc.). Insofar as these are subject to genetic influences, and interact with smoking, the removal of smokers from the sample will artefactually reduce estimates of the genetic effect. Doesn't your model presuppose that the genetic effects operate in ways that are entirely independent of the risk mechanisms affected by smoking? That seems to me unlikely.

Carlier: Many people who present with ischaemic heart disease have never smoked. If you are looking for the genetic component in this disease it appears useful to cancel the effect of smoking. However, if there is an interaction between genetic and environmental causes, as I think, both figures are of interest.

Rutter: What is your postulated mechanism for the increased correlation in your monochorionic MZ twins? This is counterintuitive in the sense that these have larger birth weight differences because of the transfusion syndrome effect. I can't think of a variable that has been shown to relate to intellectual outcome that would be indexed by monochorionic effects.

Carlier: I don't know. In the block design test from the Wechsler intelligence scales the level of resemblance is lower in dichorionic than monochorionic MZ twins. This was observed independently by two teams working on different populations (American adults and French children). It is also known that at birth the within-pair differences are greater in monochorionic MZ twins than in dichorionic MZ twins (Corey et al 1979, Vlietinck et al 1989). Fetofetal blood transfusion due to vascular communication between the fetuses, which is often present in monochorionic placentation, is the probable explanation. However, for traits measured on older populations when a chorion effect is detected, the reverse applies, i.e. the within-pair variance is greater in dichorionic MZ twins (see not only the aforementioned study on the block design test, but also studies on high-density lipoprotein measures in ageing people [Reed et al 1991a] or on personality traits [Reed et al 1991b, Karras Sokol et al 1995]).

Goldman: What I like about the discussion of intrauterine effects is that it gets us into the domain of causation, and how the genetic programme unfolds. However, I don't see that different prenatal nutritional status is going to do anything except decrease the MZ : DZ ratio, given that most of these effects are going to operate powerfully for both MZ and DZ twins. What would be the purpose of changing the design of the twin studies? Would it help us to get better estimates of heritability? If that is the sole purpose, I'm not really interested, but if the issue is that it could actually help to reveal traits that are co-inherited or something about mechanisms, then I am. Do you think that monochorionic/dichorionic differences are masking relationships between variables such as antisocial personality and conduct disorder, or are we just dealing with a new way of refining heritability estimates?

Carlier: We are not looking for heritability here, but for specific genes related to aggression.

Rutter: Let us assume that your smoking and ischaemic heart disease findings are truly valid, that they generalize beyond the sample, and so on. The importance of the findings then lies in the implication that part of the genetic effect on ischaemic heart disease is operating through something to do with smoking. That really is interesting and important, because it is informative about the mechanism. The issue is really not one of what the true heritability figure is, but rather what is the mechanism by which the genetic factor operates.

Cairns: The fact that these MZ twins are reliably different because of some intrauterine or perinatal effect raises the question of mechanism. Nichols & Broman (1974) reported that the higher similarity between MZ twins was related to the bimodality at the low end of curve. The mechanism they proposed was that the similarity was due to concordance with regard to organismic anomalies in MZ relative to DZ births. They observed that if one member of a twin pair is severely impaired, then the chances that the other member is also impaired are much higher for MZ than for DZ twins. The greater similarity at the very bottom of the scale, representing a small proportion of the twin sample, accounted for the differences in intraclass correlations between the MZ and the DZ groups.

Rutter: I don't think they had the evidence on the mechanism: they were showing that the heritability differed at the bottom end of the range, but this differed across samples.

Rowe: Is there any way you could enlarge the sample size for your groups of monochorionic and dichorionic twins? If you had, for example, 100 pairs of each, you would have a sense of how precise those numbers are.

Carlier: It is very difficult to find 100 pairs of each type of MZ twin. We found 20 monochorionic MZ and 24 dichorionic MZ pairs—our sample is small. However, with a smaller sample of 23 monochorionic MZ and nine dichorionic MZ pairs, Melnick et al (1978) found a chorion effect on IQ (the dichorionic MZ twins having greater within-pair variance than monochorionic MZ twins). Rose et al's (1981) sample was also smaller than ours (17 monochorionic MZ and 15 dichorionic MZ pairs) and, as discussed above, they found a chorion effect on block design but not on vocabulary subtests from the Wechsler Adult Intelligence Scale.

As I've said before, I'm not claiming that the chorion effect accounts for everything. It is not a general effect.

Mednick: You might be throwing out the baby with the bathwater, because it could be that the genetic effect for the variables you're considering simply determines whether you are going to have one chorion or two.

Gottesman: I want to applaud your call for innovative strategies. We don't depend just on twins reared together in the contrast with the DZ twins for our perspectives in behavioural genetics research; that's why Sarnoff Mednick and Michael Bohman used the adoption strategy to complement twin and 'ordinary' family strategies. The idea of using the offspring of discordant identical twins is a good one, and the results could surprise you. The one good example in the literature concerns schizophrenia (Gottesman & Bertelsen 1989). In this study, the twins were of an age to have had children old enough to be well-through the risk period for developing schizophrenia. The idea that discordant identical twins could give clues to aetiological heterogeneity was unsupported by our findings that the children born to the normal MZ co-twin had the same rate of schizophrenia (17%) as the offspring of the affected twin. Other explanations involving prenatal and perinatal injury were not supported, although they're still possible.

Carlier: But the other team that published a paper on this subject in the same journal issue concluded differently (Kringlen & Cramer 1989); they reported a higher frequency of schizophrenia in the offspring of schizophrenic MZ twins than in the offspring of non-schizophrenic MZ co-twins. Although the difference was not significant, the authors thought that it might be ascribed to environmental factors. The sample was, of course, quite small and, for this kind of study, collaboration between teams would be very useful.

Gottesman: It's just a question of statistical power, given the smaller simple signs in the Norwegian sample and the younger ages of the subjects.

References

Corey LA, Nance WE, Kang KW, Christian JC 1979 Effects of type of placentation on birthweight and its variability in MZ and DZ twins. Acta Genet Med Gemellol 28: 41–50

Gottesman II, Bertelsen A 1989 Confirming unexpressed genotypes for schizophrenia: risks in the offspring of Fischer's Danish identical and fraternal discordant twins. Arch Gen Psychiatry 46:867–872

Karras Sokol D, Moore CA, Rose RJ, Williams CJ, Reed T, Christian JC 1995 Intrapair differences in personality and cognitive ability among young monozygotic twins distinguished by chorion type. Behav Genet, in press

Koskenvuo M, Kaprio J, Romanov K 1992 Twin studies in metabolic diseases. Ann Med 24:379–381

Kringlen E, Cramer G 1989 Offspring of monozygotic twins discordant for schizophrenia. Arch Gen Psychiatry 46:873–877

Melnick M, Myrianthopoulos NC, Christian JC 1978 The effects of chorion type on variation in IQ in the NCPP twin population. Am J Hum Genet 30:425–433

Nichols PL, Broman SH 1974 Familial resemblance in infant mental development. Devel Psychol 10:442–446

Phillips DIW 1993 Twin studies in medical research: can they tell us whether diseases are genetically determined? Lancet 341:1008–1009

Price B 1950 Primary biases in twin study: a review of prenatal and natal differences producing factors on monozygotic pairs. Am J Hum Genet 4:293–352

Reed T, Christian JC, Wood PD, Schaefer EJ 1991a Influence of placentation on high density lipoproteins in adult males: the NHLBI twin study. Acta Genet Med Gemellol 44:353–359

Reed T, Carmelli D, Rosenman RH 1991b Effects of placentation on selected Type A behaviours in adult males in the National Heart, Lung and Blood Institute (NHLBI) twin study. Behav Genet 21:9–19

Rose RJ, Uchida IA, Christian JC 1981 Placentation effects on cognitive resemblance of adult monozygotes. Intelligence, personality and development. Twin Res 3:35–41

Spitz E 1994 Etude d'une des variables de l'environnement maternel prénatal: effets à court et à long termes du type de placenta chez les jumeaux monozygotes. PhD thesis, Université René Descartes, Paris, France

Spitz E, Carlier M, Vacher-Lavenu MC et al 1994 The effect of MZ chorion type on variation in anthropological measures, intelligence and cognitive processes. Behav Genet 24:531(abstr)

Vlietinck R, Derom R, Neale MC et al 1989 Genetic and environmental variation in the birthweight of twins. Behav Genet 19:151–161

Predisposition to criminality: Swedish adoption studies in retrospect

Michael Bohman*

Department of Child and Youth Psychiatry, University of Umeå, Sweden

Abstract. The predisposition to criminality was studied in 913 women and 862 men from the Stockholm Adoption Study. Different genetic and environmental antecedents influenced the development of criminality, depending on whether or not there was associated alcohol abuse. Male alcoholic criminals often committed repeated violent offences, whereas non-alcoholic criminals characteristically committed a small number of petty property crimes. These non-alcoholic petty criminals more often had biological fathers with histories of petty crime but no excess of alcohol abuse. The risk of criminality in alcohol abusers was correlated with the severity of their own alcohol abuse, but not with criminality in their biological or adoptive parents. Most explained variation in petty crime was due to differences between the genetic predispositions of the adoptees, but substantial contributions were also made by postnatal environment, either alone or in combination with specific genetic subtypes. There was no overlap between the congenital antecedents of alcoholism and non-alcoholic criminality, but some postnatal variables were common to this kind of criminality and type 2 or male-limited alcoholism. Low social status alone was not sufficient to lead to petty criminality, but did increase risk in combination with specific types of genetic predisposition. Unstable preadoptive placement contributed to the risks of both petty criminality and male-limited alcoholism.

1996 Genetics of criminal and antisocial behaviour. Wiley, Chichester (Ciba Foundation Symposium 194) p 99–114

Children are influenced by both the genes and the environments provided by their biological parents, which makes it difficult to judge the relative importance of nature and nurture. Besides family and twin studies, children separated from their biological relatives at an early age and reared by non-related adoptive parents have been used as a research tool to disentangle the influence of genes and environment in the development of personality traits and various mental or somatic disorders. Here I will summarize and comment

---

*Address for correspondence: Högbergsgatan 40A, S-118 26 Stockholm, Sweden

upon some Swedish adoption studies, initiated many years ago, with which we have analysed congenital and postnatal antecedents to various psychiatric disorders, including alcoholism, criminality and antisocial personality disorder (Bohman 1978, Bohman et al 1981, Cloninger et al 1982, Sigvardsson et al 1982).

These adoption studies have been accomplished in several steps over many years. They began in the early 1960s with the specific aim of evaluating, in a cross-sectional study, the adjustment of a small population of adopted and foster children to their new families (Bohman 1970, 1971). These children were later followed, in a longitudinal study, into adulthood, with data on criminal offences and alcohol abuse (Sigvardsson et al 1987, Cloninger et al 1988). In order to study specifically genetic questions concerning the predisposition to criminality, alcohol abuse and other behaviour disorders, we later collected a much larger cohort of adult adoptees and their relatives as a tool for genetic studies, a project which is still going on and has been known as the 'Stockholm Adoption Study'. Here I will mainly summarize results concerning the predisposition to criminality. However, as criminality and alcohol abuse are very much associated phenomena, it will also be necessary to discuss their interrelation and different genetic backgrounds. In view of the marked heterogeneity observed among both criminals and alcoholics in terms of their own behaviour and their biological and social background, it is clear that both are complex behaviours that are likely to involve the interaction of multiple risk factors during development. These risk factors may include genetic and/or social factors and may be measured separately by the adoption method and by cross-fostering analysis.

The Stockholm Adoption Study

The subjects studied ($n = 862$ men and 913 women) were born 1930–1950 and adopted at an early age in families with a relatively good and stable socio-economic standard. The placement agency also selected against criminality and alcohol abuse in the adoptive parents. This restricted the range of social risks, so that the environmental influence was minimized compared with the general population. Sweden is also economically prosperous and socially homogenous, which makes our population of adoptees ideal for identifying genetic risk factors. Since complete information is available about both biological and adoptive parents, the separate contributions and interactions of genetic and environmental factors can be evaluated.

In our studies, we tried to identify genetic and early environmental antecedents of adult criminal behaviour and alcohol abuse. Our index of genetic background was the behaviour and characteristics of the biological parents, whereas our index of the early environment included a description of the rearing circumstances before adoption (e.g. placement) and information about the adoptive parents. Extensive data about registered criminality, alcohol abuse, occupational status, and medical and social history were obtained for the adoptees and each biological and adoptive parent from registers of child welfare officers, temperance boards, the State Criminal Register, and the local agencies of the National Health Insurance Board.

Preliminary analysis

In a preliminary analysis of this series of adoptees (Bohman 1978), I found that the frequency of registration for criminality was approximately the same as in a comparable group from the general population (12.8% in adopted men and 2.9% in women). In contrast, the biological parents featured two to three times more often in the Criminal Register (29.0 and 6.4%, respectively). In addition, biological parents were very often registered for repeated and more serious crimes with long-term prison sentences. Similar differences were also found concerning alcohol abuse: adopted men and women had about the same frequency of registration as the general population (16.1 and 2.4%, respectively), whereas the registration among biological parents was roughly twice as high (34% among the biological fathers and 4.6% in the mothers). There was also a high correlation between crime and alcohol abuse in both biological fathers and their adopted-out sons, indicating that criminality might be a consequence of alcohol abuse, a possibility that will be discussed later in this paper. It is clear from these results that the biological parents were a negatively selected group with a high frequency of social misconduct and antisocial behaviour. In contrast, only 2.3% of the adoptive parents appeared in the register for alcohol abuse, and none was found in the Criminal Register.

There was a significant correlation between alcohol abuse in the biological parents and their adopted-out children, indicating a genetic component in the risk of developing alcoholism. There was also a correlation between criminality among the biological parents and their adopted-out children but it could not be decided whether or not this was a confounding effect of alcohol abuse, as alcohol abuse and criminality were also moderately correlated in both the biological parents and in their adopted children. Given the high correlation of alcohol abuse with number of offences, and type, severity and age of onset of criminality, in many cases it was not possible to distinguish alcoholic criminals whose abuse was symptomatic of primary alcoholism from those whose alcohol abuse was symptomatic of an antisocial personality disorder.

Genetic heterogeneity of criminality

As mentioned earlier, alcohol abuse and criminality were correlated in both the biological fathers and their sons, indicating that most criminality in this series was a *consequence* of alcohol abuse. However, in a later re-analysis of criminality with no association to alcohol abuse, we found that the 169 sons of criminal biological fathers (without alcohol abuse) were themselves significantly more often registered for criminality only, compared with the sons of all other ($n = 812$) non-criminal biological fathers (8.9 versus 4.2%; $\chi^2 = 4.1$, $P < 0.05$). This indicates that non-alcohol-related crime may have genetic determinants that are different from those leading to alcohol-related criminality (Cloninger et al 1981, 1982, Bohman et al 1982).

Further statistical analyses in which we used discriminant function analyses of the genetic heterogeneity of criminality (Cloninger et al 1982) confirmed my earlier conclusion that most criminality was a consequence of alcohol abuse (Bohman 1978). Alcoholic criminals often committed repeated violent offences, whereas non-alcoholic criminals characteristically committed a small number of petty property offences. These non-alcoholic petty criminals more commonly had biological parents with histories of petty crime but no alcoholism or only occasional teenage abuse of alcohol. In contrast, the risk of criminality in alcohol abusers was correlated with severity of their own alcohol abuse, but not with criminality in the biological or adoptive parents. Unstable preadoptive placement was associated with increased risk for petty criminality, whereas low social status was associated with alcohol-related criminality.

Familial typology of alcoholism, criminality and somatoform disorders

By a series of discriminant and cross-fostering analyses we could distinguish two relatively discrete familial types of alcohol abusers with distinct clinical features and different genetic and environmental backgrounds. These were differently associated with severity of alcohol abuse, criminality and somatoform disorders (Cloninger et al 1981, 1984). We have labelled these types 'milieu-limited' (or type 1) and 'male-limited' (or type 2) alcohol abuse (Cloninger et al 1981, Bohman et al 1981).

In families with the milieu-limited type of congenital susceptibility, both men and women were characterized by adult onset of alcohol abuse and by having no criminality requiring prolonged incarceration. Both congenital diathesis and postnatal provocation were found to be necessary for a person to express the milieu-limited type of susceptibility and the severity of alcohol abuse was determined by the type of environmental background (especially homes with low social status). In families with the male-limited (type 2) alcoholism, males often had teenage onset of recurrent alcoholism with repetitive, occasionally violent criminality. In these families, alcohol abuse increased ninefold in the adopted-out sons, regardless of their postnatal environment. In contrast, women in these families were seldom registered for alcohol abuse or criminal offences. Instead we found that, from an early age, these women took significantly more sick-leave for recurrent complaints of different bodily symptoms—these have been labelled 'diversiform somatizers' (Sigvardsson et al 1984).

A third type of family with distinct clusters of alcohol abuse, antisocial behaviour and somatization was identified in further analyses of sick-leave data. We identified a group of women with high frequency of bodily and psychiatric complaints that was distinct from both the type 1 and type 2 families described here (Bohman et al 1984). This syndrome, which was similar to that seen in Briquet's syndrome or somatization disorder (Cloninger et al 1975), we labelled 'high-frequency somatization'. Their male relatives had teenage onset of recurrent convictions for non-property crimes that were often violent. Recurrent registrations with the temperance boards were often associated with their prominent criminality, but they seldom required treatment for alcoholism. Like their male relatives, about 30% of these 'high-frequency somatizers' were criminal and/or untreated alcohol abusers (Bohman et al 1984). The type of alcoholism that characterized these families we labelled 'antisocial', as we contend that males in these families had a high frequency of antisocial personality disorder.

In a fourth type of family, property offences such as petty theft without associated alcohol abuse are the most prominent behavioural deviation in the men. The same genetic factors that predispose these men to petty criminality are expressed as petty criminality in the women with the most severe predisposition (5%) and as diversiform somatization only in the milder cases (23%). Petty criminality and type 2 alcoholism seem to share some congenital and postnatal environmental determinants, which would lead to familial association between petty criminality and type 2 alcoholism.

Recidivism and severity of disorder

A note should be made about recidivism (the tendency to relapse habitually into crime) as a measure of severity of illness. In comparisons among criminals, alcoholic criminals committed more criminal offences than non-alcoholic criminals. Also, in alcoholic criminals, the number of criminal convictions was correlated with the severity of alcohol abuse. Furthermore, the number of criminal convictions appeared to be correlated with the severity of predisposition to criminality in non-alcoholic criminals. Thus, recidivism was a measure of severity of two genetically independent disorders. Also, severity of alcoholism and hence severity of symptomatic crime, was largely determined by environmental, not genetic, factors in this population. Therefore, if recidivism is used as a measure of predisposition to criminality, highly inconsistent results may be obtained in populations that differ in the proportion of alcoholics unless the population is stratified into alcoholic and non-alcoholic subgroups. Once the heterogeneity related to alcoholism is taken into account, recidivism appears to be a useful measure of severity.

TABLE 1   Cross-fostering analysis of petty criminality in male adoptees

Classification of predisposition to petty criminality		Observed male adoptees	
Congenital	Postnatal	Total (n)	Petty criminality (%)
Low	Low	666	2.9
Low	High	120	6.7
High	Low	66	12.1
High	High	10	40.0

Cross-fostering analysis of petty criminality (without alcohol abuse) in male adoptees. 'Congenital' refers to variables derived from biological parents, whereas 'postnatal' refers to variables derived from rearing experiences and adoptive placement. Classification of predisposition depended on whether the set of background variables were more like the average characteristics of adoptees with petty criminality only (classified as high) or with no criminality and/or alcohol abuse (classified as low).

Cross-fostering analysis of gene–environment interaction in male petty criminals

The risk of petty criminality without alcohol abuse in adopted men was determined for each of four possible combinations generated by classification of both congenital and postnatal backgrounds into high- and low-risk groups (Table 1). Congenital and postnatal backgrounds were classified independently on the basis of data about biological parents and adoptive placement, respectively.

When postnatal, but not congenital factors predisposed to petty criminality, the 120 sons had more than twice the risk of petty criminality than that observed in the 666 sons with neither predisposition (6.7 versus 2.9%; $\chi^2 = 4.5$, $P < 0.05$). Similarly, when congenital, but not postnatal factors predisposed to petty criminality ($n = 66$ sons), the risk was increased fourfold (12.1 versus 2.9%; $\chi^2 = 14.5$, $P < 0.01$). The ten sons with both high congenital and high postnatal predisposition to petty criminality had a risk 14 times that of the sons with neither predisposition (40 versus 2.9%; $\chi^2 = 41.4$, $P < 0.01$) suggesting a possible non-additive interaction between congenital and postnatal factors.

Comment

Even though the postnatal antecedents partially overlapped, these environmental antecedents interacted differently with the two predispositions of criminality and alcoholism. Thus, neither the social status of the adoptive parents nor that of the biological parents were sufficient to predispose their children to petty criminality, but both did increase the risk of criminality in children when the biological parents were *themselves* petty criminals. In other words, the contribution of social status to criminality depended entirely on *interactions* with specific genetic predispositions, either facilitating or diminishing the risk of different genotypes. In contrast, the average effect of low social status increased the risk of alcohol abuse even though it had greater effect on some genotypes (e.g. type 1 alcoholic background). That is, the effect of social status on alcohol abuse had both additive and interactive components that were substantial in this population. Similarly, unstable preadoptive placements (e.g. multiple temporary placements) had both additive and interactive effects, and both were significant for petty criminality and alcoholism.

Our conclusion is that different genetic and environmental antecedents influence the development of male criminality, depending on whether or not it is associated with alcohol abuse. Consequently, it is crucial to distinguish antisocial personality disorders from criminality symptomatic of alcohol abuse in future clinical and aetiological studies. In particular, criminality without alcohol abuse is characterized by petty property offences whereas alcohol-related criminality is more violent and usually often repeated.

Sex differences in the inheritance of petty criminality

The Stockholm Adoption Study provided a unique opportunity to evaluate hypotheses about sex differences in the inheritance of criminality, as mating between the biological parents was found to be random, rather than assortative, with respect to criminality and alcohol abuse. There was a threefold excess of criminal women among the 102 daughters with a criminal background compared with the other 811 daughters (4.9 versus 1.4%; $\chi^2 = 6.62$, $P < 0.05$). Female crime mostly involved non-violent property offences and was seldom associated with alcohol abuse. Postnatal antecedents increasing the risk for criminality were different in males and females. For instance, prolonged institutional care increased the risks of criminality in women, but not in men. In contrast, multiple temporary placements and adoptive homes of very low status increased the risk of criminality in men, but not in women (Sigvardsson et al 1982).

The congenital variables that contributed to petty criminality in the two sexes were qualitatively the same, but petty criminality was more common in adopted men than in adopted women (4.5 versus 1.8%; $\chi^2 = 11.35$, $P < 0.01$). This difference reflects different thresholds for the manifestation of criminality in men and women. We compared the risk of petty criminality in the biological parents of adopted men and women who were themselves petty criminals. We observed that 21% of 39 criminal men had at least one biological parent with petty criminality (i.e. criminality and no alcohol abuse). By comparison, the risk of petty criminality in the biological parents of the criminal women was more than double that of their male counterparts (50 versus 21%; $\chi^2 = 4.78$, $P < 0.05$). Furthermore, the criminal parents of women had an average of 3.6 convictions compared with an average of 1.4 convictions for the criminal parents of the men, and significantly more criminal women had fathers with repeated convictions than the male adoptees (31 versus 5%; $\chi^2 = 6.97$, $P < 0.01$). These data indicate that the congenital predisposition to petty criminality was usually more severe in affected women than in affected men. In other words, the threshold in liability for developing petty criminality was lower (less deviant) in men than in women.

The role of personality in the risk of antisocial behaviour and alcohol abuse

Overall, our stepwise analyses have supported the distinctions between male-limited and milieu-limited alcoholism, antisocial personality with alcohol abuse and petty criminality. The separation of these groups clinically and aetiologically indicates that they are relatively discrete phenotypes. But so far our analyses of the adoptees and their two sets of families have not indicated any simple mode of inheritance of either criminality or alcohol abuse. Rather, our studies indicated that the transmission of these behaviours between generations is largely associated with personality factors, which are moderately inherited and continuously distributed in the population. Thus the variability in clinical expression according to sex and social circumstances suggested a need for characterizing underlying differences in personality or temperament. Such differences in personality or temperament are more stable traits that are involved in the adaptation of an individual with the environment, whereas

TABLE 2   Prediction of type of adult crime from personality at age 11

Characteristic at age 11 years	Percentage of variance explained	Variable means of each group of children		
		No crime (n=378)	Only property crime (n=31)	Violent crime (n=22)
Novelty-seeking (NS)	4.6	+0.1	+0.6	+1.1
Harm avoidance (HA)	1.1	+0.2	−0.1	−0.5
Reward dependence (RD)	0	+0.3	+0.2	0.0
High NS x low HA	1.7	−0.1	+0.3	+0.7

From Sigvardsson et al (1987).

criminality or alcohol abuse represent the result of this interaction. Accordingly, we may expect that personality variables will be more stable than phenomena such as criminality or alcohol abuse, and might provide an index of underlying differences in biochemical and neurophysiological function.

Further clinical studies of alcoholics according to the typology described here have revealed that male-limited alcoholism is associated with personality traits of impulsivity and sensation-seeking in combination with early onset and violent criminality (von Knorring et al 1985). In addition, these alcoholics had low platelet monoamine oxidase activity, whereas milieu-limited alcoholics had normal such activity and no associated impulsivity or sensation-seeking. In fact, type 1 and type 2 alcoholics seem to differ by being at *opposite extremes* of the same dimensions of heritable personality traits. Thus, the genetics of different alcohol-related syndromes (including antisocial behaviours) are at least partly a question of the heritability of various types of personality.

The longitudinal study

Cloninger's original theory of personality (Cloninger 1986) made specific predictions about the relationships between personality and its role in the development of anxiety states and sociopathic behaviour. Three dimensions (later four) were defined that are genetically independent but interact in modulating adaptive responses to novel stimuli. We applied this theory in the analyses of our longitudinal study of adopted children mentioned above (Sigvardsson et al 1987, Cloninger et al 1988). We made detailed behavioural assessment of 431 children at age 11, with a re-evaluation at 27 years to identify convictions for violent and property crimes, and alcohol abuse. Most personality traits derived from factor analysis in the children were found to involve the interaction of the dimensions of 'novelty-seeking', 'harm avoidance' and 'reward dependence'. In particular, aggressive behaviour at 15 years and violent criminal behaviour in adults were predicted by traits associated with antisocial personality disorder—that is, high novelty-seeking, low harm avoidance and low reward dependence. Petty criminality was associated with somewhat lower ratings but these were higher than in non-criminals, supporting our earlier findings concerning differences between these two kinds of antisocial behaviour (Table 2). In addition, high novelty-seeking and low harm avoidance were most strongly predictive of early-onset alcohol abuse, i.e. type 2 alcoholism. These two childhood variables distinguished boys who had nearly a 20-fold difference in their risk of alcohol abuse: the risk of alcohol abuse varied from 4 to 75% depending on childhood personality.

Conclusions

In this population of Swedish adoptees and their relatives, different genetic and environmental antecedents influenced the development of criminality depending on whether or not there was associated alcohol abuse. Non-alcoholic criminals mostly committed petty property offences, whereas repeated, violent crimes were characteristic of early-onset (male) alcoholics. The predisposition to different kinds of antisocial behaviour and alcohol abuse seems to be related in part to underlying inherited personality dimensions which are continuously distributed and interact with social and environmental circumstances.

Acknowledgements

The studies quoted here were in part supported by grants from the Swedish Medical Research Council and from the National Institute on Alcoholism and Alcohol Abuse and the National Institute of Mental Health, National Institutes of Health, Bethesda, MD, USA. My thanks to Dr Sören Sigvardsson for valuable advice and comments.

References

Bohman M 1970 Adopted children and their families. Proprius, Stockholm
Bohman M 1971 A comparative study of adopted children, foster children and children in their biological environment born after undesired pregnancies. Acta Paediatr Scand Suppl 221:1–38
Bohman M 1978 Some genetic aspects of alcoholism and criminality. A population of adoptees. Arch Gen Psychiatry 35:269–276
Bohman M, Sigvardsson S, Cloninger CR 1981 Maternal inheritance of alcohol abuse. Cross-fostering analysis of adopted women. Arch Gen Psychiatry 38:965–969
Bohman M, Cloninger CR, Sigvardsson S, von Knorring A-L 1982 Predisposition to petty criminality in Swedish adoptees. I. Genetic and environmental heterogeneity. Arch Gen Psychiatry 39:1233–1241
Bohman M, Cloninger CR, von Knorring A-L, Sigvardsson S 1984 An adoption study of somatoform disorders. II. Cross-fostering analysis and genetic relationship to alcoholism and criminality. Arch Gen Psychiatry 41:872–878
Cloninger CR 1986 A unified biosocial theory of personality and its role in the development of anxiety states. Psychiatr Dev 3:167–266
Cloninger CR, Reich T, Guze SB 1975 The multifactorial model of disease transmission. III. Familial relationship between sociopathy and hysteria (Briquet's syndrome). Br J Psychiatry 127:23–32
Cloninger CR, Bohman M, Sigvardsson S 1981 Inheritance of alcohol abuse: cross-fostering analysis of adopted men. Arch Gen Psychiatry 38:861–868
Cloninger CR, Sigvardsson S, Bohman M, von Knorring A-L 1982 Predisposition to petty criminality in Swedish adoptees. II. Cross-fostering analysis of gene–environment interaction. Arch Gen Psychiatry 39:1242–1247
Cloninger CR, Sigvardsson S, von Knorring A-L, Bohman M 1984 An adoption study of somatoform disorders. II. Identification of two discrete somatoform disorders. Arch Gen Psychiatry 41:863–871
Cloninger CR, Sigvardsson S, Bohman M 1988 Childhood personality predicts alcohol abuse in young adults. Alcohol Clin Exp Res 12:494–504

Sigvardsson S, Cloninger CR, Bohman M, von Knorring A-L 1982 Predisposition to petty criminality in Swedish adoptees. III. Sex differences and validation of male typology. Arch Gen Psychiatry 39:1248–1253

Sigvardsson S, von Knorring A-L, Bohman M, Cloninger CR 1984 An adoption study of somatoform disorders. I. The relationship of somatization to psychiatric disability. Arch Gen Psychiatry 41:853–859

Sigvardsson S, Bohman M, Cloninger CR 1987 Structure and stability of childhood personality: prediction of later social adjustment. J Child Psychol Psychiatry Allied Discip 28:929–946

von Knorring A-L, Bohman M, von Knorring L, Oreland L 1985 Platelet MAO as a biological marker in subgroups of alcoholism. Acta Psychiatr Scand 72:51–58

DISCUSSION

Virkkunen: You mentioned that type 2 alcoholism was only occasionally connected with violent crime and antisocial behaviour. Opinions differ on this. According to Schuckit's group (Irwin et al 1990), type 2 alcoholism is nearly always connected with antisocial personality disorder.

Bohman: Antisocial personality disorder (as defined in DSM-III-R or IV) is often connected with type 2 alcoholism, but not vice versa: type 2 alcoholism is a much broader concept. Admittedly, the risk of an individual developing type 2 alcoholism is strongly related to their possession of those independently heritable and bipolar personality traits that we associate with antisocial personality disorder: high novelty-seeking, low harm avoidance and low reward dependence. Individuals with such a combination of personality traits are prone to start to use alcohol or other drugs as stimulants at an early age, and this combination often leads to fights, arrests and sometimes to violent crimes. But from a phenomenological perspective there is no clear dichotomy between normal and abnormal behaviour. As I showed in Table 2, there was a continuum of risk for developing substance abuse and committing violent and non-violent crimes, depending on the variations in personality traits.

Virkkunen: There are some biological findings that are only applicable to the extreme group of type 2 alcoholics. We have findings that low serotonin turnover is a factor connected with impulsive violent behaviour among type 2 alcoholics. Low platelet monoamine oxidase (MAO) is possibly also in the picture.

Bohman: Yes, there seems to be an association between low platelet MAO, antisocial personality and type 2 alcoholism. Severe cases are sometimes identified as patients in clinics for alcoholics or individuals serving long prison sentences for severe violent crimes. But not all individuals who are at risk of developing type 2 alcoholism actually do so. This depends partly on the severity of their personality deviance but also on their upbringing, cultural context and other environmental influences. Our adoption research suggests that a stable adoptive placement has protective effects and neutralizes a large part of the social 'inheritance'.

Virkkunen: Cloninger et al's (1981) criteria for type 2 alcoholism differ from the criteria of von Knorring et al (1985), Gilligan et al (1988) and Sullivan et al (1990). We don't know which criteria are the most valid and reliable.

Bohman: If there are differences, they seem to be related to differences in cut-off points. In discussing this, it may also be necessary to separate the two concepts of 'risk' and 'disorder'. In principle, the risks of developing alcoholism or antisocial personality disorder are quantitative variables, not dichotomies or trichotomies. For statistical reasons, antisocial personality disorder is treated as a discrete condition in DSM-IV, but in real life there is a continuum from mild to severe depending upon the underlying combination of personality traits. From our adoption data and those from other longitudinal or follow-up studies (for instance, those by Lee Robins) it also seems clear that the development of an antisocial personality disorder is a *process* that begins in early childhood, develops into conduct disorder, and eventually leads to antisocial personality disorder. But the outcome of this process is also dependent upon social and rearing circumstances during childhood and adolescence. Our adoption studies indicate that early placement in a stable middle-class adoptive home may diminish the risk of development of antisocial behaviours and related alcohol abuse, even for those adoptees at genetic risk. For instance, type 2 biological fathers with severe alcohol abuse and violent criminality had adopted-out sons with a similar combination of crime and abuse, but to a much less severe degree.

Carlier: If we are looking for genetic markers to correlate with criminality, do you think that we should look for a marker for alcoholism?

Bohman: There has been a lot of research aiming to identify 'genetic markers' for alcoholism. For instance, it has been suggested that the restriction fragment length polymorphism markers *Taq*1A1 and B1 at the dopamine D2 receptor gene locus are associated with substance abuse. As far as I know, these suggestions have not yet been confirmed.

Heath: One can certainly look at that question from a continuum perspective. In a number of large data sets, I have tried to replicate this typology using purely alcohol symptom data. I didn't get any sort of evidence for that discrimination. Shouldn't we be giving more attention to Marc Schuckit's suggestion that perhaps what we are looking at is a continuum of impulsivity and liability to conduct problems that discriminates how people get into trouble with alcohol, rather than anything directly to do with the alcoholism process itself? In our data we find that the alcoholic symptom pattern doesn't seem to allow us to subtype at all. This is based on large epidemiological samples where we don't have to worry about selective sampling. How good is the evidence that what we're looking at in type 2 alcoholics is to do with alcoholism, rather than to do with antisocial traits?

Virkkunen: My feeling is that these antisocial traits arise first: these people start to drink possibly because of these antisocial traits, conduct disorder problems, stimulus-seeking and impulsivity.

Goldman: After having started to drink, alcoholics with antisocial behaviour may not show a different pattern of alcohol consumption or drinking career. Thus, it may not be possible to discriminate between type 1 and type 2 liability classes on the basis of alcoholic symptom patterns.

Heath: So, when we talk about type 1 and type 2, we are talking more about a continuum of liability to criminality or violent behaviour than about alcohol problems *per se*. It just happens that those people, as part of their behaviour, are very likely to develop alcohol and drug problems as well.

Bohman: I agree, if we are talking of a *continuum of liability* to criminality, violent behaviour *and* substance abuse. In my paper I tried to explain this when I emphasized the importance of the childhood personality factors, which were strongly predictive of adult criminality and alcohol abuse.

In a way I am not surprised that you did not succeed in replicating the typology in your large data sets, as you have only used information about purely alcohol symptom data. Did you have access to data on other kinds of substance abuse, arrests and violent and non-violent criminality over a large part of the lifespan? Did you rely on retrospective or prospective data?

As I mentioned in the introduction to my talk, we have recently confirmed our typology in a replication study of the genetics of alcoholism in adoptees, but this of course implies that we have used not only alcohol symptom data but also other relevant available data about antisocial behaviour and occupational status as well as information about the biological parents, etc. In addition we have also replicated the typology in clinical samples of alcoholics (von Knorring et al 1985).

I do agree with Dr Virkkunen that conduct disorder and antisocial traits *precede* substance abuse. But it may be important to remember that those who are antisocial abusers are a small minority among all alcoholics (although often a very spectacular minority).

Heath: Would you then retract the distinctions you made between type 1 and type 2 alcoholics, some of which are based on alcohol-related symptoms?

Rutter: As I understand it, Michael Bohman's findings do not concern the *defining* characteristics of type 1 and type 2 alcoholism, but rather differences in the overall *profile* of features. Are you arguing, Andrew Heath, that although there may be differences between the two types of drinking, those are not sufficiently great to be defining characteristics?

Heath: In large data sets, all we can find is just a continuum of problems.

Bohman: When you are talking of a 'continuum' of problems, I understand you to mean an increasing number of alcohol related problems, from mild to severe, among your subjects. In our analysis of the genetics of alcohol abuse and criminality, we also found a continuum of severity among both the biological parents and their adopted-out children. But severity was largely independent of typology. Our analyses suggested that severity was strongly related to environmental factors, especially among type 1 alcoholics. But the *type* of alcoholism was under the influence of the heritable traits that I have described. Admittedly, there is often some overlap between type 1 and type 2 alcoholics, depending on the combination of personality traits. But I still contend that the distinction between type 1 and type 2 alcoholism is useful and well supported by the results in the Stockholm Adoption Study and in the recently completed replication study, as well as in clinical studies of alcoholics in Sweden and in the USA.

Heath: But you can't describe the model that you have presented as a continuum, can you?

Bohman: Again, the subtypes are clinical manifestations of independent, but not mutually exclusive processes. Of course, the 'continuum' I am speaking about is related to the personality traits. These are *continuous bipolar traits* that are as predictive of the normal range of pro-social behaviours (such as maturity and leadership ability), as they are predictive of adjustment problems (such as academic underachievement and antisocial behaviour).

Rutter: As we noted earlier in our discussions (p 16), the issue of continuity/ discontinuity in aetiology cannot be tackled simply by determining whether a trait functions as a dimension in some respects. There may be different routes to the same trait outcome and it is necessary that we test for that possibility.

Heath: There are two different perspectives. The one I would agree with is that there are multiple pathways into alcoholism. However, the symptom profile expressed is purely a function of the severity of an individual along that continuum. You implied that there are quite distinctive symptom profiles, which in very large data sets we can't replicate.

Rowe: Even the age of onset differences?

Heath: Age of onset doesn't work out.

Bohman: I cannot agree with you that 'the symptom profile expressed is purely a function of the severity of an individual along that continuum'. It would be a serious error to assume that causal subtypes are not present just because alcoholism can be graded along a severity continuum. This kind of classification had already turned out to be obsolete when we published our 1981 study: severity was not related to genetic predisposition in a simple way (Cloninger et al 1981, Bohman et al 1981). In fact, 'severity' has very little to do with typology and aetiology. I contend that alcoholics do have very different profiles, especially at the beginning of their drinking careers. Admittedly, clinical differences may be much smaller after many years in cases where severe abuse has developed, when the toxic effects of alcohol and other drugs have taken their toll. When the fires have died down, the burnt-out remains look rather similar, irrespective of whether the fires were caused by arson or accident.

Carlier: You have some data that might indicate a uterine effect. In some of your papers you took into account the sex of the biological parent. When you observed different results this might have been due to a uterine effect.

Bohman: Indeed, we found very interesting differences between male and female phenotypic expressions, but it is generally difficult to draw conclusions about intrauterine effects from our results. We discussed the possible intrauterine effects of alcohol in an earlier report on maternal inheritance of alcohol abuse (Bohman et al 1981). We found that the influence of maternal inheritance on the risk of alcohol abuse in adopted women was more important than paternal inheritance. Biological mothers accounted for twice as much of the variance in alcoholic outcome for their daughters than did the fathers. This greater influence of alcoholic mothers occurred despite alcohol abuse being six times more common in the fathers than in the mothers. The alcoholic mothers also had more alcoholic children (28% of 32 sons and 10% of 51 daughters) than did alcoholic fathers (23% of 259 sons and 4% of 307 daughters). These results may indicate possible influence of alcohol in the intrauterine environment on later susceptibility to alcoholism and/or an effect of a more severe genetic predisposition among these biological mothers.

We did not have access to data on pregnancy and birth complications except in the longitudinal study, where pregnancy complications explained only a very small part of the variability of behaviours in girls at age 11.

The ratio of paternal to maternal contribution to the explained variability of petty criminality was 40:1, so, by and large, the effect of maternal intrauterine environment may have been negligible. On the other hand, the threshold in liability for development of criminality was much higher among women compared with men: more of the criminal women had biological parents with petty criminality than did their male counterparts. Thus, the congenital antecedents of criminality were the same regardless of sex, but the congenital predisposition to criminality had to be more severe for a woman to be affected.

Daly: Presumably, the question about uterine effects concerns whether there is a stronger prediction from the mother than from the father.

Bohman: Yes, as mentioned previously, there may be a possible intrauterine influence from alcoholic mothers. But our data permit only tentative conclusions. As we collected data over the lifetime of biological parents, we noticed that alcohol abuse was sometimes not known until some years after the birth of the adoptee.

Daly: Even if you did have good evidence of a stronger prediction from the biological mothers than from the biological fathers, it might not mean a uterine effect—it might simply represent a lot of misattribution of paternity in parents giving up children for adoption.

Bohman: All children were born out of wedlock, and every child had a guardian who, according to law, had to ascertain the paternity. All uncertain or unknown paternities were excluded from our analyses. Our contention is that misattribution of paternity was minimized in this adoptee population.

Heath: If women have to have a high genetic risk before they become alcoholic or criminal, then you would also expect that when there's an alcoholic mother there's a much higher risk than when there's an alcoholic father, quite apart from any possible intrauterine effect.

Gottesman: At the time that these papers were being written up, a few of us were at Washington University, St Louis, and there were discussions of whether or not the word 'genetic' would be more appropriate than the term 'congenital'. It was clear to Cloninger and the rest of us that the term genetic would be saying too much—that's why the term congenital was used so as to allow for the possibility of prenatal intrauterine effects.

Carey: One of the most fascinating aspects of this Swedish adoption work is the issue of 'restricted range' or whatever you want to call it, in the sense that the adoptive families seem to be almost criminal free. At the same time, the base rate for crime among the adoptees is about that of the population, despite the fact that their biological relatives have high rates of crime. That has to argue quite strongly that family upbringing or advantage is having a relatively high impact in this study. Do you have any data that shed light on what might be going on in these adoptive families?

Bohman: In the Stockholm Adoption Study we could not collect more detailed data about the adoptive parent families. But in our longitudinal study we collected a lot of information from several hours of interviews with the adoptive parents. So far this information has not yet been analysed, but we are planning to do this in the near future to get more detailed information about environment and rearing circumstances.

References

Bohman M, Sigvardsson S, Cloninger CR 1981 Maternal inheritance of alcohol abuse. Cross-fostering analysis of adopted women. Arch Gen Psychiatry 38:965–969

Cloninger CR, Bohman M, Sigvardsson S 1981 Inheritance of alcohol abuse: cross-fostering analysis of adopted men. Arch Gen Psychiatry 38:861–868

Gilligan SB, Reich T, Cloninger CR 1988 Alcohol-related symptoms in heterogeneous families of hospitalized alcoholics. Alcohol Clin Exp Res 12:671–678

Sullivan JL, Baenziger JC, Wagner DL 1990 Platelet MAO in subtypes of alcoholism. Biol Psychiatry 27:911–922

von Knorring A-L, Bohman M, von Knorring L, Oreland L 1985 Platelet MAO as a biological marker in subgroups of alcoholism. Acta Psychiatr Scand 72:51–58

Assessing the role of genetics in crime using adoption cohorts

Patricia A. Brennan*, Sarnoff A. Mednick*† and Bjorn Jacobsen†

*Center for Longitudinal Research, University of Southern California, Social Science Research Institute, Denney Research Building, Los Angeles, CA 90089-1111, USA, and †Institute of Preventive Medicine, Kommune Hospitalet, DK-1399 Copenhagen, Denmark

Abstract. The role of genetics in criminal behaviour can be assessed through family, twin and adoption studies. This paper discusses the major findings of adoption studies that have focused on criminal outcome. Results from adoption studies have consistently revealed a relationship between biological parent criminal behaviour and adoptee criminal outcome. This finding has been noted in the case of property crime, but not in the case of violent crime. Violent crime in adopted-away offspring is not related to violent crime in biological parents. Findings from the Danish Adoption Cohort suggest that violent crime may be genetically related to other types of behavioural deviance. In the Danish Adoption Cohort, there is an increased rate of schizophrenia in the adopted-away offspring of biological fathers who are convicted of violent crimes. This father violence–adoptee schizophrenia relationship cannot be accounted for by the potential confounding factors of rearing social status, age at transfer, knowledge of family history of crime, or biological parents' mental illness.

1996 Genetics of criminal and antisocial behaviour. Wiley, Chichester (Ciba Foundation Symposium 194) p 115–128

Adoptions provide a natural experiment which can inform us regarding the existence and strength of inherited predispositions. A newborn infant placed for adoption brings to the new family characteristics associated with the genetic materials of the biological mother and father. Few will question the heritability of biological characteristics such as hair and eye colour. In fact, adoption agencies frequently assume this heritability in their family placement. A child with blonde, blue-eyed biological parents will, if possible, be placed with blonde, blue-eyed adoptive parents.

But the child inherits many biological features. In concert with the environment, the combination of these inherited biological features may help determine the nature of his intellectual, psychological and/or social adaptation. If biological parents have heritable biological characteristics which can

TABLE 1   Conviction rates of completely identified members of adoptee families

Family member	Number identified	Conviction rate by number of convictions			
		0	*1*	*2*	*>2*
Male adoptee	6 129	0.841	0.088	0.029	0.049
Female adoptee	7 065	0.972	0.020	0.005	0.003
Adoptive father	13 918	0.938	0.046	0.008	0.008
Adoptive mother	14 267	0.981	0.015	0.002	0.002
Biological father	10 604	0.714	0.129	0.056	0.102
Biological mother	12 300	0.911	0.064	0.012	0.013

predispose them to criminal behaviour, they might transmit these biological characteristics to their offspring. Those offspring who inherit these predisposing biological characteristics would, in turn, have an increased risk of evidencing criminal behaviour. Hence, we might hypothesize that (all things being equal) children of criminal biological parents will evidence higher levels of criminal offending than the biological offspring of law-abiding parents.

The most extensive investigation of this hypothesis was completed in Denmark, studying a national total population of the 14 427 non-familial adoptions occurring between 1924 and 1947 (Hutchings & Mednick 1973). This register was established by a group of American and Danish investigators to examine the heritability of schizophrenia (Kety et al 1971). The register includes information on the adoptees, and of the adoptive and biological parents.

The investigators who established the register ascertained the psychiatric hospital admissions of the adoptees and the biological and adoptive parents. The hospital records were summarized and diagnoses made by consensus of the research group.

Court convictions were used as an index of criminal involvement. Court records were obtained for all subjects for whom date and place of birth were available ($n = 65\,516$). Table 1 presents the number of subjects in each adoption category, and the conviction records for the adoptees and their biological and adoptive parents. The biological fathers were rather severely criminal; almost 30% had been convicted of a criminal offence. The adoptive parents' conviction rates are below those of the population averages for their age, sex and time period. Of the adoptive fathers, 0.8% had two or more convictions; 10.2% of the biological fathers had two or more convictions.

As can be seen in Fig. 1, there is a significant relationship between the number of convictions of the biological parents and the rate of convictions

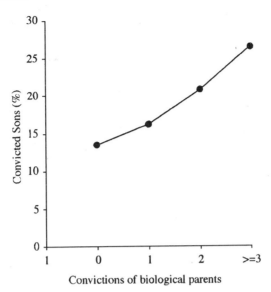

FIG. 1. Criminal convictions in the biological parents and their adopted-away offspring.

among their adopted-away sons. These data support the hypothesis that a biological characteristic which increases risk for criminal convictions is transmitted from biological parents to their sons and increases risk for criminal conviction.

The chronic offender, although infrequent, commits a markedly disproportionate number of the crimes in a cohort. In one US birth cohort, 6% of the most criminally active males committed 69.4% of the crimes. In the adoption cohort we defined a chronic offender as one with three or more convictions. This group comprises 4.09% of the male adoptees; they are responsible for 69.4% of the convictions. As can be seen in Fig. 2, chronic offending in the biological parents is significantly related to chronic offending in their adopted-away male offspring. The male chronically offending adoptees who have chronically offending biological parents comprise only 1% of the male adoptees but are responsible for **30%** of the convictions in the male adoptee cohort!

The biological parents are fertile and sometimes place more than one child for adoption. These children, both full and half-siblings, are almost always placed in separate adoptive homes. The concordance rate for convictions for unrelated, separately-reared male adoptees is 8.5%; this may be seen as a baseline. There were 126 male–male half-sibling pairs placed in separate adoptive homes; they have a 12.9% concordance rate for convictions. Forty full siblings were placed in separate adoptive homes; they have a conviction concordance rate of 20%. In those cases in which the biological parents have

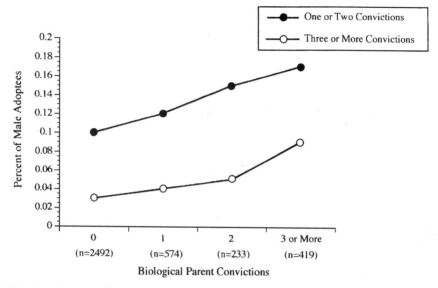

FIG. 2. Chronic offending in the biological parents and their adopted-away male offspring.

been convicted the sib and half-sib concordance rate for convictions rises to 30.8%.

The results of this population study support the hypothesis that a heritable biological factor increases risk for criminal convictions. We have not reported the data for the female adoptees because the number of females convicted was small. The relationship between biological mother convictions and adoptee convictions is significantly stronger than that between biological father convictions and adoptee convictions.

In Fig. 3 we present both the property and violent offending of the male adoptees as a function of the number of convictions of the biological parents. The increase in adoptee property offending is significantly related to biological parent offences; adoptee violent convictions are NOT significantly related to the criminal convictions of the biological parents; neither is adoptee violent offending significantly related to violent offending in the biological parents. We will return to this finding.

Other adoption projects

Crowe (1974) traced 52 adopted offspring of incarcerated women in Iowa. Seven of the 52 were convicted for a criminal offence as opposed to only one in a matched control group. Also in Iowa, Cadoret et al (1985) found that the rate

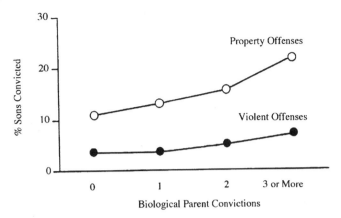

FIG. 3.   Property and violent offending of the male adoptee as a function of biological parent convictions.

of antisocial personality disorder was significantly elevated in adopted-away offspring of antisocial biological parents. Cadoret later replicated this finding in a separate group of Iowa adoptees (Cadoret et al 1987).

In Sweden, Bohman et al (1982) examined the criminal behaviour of 862 adoptees and their biological parents. Criminal biological parents had a significantly higher rate of adopted-away criminal offspring than non-criminal parents. As in the case of the Danish adoption study, Bohman did not find a relationship between biological parent crime and violent offending in the adoptees.

Violent offending

We were puzzled by the failure of crime in the biological parents to relate to violence in the adoptees. Some evidence began to suggest that perhaps serious mental illness may have a genetic relationship to violence. In Oregon, Heston (1966) followed up a sample of offspring born to schizophrenic women in a mental hospital. These children were separated from their mothers at or near birth and given foster placements. Heston noted a significant increase in schizophrenia in the offspring of the schizophrenic women, but it is of interest that he found an even higher level of antisocial behaviour, including violence (Heston 1966).

We found other indications of a possible genetic link between schizophrenia and violence. In a population study of a total birth cohort of 358 000 Danes, born 1944–1947, we noted that schizophrenics had a significantly increased level of arrests for violent offences. In another Danish birth cohort we noted

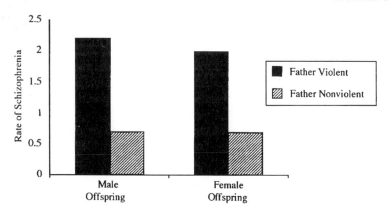

FIG. 4. Biological father violence and percentage rate of adoptee schizophrenia.

that psychiatric hospitalization in parents was related to significantly increased rates of violence in their sons. But these sons were raised by these mentally ill parents. Moffitt (1984) made an advance in the study of this question; within the Danish Adoption Cohort, she noted that the combination of crime and psychiatric hospitalization in the biological parents was significantly related to violence in their adopted-away sons. Moffitt could not analyse schizophrenic outcome in the children because of the small number of cases detected in a sweep of the Danish psychiatric register in 1976.

Fortunately, since 1976, in the context of their study of the genetics of schizophrenia, the Kety group has been regularly checking the adoptees for cases of schizophrenia in the psychiatric register. To date, they have ascertained 101 schizophrenic adoptees; they were kind enough to provide us with the identity of these subjects. The 101 schizophrenic adoptees permitted us to examine the relationship between schizophrenia in the adopted-away offspring and rates of violence in their biological parents, as in Fig. 4.

As can be seen, there is a threefold increase in the rate of schizophrenia for both male and female offspring of biological fathers convicted of violent offences. The fathers and the offspring share a heritable biological characteristic which increases risk of violence in the fathers and increases risk of schizophrenia in the offspring.

There are several possible confounding factors to be considered in assessing these and any adoption findings. Placement factors, age at transfer, assortative mating and the rearing social environment may have affected our results. We explored the possibility that the relationship between father violence and offspring schizophrenia might vary as a function of the following factors:
(1) *Socioeconomic status (SES)*. It is conceivable that the violence–schizophrenia relationship might be restricted to a specific rearing social

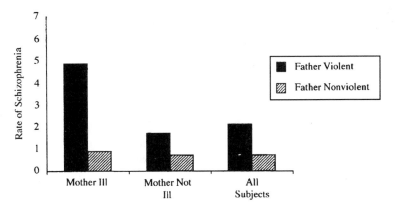

FIG. 5. Biological father violence, biological mother mental illness and percentage rate of adoptee schizophrenia.

class level. We did not find this to be the case. When subjects were divided into high and low social class level according to the income of their adoptive families, the relationship between father violence and adoptee schizophrenia was present in each of these social class levels (low SES: $\chi^2 = 9.9$, $P < 0.01$; high SES: $\chi^2 = 5.96$, $P < 0.05$).

(2) *Age at transfer*. It might be argued that the early environment of the child led to his or her increased risk for schizophrenia. Time spent with the biological parents would therefore be an important mediating factor to consider. In our study, age at transfer did not act as a mediator. The father violence–adoptee schizophrenia relationship is seen in those transferred to their adoptive homes at birth ($\chi^2 = 8.4$, $P < 0.01$), before one-year of age ($\chi^2 = 3.3$, $P < 0.05$), and for those transferred after one year of age ($\chi^2 = 5.3$, $P < 0.05$).

(3) *Biological mother's mental illness*. It is possible that violent men assortatively mate with mentally ill women. It could therefore be the mental illness in the mothers which is responsible for the increased rate of schizophrenia in the offspring. However, the father violence–adoptee schizophrenia relationship is seen even in the case where all families with mentally ill biological mothers have been removed from the analyses ($\chi^2 = 7.2$, $P < 0.01$). As Fig. 5 reveals, however, the highest rates of offspring schizophrenia are found in the case where the biological father is violent *and* the mother has been hospitalized for mental illness.

(4) *Biological father's mental illness*. One other possible explanation for our finding is that the violent fathers may have had an increased incidence of mental illness, and the mental illness resulted in the increased rates of schizophrenia in the adoptees. However, the father violence–adoptee schizophrenia relationship is seen even in the case where all families with

mentally ill biological fathers have been removed from the analyses ($\chi^2 = 13.9$, $P < 0.001$).

(5) *Biological parent schizophrenia*. Given the well-established findings on genetics and schizophrenia, we ran the analyses again, controlling for biological parent schizophrenia. Even when all biological parents with schizophrenia are removed, the father violence–adoptee schizophrenia relationship remains ($\chi^2 = 9.8$, $P < 0.01$).

(6) *Knowledge of criminal family background*. It is possible that the adoptive families may have been informed of the biological parent criminal histories, and this may have influenced their treatment or expectations for the deviant outcome of the adoptees. We controlled for this potential confounding factor by running secondary analyses including only those cases where the biological parents' criminal convictions occurred *after* the date of the adoption. Even in those cases where the biological father was not yet criminal, the adoptees evidenced an increased risk for schizophrenia ($\chi^2 = 11.0$, $P < 0.001$).

The above findings suggest that confounding factors that might be associated with adoption cohorts do not explain our results. Our findings provide preliminary evidence that the violent fathers and their offspring share a heritable biological characteristic which increases risk of schizophrenia in the offspring. Our study cannot address the question of what specific characteristic is inherited. Our findings do suggest, however, that this characteristic increases the risk for schizophrenia, but not the risk for violence in the adopted-away offspring. One possible explanation for this pattern of results is that the outcome of violence may be dependent upon a more complex combination of environmental and biological predictors than the outcome of schizophrenia. An inherited deficit in information processing, for example, may be a major component in the predictive equation for schizophrenia, and only one of several hundred possible components in the predictive equations for violence.

References

Bohman M, Cloninger CR, Sigvardsson S, von Knorring A-L 1982 Predisposition to petty criminality in Swedish adoptees. I. Genetic and environmental heterogeneity. Arch Gen Psychiatry 39:1233–1241

Cadoret RJ, O'Gorman TW, Troughton E, Heywood E 1985 Alcoholism and antisocial personality: interrelationships, genetic and environmental factors. Arch Gen Psychiatry 42:161–167

Cadoret RJ, Troughton E, O'Gorman TW 1987 Genetic and environmental factors in alcohol abuse and antisocial personality. J Stud Alcohol 48:1–8

Crowe RR 1974 An adoption study of antisocial personality. Arch Gen Psychiatry 31:785–791

Heston LL 1966 Psychiatric disorders in foster home-reared children of schizophrenic mothers. Br J Psychiatry 112:819–825

Hutchings B, Mednick SA 1973 Biological and adoptive fathers of male criminal adoptees. In: Major issues in juvenile delinquency. World Health Organization, Copenhagen, p 47–60

Kety SS, Rosenthal D, Wender PH, Schulsinger F 1971 Mental illness in the biological and adoptive families of adopted schizophrenics. Am J Psychiatry 138:302–320

Moffitt TE 1984 Genetic influences of parental psychiatric illness on violent and recidivistic criminal behaviour. PhD thesis, University of Southern California, Los Angeles, CA, USA

DISCUSSION

Gottesman: Let me try to explain the Heston findings. He and I have discussed these many times, and he agrees (Gottesman et al 1979) that the most parsimonious explanation for the high rate of antisocial behaviour in the adopted-away offspring of schizophrenic mothers concerns the characteristics of the offsprings' biological fathers. In Heston's Oregon study, the biological fathers were not examined clinically or by history. His sample of mothers were chronic schizophrenics in the state hospital and their babies were adopted away within three days of birth. Consequently, you have to ask yourself the question: what sort of man would impregnate a chronic schizophrenic woman in a state hospital? Therefore, there is a difference between the Danish (Rosenthal 1975) and the Oregon studies in what constitutes candidates for the schizophrenia spectrum. Heston was not enthusiastic, nor was David Rosenthal, about excluding antisocial personality as part of the spectrum. But your results bring this idea back to life, and it needs to be reconsidered.

Rowe: It's clear that violence is causally heterogeneous, and some of it may be related to schizophrenia. Perhaps the bottom line here is that you have to be crazy to be violent in Denmark!

In all the American literature, convictions for violence are relatively less frequent than convictions for property offences, but violent offenders often have been convicted of many property offences. You can't separate these offence types, because the people who you label as violent offenders will often have committed numerous property offences. If you took a rare property offence, such as burglary between 4 a.m. and 5 a.m., and you separated it from all other property offences, I expect you would get a very similar result to that you would obtain by separating violent and property crimes. That is, all property offences would show a statistical relationship to the property offences of the biological parent, but this rare property offence would show a very slight relationship, which could easily be statistically non-significant. Looking for the relationship between child and parental violence while controlling for other property offences is similar to controlling statistically for the very antisocial trait disposition that you are using these things to detect. I'm convinced that violence is a part of the same liability risk as general criminal behaviour. This observation goes back to the specialization/generalization debate we had yesterday (p 36).

Mednick: We find no relationship between property offending in the biological parents and schizophrenia in children; but we see a strong relationship between *violent* offending in biological parents and schizophrenia in offspring. Violent offenders are not just property offenders who got drunk one day. Violent offenders form their own group: they are very different from recidivistic property offenders. In our cohort studies we note many who commit 25–30 property offences and never once commit a violent offence.

Rutter: David Rowe, I don't quite understand the point you're making. Are you making a base-rate comparison?

Rowe: This relationship to schizophrenia suggests something different about violent crime; I agree with that. I'm saying that we don't know what percentage of the violent offences are being accounted for by the overlap of all violent offences that are occurring in this population of adoptees with schizophrenia. My general point is that violent behaviour may be something that becomes likely when somebody commits many crimes (for example, someone who steals becomes violent when a home-owner opposes him). By just breaking out one specific kind of offence that has a much lower base rate, you may lose your statistical power to detect a relationship to the characteristics of the biological parents.

Mednick: If you select a sub-group that has only 10 offenders in it, you lose a lot of statistical power. If you select a sub-group that has several hundred offenders in it, the loss of power is considerably less significant.

Maxson: Do you know anything about the abuse of women by violent offenders? Do the violent offenders abuse women more than non-violent offenders?

Mednick: We don't know. It would not be surprising if violent offenders were more abusive towards women.

Maxson: Could that abuse be the cause of the schizophrenia?

Mednick: Yes. The abuse might occur prenatally and result in fetal developmental disturbance. Or it may occur postnatally and result in pathological psychosocial learning.

Maxson: What kind of crimes have the violent offenders committed?

Mednick: Mainly assaults, just as in the Swedish studies.

Maxson: Wouldn't there be official records of spouse abuse?

Mednick: Yes, but it must be pointed out that the biological fathers did not necessarily spend a lot of time with the mothers. Some just met for 15 minutes in a doorway. For this reason, in the adoption record, some of the women state that they are unsure of the identity of the fathers. Identity of fathers is less certain than of mothers. Even in middle class families, there are alarming data on falsely assumed paternity. However, the knowledge of the biological father may be more secure in these adoptees than it is in many middle class families. The Danish state is very interested in knowing who the father is, because if the state can't find the father, then the state has to support the child; this motivates them. There is a law that says the mother must reveal the identity of the father.

Daly: Even if she doesn't know, is she still obliged to name someone?

Mednick: I have a revealing story about this. There was a woman in Jutland who gave up a child (to-be) for adoption. The officials quizzed her on the identity of the father, and she replied that it could be any one of five men. The five were given blood tests, and the officials came back a little sheepishly to tell her that none of them could be the father. So the mother thought a little harder and remembered that she had been to a party and had an encounter. All she could remember about the man was that he had a button with a number 57 on his jacket. One of these investigators happened to know there was a factory in Aarhus where all the workers are identified by means of such buttons. They went to the factory and interrogated number 57. He told them that he had indeed been at this particular party (which he had quite enjoyed). When they gave him a blood test they found out that he was the father. Most of us have never gone to that much trouble to make sure we are the fathers of our own children; I believe that the fathers are by and large accurately identified in these studies.

Waldman: How specific is the relation of biological parents' crime to adoptees' schizophrenia as opposed to its relation to personality disorders other than antisocial personality disorder?

Taylor: There's now very good evidence that schizophrenia is a risk factor specifically for violent crime among men. The evidence in relation to women is much less clear: there is far less research among women in this area. Such career and epidemiological studies as there are would suggest that the risk of crime in general is increased by schizophrenia for women, although that may have to do with the low base rates for crime among women (e.g. Lindqvist & Allebeck 1990a, Wessely et al 1994). The association for men with schizophrenia is specifically with violence rather than crime in general (Lindqvist & Allebeck 1990a, Hodgins 1992, Taylor 1993, Wessely et al 1994). Confirmatory data about a special association between violence and schizophrenia have been gathered from a variety of perspectives; including large cross-sectional samples—the Epidemiological Catchment Area survey, which had self-report data (Swanson et al 1990), and a New York-based study, which included arrest and criminal conviction data (Link et al 1992). Another approach has been to study comparative careers—looking at criminal careers side by side with illness careers. In some of the career studies, people simply noted that the criminal careers of those people with schizophrenia looked very different from those people who did not have schizophrenia (Lindqvist & Allebeck 1990a, Hodgins 1992); in others the *onset* of the of the illness and the *onset* of the violence can each be dated and compared (Coid et al 1993, Wessely et al 1994). In our study, a criterion of onset of significant violence rather than purely criminal violence was selected (Taylor 1993). In nearly 90% of cases, the onset of the violence postdated the onset of the schizophrenia. The third strand of evidence comes from an examination of phenomenological relationships. For a substantial minority of cases—nearly 50%—it would appear that symptoms, almost invariably delusions, directly drive the violence (Taylor 1985, Link & Stueve 1994). That leaves, however, just over 50% of people for whom the violence is not so directly linked to a symptom, but nevertheless seems to follow from the disorder (Taylor 1985, 1993). This is an interesting split. Hypotheses are emerging that there may be at least two distinct kinds of violence among people with schizophrenia which may have substantial organic explanations, which in turn could be very relevant. The violence that is apparently mediated through the positive symptoms of schizophrenia is, in general, the most serious violence, driven by delusions and generally emerging late in the illness (Hafner & Boker 1973, Taylor 1993, Humphreys et al 1992). This may best be accounted for by abnormalities in the dopaminergic system. The other main type of violence, which is probably less serious but tends to be more repetitive, perhaps even impulsive, may perhaps best be explained by serotonergic activity. The serotonergic system is now recognized as likely to be affected in many cases of schizophrenia. Christison et al (1991) have reviewed such differential effects and their implications for treatment. The atypical neuroleptics, which have a broader spectrum of action in the CNS, may offer advantages for those who have schizophrenia and are violent.

Waldman: In this work, have people looked at the familial relation of crime to bipolar disorders as a control?

Taylor: They hardly figure at all in the violence statistics (e.g. Hafner & Boker 1973, Taylor & Gunn 1984).

Mednick: Dr Patricia Brennan and I are studying a population of 358 000 Danes. The purpose is to study the relationship between schizophrenia and violence. Such a relationship exists. We have also looked at a variety of other disorders, and certainly affective disorders are far less related to violent crime. That is, those with affective disorders do not evidence an elevated rate of violent crimes.

Taylor: The relationship with alcohol is even more complicated—I suspect that this has to do in part with what is included in the term 'alcoholism'. Alcohol abuse may certainly complicate schizophrenia, but the problem that has probably been most commonly examined in conjunction with violence is alcohol use at the time of the attack, not necessarily a reflection of abuse more generally.

American hospital samples (e.g. Tardiff & Sweillam 1980) showed an inverse relationship between drinking, schizophrenia and violence, as did an English pre-trial prisoner study (Taylor & Gunn 1984, Taylor 1993), the latter in contrast to non-psychotic men. Alcohol abuse was not a significant problem for the psychotic men. In other words, people with schizophrenia who are violent rarely appear to drink in direct association with their violence. American prison studies, however, show something rather different (e.g. Abram & Teplin 1991). Perhaps, though, this is partly because of a tendency in such an exceptionally violent and disabled population to get ceiling effects; thus, where everyone has got everything to the most awful degree, there is an association with alcohol. In Sweden too, however, there was a positive association between violence and alcohol consumption among people with schizophrenia (Lindqvist & Allebeck 1990b). Cultural factors may be creeping into the alcohol association in ways we still do not understand.

References

Abram KM, Teplin LA 1991 Co-occurring disorders among mentally ill jail detainees. Am Psychol 46:1036–1045

Christison GW, Kirch DG, Wyatt RJ 1991 When symptoms persist: choosing among alternative somatic treatment for schizophrenia. Schizophrenia Bull 17: 217–245

Coid B, Lewis SW, Reveley AM 1993 A twin study of psychosis and criminality. Br J Psychiatry 163:87–92

Gottesman II, Shields J, Heston LL 1979 Schizoid phenotypes in the co-twins of schizophrenics: the signals and the noises. In: Roth M, Cowie V (eds) Psychiatry, genetics and pathography—a tribute to Eliot Slater. Gaskell Press, London, p 3–21

Hafner H, Boker W 1973 Crimes of violence of mentally abnormal offenders (translated into English by Helen Marshall, 1982). Cambridge University Press, Cambridge

Hodgins S 1992 Mental disorder, intellectual deficiency and crime. Arch Gen Psychiatry 4:476–483

Humphreys HS, Johnstone EC, MacMillan JF, Taylor PJ 1992 Dangerous behaviour preceding first admission for schizophrenia. Br J Psychiatry 161:501–505

Link BG, Steuve A 1994 Psychiatric syndromes and the violent/illegal behavior of mental patients compared to community controls. In: Monahan J, Steadman H (eds) Violence and mental disorder. Developments in risk assessment. University of Chicago Press, Chicago, p 137–159

Link B, Andrews H, Cullen FT 1992 The violent and illegal behavior of mental patients reconsidered. Am Sociol Rev 57:275–292

Lindqvist P, Allebeck P 1990a Schizophrenia and crime: a longitudinal follow-up of 644 schizophrenics in Stockholm. Br J Psychiatry 157:345–350

Lindqvist P, Allebeck P 1990b Schizophrenia and assultive behaviour: the role of drug and alcohol abuse. Acta Psychiatr Scand 82:191–195

Swanson JW, Holzer CE, Ganju VK, Jono RT 1990 Violence and psychiatric disorder in the community: evidence from the Epidemiological Catchment Area surveys. Hosp Community Psychiatry 41:761–770

Tardiff K, Sweillam A 1980 Assault, suicide and mental illness. Arch Gen Psychiatry 37:164–169

Taylor PJ 1985 Motives for offending among violent and psychotic men. Br J Psychiatry 147:491–498

Taylor PJ 1993 Schizophrenia and crime: distinctive patients in association. In: Hodgins S (ed) Crime and mental disorder. Sage, Beverly Hills, CA, p 63–85

Taylor PJ, Gunn J 1984 Violence and psychosis. BMJ 288:1945–1949, 289:9–12

Wessely SC, Castle D, Douglas AJ, Taylor PJ The criminal careers of incident cases of schizophrenia. Psychol Med 24:483–502

General discussion III

Waldman: Michael Bohman and Sarnoff Mednick, one of the things that I thought was under-emphasized in your papers was the role of genotype–environment interaction: could you say something about this from your adoption studies? Also, have either of you looked at genotype–environment correlations? These are two important causal influences that can be studied predominantly in adoption designs.

Bohman: Most of the explained variability in petty criminality was due to congenital or genetic factors (59%), but substantial amounts were due to additive postnatal environment (19%) and gene–environment interactions (14%). There was only a minor effect (7%) of non-random placement or other types of gene–environment correlation in this population (total explained variability only 23.6%). For further details, see Cloninger et al (1982).

Waldman: Were there specific features of the environment that seemed to interact with genetic risk in predicting antisocial behaviour?

Bohman: Environmental antecedents interacted differently with the genetic predispositions to criminality and alcohol abuse. Neither low social status of the adoptive parents, nor that of the biological parents was sufficient to predispose children to petty criminality, but both did increase the risk of criminality in the children when the biological parents were themselves petty criminals. In other words, the contribution of social status to criminality depended entirely on interactions with specific genetic predispositions, either diminishing or facilitating the risk of different genotypes. In contrast, the average effect of low social status increased the risk for alcohol abuse even though it had greater effects on some genotypes (e.g. type 1 alcoholic background). Thus, the effect of social status on alcohol abuse had both additive and interaction components that were substantial. Similarly, unstable preadoptive placements had both additive and interactive effects that were significant for both petty criminality and alcoholism. Accordingly, the cross-fostering results (shown in my Table 1, p 104) may overestimate additive contributions and underestimate gene–environment interaction. But, on the other hand, it should be stressed that most variability in the risk of criminality in this population remained unexplained; the postnatal variables that were known to us covered only a small spectrum of the human environment (Cloninger et al 1982).

Carlier: I would like to throw in a note of caution about the vocabulary we are using; it is not an interaction between genotype and environment but between the biological parent's characteristics and the adoptive parent's characteristics. We know that the biological parents give their genes to their offspring; however, we cannot assert that these parents bear genes for criminality because we do not know whether or not these genes actually exist.

You said that the family can lower the risk, so the environment can have a protective effect. This point is very important if we want to think in terms of risk factors.

Mednick: I'm not sure that's correct. I thought that Michael Bohman was saying that the adoptive family tends to have a higher social class than does the biological family.

Did you show that if an adoptee is placed with a better family this reduces their risk of criminality? We have observed this effect in the Danish adoption study (Van Dusen et al 1983).

Bohman: Yes, I think it is reasonable to say that there was a reduced risk.

Mednick: Did you show that?

Bohman: Yes, both the longitudinal study and the Stockholm Adoption Study indicate that adoption had a preventive effect. As mentioned in my answer to Irwin Waldman, social class had an influence on the predisposition to both alcohol abuse and petty criminality. But I do agree with your implicit concern that we need a better design with controls to prove this beyond doubt. Adoptees were placed with adoptive parents who were known to have been stable, well adjusted and without known alcohol abuse or antisocial behaviour. Compared with their biological parents the adoptees had much higher occupational status. As adults, the adoptees did not differ in occupational status from controls, matched for age, sex and residence. The incidence of registrations for criminal offences or substance abuse was about the same as in the general population and much less severe than among their biological parents. On the other hand, compared with the matched controls, adoptees had a significantly higher frequency of sick-leave (with somatization disorders in women), which was associated with alcoholism and criminality in their biological background (Sigvardsson et al 1984).

Bouchard: You need unadopted siblings as a match to show this.

Waldman: Phrasing my question a little more cautiously, what environmental influences interact with the putative genes for criminal and antisocial behaviour?

Mednick: Most of these studies have been done in the area of schizophrenia. There, we see very strong environmental interactions with genes. We vary genetic liability by examining subjects with zero schizophrenic parents, one schizophrenic parent or two schizophrenic parents: we assume that the genetic liability for schizophrenia increases as a function of the number of parents who are schizophrenic (Walker et al 1981). In these cases, early separation from the family really has no direct effect on rates of schizophrenia in the offspring, but in interaction with increasing genetic liability it has a strong effect. Perinatal complications also have no direct effect on rate of schizophrenia in our studies. But perinatal complications have large effects in interaction with genetic liability. We have just published a paper showing that perinatal complications in combination with disturbed familial variables predict violence, *but not property crime* (Raine et al 1994).

Virkkunen: No one has mentioned possible biological factors that contribute to the risk of petty criminality. Sarnoff Mednick has done things like skin conductance measurements. Could you say something about these, Sarnoff?

Mednick: I have been guilty of publishing a theory attempting to explain the aetiology of property crimes. The theory hypothesized that the future criminal was under-aroused and evidenced slow autonomic recovery from phasic arousal states. In childhood, when one should learn arousal behaviour, this low arousal response and slow recovery would conspire to retard passive avoidance learning. With normal children, an impudent act would lead to parental punishment which would result in an arousal (fear) response. When the child inhibits the disturbing behaviour the punishment would cease, the arousal would *quickly* dissipate, strongly reinforcing the conforming behaviour in the child. The child with a low phasic arousal would find it more difficult to learn to inhibit antisocial acts because of these predispositions.

There are several demonstrations that this 'sluggishness' of the autonomic nervous system is genetically influenced. Also, children with criminal parents evidence low phasic skin conductance and slow recovery. Such children are predisposed to the inhibition of antisocial acts. Since this type of autonomic nervous system response is heritable, this predisposition may be part of what is transmitted from the biological parent which increases the risk for criminal convictions in the adopted-away offspring.

In addition to retarding the learning of morality, the under-arousal may be a useful characteristic if you are standing in someone else's living room at 3 a.m.!

Virkkunen: We have found that cerebrospinal fluid adrenocorticotropic hormone (Virkkunen et al 1994) and urinary 24 h cortisol (Virkkunen 1985) levels are low in individuals with antisocial personality disorder. There are also Swedish findings that urinary adrenaline secretion is low among antisocial adolescents (Magnusson 1988). Then there are the British findings that the autonomic nervous system may be involved (Raine et al 1990). So can these variables be between genes and petty criminality?

Plomin: Again, I would like to go back to the theme of the usefulness of genetic research for understanding environmental influences. In addition to the distinction between shared and non-shared environment, genetics offers the possibility of exploring genotype–environment interactions, as mentioned earlier. However, it is a lot easier to talk about genotype–environment interactions than it is to find specific examples in which the effect of the environment depends on the genotype (Plomin & Hershberger 1991). Genetic research on criminality provides one of the few examples that I know about. Twenty years ago, Sarnoff Mednick showed an interaction of this sort in his adoption study of criminality. His study showed a genetic 'main effect' in that criminality was greater among adoptees who had a biological parent with a criminal record. There was also an 'environmental effect' in that regardless of their biological parents' criminality, adoptees who grew up with a criminal adoptive parent were more likely to commit a crime. Most interestingly, there was a genotype–environment interaction in that the environment had its biggest effect for those adoptees whose biological parent had a criminal record. In other words, the effect of the environment depended on genotype in the sense that the environment had its biggest effect on those adoptees with a genetic propensity towards criminality.

I have often wondered whether Mednick's finding of genotype–environment interaction for criminality would hold up in other studies. For this reason, I was struck by Michael Bohman's results (1995, this volume) because they look to me as if they replicate Mednick's findings perfectly. That is, for adoptees without a genetic propensity (that is, adoptees whose biological parents had no criminal record), the rate of criminality was 3% if their adoptive parents had no criminal record and 7% if their adoptive parents had a criminal record. This suggests some environmental effect in that the rate of criminality doubled in adoptees if their adoptive parents had a criminal record. In contrast, for adoptees with a genetic propensity (that is, adoptees whose biological parents had criminal records), the rate of criminality was 12% if their adoptive parents had no criminal records and an amazing rate of 40% if their adoptive parents had a criminal record. The greater average rate of criminality in adoptees with a genetic propensity suggests a genetic effect. However, the most striking aspect of these results is the evidence they provide for genotype–environment interaction. Just like Mednick's study, they suggest that the environment has its biggest effect on those who already have a predilection towards criminal behaviour.

Waldman: I think there is an important statistical point here too, which is that it is not a very good strategy to look at the percentage of variance accounted for in judging the magnitude or importance of the interaction. Statistically speaking, those tests have very low power. Statistical tests of interactions of the form that we typically observe—the ordinal form that Robert Plomin just mentioned—might only have 15–20% of the statistical power of the tests of the corresponding main effects.

Rutter: But more importantly, the proportion of variance explained by any variable will depend crucially on the number of cases in the sample with that variable. Thus, Down's syndrome accounts for less than 0.6% of the population variance in IQ because its base rate is so low, but the individuals with Down's syndrome show a mean IQ deficit of 60 IQ points—an immensely strong effect (Broman et al 1975). The relevance of this point to adoption studies is that they have been designed to separate nature and nurture and so provide a low gene–environment correlation. What is more important is the *difference* in rate of antisocial behaviour associated with the combination of genetic and environmental risks, rather than the proportion of variance explained.

Bohman: I agree with Irwin Waldman and Michael Rutter that it is the slope that is important, not the proportion of variance explained.

Heath: We are making strong assumptions about how genes and environments act. We are assuming that they act additively on the scale of risk. If they act additively on the scale of liability and we analyse those same data using logistic regression analysis, we might indeed find that the apparent interaction disappears. Consequently, if we look on one scale, we find important interactions, but on another scale we don't. How we assume genes and environment are acting, then, is critical. It's much more convincing when we have some sort of crossover that we can't transform away by scaling.

Plomin: But it is remarkable that the two studies that have looked at this issue come out with the same striking genotype–environment interaction. You could not 'scale away' such big effects, even though they are not crossover interactions in which the environment has completely opposite effects for different genotypes—it seems unrealistic to expect such crossover interactions anyway. Moreover, the data of interest here are criminal behaviours such as number of convictions in the biological and adoptive parents and their effects on conviction rates among the adoptees. What sense would it make to try to transform these socially relevant data to try to minimize their exceptional evidence for genotype–environment interaction?

Waldman: Evidence for genotype–environment interaction for antisocial behaviour was found in the Iowa studies by Cadoret and Crowe, as well (Cadoret et al 1983).

Rowe: If it's criminality in the adoptive parent, that looks like a pretty clear environmental variable to me. But sometimes the 'environmental' action variable is in the behaviour of the biological mother giving up the child for adoption. I find it questionable whether to regard a late adoptive placement, or mothers who give up a child and then change their minds, as purely environmental variables. They could be markers of the genetic traits of the biological parents as well as markers of environment. It's very ambiguous. When you get that kind of interaction, it may be that you have additional information about the biological mother and her traits beyond that provided by the diagnosis or the registry.

Waldman: You have to remember that in tests of interactions you are partialling out the main effects, as well as the variance in the dependent variable that they explain in common, before testing for the presence of an interaction. Therefore, the genetic influences of the biological parents should be fully controlled for in testing for the interaction, and the interaction should capture information about both genotype and environment, unless the putative environmental indicator variables are so imperfect that *all* they indicate are the indirect influences of parental genotype.

Denno: Sarnoff Mednick, didn't you show that people who were left in the adoption institution the longest were most likely to become criminal?

Mednick: Yes, level of criminal offending was elevated among offspring placed at a later age. But within each age of placement we found the genetic relationship that we noted for the entire sample (Mednick et al 1984).

Rowe: But the question is: why were they transferred later? Were they difficult babies?

Mednick: We have an idea about this, but we haven't published it. I went with a social worker and read the case reports of the children who were up for adoption but were never placed. Every weekend (at least in the 1930s) Danish people who wished to adopt would visit the orphanages and pick children. Those children who were not placed had a 7.5% rate of schizophrenia. That is a high rate of schizophrenia. This means that the adoptive parents are able to tell which of these small children is going to become schizophrenic! Children whose selection by an adoptive parent is delayed may be less attractive physically and behaviourally.

Daly: These adoption studies have been criticized in the past for the problem of selective placement.

Mednick: In Denmark, the national adoption agency had a policy of selective placement. For instance, if the biological parents had blonde hair, they would try and place the child with a blonde-haired adoptive family. If the biological family was academic, they would try to place the child with people who were more academic. However, the agency was not successful. There were too many children to be placed and not enough placements.

Daly: So those selective placement concerns are not crazy?

Mednick: Every adoption researcher is concerned about selective placement and it does exist. But the agencies weren't very successful in selective placement. The correlations between, for example, social class of the biological and adoptive families were around 0.12; they don't really explain very much. We have examined each of the selective placement factors that have been suggested. They do not explain much (if any) variance.

Gottesman: I want to show some data to fill a gap in the records (Table 1 *[Gottesman]*). We've talked a lot about the Danish twin studies, and I wanted you to see the results, because they were published in an obscure place. These results are based on convicted criminals, identified at the same time and through the same procedures used in the Danish adoption study, because both these projects were funded by the same grant to Sarnoff Mednick. His collaborators included myself, Karl Otto Christiansen and Barry Hutchings. These data complement Judy Silberg's and Michael Lyons' studies, who both took the logical next steps: instead of looking at the qualitative phenotype of

TABLE 1 (*Gottesman*) Details of concordance for registered criminality in Christiansen's Danish twin sample

Zygosity	Pairing Proband– co-twin	Number of twins Pairs	Affected	Concordant	Probandwise rates f/n	%	Tetrachoric correlation
MZ	Male–male	365	73	25	50/98	51.0	0.74 ± 0.07
MZ	Female–female	347	15	3	6/18	33.3	0.74 ± 0.12
DZ	Male–male	700	146	26	52/172	30.2	0.47 ± 0.06
DZ	Female–male	2073	30	7	7/30	23.3	0.23 ± 0.10
DZ	Male–female	2073	198	7	7/198	3.5	0.23 ± 0.10
DZ	Female–female	690	28	2	4/30	13.3	0.46 ± 0.11

MZ, monozygotic; DZ, dizygotic; f, frequency of twins; n, total count of twins. After Cloninger & Gottesman (1987).

criminality, they looked at the probable precursors—the personality disorders and the behavioural traits that may be feeding into the liability to criminality in adults.

At the same time, I want to use these results to ask Michael Rutter what he meant by saying that the Danish twin studies are at variance with the Danish adoption studies concerning antisocial behaviour. The rates in the adopted-away children of criminals in Sarnoff Mednick, Bill Gabrielli and Barry Hutching's (1984) study are in the neighbourhood of 20–23%. The rates in the comparable group of twins (those fraternal co-twins being first-degree relatives) are 30%, and 30% isn't that far away from 20–25%. So what did you have in mind?

Rutter: In making that point, I was relying on Greg Carey's (1994) review of the findings. Do you want to comment on this, Greg?

Carey: The male–male dizygotic correlation is approximately 0.47. This holds for females. If we look at the parent–offspring tetrachoric correlations from Sarnoff Mednick's study, for example, these aren't above 0.2. We can postulate shared environment and non-additive genetic effects, but we would need good databases to try to fit both models to deal with that. The major area of disagreement is on the question of violence. How come we find these data running in sibships, but in the adoption data we don't? Is it that we're using slightly different definitions for violent crimes in the two studies? The populations do not overlap contemporaneously. These twins were born around 1880–1910. Is there something that has changed in the meantime? The difference is so striking, that I think it's worthwhile sitting down and trying to explore this.

Mednick: I think the problem you mention does exist. The Swedish and Danish adoption studies are not finding violence to be heritable; Karl O.

Christiansen is. The explanation may lie with the shared intrauterine environment.

Rutter: One possible factor is that, in adoptee studies, we are dealing with different generations over a time when there have been major changes in rates of crime (Rutter & Smith 1995). I don't know whether that provides an explanation: if it does, it's not immediately clear what the underlying mechanism could be.

Rowe: One way to answer that would be to look at the base rates for violent crime in the Danish adoptees, as opposed to these twins. If the base rates are much higher in the twins, it would suggest that there has been a secular change in the expression of the trait. With higher base rates you get more statistical power and it becomes easier to show the tetrachoric correlations. But my observation of many data sets—certainly of any self-reported data set—is that violent crimes and non-violent crimes are correlated as highly as the reliability of their respective scales would permit, and form one latent construct.

Carey: Perhaps it would be a good idea to have a common type of analysis for the two data sets. Often, when a behaviour is rare, such as violence is, you can have very small effects at the percentage level that can translate into very large effects at the tetrachoric correlation level. Maybe the correlations would be the same if we were to look at them with the same type of statistical analysis. I would strongly suggest that the type of analysis should be multivariate (or at least bivariate), for example, treating the number of property crimes as one variable, the number of violent crimes as another, and then doing the full multivariate analysis on the data sets. This might be a good thing to do with the Swedish study too.

Taylor: I must re-emphasize that as long as we go on treating crime as a disorder, resulting research is in trouble. Crime is simply what the law says is a crime. This varies enormously from one country to another and over time. In Britain, for example, on 2 August 1961, suicide was a crime, but on 3 August 1961 it was not; on 26 July 1967, homosexual acts between consenting adults constituted a crime, but on 27 July 1967 they did not. Attitudes to the reporting of crime are very variable. Most car theft, for example, is reported (for insurance reasons) but very little cleared up; personal violence is least likely to be reported (because it is often between intimates), but the more serious violence at least is more likely to be cleared up. Attitudes to how seriously the police should pursue crime also vary within and between communities. Violence to a spouse, for example, was commonly disregarded but all drug crime vigorously prosecuted; now, the former is pursued but some drug crimes, like cannabis possession, are often ignored. Rich people have better lawyers than poor people. Thus, with most sorts of crime there is an enormous attrition rate between the commission of an act which could constitute a crime, and a conviction for that crime, and it is very variable between crimes. Even factors like changes in sentencing powerfully affect how many people are going to get convicted of a crime. For example, something as apparently trivial as cutting slightly the length of sentence for rape, actually resulted in more rape convictions for a period of time because juries were more prepared to convict. So, in using any sort of recorded crime figures, researchers are taking on something that is very messy indeed, and that is one reason why confusion will follow.

References

Bohman M 1995 Predisposition to criminality: Swedish adoption studies in retrospect. In: Genetics of criminal and antisocial behaviour. Wiley, Chichester (Ciba Found Symp 194) p 99–114

Broman SH, Nichols PL, Kennedy WA 1975 Preschool IQ: prenatal and early developmental correlates. Lawrence Erlbaum, Hillsdale, NJ

Cadoret RJ, Cain CA, Crowe RR 1983 Evidence for gene–environment interaction in the development of adolescent antisocial behavior. Behav Genet 13:301–310

Carey G 1994 Genetics and violence. In: Reiss AJ Jr, Miezek KA, Roth JA (eds) Understanding and preventing violence, vol 2: Biobehavioral influences. National Academy, Washington, DC, p 21–58

Cloninger CR, Gottesman II 1987 Genetic and environmental factors in antisocial behavior disorders. In: Mednick SA, Moffitt TE, Stack SA (eds). The causes of crime: new biological approaches. Cambridge University Press, New York, p 92–109

Cloninger CR, Sigvardsson S, Bohman M, von Knorring A-L 1982 Predisposition to petty criminality in Swedish adoptees. II. Cross-fostering analysis of gene–environment interaction. Arch Gen Psychiatry 39:1242–1247

Magnusson D 1988 Antisocial behavior of boys and autonomic activity/reactivity. In: Moffitt TE, Mednick SA (eds) Biological contributions to crime causation. Martinus Nijhoff, Dordrecht, p 135–146

Mednick SA, Gabrielli W, Hutchings B 1984 Genetic influences in criminal behaviour: evidence from an adoption cohort. Science 224:891–894

Plomin R, Hershberger S 1991 Genotype–environment interaction. In: Wachs TD, Plomin R (eds) Conceptualization and measurement of organism–environment interaction. American Psychological Association, Washington, DC, p 29–43

Raine A, Venables P, Williams M 1990 Relationships between central and autonomic measures of arousal at age 15 years and criminality at age 24 years. Arch Gen Psychiatry 47:1003–1007

Raine A, Brennan P, Mednick SA 1994 Birth complications combined with early maternal rejection at age one year predispose to violent crime at 18 years. Arch Gen Psychiatry 51:984–988

Rutter M, Smith D 1995 Psychosocial disorders in young people: time trends and their causes. Wiley, Chichester

Sigvardsson S, von Knorring A-L, Bohman M, Cloninger CR 1984 An adoption study of somatoform disorders. I. The relationship of somatization to psychiatric disability. Arch Gen Psychiatry 41:853–859

Van Dusen K, Mednick SA, Gabrielli WF Jr 1983 Social class and crime in an adoption cohort. J Crim Law Criminol 74:249–269

Virkkunen M 1985 Urinary free cortisol secretion in habitually violent offenders. Acta Psychiatr Scand 72:40–44

Virkkunen M, Rawlings R, Tokola R et al 1994 CSF biochemistry, glucose metabolism and diurnal activity rhythms in violent offenders, impulsive fire setters and healthy volunteers. Arch Gen Psychiatry 51:20–27

Walker EF, Cudeck R, Mednick SA, Schulsinger F 1981 Effects of parental absence and institutionalization on the development of clinical symptoms in high-risk children. Acta Psychiatr Scand 63:95–109

Direct analysis of candidate genes in impulsive behaviours

D. Goldman, J. Lappalainen and N. Ozaki

Laboratory of Neurogenetics, NIAAA, NIH, 12501 Washington Avenue, Rockville, MD 20852, USA

Abstract. Antisocial behaviour is both heterogeneous and the product of interacting genetic and environmental factors acting at different levels of causation. Heritability studies show that individual differences in predisposition to antisocial behaviour are transmitted vertically in families by genetic mechanisms. Owing to aetiological heterogeneity and complexity, study of a variety of other behavioural phenotypes may shed more light on the antecedents of antisocial behaviour than direct studies on antisocial behaviour. Identification of genetic vulnerability factors would clarify mechanisms of vulnerability and the role of the environment. Direct gene analysis and genetic linkage analysis have identifed structural variants in genes involved in neurotransmitter function, and some progress has been made towards relating these genetic variants to antisocial personality and other behaviours. Thyroid hormone receptor variants can cause attention deficit/hyperactivity disorder, and a monoamine oxidase A variant leads to aggressive behaviour in one family. Direct gene analyses have revealed non-conservative amino acid substitutions and structural variants (generally rare) at DRD2, DRD3 and DRD4 dopamine receptors and 5-HT_{1A}, 5-HT_{2A}, 5-HT_{2C} and 5-HT_7 serotonin receptors. The stage is set to identify the phenotypic significance of these as well as genetic variants at other loci which may be relevant as candidate genes for antisocial behaviour and related behavioural differences.

1996 Genetics of criminal and antisocial behaviour. Wiley, Chichester (Ciba Foundation Symposium 194) p 139–154

Interactions of genetic and environmental sources of variation underlie individual differences in behaviour. Detection of alleles of neural genes will not reduce behaviour to the nucleotide, but can help explain the origins of behavioural variation. The domain of this paper is the direct detection of candidate gene variants and the elucidation of their role in the modulation of behaviours involving impulse control, such as antisocial personality disorder and alcoholism. For this purpose, it can simply be assumed that other factors, including choice and volition, are, on a population scale, of greater importance.

Heritability studies estimate the extent to which variance in a trait is genetically determined. However, due to aetiological heterogeneity, genetic factors can be identified when heritability is low or undetectable. Also, high heritability does not preclude effective prevention or treatment. Large sociocultural effects are missed by heritability estimates derived from one time and in one population. Level of heritability is therefore largely irrelevant in terms of guiding public policy, treatment, prevention or research aimed at finding vulnerability alleles. Heritability studies can support efforts to identify and elucidate genetic factors and may help guide the design of some genetic studies.

Heritability studies on impulsive/aggressive behaviours were reviewed by Coccaro et al (1993). Including the Coccaro et al (1993) study, six out of 12 twin studies found significant heritability. Variability in results seemed dependent both on the measures used and the age of the twins. In children, three out of five studies detected significant heritability for aggressiveness and the mean was 0.80; two negative studies in children used measures of aggressiveness which may be less strongly influenced genetically (Coccaro et al 1993). In adolescents, three out of three studies were negative. In adults, three out of four studies found significant heritability. In the positive studies the heritabilities were 0.72 (Rushton et al 1986), 0.44 (Tellegen et al 1988) and 0.41 (Coccaro et al 1993).

In addition to antisocial personality, a variety of other genetically influenced psychiatric disorders are accompanied by increased liabilities for impulsive and aggressive behaviours. Identification of genetic factors contributing to these disorders would therefore contribute to an understanding of the antecedents of aggressiveness. Violent behaviour is frequently triggered by intake of relatively small amounts of alcohol, and more than half of violent crimes may occur under the influence of alcohol (Mark & Ervin 1970). Thus, alcoholism mediates liability to impulsive and aggressive behaviours. The early-onset subtype of alcoholism is itself associated with antisocial behaviour and impulsiveness (Cloninger et al 1981, von Knorring et al 1987). Other aggression/diagnosis associations include suicide in depression (Tsuang 1983), schizophrenia and alcoholism (Niskanen & Achte 1972, Tsuang 1983), self-directed violence in borderline personality disorder and self-destructive behaviours in Lesch–Nyhan syndrome and other mental retardation syndromes. Heritability of psychiatric diseases has been reviewed elsewhere (for example, schizophrenia [Gottesman & Shields 1982], affective illness [Berrettini et al 1984, Loehlin et al 1988], alcoholism [Goldman 1993a] and sociopathy [Coccaro et al 1993]).

Recently, linked (or associated) genetic markers and functionally significant alleles for impulsive and aggressive behaviours have been discovered in the human. The oxidation of serotonin (5-hydroxytryptamine; 5-HT) to 5-hydroxyindoleacetic acid (5-HIAA) is catalysed by monoamine oxidase A (MAOA) in raphe neurons. A family with X-linked non-dysmorphic borderline mental retardation was described. Behaviour of affected males was markedly abnormal. They were shy, withdrawn, often without friends and had unprovoked or minimally provoked aggressive outbursts. Reduced excretion of metabolites of dopamine, noradrenaline and 5-HT was detected in urine. Linkage was detected to a CA-repeat polymorphism located in the Xp11-21 region (Brunner et al 1993a). A stop codon mutation was identified within the MAOA gene (Brunner et al 1993b). MAOA and MAOB had previously been localized to this region of the X chromosome (Kochersperger et al 1986, Ozelius et al 1988). The same MAOA defect or other inactive MAOA alleles may be detected in other families. However, preliminary data indicate that the MAOA stop codon mutation is rare in individuals with aggressivity/ impulsivity and low cerebrospinal fluid (CSF) 5-HIAA levels (D. Goldman, M. Dean, M. Virkkunen, H. Naukkarinen, M. Eggert & M. Linnoila, unpublished data).

Identification of the MAOA variant as well as a series of thyroid hormone receptor variants which can cause attention deficit/hyperactivity disorder (Hauser et al 1993) has encouraged the scanning of additional candidate genes for alleles significant for impulsive behaviours. As will be described in this paper, direct gene analyses have revealed non-conservative amino acid substitutions and structural variants (generally rare) at three dopamine receptors and, as reported here, at four 5-HT receptors. This paper will discuss possible relationships of genetic variation in 5-HT function to impulsive and aggressive behaviours and describe direct gene analysis approaches and their limitations.

Genetic linkage and direct gene analysis

For behavioural traits, incomplete penetrance, genetic heterogeneity and the presence of phenocopies make the identification of determinant alleles difficult. Incomplete penetrance can be dealt with conservatively by studying only affected individuals, but this diminishes the power of family linkage. Phenocopies complicate linkage analyses for common disorders such as alcoholism in which many cases are sporadic. A high level of genetic heterogeneity should be presumed for behavioural traits. The problem of heterogeneity is ameliorated by using traits and markers which isolate more homogeneous subgroups and by identifying large, high-density families and genetically more-homogeneous populations.

Direct scanning of large DNA sequences across many individuals is practical because of the cloning of numerous candidate genes, and the advent of rapid methods for detecting the genetic variants and automated sequencing to characterize them. The main scanning methods are single-strand conformational polymorphism (SSCP) analysis (Orita et al 1989) and denaturing gradient gel electrophoresis (DGGE; Myers et al 1987).

Of the several mutation detection techniques, SSCP analysis is probably the simplest; it is also one of the most sensitive. SSCP has been successfully used to identify alleles for cystic fibrosis and amyotrophic lateral sclerosis, and also to detect somatic mutations in proto-oncogenes. Unfortunately, neither SSCP nor any other mutation detection technique is 100% sensitive. Sensitivity of SSCP has been reported to range from 33 to 100%. However, the use of a combination of techniques and careful optimization of the conditions yields 90–100% sensitivity. Recently, SSCP was utilized to identify functional variants in the angiotensin gene which predispose to essential hypertension. This demonstrates the usefulness of SSCP for finding alleles in a trait which is regarded as multigenic.

Direct scanning for genetic variants turns the problems of genetic heterogeneity and polygenicity into advantages, because both 'problems' increase the likelihood that analysis of a particular candidate gene will detect an allele affecting function. In this way, the direct scanning of candidate genes has very different advantages as compared with genetic linkage using markers at candidate genes. Also, although it is not possible to scan regions of the size covered by linkage analysis by direct scanning, the exclusions which are produced are valid under realistic models.

Analyses of genes involved in dopamine and 5-HT function

Dopamine

Dopamine has been directly implicated in aggressive behaviour (reviewed in Brunner et al 1993b). Dopamine is also of interest due to its hypothesized involvement in schizophrenia, affective disorder and alcoholism, all of which are associated with impulsivity and aggressiveness. Many genes involved in brain dopamine function have been cloned, including those for tyrosine hydroxylase, dopamine receptors (D1–D5), the dopamine transporter, dopamine β hydroxylase, and MAOA and B (Table 1). Polymorphic markers identified within and near these genes allow linkage studies. Gene product structural variants which have been identified include a 16 amino acid repeat sequence within the D4 receptor, three rare amino acid substitutions in the D2 receptor (Gejman et al 1993, Itokawa et al 1993) and a $Ser^9 \rightarrow Gly^9$ substitution in the D3 receptor (Rietschel et al 1993). To date, linkage and population association studies on dopamine D1 (D1 and D5) and D2 class receptors (D2, D3 and D4), including the ones which utilized functional polymorphisms within these genes, have yielded negative results in schizophrenia and affective disorders. These genes have apparently not been scanned in individuals identified as impulsive.

For the D2 receptor, the Taq1A1 marker has been repeatedly tested for associations to behaviours. The A1 allele, as far as is known, is itself not functionally significant. Following the finding by Blum et al (1990), the D2/Taq1A1 allele association was not as strong in subsequent positive reports (Blum et al 1991, 1993, Parsian et al 1991) or in negative reports (Bolos

TABLE 1 Candidate genes involved in dopamine function

Gene	Location	
Tyrosine hydroxylase	11p15.5	
Dopamine β hydroxylase	9q34.3	
Dopamine receptor 1	5q35.1	
Dopamine receptor 2	11q22-q23	*
Dopamine receptor 3	3q13.3	*
Dopamine receptor 4	11p15.5	*
Dopamine receptor 5	4p16.1	
Monoamine oxidase A	Xp11.4-p11.3	*
Monoamine oxidase B	Xp11.4-p11.3	
Aromatic L-amino acid decarboxylase	7p11	
Dopamine transporter	5p15.3	

*Structural variant has been identified.

et al 1990, Gelernter et al 1991, Schwab et al 1991, Goldman et al 1992, 1993b, Turner et al 1992, Cook et al 1992, Arinami et al 1993, Suarez et al 1994). Despite possible publication bias, the D2 association to alcoholism may overall be non-significant (Gelernter et al 1993) but this is an active area of research. Associations of D2 to other traits, including substance abuse (Smith et al 1992, Noble et al 1994), P300 latency (Noble et al 1993) and other conditions (Comings 1991) are not refuted. Chance associations may be difficult to invalidate. It may be observed that if D2 is a candidate gene, the most logical step is to scan its sequence for alleles altering receptor structure or expression. Using DGGE, the D2 coding sequence was scanned in large samples of alcoholics and schizophrenics without detection of a functional variant that can account for the associations named above (Gejman et al 1994). However, the DGGE analysis (which detected three rare, possibly functional variants) cannot completely rule out the possibility that there exists an abundant functional variant within the *DRD2* promoter region, in an intron, or in a completely different, but genetically linked gene.

Spurious associations arise by chance or ethnic stratification. Ethnic stratification may explain some conflicting D2 reports because fourfold *DRD2* allele frequency differences are found between ethnic groups (Goldman et al 1993b). Furthermore, D2 association studies conducted in ethnically well-defined populations have generally been negative (Schwab et al 1991, Goldman et al 1992, 1993b, Arinami et al 1993) as have linkage studies in families (Bolos et al 1990, Parsian et al 1991).

5-HT

The role of 5-HT in behavioural inhibition has been reviewed elsewhere (Soubrie 1986), as have widely replicated observations that diminution of 5-HT activity releases punishment-suppressed behaviours (Linnoila et al 1983) and disinhibits aggression directed against both self and others (Asberg et al 1987). Impulsive/violent Finns with exceptionally low CSF 5-HIAA concentrations were almost all alcoholic, and more than half had a history of suicide attempts (Linnoila et al 1983, Linnoila & Virkkunen 1992). Impulsive subjects studied by Brown et al (1979, 1982, 1985) had low CSF 5-HIAA and, although young, were also generally alcoholic. The tendency of alcoholism, suicidal behaviour and impulsive behaviours to aggregate within the same individuals and to be transmitted from parent to offspring (Cloninger et al 1981, 1985, Bohman 1978) may indicate a shared underlying serotonergic mechanism.

Heritability studies on 5-HT are limited by the relative inaccessability of 5-HT in the brain. Oxenstierna et al (1986) calculated a heritability for CSF 5-HIAA of 0.35 from a small sample. This result was not non-significant. However, in a larger study on rhesus macaque monkeys in which CSF 5-HIAA also correlates with impulsivity and aggression (Mehlman et al 1994) and in which repetitive measures were available, Higley et al (1993) found significant heritability for CSF 5-HIAA. In human twins, platelet 5-HT uptake was significantly heritable (Meltzer & Arora 1988).

We have identified variant alleles in genes involved in 5-HT function because of the possible involvement of this neurotransmitter in a form of alcoholism (Cloninger type 2 alcoholism) with high genetic liability. To increase the efficiency of the search for the alleles and to establish phenotypic specificity, we have also analysed a spectrum of other diseases in which 5-HT has been implicated, including obsessive compulsive disease, autism, hereditary myoclonus, schizophrenia and anorexia nervosa.

For type 2 alcoholism, a large collection of DNA samples from Finnish alcoholic violent offenders has been assembled (Virkkunen et al 1990), including large multiplex families and healthy psychiatrically interviewed controls (M. Linnoila, D. Goldman, H. Naukkarinen, M. Eggert & M. Virkkunen, unpublished results). This study was carried out at the Department of Forensic Psychiatry at the University of Helsinki, Finland. Finns mostly descend from a small population of founders who settled Finland only 80–100 generations ago (Nevanlinna 1972, Norio et al 1973). The combination of a genetically isolated population and a high-quality health-care system with accurate national registers of diseased individuals makes this population close to ideal for genetic studies. The characteristics of these alcoholic violent offenders and healthy volunteers and the assessment methods have been published elsewhere (Virkkunen et al 1994).

TABLE 2   Polymorphic candidate genes involved in 5-HT function

Gene	Protein variant(s)	Frequency	DNA variant	Reference
5-HT$_{1A}$	Yes (2)	< 0.01 (both)	Yes	Nakhai et al 1995
5-HT$_{1D\alpha}$			Yes	Ozaki et al 1995a
5-HT$_{1D\beta}$			Yes	Lappalainen et al 1995a
5-HT$_{1E}$			Yes	J. Lappalainen, D. Goldman & M. Dean, unpublished
5-HT$_{1F}$			Yes	J. Lappalainen, D. Goldman & M. Dean, unpublished
5-HT$_{2A}$	Yes (2)	< 0.01; 0.09	Yes	Ozaki et al 1995b
5-HT$_{2C}$	Yes (1)	0.13	Yes	Lappalainen et al 1995b
5-HT$_7$	Yes (1)	< 0.01	Yes	U. Pesonen, M. Koulu, M. Virkkunen, H. Naukkarinen, M. Eggert, M. Linnoila & D. Goldman, unpublished
TPH			Yes	Nielsen et al 1994
MAOA	Yes	< 0.01	Yes	Brunner et al 1993b
MAOB			Yes	Grimsby et al 1992
GTPCI	Yes (4)	< 0.01 (all 4)	Yes	Ichinose et al 1995

5-HT$_{1A}$ etc., various 5-HT receptor genes; TPH, tryptophan hydroxylase; MAO, monoamine oxidase; GTPCI, GTP cyclohydrolase I.

A panel of 5-HT candidate genes is being scanned for variant alleles (Table 2) across 300–500 Finnish alcoholic offenders and in the other patient populations named above. Due to their roles in 5-HT synthesis, neurotransmission and reuptake, many or most of these genes may alter behaviour. The functionally variant alleles may generally be infrequent, requiring efficient screening technology. These genes are being scanned regardless of whether associations or linkages to markers have been reported. A population association between a DNA marker within intron seven of the tryptophan hydroxylase (*TPH*) gene to CSF 5-HIAA concentration and to suicidal behaviour was found in alcoholic impulsive Finns studied as inpatients at the University of Helsinki (Nielsen et al 1994). The association of genotype to 5-HIAA concentration was observable only in individuals who, by the nature of their crimes, were impulsive. This could indicate that functional TPH variants capable of altering 5-HIAA concentration may be rare (too rare to yield an association) in the general population and in non-impulsive individuals. The TPH association was found in a sample which was behaviourally relatively extreme and genetically relatively homogeneous. Although these factors may enhance the plausibility of the finding, a structural variant of TPH was not observed within the coding sequence of a very small sample of these individuals (D. Nielsen, M. Virkkunen, M. Linnoila & D. Goldman, unpublished observations).

Primarily using the SSCP method, we detected naturally occurring amino acid substitutions at four out of eight 5-HT receptors we scanned (Table 2). The other 5-HT receptors had synonymous nucleotide substitutions. All of the variants were observed in more than one unrelated individual. However, only the 5-HT$_{2A}$ and 5-HT$_{2C}$ protein sequence variants are abundant (0.09 and 0.13), as compared with rare sequence variants which have been detected at GTP cyclohydrolase I, MAOA and the other 5-HT receptors listed in Table 2. Using direct gene analysis, a panel of 5-HT gene alleles which could be capable of causing variation in behaviour can be assembled and tested. The gene-scanning approach obviously becomes more powerful as remaining members of the 5-HT receptor family are cloned.

Detailed description of the SSCP screening procedures can be found in individual articles. Genomic DNA is generally isolated from Epstein–Barr-virus-immortalized lymphoblastoid cell lines, and DNA amplifications are typically from 30 ng of DNA. To increase the sensitivity of the SSCP analysis, the amplified fragments are further digested with restriction enzymes to yield subfragments 80–250 bp in length. Amplified DNA is diluted with 15 ml of 95% formamide, 10 mM NaOH, 0.05% xylene cyanol and 0.05% bromphenol blue, incubated at 95 °C for 3 min and then placed on ice. The denatured DNA (4 ml) is loaded in each lane of a mutation detection enhancement gel (AT Biochem, Malvern, PA). Electrophoresis is carried out at 4 °C for 16 h at 6 W. Detection of DNA fragments is by autoradiography. We have found that use of other gel compositions does not provide higher SSCP sensitivity. However, incorporation of [33]P (as opposed to ^{32}P) into PCR fragments and effective cooling during the SSCP run produces substantially higher resolution.

The identified variants are directly sequenced using cycle sequencing, and are converted to restriction fragment length polymorphisms or allele-specific amplifications (ASAs) to facilitate their further use in association and family studies, and also to confirm the sequencing result. For genetic localization of the genes the markers were typed in all informative CEPH (Centre d'Etudes du Polymorphisme Humain) families and mapped by the linkage approach against markers of known location.

Two rare amino acid substitutions were detected in the 5' N-terminal, extracellular domain of the 5-HT$_{1A}$ receptor (Nakhai et al 1995). 5-HT$_{1A}$ agonists reduced aggressive and defensive behaviour and increased passivity in wild rats in anxiety-producing situations (Blanchard et al 1988). Thus, these alleles may be of considerable interest for impulsive behaviours. The frequencies of the rare 5-HT$_{1A}$ alleles have been determined by screening of large populations with sample pooling, allele-specific amplification and electrochemiluminescence detection (mass allele detection) (Bergen et al 1995).

Mice in which the 5-HT_{1B} receptor (equivalent to the human 5-$HT_{1D\beta}$) have been 'knocked out' show greatly enhanced intruder confrontation aggression (Saudou et al 1994) without other behavioural or developmental abnormalities. In rodents, both 5-HT_{1B} agonists and antagonists reduce aggression in intruder confrontation paradigms. 5-$HT_{1D\beta}$ is the terminal 5-HT autoreceptor, and abnormal function of this receptor could diminish 5-HT turnover and produce low 5-HIAA concentrations such as are seen in impulsive individuals. However, only a synonymous substitution and no amino acid substitutions were detected when we screened a large population of impulsive alcoholic Finns (Lappalainen et al 1995a). Cloning studies have revealed the existence of another 5-HT_{1D} subtype designated 5-$HT_{1D\alpha}$. Although the two 5-HT_{1D} receptors are only 63% identical, they are pharmacologically and physiologically almost indistinguishable. Both genes are intronless and widely expressed in human brain, with the highest levels of expression observed in limbic regions and striatum. Amino acid substitutions were not detected in 5-$HT_{1D\alpha}$.

The 5-HT_{2C} receptor is widely distributed in the brain, where it is involved in the regulation of endocrine responses, including production and secretion of adrenocorticotropic hormone, oxytocin and prolactin. Genes for rodent (Julius et al 1988) and human (Saltzman et al 1991) 5-HT_{2C} receptors have been cloned. The functional state of 5-HT_{2C} receptors in normal controls and patients with various psychiatric disorders has been assessed *in vivo* by the administration of metachlorophenylpiperazine (mCPP), a non-selective 5-HT_{2C} agonist, and the measurement of hormonal and psychological responses. In alcoholics, but not controls, mCPP induced alcohol craving (Benkelfat et al 1991, George et al 1995). Alcoholics also showed blunted response to mCPP-induced increases in adrenocorticotropic hormone and prolactin (George et al 1995). In addition, Moss et al (1990) suggested that mCPP-induced cortisol and prolactin release are abnormal in patients with antisocial personality disorder and substance abuse. A common, non-conservative amino acid $Cys^{23} \rightarrow Ser^{23}$ substitution was identified in the 5-HT_{2C} gene (Lappalainen et al 1995b). The substitution is located in the C-terminal, extracellular domain of the receptor and has been expressed in oocytes where preliminary data indicate that affinity for mCPP may be altered (L. Zhang, J. Lappalainen, M. Oz, N. Ozaki, M. Linnoila, D. Goldman & F. Weight, unpublished results). This allele is currently being evaluated for effects on clinical phenotype in family- and population-association studies.

Two amino acid substitutions were detected at the 5-HT_{2A} receptor and one was also found at 5-HT_7. The 5-HT_{2A} receptor is widely distributed postsynaptically in the brain and has affinity for clozapine, whereas the 5-HT_7 receptor is more localized in its distribution. One area with a high density of 5-HT$_7$ receptors is the suprachiasmatic nucleus, possibly implicating this 5-HT receptor in circadian rhythm disruption. One of the novel 5-HT$_{2A}$ alleles is a non-conservative substitution and the 5-HT$_{2A}$ allele frequencies are 0.01 and 0.09.

Methodological considerations and prospects for future research

Genetic linkage has the ability to detect phenotypically significant alleles wherever they exist in the genome, including regions involved in gene regulation. However, identification of loci by genetic linkage may falter if, for example, genetic heterogeneity is extensive. One solution to this problem is to screen large samples for genetic association using a dense map of genetic markers. Spurious associations due to ethnic stratification (*vide supra*) can be avoided by careful matching for ethnicity or by sampling parents and using their non-transmitted alleles for population allele frequencies.

Direct analysis of the genes which could contribute to the phenotype is a definitive and in some ways more comprehensive strategy. Like linkage, direct gene analysis permits exclusion mapping. Linkage analysis excludes regions of the genome; direct gene analysis generally excludes only the region scanned, usually the coding sequences of genes. Linkage analysis scans much larger regions of DNA, but the scanning is more vulnerable to false negative results. With direct gene analysis, the problem of heterogeneity is turned on its head because an 'n' of one is in some cases sufficient to identify a functional allele, although other steps, such as *in vitro* expression and association and linkage studies, will generally be required to show that function is altered.

Conclusions

(1) A multiplicity of genetic and non-genetic variables are likely to underlly interindividual variability in the propensity to impulsive and aggressive behaviours.

(2) Genetic linkage and direct gene scanning are two general approaches for identifying the alleles which have different advantages and limitations. The direct gene analysis strategy benefits from genetic heterogeneity and polygenicity, factors that make linkage analysis more difficult.

(3) The neurochemistry, occurrence in various psychiatric diseases and neuropharmacology of impulsivity point to a major role for 5-HT and other monoamines. A large number of the candidate genes for these neurotransmitter systems have been cloned.

(4) Protein structural variants are identified for MAOA, three dopamine receptors and, as reported here, four 5-HT receptors (5-HT$_{1A}$, 5-HT$_{2A}$, 5-HT$_{2C}$ and 5-HT$_7$). Four other 5-HT receptors (5-HT$_{1D\alpha}$, 5-HT$_{1D\beta}$, 5-HT$_{1E}$, 5-HT$_{1F}$) did not exhibit variants which would alter protein structure.

References

Asberg M, Schalling D, Traskman-Bendz L et al 1987 Psychobiology of suicide, impulsivity and related phenomena. In: Meltzer HY (ed) Psychopharmacology: the third generation of progress. Raven Press, New York, p 655–668

Benkelfat C, Murphy DL, Hill JL, George DT, Nutt D, Linnoila M 1991 Ethanol-like properties of the serotonergic partial agonist *meta*-chlorophenylpiperazine in chronic alcoholic patients. Arch Gen Psychiatry 48:383

Bergen A, Wang CY, Nakhai B, Goldman D 1995 Mass allele detection (MAD) of rare 5HT1A structural variants with allele specific amplification and electrochemi-luminescence detection. Hum Mutat, in press

Berrettini WH, Goldin LR, Nurnberger JI Jr, Gershon ES 1984 Genetic factors in affective illness. J Psychiatr Res 18:329–350

Blanchard D, Shepherd JK, Rodgers RJ, Blanchard RJ 1992 Evidence for differential effects of 8-OH-DPAT on male and female rats in the anxiety/defense test battery. Psychopharmacol Ser (Berl) 106:531–539

Blum K, Noble EP, Sheridan PJ 1990 Allelic association of human dopamine D2 receptor gene in alcoholism. JAMA 263:2055–2060

Blum K, Noble EP, Sheridan PJ et al 1991 Association of the A1 allele of the D2 dopamine receptor gene. Alcohol 8:409–416

Blum K, Noble EP, Sheridan PJ et al 1993 Genetic predisposition in alcoholism: association of the D2 dopamine receptor TaqI B1 RFLP with severe alcoholics. Alcohol 10:59–67

Bohman M 1978 Some genetic aspects of alcoholism and criminality. A population of adoptees. Arch Gen Psychiatry 35:269–276

Bolos AM, Dean M, Lucas-Derse S, Ramsburg M, Brown GL, Goldman D 1990 Population and pedigree studies reveal a lack of association between the dopamine D2 receptor gene and alcoholism. JAMA 264:3156–3160

Brown GL, Goodwin FK, Ballenger JC, Goyer PF, Major LF 1979 Aggression in humans correlates with cerebrospinal fluid metabolites. Psychiatry Res 1:131–139

Brown GL, Ebert MH, Goyer PF et al 1982 Aggression, suicide and serotonin: relationships to CSF amine metabolites. Am J Psychiatry 139:741–746

Brown GL, Kline WJ, Goyer PF, Minichiello MD, Krusei MJP, Goodwin FK 1985 Relationship of childhood characteristics to cerebrospinal fluid 5-hydroxyindoleacetic acid in aggressive adults. In: Chagass C (ed) Biological psychiatry. Elsevier, New York, p 177–179

Brunner HG, Nelen MR, van Zandvoort P et al 1993a X-linked borderline mental retardation with prominent behavioural disturbance: phenotype, genetic localization, and evidence for disturbed monoamine metabolism. Am J Hum Genet 52:1032–1039

Brunner HG, Nelen M, Breakefield XO, Ropers HH, van Oost BA 1993b Abnormal behaviour associated with a point mutation in the structural gene for monoamine oxidase A. Science 262:578–580

Cloninger CR, Bohman M, Sigvardsson S 1981 Inheritance of alcohol abuse: cross-fostering analysis of adopted men. Arch Gen Psychiatry 38:861–868

Cloninger CR, Bohman M, Sigvardsson S, von Knorring A-L 1985 Psychopathology in adopted-out children of alcoholics: The Stockholm Adoption Study. Recent Dev Alcohol 3:37–51

Coccaro EF, Bergeman CS, McClearn GE 1993 Heritability of irritable impulsiveness: a study of twins reared together and apart. Psychiatry Res 48:229–242

Comings DE, Comings BG, Muhleman D et al 1991 The dopamine D2 receptor locus as a modifying gene in neuropsychiatric disorders. JAMA 56:1793–1800

Cook BL, Wang ZW, Crowe RR, Hauser R, Freimer M 1992 Alcoholism and the D2 receptor gene. Alcohol Clin Exp Res 16:806–809

Gejman PV, Ram A, Gelernter J et al 1994 No structural mutation in the dopamine D2 receptor gene in alcoholism or schizophrenia: analysis using denaturing gradient gel electrophoresis. JAMA 271:204–208

Gelernter J, O'Malley S, Risch N et al 1991 No association between an allele at the D2 dopamine receptor gene (DRD2) and alcoholism. JAMA 256:1801–1807

Gelernter J, Goldman D, Risch N 1993 The A1 allele at the D2 dopamine receptor gene and alcoholism: a reappraisal. JAMA 269:1673–1677

George DT, Benkelfat C, Hill C et al 1995 A comparison of behavioral and biochemical responses to metachlorophenylpiperazine in subtypes of alcoholics. Submitted

Goldman D 1993 Alcoholism: genetic transmission. Recent Dev Alcohol 11:231–248

Goldman D, Dean M, Brown GL et al 1992 D2 dopamine receptor genotype and cerebrospinal fluid homovanillic acid, 5-hydroxyindoleacetic acid and 3-methoxy-4-hydroxyphenylglycol in Finnish and American alcoholics. Acta Psychiatr Scand 86:351–357

Goldman D, Brown GL, Albaugh B et al 1993 DRD2 dopamine receptor genotype, linkage disequilibrium and alcoholism in American Indians and other populations. Alcohol Clin Exp Res 17:199–204

Gottesman II, Shields J 1982 The epigenetic puzzle. Cambridge University Press, Cambridge

Grimsby J, Chen K, Devor EJ, Cloninger CR, Shih JC 1992 Dinucleotide repeat (TG)23 polymorphism in the MAOB gene. Nucleic Acids Res 20:294

Hauser P, Zametkin AJ, Martinez P et al 1993 Attention deficit–hyperactivity disorder in people with generalized resistance to thyroid hormone. N Engl J Med 328:997–1001

Higley JD, Thompson WW, Champoux M et al 1993 Paternal and maternal genetic contributions to cerebrospinal fluid monoamine metabolites in rhesus monkeys (*Macaca mulatta*). Arch Gen Psychiatry 50:615–623

Ichinose H, Ohye T, Takahashi E et al 1995 Hereditary progressive dystonia with marked diurnal fluctuation caused by mutations in the GTP cyclohydrolase gene. Nat Genet, in press

Itokawa M, Arinami T, Futamura N, Hamaguchi H, Toru M 1993 A structural polymorphism of human dopamine receptor D2 (Ser311–Cys). Biochem Biophys Res Commun 196:1369–1375

Kochersperger LM, Parker EL, Siciliano M, Park M, Darlington DJ, Denney RM 1986 Assignment of genes for human monoamine oxidases A and B to the X chromosome. J Neurosci Res 16:601–616

Lappalainen J, Dean M, Charbonneau L, Virkkunen M, Linnoila M, Goldman D 1995a Mapping of the 5-HT1Dβ autoreceptor gene on chromosome 6 and direct analysis for sequence variants. Am J Med Genet 60:157–161

Lappalainen J, Zhang L, Dean M et al 1995b Identification, expression, and pharmacology of a Cys[23]–Ser[23] substitution in the human 5-HT2C receptor gene (HTR2C). Genomics 27:274–279

Linnoila VM, Virkkunen M 1992 Biologic correlates of suicidal risk and aggressive behavioral traits. J Clin Psychiatry 12:S19–S20

Linnoila M, Virkkunen M, Scheinin M, Nuutila A, Rimon R, Goodwin FK 1983 Low cerebrospinal fluid 5-hydroxyindoleacetic acid concentration differentiates impulsive from nonimpulsive violent behaviour. Life Sci 33:2609–2614

Loehlin JC, Willerman L, Horn JM 1988 Human behavior genetics. Annu Rev Psychol 39:101–233

Mark VH, Ervin FR 1970 Violence and the brain. Harper & Row, New York

Mehlman PT, Higley JD, Faucher I et al 1994 Low CSF 5-HIAA concentrations and severe aggression and impaired impulse control in nonhuman primates. Am J Psychiatry 151:1485–1491

Meltzer HM, Arora RC 1988 Genetic control of serotonin uptake in blood platelets: a twin study. Psychiatr Res 24:263–269

Moss HB, Yao JK, Panzak GL 1990 Serotonergic responsivity and behavioral dimensions in antisocial personality disorder with substance abuse. Biol Psychiatry 28:325–328

Myers RM, Maniatis T, Lerman LS 1987 Detection and localization of single base changes by denaturing gradient gel electrophoresis. Academic Press, New York

Nakhai B, Nielsen D, Goldman D 1995 Two naturally occurring amino acid substitutions in the human 5HT1A receptor: 5HT1A-22→Ser and 5HT1A-28→Val. Biochem Biophys Res Commun 210:530–536

Nevanlinna HR 1972 The Finnish population structure: a genetic and genealogical study. Hereditas 71:195–236

Nielsen DA, Goldman D, Virkkunen M, Tokola R, Rawlings R, Linnoila M 1994 Suicidality and 5-hydroxyindoleacetic acid concentration associated with a tryptophan hydroxylase polymorphism. Arch Gen Psychiatry 51:34–38

Niskanen P, Achte KA 1972 The course and prognoses of schizophrenic psychoses in Helsinki: a comparative study of first admissions in 1950, 1960 and 1965. Monogr Psychiatr Clin Helsinki Univ Centr Hosp

Noble EP, Blum K, Khalsa ME et al 1993 Allelic association of the D2 dopamine receptor with cocaine dependence. Drug Alcohol Depend 33:271–285

Noble EP, Berman SM, Ozkaragoz TZ, Titchie T 1994 Prolonged P300 latency in children with the D2 dopamine receptor A1 allele. Am J Hum Genet 54:658–668

Norio R, Nevanlinna HR, Perheentupa J 1973 Hereditary diseases in Finland: rare flora in rare soil. Ann Clin Res 5:109–141

Orita M, Suzuki Y, Sekiya T, Hayashi K 1989 Rapid and sensitive detection of point mutations and DNA polymorphisms using the polymerase chain reaction. Genomics 5:874–879

Oxenstierna G, Edman G, Iselius L, Oreland L, Ross SB, Sedvali G 1986 Concentrations of monoamine metabolites in the cerebrospinal fluid of twins and unrelated individuals: a genetic study. J Psychiatr Res 20:19–29

Ozaki N, Lappalainen J, Dean M, Virkkunen M, Linnoila M, Goldman D 1995a Mapping of the human 5-HT1Dα autoreceptor gene (HTR1D) on chromosome 1 using a silent polymorphism in the coding region. Am J Med Genet 60:162–164

Ozaki N, Rosenthal N, Pesonen U et al 1995b Identification of two naturally occurring amino acid substitutions of the 5-HT2A receptor in patients with seasonal affective disorders and in controls. Submitted

Ozelius L, Hsu Y-P, Bruns G et al 1988 Human monoamine oxidase gene (MAOA): chromosome position (Xp21-pl 1) and DNA polymorphism. Genomics 3:53–58

Parsian A, Todd RD, Devor EJ, O'Malley KL, Suarez BK, Reich T, Cloninger CR 1991 Alcoholism and alleles of the human D2 dopamine receptor locus. Arch Gen Psychiatry 48:655–663

Rietschel M, Nöthen MM, Lannfelt L et al 1993 A serine to glycine substitution at position 9 in the extracellular N-terminal part of the dopamine D3 receptor protein: no role in the genetic predisposition to bipolar affective disorder. Psychiatry Res 46:253–259

Rushton JP, Fulker DW, Neale MC, Nias NKB, Eysenck HJ 1986 Altruism and aggression: the heritability of individual differences. J Pers Soc Psychol 50:1192–1198

Sadou F, Amara DA, Dierich A et al 1994 Enhanced aggressive behaviour in mice lacking 5-HT$_{1B}$ receptor. Science 265:1875–1878

Saltzman AG, Morse B, Whitman MM, Ivanshchenko Y, Jaye M, Felder S 1991 Cloning of the human serotonin 5-HT2 and 5-HT1C receptor subtypes. Biochem Biophys Res Commun 181:1469–1478

Schwab S, Soyka M, Niederecker M, Ackenheil M, Scherer J, Wildenauer DB 1991 Allelic assocation of human dopamine D2-receptor DNA polymorphism ruled out in 45 alcoholics. Am J Hum Genet 49 (suppl):203(abstr)

Smith SS, O'Hara BF, Persico AM et al 1992 Genetic vulnerability to drug abuse: the D2 dopamine receptor Taq1 restriction fragment length polymorphism appears more frequently in substance abusers. Arch Gen Psychiatry 49:723–727

Soubrie P 1986 Reconciling the role of central serotonin neurons in human and animal behaviour. Behav Brain Sci 9:319–364

Suarez BK, Parsian A, Hampe CL,Todd RD, Reich T, Cloninger CR 1994 Linkage disequilibria at the D2 dopamine receptor locus (DRD2) in alcoholics and controls. Genomics 19:12–20

Tellegen A, Lykken DT, Bouchard TJ, Wilcox K, Seagal N, Rish S 1988 Personality similarity in twins reared apart and together. J Pers Soc Psychol 54:1031–1039

Tsuang MT 1983 Risk of suicide in relatives of schizophrenics, manic depressives and controls. J Clin Psychiatry 44:396–400

Turner E, Ewing J, Shilling P et al 1992 Lack of association between an RFLP near the D2 dopamine receptor gene and severe alcoholism. Biol Psychiatry 31:285–290

Virkkunen M, Linnoila M 1990 Serotonin in early onset, male alcoholics with violent behaviour. Ann Med 22:327–331

Virkkunen M, Rawlings R, Tokola R et al 1994 CSF biochemistries, glucose metabolism, and diurnal activity rhythms in alcoholic, violent offenders, fire setters, and healthy volunteers. Arch Gen Psychiatry 51:20–27

von Knorring L, von Knorring A-L, Smigan L, Lindberg U, Edholm M 1987 Personality traits in subtypes of alcoholics. J Stud Alcohol 48:523–527

DISCUSSION

Gottesman: If what you have said is correct, then we should expect that each family will have a pedigree consistent with Mendelian inheritance for the trait of interest, and this is not what we see.

Goldman: Transmission studies are normally performed on an assemblage of families. If one estimates mode of transmission in a heterogeneous assemblage of families with different modes of transmission, a clear mode of transmission may not emerge, even if there is a major gene effect in some families

Even if a single locus is involved in the different families, differences in penetrance and variations in phenotype expression may occur.

Furthermore, there are clear indications that there may be major gene effects. For example, Cloninger and co-workers found a major gene effect for early-onset alcoholism associated with features of antisocial personality (Gilligan et al 1987). When we look at the adoption data or the twin data, we can see signs that there may be major gene effects. When the biological parent has the trait, surprisingly often the offspring has the trait—surprisingly often, that is, if the trait really is due to the action of several alleles at different genes.

Gottesman: That makes it easier for me to accept what you said. You haven't refuted the usefulness of the quantitative trait loci approach proposed by Plomin et al (1994) to find these posited individual genes for complex traits.

Goldman: If the polygenic model were correct, it would not be discouraging for the direct gene analysis approach. If it were to turn out that the traits were polygenic, this would actually be an advantage for direct gene scanning, because if affected individuals all have four or five variant alleles instead of one, one is then more likely to find variant alleles by this approach.

Carey: It seems that some systems, like red blood cells, have a large number of common polymorphisms (where the allele frequency is about 0.3), whereas when a polymorphism occurs in a brain protein, one with an allele frequency of 0.01 is considered to be very common. Is this just my misperception of the field?

Goldman: We don't know exactly. There are examples of highly polymorphic brain proteins. The *DRD4* gene has a 16 amino acid repeated sequence that is extremely polymorphic. There are seven or eight *DRD4* alleles. Erythrocyte protein polymorphisms were identified early because of the accessibility of the cell and the proteins, whereas it's only recently, as we have been able to do the genetics at the level of the DNA, that we have begun to find polymorphisms in the previously inaccessible brain proteins.

Carey: With some of these relatively rare polymorphisms, it might not be the best strategy just to pick a disorder and then go after the molecules, for example, the serotonin system. It might be useful to complement that by finding a family that has the polymorphism in it, and then examining the behaviour in that family. That is, to identify an important receptor, and then try to see what behaviours it might affect.

Goldman: I agree. There are two things we're doing along those lines. First, we have taken a whole series of disorders in which we think variation in serotonin functions may be involved: alcoholism with antisocial personality, autism, obsessive compulsive disorder, seasonal affective disorder and anorexia nervosa. We are simultaneously screening the coding sequences of serotonin receptor genes in all of these disorders. Second, we are collecting families that have a trait of interest and also have a genetic variant. Amino acid substitutions can be phenotypically neutral. Linkage analysis in families is one strategy for demonstrating effect of an allele on phenotype.

Brunner: I'm not sure that I understood your strategy for detecting these polymorphisms. The impression I got was that you are screening for polymorphisms in a control population, and then applying the polymorphisms that you find to specific disorders. Wouldn't it be more effective to look at patients first, to see whether you find abnormalities, and then to go back to the population to see whether or not they're present at any appreciable frequency in the general population?

Goldman: The screening is being performed in patients first, as you suggest. By screening clinical populations such as Matti Virkkunen's antisocial impulsive alcoholics and other subjects with diseases such as anorexia nervosa, autism and obsessive compulsive disorder, we think that we're more likely to find the variants than if we screened controls. Having found them, it is very important for us to determine population frequencies and clinical specificity.

Rowe: If you look at the mutation rates at neutral sites in the genome, they're also very much depressed in some regions downstream from genes, in some regions within introns and in some regions upstream. This implies that a lot of selective pressure may exist on non-coding areas. Some of these 'neutral' mutations may actually have functional importance.

Cairns: David Goldman, you seem to be arguing that it is important to try to identify specific pathways and to be open to the possibility that multiple pathways could contribute to some behavioural phenotypes. In this regard, when we talk about serotonin and dopamine concentrations in the CSF, that is a rather general specification. Would localizing the activity of these neurotransmitters in the brain facilitate your job?

Goldman: The linkage approach with markers doesn't depend upon any knowledge of mechanism or physiology. With the genetic markers and a genetic trait that's well enough behaved, the gene can be found by tracing inheritance of the marker and the trait. I recently heard a talk by Francis Collins who presented a list of disease genes identified to date strictly by the linkage approach (positional cloning) and with no information whatever about physiology or underlying mechanism. This list of positionally cloned disease genes fits nicely on a single piece of paper, whereas there are now hundreds of disease genes that have been identified by analysis of candidate genes. Both approaches are getting more powerful as the human genome mapping project advances. The genetic map is denser and when you find the genetic linkage it is more likely that a candidate gene will have already been located nearby. On the other hand, if we wish eventually to identify even the genes that account for a small portion of the total variance in a trait, I think it's going to be necessary for us to think about the processes, predict the candidate genes, identify the functional variants of the candidate genes, and test whether those variants have a role in the phenotypes in which we're interested.

References

Gilligan SB, Reich T, Cloninger CR 1987 Etiologic heterogeneity in alcoholism. Gen Epidemiol 4:395–414
Plomin R, Owen MJ, McGuffin P 1994 The genetic basis of complex human behaviors. Science 264:1733–1739

MAOA deficiency and abnormal behaviour: perspectives on an assocation

Han G. Brunner

Department of Human Genetics, Nijmegen University Hospital, PO Box 9101, 6500HB Nijmegen, The Netherlands

Abstract. We have recently described an association between abnormal behaviour and monoamine oxidase A (MAOA) deficiency in several males from a single large Dutch kindred. Affected males differed from unaffected males by borderline mental retardation and increased impulsive behaviour (aggressive behaviour, abnormal sexual behaviour and arson). Nevertheless, a specific psychiatric diagnosis was not made in four affected males who had psychiatric examination. Since MAOA deficiency raises 5-hydroxytryptamine (5-HT) levels, it provides an interesting exception to the low 5-HT paradigm of impulsive aggression. Even if the possible relationship between MAOA deficiency and abnormal behaviour is confirmed in other kindreds, the data do not support the hypothesis that MAOA constitutes an 'aggression gene'. In fact, because genes are essentially simple and behaviour is by definition complex, a direct causal relationship between a single gene and a specific behaviour is highly unlikely. In the case of MAOA deficiency, some of the complexities are illustrated by the variability in the behavioural phenotype, as well as by the highly complex effects of MAOA deficiency on neurotransmitter function. Thus, the concept of a gene that directly encodes behaviour is unrealistic.

1996 Genetics of criminal and antisocial behaviour. Wiley, Chichester (Ciba Foundation Symposium 194) p 155–167

Monoamine oxidase (MAO) is a mitochondrial enzyme that is responsible for the breakdown of several neurotransmitters, including dopamine, nor-adrenaline and serotonin (5-hydroxytryptamine; 5-HT). There are two MAO isozymes, called MAOA and MAOB, that have different substrate specificities as well as different localization in the brain. MAOA and MAOB are encoded by distinct genes that lie in close proximity on the short arm of the X chromosome.

Pharmacological inhibition of MAO (especially MAOA) is an effective treatment for endogenous depression, which suggests that altering MAO enzymic activity can have profound influences on brain function. Interest in the possible relationship between the naturally occurring variation in MAO activity and behaviour stems from the finding that altered neurotransmitter levels are found in the cerebrospinal fluid of patients with various psychiatric disorders. Such alterations in neurotransmitter levels may reflect alterations in production, release, re-uptake or degradation. A number of studies have attempted to correlate variations in MAOB activity to susceptibility to alcoholism, to sensation-seeking behaviour, to impulsivity and to Parkinson's disease (Hsu et al 1989). However, none of these associations has been consistently replicated.

We have recently described a large Dutch kindred, spanning four generations, in which 14 males are affected by a complex behavioural syndrome that manifests itself by borderline mental retardation and prominent behavioural abnormalities (Brunner et al 1993a,b). The most consistent findings, among eight affected males for whom adequate documentation is available, were borderline mental retardation and impulsive aggressive behaviour. Aggressive behaviour was usually restricted to verbal threats or aggressive posture, although isolated instances of physical aggression have also occurred.

Other impulsive behaviours that were noted in affected males included arson, attempted rape and exhibitionism. The syndrome affected only males, but the gene was apparently transmitted through normal female carriers. This suggested that the genetic defect was located on the X chromosome. The defective gene would be masked in 46 XX females, but its effect would become manifest in 46 XY males, since they have only a single X chromosome. This hypothesis was supported by use of genetic markers from the X chromosome, which indicated that the abnormal gene was located very close to the MAOA and MAOB genes. Subsequent biochemical analyses indicated that affected males had a severe impairment of neurotransmitter metabolism, affecting the breakdown of 5-HT, noradrenaline and dopamine (Brunner et al 1993a). It was hypothesized that MAOA, MAOB or both were defective in these patients. As it turned out, MAOB was normal in affected males, whereas MAOA activity was completely absent. Sequencing of the MAOA gene then showed a single base substitution which converts the code for glycine to a termination codon at position 296 of the amino acid sequence. This mutation in the MAOA gene leads to the production of an incomplete MAOA enzyme which has no functional activity (Brunner et al 1993b).

Phenotypic considerations

The discovery of an association between abnormal behaviour and an inherited genetic abnormality raises a number of questions regarding the specificity of the behavioural patterns. In this regard, several points need to be addressed. First, we emphasize that the genetic studies were prompted by the fact that a very clear dichotomy exists in this family between affected and unaffected males. This dichotomy had been recognized by the family for many years, and there was a complete consensus between family members (including the patients) as to who was affected and who was not. In fact, more than 35 years ago, one family member visited all his then living family members in order to investigate this problem. He wrote a report which he ended by stating: 'From this I concluded that mental deficiency was hereditary in this kindred, and that it was transmitted by females. However, only males were affected'. The dichotomy between affected and unaffected males was confirmed in personal interviews with many family members, during the course of our genetic studies. The distinction between affected and unaffected males did not depend on physical characteristics. Moreover, the behavioural abnormalities were clearly much more prominent than could be explained on the basis of the cognitive deficit. In fact, the difference in cognitive functioning between affected and unaffected males (although consistently present) is small. Thus, the unambiguous distinction between affected and unaffected males is based on the consistent association of borderline mental retardation (defined as a low–normal IQ and learning difficulties) and abnormal behaviour. A much more difficult question concerns the specificity and consistency of this 'recognizable behavioral phenotype' (Brunner et al 1993a,b), especially in further cases of MAOA deficiency outside the original kindred that we described. No further cases of MAOA deficiency have yet been described, and therefore this question cannot be answered. Nevertheless, a number of comments can be made at this preliminary stage. The combination of borderline mental retardation and abnormal behaviour is by no means specific for MAOA deficiency. In fact, the observed behavioural abnormalities occur with appreciable frequency in the general population. Moreover, they occur more frequently in individuals with learning disability (e.g. Harris 1993, Sigafoos et al 1994).

A specific psychiatric diagnosis was not made in each of four affected MAOA-deficient males who were seen by a psychiatrist prior to or during our studies. One of these cases had more extensive psychiatric and neuro-psychological evaluation after the conclusion of our genetic studies, but also failed to fulfil the necessary criteria for any specific DSM-IV diagnostic category (W. M. A. Verhoeven, personal communication). We are unable to rule out the possibility that systematic psychiatric evaluation of other affected and unaffected family members might have yielded a more specific psychiatric diagnosis. Nevertheless, as the observed behavioural patterns are strikingly similar in all affected males, this seems unlikely. The fact that this family was ascertained through a request for genetic counselling has limited the possibilities for more extensive psychiatric and neuropsychological investigations. A review of the family data, as well as an account of detailed neuropsychological and psychiatric findings in one affected male is to be reported elsewhere (Tuinier et al 1995). Since MAOA deficiency is uncommon, and the types of behaviour that we observed are relatively frequent, the detection of additional singleton cases based on our phenotypic description is likely to be unrewarding. Adding the requirement of a family history consistent with X-linkage (i.e. affected males linked through unaffected females) might be helpful, but would still not be very selective since abnormal behaviour as reported by us (sexual, aggressive and firesetting behaviour) is more common in males than in females in the general population.

How certain can we be that there is a genetic factor underlying (or at least influencing) the behaviour in the affected males in this kindred? As stated previously (Brunner et al 1993a), the strongest argument for a genetic factor has been that similar behavioural patterns were observed in different sibships in the family, living in different regions of the country and in different parts of the century. This argues against shared environmental factors to explain the clustering of cases in this single family.

Nevertheless, it should also be emphasized that no effort was made to rigidly exclude environmental factors. In fact, as might be expected, the phenotype appears to be definitely influenced by environmental factors. Frequency and severity of abnormal behaviour was seen to vary among affected individuals, and also in the same individual over time. In some cases, abnormal behaviour occurred more frequently during times of emotional stress, and appeared to be favourably influenced by a change from living independently to living in a sheltered environment.

Is MAOA deficiency a plausible explanation for abnormal behaviour?

A number of previous studies have attempted to link behavioural characteristics to variation in MAO activity. It has been suggested that susceptibility to alcoholism, to sensation-seeking behaviour, to impulsivity and to Parkinson's disease are all in some way related to variation in MAO activity (Hsu et al 1989). It is relevant to note here that these studies were comparing variation in behaviour to variability in MAOB activity. None of these studies involved MAOA. This is not because MAOB is a better candidate for influencing behaviour than MAOA. In fact, MAOA is known to be important for metabolism of monoamine neurotransmitters following neuronal re-uptake, but the functional importance of MAOB remains largely to be defined (Berry et al 1994). Moreover, isolated MAOB deficiency, studied by us in two brothers, does not lead to any behavioural or cognitive defects (Berger et al 1992 and our unpublished observations). Finally, selective MAOA inhibitors show more pronounced effects on psychological functioning than do MAOB inhibitors (Fowler & Ross 1984). The main reason for the emphasis on MAOB rather than MAOA in these studies appears to be the fact that MAOB activity can be readily assayed from platelets, whereas MAOA activity measurement requires a skin biopsy for fibroblast culture. Thus, deficiency of

MAOA was a better candidate for causing abnormal behaviour than deficiency
of MAOB, even before our studies began.

How might MAOA deficiency influence behaviour?

The known biochemical affects of blocking MAOA activity do not support a
simple causal relationship between the metabolic abnormality and the
behavioural disturbance that we observed. MAO-inhibiting drugs have been
used extensively to treat psychiatric patients with endogenous depression.
Abnormal behaviour as noted by us in the patients with inherited MAOA
deficiency has not been a prominent side effect of these drugs (Murphy 1977,
Pickar et al 1982, Murphy et al 1983, Bougerol et al 1992). This raises the
question of whether the presumed relationship between MAO deficiency and
abnormal behaviour might be more indirect, and perhaps even involve prenatal
influences.

One of the most consistent biochemical findings in studies of impulsive
aggression has been a low level of 5-HT (Brown et al 1979, Coccaro 1989,
Coccaro et al 1994, Depue & Spoont 1986, Kruesi et al 1986, Linnoila et al
1983, van Praag 1991, van Praag et al 1990). This relationship has received
powerful support from the observation that 5-HT_{1B} receptor-stimulating drugs
(serenics) can be used to decrease aggressive behaviour in animals (Olivier et al
1990), and that mutant mice lacking a functional 5-HT_{1B} receptor have
increased aggressive behaviour (Saudou et al 1994).

In view of the low 5-HT paradigm of (impulsive) aggression in humans and
animals (Brown et al 1979, Coccaro 1989, Coccaro et al 1994, Depue & Spoont
1986, Kruesi et al 1990, Linnoila et al 1983, van Praag 1991, van Praag et al
1990), the finding that 5-HT levels are actually higher than normal in males
with isolated MAOA deficiency does not appear consistent (Brunner et al
1993b). However, one might speculate that if brain serotonin levels are elevated
throughout life (including a significant part of prenatal life), this may alter
receptor densities and/or serotonergic innervation in such a way that the net
effect is a decrease in activity of 5-HT receptor-mediated activity. It is quite
clear that MAOA inhibition leads to significant elevation of 5-HT levels in the
brain (e.g. Sleight et al 1988, Blier et al 1986) and that this causes secondary
adaptations (Manrique et al 1994, van Huizen et al 1993). In fact, the efficacy
of MAO inhibitors to treat depression probably involves exactly this
mechanism of 5-HT receptor down-regulation caused by high levels of 5-HT
(Stahl 1994). This decrease does not necessarily involve all 5-HT receptors to
the same extent. One might speculate that a relative decrease in only one or a
few 5-HT receptors (especially involving the $5\text{-HT}_{1D\beta}$ receptor, which is the
human counterpart of the 5-HT_{1B} receptor in mice) would give rise to an
interesting parallel with the 5-HT_{1B} receptor knockout mice described by

Saudou et al (1994). So far, data on the status of 5-HT receptor subtypes in MAOA-deficient males are unavailable.

If MAOA deficiency causes down-regulation of specific neurotransmitter receptors, or even changes in innervation, this could help resolve the discrepancy between the paradoxical biochemical findings in impulsive aggression in the literature, and the findings in the kindred with abnormal behaviour associated with MAOA deficiency reported by us.

Whitaker-Azmitia et al (1994) have recently reported studies in rats that were treated during pregnancy with a combination of drugs that inhibit both MAOA and MAOB. They found that this regimen caused a significant change in serotonergic innervation in the cortex of offspring rats compared with controls. Although similar experiments with drugs that inhibit MAOA alone have yet to be performed, this suggests that prenatal MAO deficiency may interfere with normal brain development (Whitaker-Azmitia et al 1994). Progress in defining the various effects of inherited MAOA deficiency on cerebral functional anatomy and biochemistry is to be expected from genetically engineered MAOA knockout mice. Several groups have started projects that aim at creating a mouse model of MAOA deficiency, and the results are awaited with keen interest. Nevertheless, animal models of metabolic disorders may not always have identical functional deficits. It has recently been demonstrated that mice lacking a functional hypoxanthine phosphoribosyltransferase (*HPRT*) gene do not develop an equivalent clinical phenotype to humans with HPRT deficiency (Lesch–Nyhan syndrome). The much milder phenotype associated with HPRT deficiency in mice compared with humans is explained by compensation through the related adenine phosphoribosyltransferase (APRT) enzyme (Wu & Melton 1993).

Is MAOA an aggression gene?

Broad popular support apparently exists for the concept that specific emotions and behaviours can be genetically encoded by single genes. In fact, our studies described above have been repeatedly quoted as evidence for an aggression gene (e.g. Morell 1993). This concept is unlikely to be productive, and in the case of MAOA deficiency it is not in keeping with the data as they were reported.

MAOA deficiency is not the first genetic metabolic abnormality to be linked to more-or-less specific abnormal behaviour. Examples of previously reported associations include severe mental retardation and self-mutilation due to HPRT deficiency (Lesch & Nyhan 1964), attention deficit hyperactivity disorder and thyroid hormone resistance (Hauser et al 1993), aggressive behaviour and other disorders of conduct and homocystinuria (Abbott et al 1987), and generalized anxiety disorder and acute intermittent porphyria due to porphobilinogen deaminase deficiency (Patience et al 1994). What these conditions have in common is a very general disturbance of brain metabolism, which must affect a broad range of physiological functions. These examples indicate that even rather specific and reproducible behavioural abnormalities arise from an extremely complex interplay between many functional units or circuits in the brain, rather than from dysfunction of a single functional brain unit that is uniquely responsible for this type of behaviour.

This is not to say that behaviour is not influenced by genetic factors. On the contrary, genetic influences have been demonstrated for a wide range of behavioural patterns, both normal and abnormal (Bouchard 1994, Plomin et al 1994). However, the notion of an 'aggression gene' does not make sense, because it belies the fact that behaviour should and does arise at the highest level of cortical organization, where individual genes are only distantly reflected in the anatomical structure, as well as in the various neurophysiological and biochemical functions of the brain. This controversy between reductionism and holism is reminiscent of Hofstadter's description (1979; p 311–316) of an intelligent ant colony which carries the name of Aunt Hillary. In spite of Aunt Hillary's intelligent behaviour, the ants themselves were found to be very dumb by the anteater. Although the analogy applies to the different functional levels on which the brain can be described (from neuronal firing, through coordinated signals to abstract thought), it is easy to see how a similar argument could be made for the difference in level of genes, of neurotransmitters and behaviour. Thus, although a multitude of genes must be involved in shaping brain function, none of these genes by itself encodes behaviour.

Implications of the MAOA deficiency state
for understanding abnormal impulsive behaviour

Should our initial observation of increased impulsive behaviour (aggressive, sexual and firesetting behaviour) with MAOA deficiency be confirmed in other kindreds, will this tell us anything about the regulation of impulsive behaviour in general?

MAOA deficiency is unlikely to be a significant factor in a strict sense, since it must be extremely uncommon. Also, the use of MAOA deficiency as a model for understanding impulsive behaviour may be limited by the fact that having a complete deficiency of a key enzyme in neurotransmitter catabolism may unbalance the system so severely that few conclusions about normal brain function and regulatory pathways are possible.

Despite such limitations, I believe that at a much more modest level, the association of MAOA deficiency and abnormal behaviour is important, because it demonstrates that the low 5-HT paradigm of impulsive aggression (Coccaro 1989, Coccaro et al 1994, Depue & Spoont 1986, Kruesi et al 1990, Linnoila et al 1983, van Praag 1991, van Praag et al 1990) needs to be refined.

Because the MAOA deficiency state alters brain neurotransmitter levels (and increases 5-HT) throughout life, understanding the secondary effects on neurotransmitter receptors is essential in order to understand the pathogenic basis of the association with abnormal behaviour. Future studies of MAOA deficiency (both in humans and in experimental animals) may add to the growing body of experimental data in animals that implicates specific 5-HT receptor subtypes in the regulation of aggression (Olivier et al 1990, Saudou et al 1994).

Conclusion

Our studies suggest that MAOA deficiency in human males is associated with increased impulsive aggression and with other types of abnormal behaviour. Additional kindreds with MAOA deficiency have to be studied in order to test the validity and reproducibility of this association. Moreover, the pathogenetic basis of this association is not at all clear, which further limits the conclusions that can be drawn from our studies. At the same time, the fact that MAOA-deficient patients have elevated levels of 5-HT provides an exception to the low 5-HT paradigm of impulsive aggression. Resolution of this paradox could potentially be of importance for defining additional functional and/or structural aspects of brain functioning that are reflected in impulsive behavioural disturbance.

Although genetic studies cannot explain *why* impulsive aggression occurs, they may still help to improve our understanding of *how* impulsive behaviour happens. Studying the pathogenesis of abnormal behaviour could prove more rewarding than trying to define its ultimate causes.

References

Abbott MH, Folstein SE, Abbey H, Pyeritz RE 1987 Psychiatric manifestations of homocystinuria due to cystathione β-synthase deficiency—prevalence, natural history, and relationship to neurologic impairment and vitamin B6 responsiveness. Am J Med Genet 26:959–969

Berger W, Meindl A, van de Pol TJ et al 1992 Isolation of a candidate gene for Norrie disease by positional cloning. Nat Genet 1:199–203

Berry MD, Juorio AV, Paterson IA 1994 The functional role of monoamine oxidases A and B in the mammalian central nervous system. Prog Neurobiol 42:375–391

Blier P, de Montigny C, Azzaro AJ 1986 Modification of serotonergic and noradrenergic transmissions by repeated administration of monoamine oxidase inhibitors: electrophysiological studies in the rat central nervous system. J Pharmacol Exp Ther 237:987–994

Bouchard TJ 1994 Genes, environment and personality. Science 264:1700–1701

Bougerol T, Uchida C, Gachoud J-P, Köhler M, Mikkelsen H 1992 Efficacy and tolerability of moclobemide compared with fluvoxamine in depressive disorder (DSM III)—a French/Swiss double-blind trial. Psychopharmacology 106 (suppl): S102–S108

Brunner HG, Nelen MR, van Zandvoort P et al 1993a X-linked borderline mental retardation with prominent behavioral disturbance: phenotype, genetic localization, and evidence for disturbed monoamine metabolism. Am J Hum Genet 52:1032–1039

Brunner HG, Nelen M, Breakefield XO, Ropers HH, van Oost BA 1993b Abnormal behaviour associated with a point mutation in the structural gene for monoamine oxidase A. Science 262:578–580

Brown GL, Goodwin FK, Ballenger JC, Goyer PF, Major LF 1979 Aggression correlates with cerebrospinal fluid amine metabolites. Psychiatry Res 1:131–139

Coccaro EF 1989 Central serotonin and impulsive aggression. Br J Psychiatry 155 (suppl 8):52–62

Coccaro EF, Silverman JM, Klar HM, Horvath TB, Siever LJ 1994 Familial correlates of reduced central serotonergic system function in patients with personality disorders. Arch Gen Psychiatry 51:318–324

Depue RA, Spoont MR 1986 Conceptualizing a serotonin trait. A behavioral dimension of constraint. Ann N Y Acad Sci 487:47–62

Fowler CJ, Ross SB 1984 Selective inhibitors of monoamine oxidase A and B: biochemical, pharmacological, and clinical properties. Med Res Rev 4:323–358

Harris P 1993 The nature and extent of aggressive behavior amongst people with learning difficulties (mental handicap) in a single health district. J Intellect Disabil Res 37:221–242

Hauser P, Zametkin AJ, Martinez P et al 1993 Attention deficit–hyperactivity disorder in people with generalized resistance to thyroid hormone. N Engl J Med 328:997–1001

Hofstadter DR 1979 Gödel, Escher, Bach. Vintage, New York, p 311–336

Hsu Y-PP, Powell JF, Sims KB, Breakefield XO 1989 Molecular genetics of the monoamine oxidases. J Neurochem 53:12–18

Kruesi MJP, Rappoport JL, Hamburger S et al 1990 Cerebrospinal fluid monoamine metabolites, aggression, and impulsivity in disruptive behavior disorders of children and adolescents. Arch Gen Psychiatry 47:419–426

Lesch M, Nyhan WL 1964 A familial disorder of uric acid metabolism and central nervous system function. Am J Med 36:561–570

Linnoila M, Virkkunen M, Scheinin M, Nuutila A, Rimon R, Goodwin FK 1983 Low cerebrospinal fluid 5-hydroxyindoleacetic acid concentration differentiates impulsive from nonimpulsive behavior. Life Sci 33:2609–2614

Manrique C, François-Bellan AM, Segu L et al 1994 Impairment of serotonergic transmission is followed by adaptive changes in 5HT$_{1B}$ binding sites in the rat suprachiasmatic nucleus. Brain Res 663:93–100

Morell V 1993 Evidence found for a possible 'aggression gene'. Science 260:1722–1723

Murphy DL 1977 The behavioral toxicity of monoamine oxidase inhibiting antidepressants. Adv Pharmacol Chemother 14:71–105

Murphy DL, Garrick NA, Cohen RM 1983 Monoamine oxidase inhibitors and monoamine oxidase: biochemical and physiological aspects relevant to human psychopharmacology. In: Burrows GD, Norman TR, Davies B (eds) Antidepressants. Elsevier Science, New York, p 209–227

Olivier B, Mos J, Hartog J, Rasmussen D 1990 Serenics. Drugs News Perspect 3:261–271

Patience DA, Blackwood DHR, McColl KEL, Moore MR 1994 Acute intermittent porphyria and mental illness—a family study. Acta Psychiatr Scand 89:262–267

Pickar D, Murphy DL, Cohen RM, Campbell IC, Lipper S 1982 Selective and nonselective monoamine oxidase inhibitors. Arch Gen Psychiatry 39:535–540

Plomin R, Owen MJ, McGuffin P 1994 The genetic basis of complex human behaviors. Science 264:1733–1739

Saudou F, Amara DA, Dierich A et al 1994 Enhanced aggressive behavior in mice lacking 5-HT$_{1B}$ receptor. Science 265:1875–1878

Sigafoos J, Elkins J, Kerr M, Attwood T 1994 A survey of aggressive behaviour among a population of persons with intellectual disability in Queensland. J Intellect Disabil Res 38:369–381

Sleight AJ, Marsden CA, Martin KF, Palfreyman MG 1988 Relationship between extracellular 5-hydroxytryptamine and behaviour following monoamine oxidase inhibition and L-tryptophan. Br J Pharmacol 93:303–310

Stahl S 1994 Is serotonin receptor down-regulation linked to the mechanism of action of antidepressant drugs? Psychopharmacol Bull 30:39–43

Tuinier S, Verhoeven WMA, Pepplinkhuizen L, Scherders MJWT, Fekkes D 1995 Neuropsychiatric and biological characteristics of X-linked MAOA deficiency syndrome: a single-intervention case study. Submitted

van Huizen F, Bansse M-T, Stam NJ 1993 Agonist-induced down-regulation of human 5HT$_{1A}$ and 5-HT$_{2}$ receptors in Swiss 3T3 cells. NeuroReport 4:1327–1330

van Praag HM 1991 Serotonergic dysfunction and aggression control. Psychol Med 21:15–19

van Praag HM, Asnis GM, Kahn RS et al 1990 Monoamines and abnormal behaviour, a multiaminergic perspective. Br J Psychiatry 157:723–734

Whitaker-Azmitia PM, Zhang X, Clarke C 1994 Effects of gestational exposure to monoamine oxidase inhibitors in rats: preliminary behavioral and neurochemical studies. Neuropsychopharmacology 11:125–132

Wu C-L, Melton DW 1993 Production of a model for Lesch–Nyhan syndrome in hypoxanthine phosphoribosyltransferase-deficient mice. Nat Genet 3:235–240

DISCUSSION

Goldman: Even though we clearly don't have a gene for antisocial personality here, the family you have studied clearly displays a distinctive syndrome that includes many of the sorts of behaviours in which we're interested. In that sense, this is one of the first examples of a class of situations in which scientists will be faced with decisions about what to do with genetic information concerning these types of behaviours. I would like to ask about how you have handled some of the bioethical problems.

First, in terms of actually studying the family, how did you contact them, and what decisions did you make about how you would get back to them with information subsequently?

Brunner: We did not start this as a scientific study, but as patient care within the clinical genetics department: we were trying to answer the family's questions. At the time we offered the linkage analysis, it wasn't clear to us that the behaviour was such a central part of this syndrome. Consequently, the family members who participated in the linkage analysis were mostly recruited through the one female who came to us in the first place. We explained to her that to do the study we would have to compare the affected and the unaffected males within the family. She went back to the family with that information and got most of them to cooperate, although a few declined to participate.

When we found the MAOA mutation, we decided to explain this to the family. However, we allowed each individual family member to decide whether they wanted to know their status with respect to this mutation. We've not initially given any information on carrier status to females who didn't already know it. We have given them the opportunity to ask for that information.

Goldman: What decisions did you make on keeping information confidential? For example, you have published a pedigree: did you make a decision to disguise it?

Brunner: One thing I would do differently today is that I would change the pedigree in order to make it less recognizable. However, the specific examples of behaviour that I've given all took place many years ago—I've avoided giving specific examples of behaviours that have occurred in the last 10–15 years. I have not indicated in the pedigree who had which behaviour, as an attempt to retain confidentiality. Having seen how much this pedigree has been publicised, I should perhaps not have published a pedigree at all, but then you might not have believed me. There's a conflict here—I've tried to avoid giving enough information to make individuals recognizable, but I've tried to give enough information to convince people on a scientific level that this was a real finding. The two are difficult to reconcile.

Virkkunen: I think your finding is very important because it is the first real mutation to be connected with criminality. Have any of these men had alcohol problems?

Brunner: None of them have had alcohol problems that I'm aware of.

Virkkunen: There is the problem of how much the mild mental retardation these men had was connected with these criminal acts. The antisocial behaviour (exhibitionism, rape, arsons) these individuals displayed are typical of mentally retarded patients.

How do you explain the fact that no females displayed this phenotype? Is it just that they have two X chromosomes?

Brunner: Since we don't know what the link is between the mutation and the behaviour in the males, I cannot answer your question for the females. There are many X-linked conditions where you never, or only very rarely, see any expression in the females, but there are other X-linked conditions where expression in females is common. Just on the basis of this family, it looks as though there's no expression at all in the carrier females.

Carlier: You only analysed three of the males. How did you chose these three?

Brunner: This research was done in two phases. The first was the linkage study in which we asked for a blood sample from everyone. Having found linkage to MAOA, we then asked affected and unaffected males and carrier females whether they would be prepared to give a skin biopsy, a 24 h urine sample and an additional blood sample. Three of the affected males were willing to do this, the other two weren't.

Carlier: Are you sure that the same results will be observed in the five affected males who did not agree to have their MAOA levels tested?

Brunner: We have shown that the five affected males in the pedigree all have the same mutation. It is a termination mutation, which means that even if you had only the mutation you will still be confident that it's impossible to have a functional MAOA enzyme. Out of those five, we have confirmed that hypothesis by actually measuring MAOA activity in three of them. We're not at all worried that the two who have the mutation and who have not been tested enzymically could have any functional MAOA activity.

Rowe: I used Hotamisligil & Breakefield's (1991) MAOA markers to test some adolescents in Tuscon. One marker significantly predicted their self-reported delinquent behaviour, but I didn't write this up for publication because it was contrary to what I had predicted. There are two alleles: one is associated with low activity of the MAOA enzyme (*Eco*RV site negative), the other with high activity (*Eco*RV site positive). I found that in this group of adolescents there was a significant positive relationship between the allele activity and greater delinquency. I had expected a negative relationship.

Brunner: It's extremely important that these sorts of negative findings are published to avoid the meta-analyses later coming up with the wrong answer.

Plomin: Is the MAOA marker functional? That is, does the DNA difference among individuals produce a direct (pleiotropic) effect or is it just a non-functional (non-coding) difference that serves as a marker for some other functional bit of DNA? In other words, is it likely that the MAOA marker is itself the causal genetic mechanism that is responsible for the behavioural phenomenon?

Rowe: It's a functional polymorphism and it does predict delinquency, but it's not the prediction I anticipated. I expected the low-activity allele to be associated with higher delinquency.

It's not a truly functional polymorphism, but it has been linked in cell lines to high and low activity. It's not the polymorphism itself which is important, it's presumably linked to a functional thing elsewhere in the gene.

Goldman: I would like to comment on the potential abundance of the MAOA stop codon mutation. We've looked for it in several hundred of Matti Virkkunen's impulsive antisocial alcoholic Finns. Other people have looked for it also. We verified its presence in DNA kindly supplied by Dr Brunner, but we haven't found it in a second genetically independent individual yet. We haven't looked for this variant in individuals who strongly resemble the individuals in your family, for example, ones with mild mental retardation and the specific constellation of behaviours that you observed. This MAOA mutation may be uncommon, but perhaps we should look in individuals with a similar phenotype before we conclude that it's not there.

Brunner: I don't think it's going to be much use looking for this mutation outside the region in The Netherlands that this family comes from. Out of eight affected males that I mentioned, only one has married and has offspring, which in genetic terms means this mutation behaves as an X-linked semi-lethal, because only the females transmit the mutation. It is exceptional that this family should be as large as it is. Also, you will not find the same mutation twice in any gene for any condition unless there is a specific reason for that. My hypothesis would be that if there is MAOA deficiency elsewhere in the world, it's going to be a different mutation, so there's really no great use in looking at this one mutation. If you are interested in finding other cases of MAOA deficiency, and then looking for any behavioural phenotype attached to this, I would suggest that a much more efficient way do this would be to do urine screening and look for the metabolites. We've demonstrated great differences on 24 h urine screening, but they're also there if you take single urine samples.

Goldman: We did directly scan the MAOA coding sequence for other variants, and so far have not detected another coding substitution. I agree with you that mutations altering MAOA function are likely to be different in other families. A good analogy would be HPRT (hypoxanthine guanine phoshporibosyl transferase) deficiency in Lesch–Nyhan syndrome. There are not very many males with severe HPRT deficiency and the mutations tend to be completely different from one Lesch–Nyhan patient to the next.

Reference

Hotamisligil GS, Breakefield XO 1991 Human monoamine oxidase A gene determines levels of enzyme activity. Am J Hum Genet 49:383–392

Serotonin in alcoholic violent offenders

Matti Virkkunen, David Goldman* and Markku Linnoila*

Department of Psychiatry, Helsinki University Central Hospital, 00180 Helsinki, Finland, and *Division of Intramural Clinical and Biological Research, National Institute on Alcohol Abuse and Alcoholism, Bethesda, MD 20892, USA

Abstract. Finnish alcoholic, impulsive, habitually violent offenders have been found to have low brain serotonin (5-hydroxytryptamine; 5-HT) turnover which is associated with impaired impulse control, a history of suicide attempts, hypoglycaemic tendency after an oral glucose load and diurnal activity rhythm dysregulation or hyperactivity. Relatively high cerebrospinal fluid (CSF) free testosterone concentration is a further characteristic of the offenders with antisocial personality disorder. The impulsive offenders may represent a behaviourally extreme group of type 2 alcoholics as defined by Cloninger. A large cohort of 800 subjects, including alcoholic violent offenders, their relatives and male controls, has now been gathered from Finland with support from the National Institute on Alcohol Abuse and Alcoholism. About 200 subjects have provided CSF samples. Leukocytes from the whole cohort have been harvested and immortalized. Genes regulating 5-HT functions are now being systematically analysed from these samples. Thus far, polymorphisms of the tryptophan hydroxylase (*TPH*) and *5-HT$_{2C}$* receptor genes have been the most informative findings.

1996 Genetics of criminal and antisocial behaviour. Wiley, Chichester (Ciba Foundation Symposium 194) p 168–182

During the past few years increasing evidence has implicated low brain serotonin (5-hydroxytryptamine; 5-HT) turnover rate and 5-HT receptor function in vulnerability to impulsive violent behaviour, including various crimes of violence.

According to Mossman (1994), during the past few years, long-term (>1 year) predictions of violence have become nearly as accurate as short-term (1–7 days) predictions when we use $AUC \pm SEM$ values of receiver operating characteristic (ROC) analyses. (An AUC value in an ROC analysis equals the likelihood that a clinician would rate a randomly selected, actually violent person as more likely to be violent than a randomly selected, actually non-violent person. The area under the ROC curve [AUC] is a succinct and commonly used method for summarizing overall discriminatory power.) During the 1970s and early 1980s these long-term predictions about outpatients were very inaccurate (Monahan 1984). The improvement in these predictions is partly due to the inclusion of 5-HT-related variables to the predictive equations (Mossman 1994).

In a series of studies on Finnish violent offenders with antisocial personality or intermittent explosive disorder, we have found low cerebrospinal fluid (CSF) 5-hydroxyindoleacetic acid (5-HIAA) concentration to be associated with impaired impulse control, a history of suicide attempts, hypoglycaemic tendency after an oral glucose load and diurnal activity rhythm dysregulation or hyperactivity.

Antisocial personality (ASP) disorder is the most common personality disorder diagnosis among prisoners in Western industrialized countries. It has been suggested that over 30% of new prisoners have ASP disorder (American Psychiatric Association 1994). In Finland, 80–85% of all recidivist severe violent crimes (homicides) are thought to be committed by criminals with ASP disorder (Tiihonen & Hakola 1994). Another large group of impulsive violent offenders have intermittent explosive disorder. These offenders do not fulfil the criteria of ASP disorder when they are abstinent (American Psychiatric Association 1994), but respond repeatedly with disproportionate violence to minor or no provocation when under the influence of alcohol or other substances of abuse.

We have found that offenders with intermittent explosive disorder, who as a group have low mean CSF 5-HIAA concentration, also have very disturbed diurnal activity rhythms. Offenders with ASP disorder who also have low mean CSF 5-HIAA concentrations show greater physical activity throughout the 10 day–night monitoring period than healthy volunteers. Thus, a low CSF 5-HIAA concentration is not *per se* conducive to diurnal activity rhythm disturbances but within certain diagnostic groups it is strongly associated with a striking diurnal activity rhythm disturbance (Virkkunen et al 1994a). The primary behavioural traits which correlate with low CSF 5-HIAA are increased irritability, impaired impulse control, stimulus seeking and psychasthenia among violent alcoholics with ASP disorder or intermittent explosive disorder (Virkkunen et al 1994b). Interestingly, low orbitofrontal glucose metabolism has also been reported among impulsive psychiatric patients with personality disorders (Goyer et al 1994).

A discriminant function analysis between impulsive and nonimpulsive alcoholic offenders and between alcoholic offenders and healthy volunteers revealed that low CSF 5-HIAA is clearly a concomitant of impaired impulse control, and CSF free testosterone explains most of the variance for interpersonal aggressiveness or violence. A high CSF free testosterone concentration is a biochemical characteristic of young, violent alcoholic men with ASP disorder. How CSF testosterone concentrations and brain 5-HT metabolism are interrelated is currently poorly understood. Men tend, however, to have a lower central 5-HT turnover rate than women (Nordin et al 1993).

Heritability

Oxenstierna et al (1986) examined CSF monoamine metabolite concentrations in monozygotic (MZ) and dizygotic (DZ) twins and found a higher intrapair correlation for 5-HIAA in the MZ twins. They did not, however, find significant heritability of CSF 5-HIAA. In a large-scale study on rhesus monkeys, designed to investigate genetic and environmental influences on CSF monoamine metabolites, Higley et al (1993) found significant maternal and paternal genetic contributions to CSF 5-HIAA concentration. Rather drastic environmental manipulations, such as rearing in peer groups or by an unrelated female monkey, did not significantly influence CSF 5-HIAA concentrations in prepubertal monkeys. Thus, it appears that, at least in young non-human primates, CSF 5-HIAA concentration may be a useful phenotypic marker (Higley et al 1993).

Type 2 alcoholism and brain 5-HT turnover

Cloninger et al (1981), in a large-scale adoption study, defined male-limited, type 2 alcoholism. This is characterized by high heritability from fathers to sons, early onset, and is related to antisocial, often violent behavioural traits. Later, von Knorring et al (1985) clarified clinical criteria to permit classification of alcoholics into types 1 and 2 (von Knorring et al 1985). We have found among alcoholics that a majority of the type 2 patients are characterized by low CSF 5-HIAA (Roy et al 1987, Virkkunen & Linnoila 1993). This subtype of alcoholism is associated with hereditary factors and impulsive, often violent personality disorders, especially with ASP disorder. Some investigators, for instance, the group of Schuckit, who have studied primary alcoholism, postulate that type 2 alcoholism and ASP disorder may share the same genetic aetiology (Irwin et al 1990).

That type 2 alcoholics are prone to violence during intoxication has been suggested by many investigators (von Knorring et al 1985, Cloninger 1987, Virkkunen et al 1989, 1994a, Virkkunen & Linnoila 1993, Tiihonen & Hakola 1994). This is, to a certain extent, expected if a large proportion of this subgroup of alcoholics actually have ASP disorder (Irwin et al 1990). Among all perpetrators of recidivist homicides in Finland, 85% have type 2 alcoholism and ASP disorder (Tiihonen & Hakola 1994).

The clinical criteria for type 2 alcoholism have, however, not yet been completely agreed upon (von Knorring et al 1985, Gilligan et al 1988, Sullivan et al 1990, Lamparski et al 1991). The early onset of alcohol abuse is, however, a central characteristic. Aggressivity and conduct disorder problems starting before the age of 10 and continuing into adulthood have been found to precede this early-onset alcohol abuse in a prospective follow-up study in Finland (Pulkkinen & Pitkänen 1994). Because conduct disorder problems are always part of ASP disorder (American Psychiatric Association 1994) and precede the onset of type 2 alcoholism, Schuckit's group have called type 2 alcoholism in most patients 'secondary' (Irwin et al 1990, Anthenelli et al 1994).

We have found that among early-onset alcoholic, habitually violent male offenders, those who do not have alcoholic violent fathers often have alcoholism among their mother's first-degree male relatives (i.e. brothers and fathers) (Virkkunen et al 1989). Thus, these patients do not have type 2 alcoholism according to the original Cloninger criteria, but alcoholism which may be X-chromosome linked. They represent a minority of the violent male alcoholics.

5-HT receptors

At present we do not know which subtypes of 5-HT receptors are most important in mediating the effects of central 5-HT on impulse control. It is hoped that the ongoing molecular genetic studies will provide an answer to this question. There are at least 18 different 5-HT receptors currently known and more are likely to be discovered (Glennon & Dukat 1995). Many of the human 5-HT receptor variants are under investigation in the Laboratory of Neurogenetics in the National Institute on Alcohol Abuse and Alcoholism (NIAAA). Our preliminary findings implicate presynaptic receptors and tryptophan hydroxylase as particularly important for impaired impulse control (Nielsen et al 1994a, Lappalainen et al 1995a, Ozaki et al 1995).

5-HT receptor challenges in early- versus late-onset male alcoholics

Recent challenge studies suggest that serotonergic dysregulation may be more prominent in type 2 alcoholics than in type 1 alcoholics and healthy subjects (Benkelfat et al 1991, Krystal et al 1994). Metachlorophenylpiperazine (mCPP), a primarily $5\text{-}HT_{2C}$ receptor agonist, has been found to produce limited hormonal (prolactin, cortisol) responses in all alcoholics but to have alcohol-like effects among type 2 alcoholics (Benkelfat et al 1991, Krystal et al 1994). In addition to the $5\text{-}HT_{2C}$ receptor, mCPP may also interact with at least the $5\text{-}HT_{1A}$, $5\text{-}HT_{1D}$, $5\text{-}HT_{2A}$, $5\text{-}HT_3$ and $5\text{-}HT_7$ receptors (see Krystal et al 1994).

Abnormal hormonal responses to mCPP have also been observed in ASP disorder by Moss et al (1990). Furthermore, low platelet monoamine oxidase (MAO) activity has been found in type 2 alcoholics by von Knorring (1985) and Sullivan et al (1990).

Follow-up studies

In a prospective follow-up study, low CSF 5-HIAA and a low blood glucose nadir after an oral glucose challenge were predictive of recidivism of violent crimes under the influence of alcohol (Virkkunen et al 1989). Particularly low CSF 5-HIAA was associated with a family history positive for paternal alcoholism and violence (Linnoila et al 1989). This finding is compatible with Cloninger's genetic model of type 2 alcoholism being 'male limited'. Our unpublished studies on alcoholic violent sib-pairs also strongly support Cloninger's original observations.

A prospective follow-up study among American children and adolescents with disruptive behavioural disorders (mainly conduct disorders) (Kruesi et al 1992) also found low CSF 5-HIAA to be predictive of future violent behaviour.

Molecular genetic studies of alcoholic violent offenders in Finland

Dr Virkkunen's group in Helsinki, in collaboration with investigators at NIAAA, have now studied 250 relatives of impulsive, male, alcohol-abusing, violent offenders and firesetters who have a low CSF 5-HIAA (less than 50 pmol/ml) concentration. Altogether, 30 informative pedigrees have been studied. Also, a random population sample of 250 men, 60 with CSF measurements, has been characterized to serve as controls in genetic association and linkage studies.

To fulfil the assumptions of statistical power calculations we gathered 160 still-affected sib-pairs (usually brothers) exhibiting alcohol abuse or dependence or impulsive violence-related problems. Blood samples from all these have been sent to the Laboratory of Neurogenetics at NIAAA. The leukocytes have been harvested and immortalized by transformation with the Epstein–Barr virus. The 5-HT_{1A}, $5\text{-HT}_{1D\alpha}$, $5\text{-HT}_{1D\beta}$, 5-HT_{2A}, 5-HT_{2C}, 5-HT_3, 5-HT_4 and 5-HT_7 receptor and 5-HT transporter genes have been investigated thus far.

Because of the findings of Dutch investigators published at the end of 1993 that *MAOA* gene abnormality is linked to violent (sexual) tendencies among mildly mentally retarded males (Brunner et al 1993a,b), we are also investigating *MAOA* and *MAOB* genes. This *MAOA* gene defect cannot, however, be a common cause of impulsive violence, because most impulsive offenders do not come from X-linked families (Morell 1993).

All these genes have been cloned during the past couple of years and all are thought to be important in controlling aspects of 5-HT metabolism and transmission.

Tryptophan hydroxylase

Thus far, we have published data on a tryptophan hydroxylase intronic polymorphism. This polymorphism seems to be strongly associated with low CSF 5-HIAA and increased lifetime risk for suicide attempts among alcoholic impulsive offenders (Nielsen et al 1994a,b). Recently, Siever et al (1994) have reported preliminary findings that the variant found by us to be associated with self-injurious behaviour is also associated with impulsiveness and high risk-taking among patients with mood and personality disorders.

5-HT$_{2C}$

We have also found a mutation in the *5-HT$_{2C}$* receptor gene which is on the X-chromosome. We identified a Cys→Ser substitution in the extracellular domain of the human 5-HT$_{2C}$ receptor (Lappalainen et al 1995b).

According to our preliminary findings, the frequency of the serine allele is lower among alcoholic offenders (10%) than among Finnish male volunteers (18%). This is especially true among non-ASP alcoholic offenders (7%). Among the offenders with ASP disorder, the frequency was 13%.

5-HT$_{1D\alpha}$ and 5-HT$_{1D\beta}$

5-HT$_{1D}$ receptors are autoreceptors in the human brain that regulate 5-HT release. Recent cloning studies have revealed two 5-HT$_{1D}$ receptor subtypes: 5-HT$_{1D\alpha}$ and 5-HT$_{1D\beta}$, the latter being the human homologue of the rodent 5-HT$_{1B}$ receptor (Glennon & Dukat 1995).

The human *5-HT$_{1D\alpha}$* receptor gene has previously been localized to chromosome 1 (Glennon & Dukat 1995). We have found a polymorphism in this gene (Ozaki et al 1995). It does not, however, produce an amino acid substitution in the protein. The silent T→C substitution at nucleotide 1350 is more common among offenders with ASP disorder (10.7%) or its precursor, conduct disorder (33.3%), than among normal controls (4.5%). It is also interesting that the same impulsive, habitually violent offenders with ASP disorder have behaved aggressively not only towards others, but also have made impulsive suicide attempts, such as slashing, taking overdoses of medicines, and attempting to hang themselves.

The gene for the human 5-HT$_{1D\beta}$ receptor has been previously localized to chromosome 6. We have also found a silent polymorphism in this gene with allele frequencies of 0.72 and 0.28 (Lappalainen et al 1995a). The variant is caused by a G→C substitution at nucleotide 861 of the coding region. This mutation is also associated with ASP disorder, the rarer allele being much less common among patients with ASP disorder (13%). We are further elucidating these findings in our pedigrees.

Summary of the molecular genetic findings

So far, we have already found many polymorphisms of 5-HT metabolism and function-related genes among impulsive violent offenders and healthy volunteers. However, many of these are rare, and most of them are silent.

The ultimate significance of these mutations will be elucidated in future linkage studies.

Future research

It is likely that several new gene markers linked to and associated with impulsive violence, alcoholism and related behaviours will be characterized within the next few years. The next phase of research will then be to elucidate environmental risk and protective factors and their interactions with these alleles. Hopefully, these research efforts will then lead to rational prevention and treatment strategies. Longitudinal follow-up studies will elucidate phenomena such as why patients with ASP disorder 'burn out' in their forties. The polymorphic alleles of the vulnerability genes may also help us to develop new, more-specific medicines to reduce impulsive violence. Identification of genetic markers could facilitate early detection of individuals at risk and implementation of preventive behavioural and environmental interventions.

Ethical concerns of molecular genetic research on violent offenders

The ethical issues concerning biological research on criminals and violent offenders have been discussed in an editorial in *Forensic Psychiatry* (Virkkunen 1991).

Initially, it was thought that it was unethical to conduct biological and molecular genetic studies on prisoners. The consensus attitude is, however, changing towards acceptance of the idea that *it would even be unethical for these studies not to be conducted* because the biological findings seem to have a role in the prediction of future violence (Virkkunen et al 1989, Kruesi et al 1992).

Double-blind studies are also in progress at many centres to verify whether habitually violent behaviour and impulsivity can be reduced using pharmacotherapy (specifically, the new 5-HT re-uptake inhibitors, lithium, carbamazepine, tryptophan, beta-blockers, etc.). All these medicines have an effect on brain 5-HT metabolism. Thus, previously 'incurable psychopaths' may in the future come into the sphere of medical treatment, at least when there is evidence that they have abnormal brain 5-HT metabolism.

These biological findings are also related to 'free will', if, by this, we mean a person's ability to control him/herself (impulsivity). It will be important for forensic psychiatry in the future to make decisions concerning, for example, diminished responsibility and dangerousness not only on the basis of descriptive criteria of personality disorders and psychological tests, but also using biological and even molecular genetic data as additional sources of information.

At present only two forensic psychiatric units in the world perform, for instance, CSF monoamine measurements on violent criminal offenders (the Department of Forensic Psychiatry, Helsinki University Central Hospital, Finland, and the Department of Social and Forensic Psychiatry, Karolinska Institute, Huddinge, Sweden). A possible reason for this small number is that these studies are somewhat complicated and forensic psychiatrists have not been very interested in biological variables. The difficulties are also compounded by the 'old battle' between sociological, sociopsychological and biological theories of criminality and violence.

References

American Psychiatric Association Committee on Nomenclature and Statistics 1994 Diagnostic and statistical manual of mental disorders, 4th edn. American Psychiatric Association, Washington, DC

Anthenelli RM, Smith TL, Irwin MR, Schuckit MA 1994 A comparative study of criteria for subgrouping alcoholics: the primary/secondary diagnostic scheme versus variations of the type 1/type 2 criteria. Am J Psychiatry 151:1468–1474

Benkelfat C, Murphy DL, Hill JL, George DT, Nutt D, Linnoila M 1991 Ethanollike properties of the serotonergic partial agonist *meta*-chlorophenylpiperazine in chronic alcoholic patients. Arch Gen Psychiatry 48:383

Brunner HG, Nelen MR, van Zandvoort P et al 1993a X-linked borderline mental retardation with prominent behavioral disturbance: phenotype, genetic localization, and evidence for disturbed monoamine metabolism. Am J Hum Genet 52:1032–1039

Brunner HG, Nelen M, Breakefield XO, Ropers HH, van Oost BA 1993b Abnormal behavior associated with a point mutation in the structural gene for monoamine oxidase A. Science 262:578–580

Cloninger CR 1987 Neurogenetic adaptive mechanisms in alcoholism. Science 236: 410–416

Cloninger CR, Bohman M, Sigvardsson S 1981 Inheritance of alcohol abuse: cross-fostering analysis of adopted men. Arch Gen Psychiatry 38:861–868

Gilligan SB, Reich T, Cloninger CR 1988 Alcohol-related symptoms in heterogeneous families of hospitalized alcoholics. Alcohol Clin Exp Res 12:671–678

Glennon RA, Dukat M 1995 Serotonin receptor subtypes. In: Ploom FE, Kupfer DJ (eds) Psychopharmacology: the fourth generation of progress. Raven Press, New York, p 415–429

Goyer PF, Andreason PJ, Semple WE et al 1994 Positron-emission tomography and personality disorders. Neuropsychopharmacology 10:21–28

Higley JD, Thomson WT, Champoux M et al 1993 Paternal and maternal genetic and environmental contributions to cerebrospinal fluid monoamine metabolite concentrations in rhesus monkeys (*Macula mulatta*). Arch Gen Psychiatry 50:615–623

Irwin M, Schuckit MA, Smith TL 1990 Clinical importance of age at onset in type 1 and type 2 primary alcoholics. Arch Gen Psychiatry 47:320–324

Kruesi MJP, Hibbs EDL, Zahn TP et al 1992 A 2-year prospective follow-up study of children and adolescents with disruptive behavior disorders: prediction by cerebrospinal fluid 5-hydroxyindoleacetic acid, homovanillic acid, and autonomic measures? Arch Gen Psychiatry 49:429–435

Krystal JH, Webb E, Cooney N, Kranzler HR, Charney DS 1994 Specificity of ethanol-like effects elicited by serotonergic and noradrenergic mechanisms. Arch Gen Psychiatry 51:898–911

Lamparski DM, Roy N, Nutt DJ, Linnoila M 1991 The criteria of Cloninger et al. and von Knorring et al. for subgrouping alcoholics: a comparison in a clinical population. Acta Psychiatr Scand 84:497–502

Lappalainen J, Dean M, Charbonneau L, Virkkunen M, Linnoila M, Goldman D 1995a Mapping of the serotonin 5-HT1Dβ autoreceptor gene on chromosome 6 using a coding region polymorphism. Am J Med Genet 60:157–161

Lappalainen J, Zhang L, Dean M et al 1995b Identification, expression, and pharmacology of a Cys^{23}–Ser^{23} substitution in the human 5-HT2C receptor gene (HTR2C). Genomics 27:274–279

Linnoila M, DeJong J, Virkkunen M 1989 Family history of alcoholism in violent offenders and impulsive fire setters. Arch Gen Psychiatry 46:613–616

Monahan J 1984 The prediction of violent behavior: toward a second generation of theory and policy. Am J Psychiatry 141:10–15

Morell V 1993 Evidence found for a possible 'aggression gene'. Science 260:1722–1723

Moss HB, Yao JK, Panzak GL 1990 Serotonergic responsivity and behavioral dimensions in antisocial personality disorder with substance abuse. Biol Psychiatry 28:325–328

Mossman D 1994 Assessing predictions of violence: being accurate about accuracy. J Consult Clin Psychol 4:783–792

Nielsen DA, Goldman D, Virkkunen M, Tokola R, Rawlings R, Linnoila M 1994a Suicidality and 5-hydroxyindoleacetic acid concentration associated with a tryptophan hydroxylase polymorphism. Arch Gen Psychiatry 51:34–38

Nielsen D, Nakhai B, Schuebel K et al 1994b Tryptophan hydroxylase and the 5HT$_{1A}$ receptor: behavioral and gene expression studies. Abstr Am Coll Neuropsychopharmacol, 33rd Annu Meet, 12–16 December, San Juan, Puerto Rico

Nordin C, Swedin A, Zauhau AC 1993 Tapping-time influences concentrations of 5-HIAA in the CSF. J Psychiatr Res 27:409–414

Oxenstierna G, Edman G, Iselius L, Oreland L, Ross SB, Sedvall G 1986 Concentrations of monoamine metabolites in the cerebrospinal fluid of twins and unrelated individuals: a genetic study. J Psychiatr Res 20:19–29

Ozaki N, Lappalainen J, Dean M, Virkkunen M, Linnoila M, Goldman D 1995 Mapping of the serotonin 5-HT$_{1D\alpha}$ autoreceptor gene (5-HTRID) on chromosome 1 using a silent polymorphism in the coding region. Am J Med Genet 60:162–164

Pulkkinen L, Pitkänen T 1994 A prospective study of the precursors to problem drinking in young adulthood. J Stud Alcohol 55:578–587

Roy A, Virkkunen M, Linnoila M 1987 Reduced central serotonin turnover in a subgroup of alcholics? Prog Neuropsychopharmacol Biol Psychiatry 11:173–177

Siever L, Trestman R, Silverman J, Erdos J, Gelertner J 1994 Impulsivity and tryptophan hydroxylase allelic status in personality disordered patients. Abstr Am Coll Neuropsychopharmacol, 33rd Annu Meet, 12–16 December, San Juan, Puerto Rico

Sullivan JL, Baenziger JC, Wagner DL, Rauscher FP, Nurnberger JJ, Holmes JS 1990 Platelet MAO in subtypes of alcoholism. Biol Psychiatry 27:911–922

Tiihonen J, Hakola P 1994 Psychiatric disorders and homicide recidivism. Am J Psychiatry 151:436–438

Virkkunen M 1991 Brain serotonin and violent behaviour. Forensic Psychiatry 3:371–374

Virkkunen M, Linnoila M 1993 Brain serotonin, type II alcoholism and impulsive violence. J Stud Alcohol 11:163–169

Virkkunen M, DeJong J, Bartko J, Goodwin FK, Linnoila M 1989 Relationship of psychobiological variables to recidivism in violent offenders and impulsive fire setters: a follow-up study. Arch Gen Psychiatry 46:600–603

Virkkunen M, Rawlings R, Tokola R et al 1994a CSF biochemistries, glucose metabolism, and diurnal activity rhythms in alcoholic, violent offenders, fire setters, and healthy volunteers. Arch Gen Psychiatry 51:20–27

Virkkunen M, Kallio E, Rawlings R et al 1994b Personality profiles and state aggressiveness in Finnish alcoholic, violent offenders, fire setters, and healthy volunteers. Arch Gen Psychiatry 51:28–33

von Knorring A-L, Bohman M, von Knorring L, Oreland L 1985 Platelet MAO activity as a biological marker in subgroups of alcoholism. Acta Psychiatr Scand 72:51–58

DISCUSSION

Goldman: It's going to be crucial that we have available the sib-pair data set of approximately 160 pairs, which we have jointly collected with you, to validate the associations you discussed—especially the associations to the non-functional markers. It is important to move beyond the paradigm of marker association to verify effects of genes on phenotypes, since the marker associations have historically frequently proven to be fragile and unreplicable.

Plomin: Allelic association is much more powerful than linkage in the sense that allelic association can detect very small effects of quantitative trait loci that operate in multiple-gene systems (Plomin et al 1994). The strength of linkage is that it looks at the association between a marker allele and a disorder as they are transmitted within a family. Because there is so little recombination within a few generations in a family, a marker is able to scan a wide span of the chromosome, at least 10 million base pairs. For this reason, with about 300 markers, linkage can be used to search systematically the entire genome of 3 billion base pairs. But its search is limited to genes of major effect size. It would be marvellous if such major genes could be found in the population for complex behavioural traits, but it seems unlikely to me. In contrast, allelic association is myopic in that a marker can 'see' only a few hundred thousand base pairs away because it looks for associations in an outbred population rather than within a family, so that all but the tightest linkages between a marker and a quantitative trait locus have been eliminated by recombination. Rather than arguing which approach is better, however, I think we can agree that we need all the help we can get in identifying genes responsible for the ubiquitous heritability of behaviour, and that it is best to consider linkage and association as complementary (Owen & McGuffin 1993).

Goldman: If you have a genetic marker that is located very close to the gene acting to cause a trait difference, then you have the power to get a linkage signal in a population study. This association approach can be very powerful because you can collect very large association data sets and detect small but important effects. But then having found the association, what do you do next?

Plomin: The problem with linkage is that the closer you get to a gene, the harder it is to get any closer because there are fewer and fewer recombinations within a family. Association is not limited in this way: the closer you get to the gene, the easier it is to find association. We already have several examples in which linkage was used to find the general neighbourhood of a gene, and association was used to pinpoint the gene's address. None the less, it is no easy matter to find the gene, even when the search has been narrowed to a million base pairs. I believe that the indirect methods used now, such as exon trapping, will give way to association studies. That is, most genes will be mapped and cloned so that we can proceed directly to search an area for association with these known genes. One problem is that association is limited to finding old mutations that have been around for many generations—it will not help to find recent mutations or frequently occurring mutations. Moreover, there is the issue of false positive results. If many markers are examined for association, some positive associations will be found on the basis of chance alone. Precautions must be taken to avoid false positives but, at the same time, we must not go overboard and increase the risk of false negatives at this early stage of exploration. Rather than setting extremely high probability values, which make it impossible to find an effect unless it is essentially a major gene effect, I am much more in favour of replication.

Goldman: What bothers me is how easily we can detect 'significant' associations. We haven't published most of the statistically significant associations that we've seen. In this talk, a tryptophan hydroxylase association, a $5\text{-HT}_{1D\alpha}$ association, a $5\text{-HT}_{1D\beta}$ association and a 5-HT_{2C} association were all described. This seems like rather too much to hope for, on the basis of the biology.

Brunner: You've been showing us 5-HIAA data throughout, and the assumption is that this tells us about 5-HT metabolism. Do you have any direct evidence for this? What's happening to the other neurotransmitters, such as dopamine and noradrenaline?

Virkkunen: The levels of the dopamine metabolite, homovanillic acid, and 5-HIAA in CSF are interconnected. Usually, low 5-HIAA levels indicate low levels of CSF homovanillic acid. These levels need to be measured in CSF because urine measurements are not reliable. CSF 5-HIAA is thought to give a picture of the 5-HT turnover in the brain.

Brunner: Have you any direct information on CSF 5-HT levels in your patients, as opposed to 5-HIAA?

Virkkunen: It's very difficult to measure 5-HT from CSF.

Maxson: I have a question about the taxonomy of human aggression. What is the difference between impulsive and non-impulsive aggressive acts? How can you tell whether or not the aggressive acts are impulsive?

Virkkunen: We have used the Karokinska Scale of Personality for measuring impulsivity. There are also other impulsivity scales. But mainly we have defined impulsive violent crimes as violent acts that occur with no provocation at all or with very small (usually verbal) provocation, and where there is no monetary gain (i.e. excluding robbery).

Maxson: In the mouse studies, if a mouse is aggressive, you get endocrine and neurotransmitter changes. Is it possible that some of the neuroendocrine changes that you see in association, like the testosterone levels, are a consequence of their aggressive behaviour rather than a cause?

Virkkunen: It is difficult to say how important testosterone is because, even among normal males, testosterone concentration varies quite a lot. Testosterone is usually connected with verbal aggression, masculinity and dominant tendencies (leadership). Leaders of groups of apes have higher testosterone levels than group members. So having high levels of testosterone can be a good thing. Still, we have found very high levels of CSF free testosterone among habitually violent antisocial young adults (Virkkunen et al 1994).

Rutter: The point is that if you manipulate behaviour, there are effects on hormones, both in animals and in humans. The question is: given the sort of finding you have, how do you tell in which direction the causal effect operates?

Virkkunen: I cannot say, but we have made measurements in neutral situations.

Daly: Recent studies on short-term testosterone responses to competitive interactions in humans have produced interesting results. My favourite is Allan Mazur's finding that in the aftermath of a chess game between two closely matched men, the guy who wins has a massive elevation in his testosterone levels, whereas those of the guy who loses plummet (Mazur et al 1992). However, in a one-sided game in which there's no question about who's going to win, there are no consequences of winning or losing.

Goldman: Raleigh & McGuire (1991) have shown that 5-HIAA levels in vervet monkeys change with changes in social status. So the primate data cut both ways—5-HIAA levels are heritable, but they are also responsive to forces in the environment.

Virkkunen: Females also secrete testosterone, but only in very small amounts. There are preliminary Swedish findings that those females who are dysphoric and aggressive secrete more testosterone (Eriksson et al 1992).

Maxson: There are also suggestions that female aggression in mice is related to testosterone (Simon et al 1993).

Bohman: You (Dr Virkkunen) referred to Mark Schuckit's study of men at risk of developing alcohol abuse. It may be difficult and not very meaningful to compare his study with our adoption study where the biological parents were very much biased towards antisocial behaviours and low social status. In contrast, his subjects consisted of university students or non-academic personnel at a university or a hospital. These men will most likely be at very low risk of developing type 2 alcoholism or antisocial personality disorders. The same bias is also present in Vaillant's study of 456 non-delinquent male controls used by Sheldon and Glueck in their study of juvenile delinquency.

Dr Virkkunen, in your paper you have described a very special group of males with violent criminality and alcohol abuse. As you remember from my paper (p 99), we were able to identify among the biological fathers a subtype of alcoholic males with severe violent criminality who were serving long prison sentences, and who seem to resemble your subjects. These biological fathers had daughters with 'high-frequency somatization disorder', which was very similar to Briquet's syndrome. It would be interesting to know if you have information about somatization disorders or other disabilities among the female relatives of the males you have described.

Virkkunen: In our new cohort we have studied about 800 Finns (violent offenders with type 2 alcoholics and their relatives) as thoroughly as possible. We haven't found somatization disorders in these pedigrees. We have studied all relatives very thoroughly by SCID interviews.

Taylor: Once again I want to return to the issue of definition of behaviours. As an act of interest here, what is violence? And how does impulsiveness define it further? It seemed to me that we came close to the latter yesterday, when considering mice; perhaps similar parameters could be applied to humans. As I recall it, the definition had to do with the latency period between the received stimulus (to attack) and the act. Now, a problem with human beings and research is that, in most cases, the violence of interest occurred some time in the past. There may or may not be a corroborative account of the act itself, but the internal state of the patient is only questioned at best hours and at worst years after a significant index event or events. It then becomes extremely difficult to get an accurate description of what went on, not least because, in relation to much of the more serious and unlawful violence, the subject will have been given various messages about how it may be construed—for example, by law enforcers or lawyers. That said, in a hospital setting at least, it does appear possible to see differences in acts of violence, and impulsive violence does not equate with violence which has no obvious provocation. Much delusionally driven violence, for example, has no obvious external provocation, and may be extremely well planned and long considered; it is not impulsive at all. At the other extreme, some people with a psychosis may be exceptionally vulnerable to provocation, lashing out at the least stimulus from another patient or a member of staff, the latter for example trying to get the patient out of bed. Such a low threshold and rapid recourse to violence does not necessarily have to do with frequency, although that could be another indicator. The development and use of specific rating scales would help here, at the least having the advantage that one researcher would clearly know what another meant by the use of certain terminology and ratings, but still there is a need for caution.

Scales which measure traits or propensities, for example, which are often applied, may yield scores which correlate very poorly with acts (e.g. Gunn & Gristwood 1975).

Mednick: Pamela Taylor and Matti Virkkunen work with populations that are highly selective. If (as we do) you take large unselected populations, then the problem of differentiating between someone who has taken 10 s to decide to attack versus someone who has taken 30 s is impossible to determine and may not be critical. If you know the person has committed two violent offences and you can compare that violent individual with an individual who has not committed any offences, that is sufficient. But if you're looking within a population where everybody has been a murderer, then perhaps these greater details are important.

Taylor: We very much need enormous samples like yours, and the size of the sample may have to dictate that detailed, verified ratings cannot be made on all the people in such samples. Because, however, in any community sample, the vast majority of people included are not usually significantly violent, this should not be a great problem (on self-report, Swanson et al 1990 said 98% had not been violent over one 12 month period). It ought to be possible to investigate the violent subgroup further and clarify the qualities of the violence, and, for good measure, to apply similar ratings to a random same-size sample of the supposedly non-violent to check their status. The reason I am advocating this is because violence is not a homogeneous phenomenon any more than crime is. Precision with the genetic and uterine environmental configuration is important, and we have heard of the efforts expended to establish not only how many placentae but also how many amnitoic sacs were involved in multiple births, but all this sophistication is pointless unless the same intensity of effort is put into definition on the other side of the equation— definition of the behaviour or behaviours of interest.

References

Eriksson E, Sundblad C, Lisjo P, Modigh K, Andersch B 1992 Serum levels of androgens are higher in women with premenstrual irritability and dsyphoria than in controls. Psychoneuroendocrinology 17:195–204

Gunn J, Gristwood J 1975 Use of the Buss–Durkee hostility inventory among British prisoners. J Consult Clin Psychology 43:590

Mazur A, Booth A, Dabbs JM 1992 Testosterone and chess competition. Social Psychol Quart 55:70–77

Owen MJ, McGuffin P 1993 Association and linkage: complementary strategies for complex disorders. J Med Genet 30:638–639

Plomin R, Owen MJ, McGuffin P 1994 The genetic basis of complex human behaviors. Science 264:1733–1739

Raleigh M, McGuire MT 1991 Bidirectional relationships between tryptophan and social behavior in vervet monkeys. Adv Exp Med Biol 294:289–298

Simon NG, Lu SF, McKenna SE, Chen X, Clifford AC 1993 Sexual dimorphisms in regulatory systems for aggression. In: Haug M et al (eds) The development of sex differences and similarities in behaviour. Kluwer Academic, The Netherlands, p 389–408

Swanson JW, Holzer CE, Ganju VK, Jono RT 1990 Violence and psychiatric disorder in the community: evidence from the Epidemiological Catchment Area surveys. Hosp Community Psychiatry 41:761–770

Virkkunen M, Rawlings R, Tokola R et al 1994 CSF biochemistry, glucose metabolism and diurnal activity rhythms in violent offenders, impulsive fire setters and healthy volunteers. Arch Gen Psychiatry 51:20–27

Evolutionary adaptationism: another biological approach to criminal and antisocial behaviour

Martin Daly

Department of Psychology, McMaster University, Hamilton, Ontario L8S 4K1, Canada

Abstract. Although in a sense 'genetic', the conceptual framework of evolutionary psychology, behavioural ecology and sociobiology is distinct from that of behaviour genetics. Considerable confusion has resulted from failures to recognize the distinctions. These disciplines are primarily concerned with the characterization of evolved adaptations, which are usually species-typical and environmentally contingent, so theory and research in these fields mainly concerns environmental rather than genetic sources of behavioural variation. Heritable behavioural variation is in general neither predicted by nor supportive of adaptationist theories. One might even say that substantial heritability of an apparently consequential attribute is a datum that challenges the tenets of adaptationism. Behaviour genetics and evolutionary adaptationism have had only limited mutual influence, but increasing knowledge of the processes by which genotypes affect behavioural phenotypes should facilitate development of a more synthetic approach.

1996 Genetics of criminal and antisocial behaviour, Wiley, Chichester (Ciba Foundation Symposium 194) p 183–195

'Genetics of criminal and antisocial behaviour' can be broadly interpreted as encompassing research quite different in aims and methods from that of behaviour geneticists. Margo Wilson and I study homicidal violence, which is assuredly 'criminal and antisocial', and since our hypotheses come from 'evolutionary psychological' (or 'sociobiological') theories, they are in a sense 'genetic' (e.g. Daly & Wilson 1988a,b, Wilson et al 1993, 1996). Nevertheless, our expertise and interests are tangential to this conference's titular theme, and it may be useful to consider why. An explicit look at what distinguishes aims and claims of evolutionary psychologists from those of behaviour geneticists may clarify certain issues and help defuse some of the contention that surrounds 'biological' approaches in criminology.

Evolutionary psychologists, sociobiologists and behavioural ecologists share a paradigm, which we may describe as *evolution-minded, adaptationist behavioural science*. We shall call it EMABS for short, for although acronyms are abominations, we need a single label that avoids the distracting and often false connotations of the existing ones. The hallmark of EMABS is a certain kind of 'functional explanation' (Tinbergen 1963): researchers ask 'Why do the attributes of organisms take the forms they do and not others?', and seek answers in terms of adaptive function and natural selective pressures and history.

EMABS practitioners are fond of informational/control theory terms like 'algorithm' and of pseudomechanistic jargon like 'optimal memory window' or 'mental architecture'. It is tempting to mock this language as an attempt to claim the prestige of scientific materialism without its substance. However, the materialistic stance reflects a serious effort to characterize behavioural control mechanisms and processes with sufficient precision that hypotheses about functional 'design' can be rigorously evaluated. EMABS is (or aspires to become) the 'functional morphology' of mind and behaviour.

The EMABS approach has been so successful that it now dominates the study of non-human animal behaviour (see recent isues of *Animal Behaviour*, *Behavioral Ecology*, *Behavioral Ecology & Sociobiology*, *Behaviour* and *Ethology*). Nevertheless, adaptationist thinking has been caricatured and attacked as *post hoc* and unscientific, necessitating a digression in its defence. It seems to me that adaptationism is not merely useful, but inescapable, for it is hard to imagine how biological research could proceed without notions of adaptive function (Mayr 1983). There could be no neuroscience, for example, until the relatively recent discovery that information processing is what the nervous system is 'for'. Similarly, the very words 'digestion', 'vision' and 'respiration' embed hypotheses about what these processes are organized to accomplish.

Adaptationist thinking is most effective when it is guided by current understanding of selection, the process that creates adaptations. Psychologists have wandered down innumerable garden paths by imagining that adaptations are organized merely to promote homeostatic quietude, or personal growth, or longevity, or 'the reproduction of the species', or even death, when they are in fact organized to promote Darwinian fitness: the replicative success of one's genes, relative to their alleles, in a statistical aggregate of the environments encountered by one's ancestors. The realization that fitness is the final arbiter of adaptation often renders expectations generated by non-selectionist adaptationist thinking suspect. Can we expect, for example, that evolved mechanisms of maternal–fetal interaction will promote fetal well-being with minimal energetic and material wastage? Not if reproduction is sexual, so that maternal and fetal fitnesses are disjunct (Trivers 1974); this insight has illuminated a host of otherwise puzzling phenomena in human pregnancy (Haig 1993).

Adaptationist hypotheses are not claims about heritability

Similarly to functional morphologists, EMABS scientists strive to identify adaptations and to assess the validity of detailed notions about their functions by the criterion of 'good design' (Williams 1966, 1992). A sophisticated engineering analysis of design quality is occasionally possible, but even without mathematical criteria of good design, the functional integration of a complex whole may be sufficient to affirm exquisite precision of adaptation. The classic example is the vertebrate eye. Certain tissues must be transparent and others photosensitive for us to see. The adjustable iris usefully regulates incoming light while the adjustable lens usefully regulates focal distance. And so on and on, with details of musculature and lubricatory glands and visual pigment chemistry and (especially) neural processing all mutually coordinated and demonstrably fitted to their roles in the immensely complex task of vision.

Those components and attributes of eyes that play clear roles in the business of seeing are more or less species-typical. Significant departures from the prototype are 'pathologies': cataracts, colour blindness and detached retinas are variants that entail diminished visual capability and are likely to be selected against. We may therefore expect them to be rare (detached retinas) and/or late developing (cataracts); or to be otherwise subject to only weak selection, perhaps because of evolutionarily recent changes in selective forces (colour blindness?); or to have little if any heritability (other injury-induced pathologies).

It follows that heritable variation is decidedly *not* a criterion of adaptation. Quite the contrary, in fact: significant heritable variation is prima facie evidence (though by no means conclusive evidence) that the variable trait is irrelevant to proper functioning (Falconer 1960). For example, human iris colour ('eye colour') is both highly variable and highly heritable (in some populations), and it is no accident that it is also missing from our list of 'well designed' attributes above. Heritable variations in eye colour can persist because they are irrelevant to visual function.

This point is often misunderstood. Perhaps because the evolution of adaptation requires genetically based phenotypic variants as its raw material, it is often claimed that the positive demonstration of heritable variation provides support for—or is even a necessary condition for—an adaptationist hypothesis. An example comes from the literature on 'sexually selected infanticide'. In several species, a male who 'takes over' an already nursing female is likely to kill the young sired by his predecessor, with the result that the female soon returns to oestrus and reproduces with the killer. In an otherwise sophisticated discussion, Hrdy & Hausfater (1984) mistakenly assert that one of the implications of the hypothesis that such infanticide constitutes a sexually selected adaptation is that it should be 'heritable'.

Not so. If infanticide has been favoured by selection, the most likely state of affairs is that it will have gone to fixation, and even if we find that infanticide occurs after some but not other takeovers, the preferred adaptationist hypothesis would still be that males are alike in obeying an environmentally contingent 'decision' rule. Maybe infanticidal decisions are sensitive to cues of the females' willingness and ability to defend their young, for example, or to cues indicative of the predecessor male's relatedness to the usurper. Such hypotheses are our first resort both because they are testable and because the maintenance of a polymorphism of infanticidal and non-infanticidal phenotypes is not readily accounted for by the usual candidate processes such as frequency-dependent selection (see below). In any event, far from constituting support for the sexual selection hypothesis, substantial heritable variation would constitute reason to suspect that infanticidal behaviour had not been a target of selection after all.

Perhaps because the conceptual framework of EMABS is avowedly 'biological' and its theorists are apt to invoke 'genes' when explaining behavioural phenomena, many people seem to think that the 'explanations' sought by EMABS are of the same sort as those sought by behaviour genetics (BG). Herzog (1986) has documented how such a misrepresentation of 'sociobiology' has become a seemingly ineradicable 'meme' in introductory psychology textbooks. But in fact, theory and research in EMABS are overwhelmingly focused on predicting and explaining the detailed nature of environmental, not genetic, sources of behavioural variation (Crawford & Anderson 1989).

Our homicide research, for example, tests hypotheses about the social and circumstantial factors that might be expected to exacerbate or mitigate the conflicts characteristic of certain relationships and hence to elevate or reduce the risk of murder. The relevant theory concerns the prototypical attributes of certain relationships (mates, parent–offspring, unrelated same-sex acquaintances, and so on), and the responses of prototypical women and men to their immediate and chronic situations. The tests reside in demographic risk patterns. For example, lethal violence between unrelated men varies as a function of the protagonists' marital and employment status, life expectancy and prospects, in ways that bespeak modulation of competitiveness and risk-proneness in relation to expected gains and losses of fitness-relevant social and material resources (Daly & Wilson 1990, Wilson & Daly 1985). Constitutional differences among individuals are not what is at issue, and are ignored, either washing out statistically or remaining as 'noise'. This is also the dominant research strategy in studies of perception, memory, physiology, social psychology, or wherever the focus is on the shared substance of human nature, and although BG researchers may disparage it as 'essentialistic', it is an appropriate strategy for such questions.

This is not to deny that there are points of contact between EMABS and BG (perhaps especially in the study of sexual selection; see Andersson 1994), nor that further interchange and synthesis would be salutary. By and large, however, EMABS and BG are distinct paradigms with different questions, concepts and methods. Failure to recognize their distinctness has engendered a good deal of unnecessary confusion, not only among people who know little about either approach and are prejudicially hostile to both, but even among sophisticated life scientists.

And 'kin selection' theory isn't about heritability either

A seminal event in the rise of EMABS was Hamilton's (1964) analysis of 'the genetical evolution of social behaviour'. By extending the concept of fitness to include the actor's effects on the expected reproduction of collateral as well as descendant kin, Hamilton solved the paradox of the evolution of 'altruistic' actions that reduce the actor's expected reproductive success while enhancing that of another, and thereby replaced the classical Darwinian concept of organisms as 'reproductive strategists' with the notion that they have evolved to be 'nepotistic strategists', instead.

Hamilton's theory suggests that people, like other creatures, should possess an effectively nepotistic evolved social psychology, and it therefore seemed to us paradoxical that researchers had proclaimed the 'family' to be an arena uniquely imbued with violence. So we set out to assess whether genetic relationship might actually be associated with reduced risks of homicidal violence, other things being equal, instead; the evidence turned out to be fully supportive of this Hamiltonian expectation (Daly & Wilson 1988a,b). To our surprise and dismay, however, our demonstrations that the risk of lethal violence is reduced within genetic relationships have sometimes been portrayed, in both academic and popular writings, as BG claims about genetic differences between killers and other people.

This sort of misunderstanding afflicts EMABS research on non-human animals, too. Consider Sherman's (1977) classic study of alarm calling by ground squirrels, a textbook case of the problem of 'altruism'. Having detected a predator, the calling squirrel expends effort and draws attention to itself by a vocal act that seems designed to alert neighbours to the threat. Why not stay mum and let the neighbours take care of themselves? The plot thickens: some squirrels do just that. What Sherman then predicted and confirmed is that the probability that a given squirrel will call increases the closer its genealogical relationship to the neighbours who might benefit. In other words, alarm calling is facultatively deployed exactly as it should be if its function is nepotistic.

In an influential BG 'primer', this study was presented as a prototype of sociobiological research, which indeed it is. After a brief description of the research (which, despite omitting the most important results and misrepresenting others, conveyed much of its gist accurately), Plomin et al (1980, p 62) came to this conclusion:

> In this study, variation was observed in alarm calls within a species. The kinship selection theory [i.e. Hamilton's inclusive fitness theory] prediction that such altruism will be more common among individuals who have more relatives was confirmed for females. However, this does not prove that altruism has a genetic base, because relatives share environments as well as genes. For example, it is possible that females who rear young learn to protect them as they were themselves protected. If kinship selection theory is to be accurately applied, it is necessary to determine the extent to which observed variability is genetic in origin.

Apparently, Plomin et al (1980) suppose that the research must have been designed to address issues of (1) nature versus nurture (witness their comment about 'learning'), and/or (2) the role of genetic differences in determining behavioural differences. But Sherman's research was concerned with neither of these things.

Similarly to the eye and other important adaptations, the putative nepotistic adaptation whose properties Sherman explored was conceptualized as species-typical. His results confirmed that alarm-calling is a facultative behaviour, whose performance is contingent on the presence of relatives. What Sherman did *not* conclude is that 'altruism has a genetic base' in the BG sense, that is, that the difference between those squirrels who call and those who do not is a genetic difference.

But wait. Doesn't Hamilton's notion that apparent altruism is really 'nepotism' demand heritable variation? If non-relatives weren't systematically different from relatives at relevant genetic loci, how could nepotistic discrimination have any selective consequences? This tempting but erroneous line of thought is 'Washburn's fallacy'. According to Washburn (1978, p 415), 'Individuals whom sociobiologists consider unrelated share, in fact, more than 99% of their genes', and Hamilton's 'kin selection' theory therefore predicts extreme altruism towards all conspecifics and considerable favouritism even towards other related species.

But of course it is Washburn's reasoning that was fallacious, not Hamilton's, and perhaps the clearest refutation of the fallacy is that provided by Dawkins (1979), who notes that the issue is not overall genetic similarity, but evolutionary stability. A population of indiscriminate altruists is vulnerable to invasion by an initially rare 'nepotistic allele', but a population of nepotists cannot be invaded by a gene for indiscriminate altruism. Thus, alleles engendering nepotistic phenotypes should routinely go to fixation and stay there.

Population genetical theories such as Hamilton's are central to EMABS, but it does not follow that EMABS researchers are interested in tracing variation to genetic differences. The genetical models serve to address how selection would be expected to affect a trait, and to predict equilibrial states, but in those equilibrial states, heritable variation may be negligible. Again, the point is that both theory and research in EMABS are directed largely toward the discovery of species-typical adaptations, often expressed as contingent decision rules, so that environmental rather than genetic sources of behavioural variation provide the crucial evidence.

So what do adaptationists make of heritability?

Discoveries of heritable behavioural variation are in general neither predicted by nor supportive of EMABS theories. One might even say that substantial heritability of a seemingly consequential attribute is a datum that challenges the tenets of adaptationism rather than supporting them. Yet substantial heritabilities have been repeatedly documented by BG researchers, and many of these heritable traits seem likely to have important fitness consequences. How can these findings be reconciled?

Perhaps the least interesting possibility is that the variation in question is not in fact consequential, but 'neutral'. Much demonstrably heritable personality variation is likely to be functionless, for even heritable differences with seemingly dramatic behavioural consequences may have been subject to weak selection if evolutionarily novel aspects of the modern world have released or elicited novel phenotypic effects of genotypic variants that were inconsequential in ancestral environments—consider heritable variation in sensitivity to modern synthetic chemicals. Another way that heritable variation could be an artefact of evolutionarily novel conditions is if it is a product of recent mixing of formerly isolated and perhaps locally adapted populations; this conjecture would be strenghtened if temperament and behaviour were found to be less heritable within ethnically homogeneous populations than elsewhere. Finally, some heritable variation is surely the product of recent relaxation of particular selective forces. The congenitally blind, for example, now survive into adulthood and reproduce; what is less often remarked is that differential reproduction, and hence opportunity for selection of *any* sort, has plummeted in the western world in recent decades. All of these 'modern environments' arguments raise the question of whether measured heritabilities of personality, temperament and so forth would be smaller if assessed within foraging peoples living in circumstances more like those of our evolutionary past.

Perhaps more interesting is the idea that heritable diversity might often bespeak multiple adaptively significant behavioural phenotypes, somehow maintained by selection for their distinct utilities. However, this hypothesis is more onerous than some of its advocates have realized. It is not enough that each phenotype is sometimes fittest, for a selective advantage need only be an average advantage (and a very small one at that) to proceed to fixation.

Moreover, if the respective advantages are in any way correlated with environmental cues, a polymorphism of 'dumb' obligates will be evolutionarily unstable against invasion by 'cleverer' adaptively contingent phenotypes. Nevertheless, Wilson et al (1994) show that a polymorphism of specialists or even a range of continuous quantitative variation might in principle be maintained in a species having multiple niches if individuals can recognize and selectively occupy the niches to which their adaptations are best fitted. Wilson (1994) has speculated that human personality variability might reflect several such functional polymorphisms.

Perhaps a likelier process for the maintenance of at least some polymorphisms in human behaviour, including criminal and antisocial behaviour, may be 'frequency-dependent selection', whereby a variant is especially successful when it is rare. Mealey (1995) discusses the evidence that 'psychopaths' may be an adaptive type maintained at low frequencies by such selection. Gangestad & Simpson (1990) argue that diversity in human female sexuality may be maintained by the same force. How such ideas will fare is very much up in the air. Frequency-dependent selection is also a strong candidate for the maintenance of non-adaptive variation in personality and behaviour as a by-product of biochemical variation maintained by rapidly evolving disease organisms that impose disproportionate selective penalties on whichever alleles happen to be locally prevalent (Tooby & Cosmides 1990).

If this latter effect is important, then much of the heritable variation studied by BG researchers may be incidental to the selective maintenance of variation at an entirely different phenotypic level. And the question of which aspect of the phenotype has been the real target of selection is broader still. Familial concordance in aggressivity, for example, does not necessarily mean that there are heritable differences in the psychological mechanisms of aggression; in principle, everyone might be operating on the same contingent decision rule — if bigger than average be mean, say, and if smaller be conciliatory — with the result that whatever engenders heritability of height produces a 'reactive' heritability of meanness, too. Of course, all heritability of overt traits is 'reactive' in this way (i.e. traceable to some mediating proximate cause), but adaptationists will want to know which variations have been specifically maintained by virtue of their natural selective consequences, and which ones have hitched a ride. Studies elucidating the precise developmental and physiological factors mediating behavioural heritabilities (e.g. see other papers in this volume) may thus address EMABS hypotheses where mere demonstrations of heritability do not.

Acknowledgements

Thanks to Margo Wilson for critical discussion and research collaboration. Our homicide research has been supported by the Harry Frank Guggenheim Foundation, the Natural Sciences & Engineering Research Council of Canada, and the Social Sciences & Humanities Research Council of Canada.

References

Andersson M 1994 Sexual selection. Princeton University Press, Princeton, NJ

Crawford CB, Anderson JL 1989 Sociobiology: an environmentalist discipline? Am Psychol 44:1449–1459

Daly M, Wilson MI 1988a Evolutionary social psychology and homicide. Science 242:519–524

Daly M, Wilson MI 1988b Homicide. Aldine de Gruyter, Hawthorne, NY

Daly M, Wilson MI 1990 Killing the competition. Hum Nat 1:81–107

Dawkins R 1979 Twelve misunderstandings of kin selection. Z Tierpsychol 51:184–200

Falconer DS 1960 Introduction to quantitative genetics. Ronald Press, New York

Gangestad SW, Simpson JA 1990 Toward an evolutionary history of female sociosexual variation. J Pers 58:69–96

Haig D 1993 Genetic conflicts in human pregnancy. Q Rev Biol 68:495–532

Hamilton WD 1964 The genetical evolution of social behaviour. I & II. J Theor Biol 7:1–52

Herzog H 1986 The treatment of sociobiology in introductory psychology textbooks. Teach Psychol 13:12–15

Hrdy SB, Hausfater G 1984 Comparative and evolutionary perspectives on infanticide: introduction and overview. In: Hausfater G, Hrdy SB (eds) Infanticide. Aldine de Gruyter, Hawthorne, NY, p xiii–xxxv

Mayr E 1983 How to carry out the adaptationist program? Am Nat 121:324–334

Mealey L 1995 The sociobiology of sociopathy: an integrated evolutionary model. Behav Brain Sci 18:401–477

Plomin R, DeFries JC, McClearn GE 1980 Behavioral genetics: a primer. W. H. Freeman, San Francisco, CA

Sherman PW 1977 Nepotism and the evolution of alarm calls. Science 197:1246–1253

Tinbergen N 1963 On aims and methods of ethology. Z Tierpsychol 20:410–433

Tooby J, Cosmides L 1990 On the universality of human nature and the uniqueness of the individual: the role of genetics and adaptation. J Pers 58:17–67

Trivers RL 1974 Parent–offspring conflict. Am Zool 14:249–264

Washburn SL 1978 Human behavior and the behavior of other animals. Am Psychol 33:405–418

Williams GC 1966 Adaptation and natural selection. Princeton University Press, Princeton, NJ

Williams GC 1992 Natural selection: domains, levels and challenges. Oxford University Press, New York

Wilson DS 1994 Adaptive genetic variation and human evolutionary psychology. Ethol Sociobiol 15:219–235

Wilson DS, Clark AB, Coleman K, Dearstyne T 1994 Shyness and boldness in humans and other animals. Trends Ecol & Evol 9:442–446

Wilson MI, Daly M 1985 Competitiveness, risk-taking and violence: the young male syndrome. Ethol Sociobiol 6:59–73

Wilson MI, Daly M, Wright C 1993 Uxoricide in Canada: demographic risk patterns. Can J Criminol 35:263–291

Wilson MI, Daly M, Scheib J 1996 Femicide: an evolutionary psychological perspective. In: Gowaty PA (ed) Feminism and evolutionary biology. Chapman & Hall, New York, in press

DISCUSSION

Rutter: Kinship selection theory, as I understand it, is a theory: it is proposing a mechanism; it's not simply a descriptor. In so far as it is a theory, it is concerned with intergenerational change as it operates in relation to evolution. If you're not putting forward a Lamarckian view, what is the mechanism you're proposing?

Daly: Well, I'm not fond of the word 'mechanism' in this context, as it implies a device that is designed to achieve something—a goal-directed device, if you will—and the evolutionary process has no goals. But be that as it may.

Inclusive fitness theory—or kin selection theory, if you like—is a theory of the nature of evolved adaptations; it's a theory of the selection pressures to which they're adapted.

Explaining nepotistic behaviour in terms of inclusive fitness theory is analogous to explanations of functional morphology. You don't test the idea that our skeletal structure has become adapted evolutionarily to the demands of upright posture by measuring heritabilities or intergenerational changes; you do it by evaluating the fit between the hypothesized demands of upright posture and the observed structure. Similarly, the critical test of a hypothesis about a putatively nepotistic behavioural adaptation is whether its forms and its proximate causation are 'well designed' to bestow benefit discriminatively on kin.

Rutter: If it's evolutionary, it seems necessary that the mechanism involves genetically influenced variable traits, otherwise how will evolutionary change come about?

Rowe: The theory does postulate alleles that promote these behaviours, but for any species-characteristic adaptation like discriminative alarm calling, they are likely to have gone to fixation, and to be more-or-less monomorphic at any moment in time. Evolutionarily, these mutations must have occurred and risen in frequency up to 100%: that's where they stand now.

Goldman: We should be careful not to look at behaviours (as opposed to genes) as having been the individual objects of evolutionary pressure. For example, vulnerability to suicide could have been selectively maintained, not because suicide is somehow selectively advantageous (which is hard for me to imagine), but because suicidal behaviour is a consequence of something else that was selected for. Also, Stephen Jay Gould (1982) has pointed out that many of the behaviours we exhibit may not be adaptations but 'exaptations'. I think that many or most social behaviours have been subject to selection but, on the other hand, people living in different cultures and locales are being exposed to different pressures.

Daly: That was very much my point—the pressures are different. But I didn't want to treat homicide as a hypothesized adaptation analogous to discriminative alarm calling by ground squirrels. We are treating homicide as a rare conflict assay. I assume there's some functional significance to the psychology of interpersonal conflict and anger and aggressivity, and that there is adaptation in the ways in which conflictual inclinations are facultative or contingent, but that doesn't necessarily imply that homicide itself is adaptive.

Bouchard: In some populations half the people are killed by homicide, and these are populations that live in the environment of evolutionary adaptation. In some of the New Guinea tribes Napoleon Chagnon refers to, 40% of the men have killed someone. If that's representative of the environment of evolutionary adaptation, homicide is an adaptation.

Daly: There's been an odd debate among those who attend the Human Behaviour and Evolution Society meetings. The two largest disciplinary factions in this organization are psychologists and anthropologists. The debate concerns whether counting babies or studying mind design is the best way to do this research. I lean towards the mind design perspective, but there are people who think you can't make a good evolutionary argument without assessing the fitness consequences. The problem is, as you say, that the fitness consequences of some evolutionarily novel, unanticipated-in-ancestral-environments kind of circumstance are neither here nor there with respect to whether some aspect of the psyche is an adaptation. You could imagine selection designing the males of some species to be interested in not much else than maximizing the number of copulatory partners. Then somebody vulcanizes rubber and introduces an evolutionary novelty into such a population, and the males carry on happily maximizing utility but no longer promoting their fitness. The argument that sexual motivation was an adaptation is not gainsaid by this maladaptive response to novelty.

Rutter: With respect to the question of whether the age differences in crime reflect biological ageing, I do not know of any research findings that address that issue directly. However, the data on suicide carry a warning that we should test for biological ageing effects and not just assume them. It used to be argued that the suicide rate showed an invariant increase with age, but it is now apparent that it doesn't. Norman Kreitman (1988) re-analysed age changes in suicide rates after controlling for family circumstances. The curves for people who were single, married, divorced and widowed were quite different. Once family circumstances were controlled for, the age curve was lost after the early thirties. The age effect was not invariant.

Daly: There are many reasons to think that we've been designed to be maximally competitive and conflictual in young adulthood. Muscle strength is maximal in males and maximally sexually differentiated shortly after puberty, and then the sex difference declines. Aerobic capacity does the same. One interpretation is that males are in various ways specialized for conflict and competition in young adulthood. And there's research on 'taste for risk' that seems to imply the same. I'd be very surprised if age effects were to completely evaporate when we take out all social correlates.

Bouchard: The adaptationist argument falls off after a certain age. In the environment of evolutionary adaptation, we didn't survive into old age, so many of the behaviours that we see in old age may be quite irrelevant.

Daly: In a sense that's true, although you could say that if males have an evolved lifespan developmental trajectory of some functional significance, then there should be some organization to it, up to however late in life selection was significant. You often hear the argument that selection in middle age can't have been important because somebody has computed that the age of past populations was 30 or whatever, on the basis of archaeological skeletal samples. But those means are averages that include all the infant mortalities. In early societies, if you made it to adulthood, the chance of making it into your forties probably wasn't all that bad.

Hinde: Having established that a given pattern of behaviour is adaptive, what criteria do you use to differentiate that this behaviour is itself an adaptation, rather than representing the expression of propensities adaptive in other contexts? You need some additional argument.

Daly: Yes, I think you need to get psychological. You have got to back up from the behavioural level to some other level of abstraction. Does the emotional/motivational state of anger, for example, actually focus attention in ways that help us process the particular kinds of information that we need to process quickly in aggressive conflicts? Does it mobilize capability for a fight both peripherally and centrally? That sort of thing.

Heath: Is there any work by economists on rational theories of crime? They tend to be very quantitative in their thinking.

Daly: There is indeed. There's a whole school of criminology that is more-or-less economic in its ideas and language, whose practitioners treat property crime in particular as a rational choice. Unfortunately, there is a tendency to treat rationality as the antithesis of emotion. For example, there is a very interesting book called *The seductions of crime* by Jack Katz, in which he argued that criminologists have badly neglected the thrill-seeking aspect of being a 'bad dude', and the 'fun' that it is to do robbery and violence. He framed this as a critique of rational choice theories. For example, people often do vandalism when they do burglary, and the vandalism seems superfluous: he argued that this runs counter to any rational choice theory. However, if you think of there being a rationality to the emotions and the structure of the mind, that dichotomy seems less convincing. Katz describes cases of impulsive violence, for example, which he sees as impassioned and therefore irrational, but it seems to me that there is a social display function to the violence. For instance, three or four guys rob a convenience store together. They're all armed. They take the money and then one of them gets all angry and shoots the people that they've robbed when they are lying on the floor putting up no resistance. This seems like absolutely crazy behaviour on his part, and yet the reaction of his fellows is that they don't want to mess with him. In certain social contexts, the inclination to engage in dangerous displays of rage is not necessarily dysfunctional.

Mednick: You surprised me by saying that some social changes have no natural selective consequences.

Daly: There's been a lot of relaxed selection in the recent western world simply in the sense that variance in reproductive success has plummeted to nearly zero.

Mednick: That seems like an 'ethnocentric' view of the issue. Selection, I would guess, is still going on, but it may not be for what you think should be selected for.

Daly: The opportunity for selection is differential reproductive success. If *everybody* survives childhood and has 2.2 kids, there is no selection. In the western world we've moved a lot in that direction in the past 60 or 80 years. It also appears that differential survival and reproductive success were more extreme in the recent western world, such as in the 19th century, than they are in face-to-face and hunter–gathering societies. Perhaps differential reproduction got more extreme with the invention of agriculture, but has come down again in this century. This is what demographic data suggest. This doesn't mean that there can't be a lot of interesting selection going on, but the opportunity for selection has certainly diminished.

Mednick: Can you see any possibility of selection moving in ways that you wouldn't have anticipated, say, 100 years ago?

Daly: I'm sure there has been relaxed selection for vulnerability to various kinds of insults as a result of medical intervention, for example.

Bouchard: For instance, myopia.

Daly: Myopia could be a good example of a heritable phenomenon becoming phenotypically significant only because of evolutionarily novel circumstances. The argument has been made that only when small children do close work—reading, in particular—do they develop myopia. The vulnerability for myopia is highly heritable, but there's essentially no myopia in illiterate societies.

Hinde: One case that comes near to meeting this point is surely the fact that in many agricultural and preindustrial societies wealth is related to reproductive success, whereas it isn't in western Europe and North America (Vining 1986).

References

Gould SJ 1982 Darwinism and the expansion of evolutionary theory. Science 216:380–387

Kreitman N 1988 Suicide, age and marital status. Psychol Med 18:121–128

Vining DR 1986 Social versus reproductive success. Behav Brain Sci 9:167–216

General discussion IV

Rutter: I would like to raise the issue of whether an 'individual differences' approach is incompatible with one based on looking at social interactions and organization. Stealing might provide a sample model with which to start to address this question. The individual differences approach simply involves asking whether or not a person's overall propensity to engage in stealing is due to certain identifiable individual risk factors, and whether this is so across circumstances: the analyses deal with this by averaging behaviours across situations. There is then the very different question of whether, irrespective of those individual differences, stealing is more likely to take place in some situations than others. There is a substantial literature showing that theft is indeed more likely to occur in certain circumstances than in others. This takes for granted individual differences and averages across them. These approaches don't seem to be in contradiction at all, they're simply asking different questions; one on individual differences, one on level.

There is then a third question, which is whether the individual differences are specific either to particular types of behaviour or to behaviours that arise only in particular situations. In relation to crime, one might ask, for example, whether the explanations for the individual differences in liability to homicide are the same as for shoplifting in adolescence or for infanticide. I can't see that there's any paradox here.

Hinde: I like the way you put it about stealing, but there's one gloss that has to be added to this. If you're going to kill somebody, you may be influenced by what he thinks of you, or by what you expect him to do next on the basis of his past behaviour. Your relationship with him has properties that are more than his characteristics plus your characteristics, which is not true of the stealing case.

Cairns: I would like to insert development into this discussion. For many of the issues that we've talked about here, the time of exposure in any relationship has a great deal of predictive and explanatory power if one looks at what happens during that time interval.

How individual differences interact in a significant way with context and how the individual differences may contribute to the creation of the context, is a key area for future investigation. For instance, it's well known that there are strong links between aggressive and violent behaviour in an individual and the aggression for those with whom he/she associates. This holds throughout the literature. It's focused upon adolescents, but it is just as strong in school-age kids and continues on through adulthood. The social worlds created by individuals help support and maintain their ongoing behaviour. These outcomes of relationships can accentuate individual differences that brought people into relationships in the first place. We need to understand better how external supports—the relational contexts in which we live—are synchronized with the internal biases and preferences which are formed across development in individuals.

Carey: The generic problem of a person–time situation issue has actually been addressed in personality literature. It was a very heavy duty topic in the 1970s. The bottom line was generally that both personality traits and situations contribute to the way that one acts. Even an extrovert will behave slightly differently at a cocktail party than if he or she were meeting the Queen. But, surprisingly, very little interaction was found. You could sometimes find the interactions, but statistically they tended not to be very large.

Rutter: The other thing that came out of that debate was the problem of an inadequate classification of situations. There were lots of studies looking at situational effects, but in terms of deriving a general principle (i.e. this kind of situation has this kind of effect) they were not very successful.

Hinde: The personality measures you've used are designed to be cross-situational. That is, the questions covered a range of situations, so that they inevitably give a very superficial prediction of behaviour in any particular situation.

Rutter: Another issue we haven't talked about at all, is the association between crime and drug-taking. We've talked about the association with alcoholism, but we've said remarkably little about other drugs, even though there are well established associations.

Denno: I'm part of a Drugs/Violence Task Force, which was organized to work with and advise members of the United States Sentencing Commission on the current Federal Sentencing Guidelines for drug offenders. Each time our Task Force meets, we invite experts to tell us what they know about the alleged drugs–violence connection. Our preliminary conclusion is that most of the violence associated with drugs has to do with their marketing. It's much rarer to find violence associated with an individual's actual ingestion of drugs. We are examining this issue because the Federal Sentencing Guidelines are very stringent for drug offenders on the basis of, in part, an assumed drugs–violence link that doesn't appear to exist in any substantial way.

Carey: In our work, we're ascertaining a number of substance abusing adolescents. They tend to have substance abuse severe enough that they either get remanded or placed into a nine-month in-patient treatment setting. However, in both these adolescents and in our control group selected from the general population, aggressive behaviour tends to predate the onset of drug use, specifically with conduct disorder. As Deborah Denno has pointed out, many of the more serious types of crime associated with drugs are largely to do with marketing. We need to look at who is going to get into the marketing business to begin with and commit those crimes. There could be a very important link between conduct disorder and future drug use, and then future crime coming from participation in the drug world.

Daly: Presumably there are also very specific pharmacological drug effects on violence?

Denno: Yet experts will say that the ingestion of drugs typically doesn't cause individuals to become violent. If there is any cause–effect relationship at all, it appears to be in the opposite direction. Violent, aggressive or behaviourally disturbed individuals are relatively more likely to use drugs.

Rowe: These factors can easily be mutually reinforcing. There are experimental studies using some of the older aggression paradigms which show that individuals are more aggressive when they're given alcohol rather than a placebo.

Denno: Alcohol is an exception. There seems to be a link between the ingestion of alcohol and violence.

Daly: What about 'angel dust'?

Carey: There are deleterious side effects from drugs such as amphetamines. Irritability can certainly be a symptom of ingesting too much cocaine. In terms of proportions of variance, however, this type of statistical association between crime and substance abuse is relatively small.

Rutter: The Virginia Twin Study of Adolescent Behavioral Development has looked at the co-occurrence of antisocial behaviour and drug misuse in eight- to 16-year-olds. Judy Silberg, would you like to say something about the findings so far?

Silberg: The conclusions must necessarily be tentative both because the analyses are at an early stage and because data are still cross-sectional. The availability now of the first follow-up, some 15–18 months after the first assessment, will greatly facilitate the testing of hypotheses about causal mechanisms. Nevertheless, the latent class analyses undertaken so far bring out four important points (L. Eaves, personal communication). First, our findings confirm the frequency with which antisocial behaviour co-occurs with substance misuse, but also show that there is a substantial proportion of adolescents who use drugs but who do not engage in delinquent or other antisocial activities. Second, in line with other studies (e.g. Robins 1986), the latent class of multisymptomatic individuals who use drugs was similar in males and females in terms of the finding that the main co-occurrence was with oppositional defiant and antisocial behaviour, but different in that this extreme multisymptomatic class was more likely to include affective disturbances in females. Third, shared environmental effects predominated in this extreme multisymptomatic group. The finding constitutes an important reminder that the most deviant behaviours are not necessarily the most genetic. Fourth, the class of relatively 'pure' substance misuse (without antisocial behaviour) had a much stronger genetic component. This finding is interesting because, on the face of it, this recreational use of drugs by young people without major psychopathology seems both more normal and more sociocultural in origin. Despite that, genetic factors were important in individual differences.

Cairns: In agreement with what's been said, aggression in childhood has been identified across a whole range of longitudinal studies as being a primary risk factor for a number of problems, including hard drug use. It's not only that aggressive kids are at risk of harming other persons, they harm themselves. And the females are at risk of harming their offspring, which is a problem for adoptive models. But what about the issue that a couple of longitudinal studies have identified: the differential association of males and of females with others like themselves in aggression and violence. In adolescence, this leads immediately to the 'musical chairs' that you have in assortative mating. This provides a mechanism for transmission to the next generation. It looks like there is differential association in terms of aggression, not only with members of the same sex, but there also appears to be differential association across sexes during this reproductive phase.

Bouchard: The data on personality show much less assortative mating than everyone expected.

Hinde: I do not agree. The evidence in favour of some similarity in personality between mates is considerable, though the degree of similarity may not be great. This applies even to the trait of 'dominance' (Katz et al 1960).

Rowe: I analysed this in the London study that David Farrington did (D. C. Rowe & D. F. Farrington, unpublished results). The tetrachoric correlation for convictions in husbands and wives is about 0.50.

Bouchard: That's a higher level of assortative mating than for IQ. I find that hard to believe.

Rowe: I don't think that this correlation implies that criminal men seek criminal wives. It's more that the social availability of people creates this: because our society is very good at moving people with different kinds of traits into different social settings where they can find their mates. I'm unconvinced that people screen their mates as strongly as most assortative mating models would suggest.

Rutter: Certainly, our data on antisocial behaviour show strong assortative mating (Quinton et al 1993). Antisocial behaviour is the one variable where assortative mating is very powerful, and it is very important to take this into account in analyses.

Bouchard: You would expect to see assortative mating for Eysenck's measure of psychoticism.

Heath: For Eysenck's personality variables, I think the marital correlations are zero to the third decimal place. That may just be a reflection of the fact that psychoticism as measured by Eysenck has almost nothing to do with antisocial behaviour.

Cairns: When we compute intraclass correlations to determine levels of within-social-group similarity, we find that aggressive behaviour is the dominant behavioural dimension upon which group members are similar. This effect holds for males and females. So it's fairly general—we're talking about overt and highly salient activity that tends to provide a basis for mutual association among same-sex kids in adolescence.

Bouchard: The trouble-makers hang around together and the nerds hang around together: is that it?

Cairns: Yes, except the evidence for 'nerd' homophily is less strong.

Rowe: It is striking that interaction effects are absent in behaviour genetic data on natural populations. There are three reasons why I think they're absent. First, a lot of homeostasis exists in physiological and behavioural systems, where both tend to return to some kind of norm when deflected by the environment. A second process is these correlational effects. If we could randomly assign kids to different neighbourhoods, we might actually discover interactions. For instance, timid kids in tough neighbourhoods would be very anxious. This would show up as a big interaction. But because children (and adults—consider political orientation similarity among friendship networks) self-select their companions, these interactions are obviated. The third reason is genetic: any gene is thrown in with a different genetic background every generation. It must be, on average, able to produce its effect in the presence of many backgrounds.

Rutter: Bob Cairns, in relation to your developmental concern, there are two very striking, but utterly different, examples that illustrate the point that there may be different causal mechanisms operating at different points in the causal chain.

The first example is provided by Lee Robins' study of Vietnam veterans (Robins et al 1977). When she considered heroin addiction at follow-up sometime after return to the USA as her dependent variable, sociodemographic variables had no effect on the endpoint behaviour. When she analysed it on a step-by-step basis, however, there were two strong correlates, but they worked in opposite directions at different points in the causal process. Thus, inner-city blacks constituted the group with the greatest likelihood of taking heroin in Vietnam. By contrast, of those who took heroin in Vietnam, it was the group of rural whites who were most likely to be addicted a year later. Sociodemographic variables *did* have an effect but they worked in different ways at different points in the chain leading from taking heroin in Vietnam, through continuing to take it on return to the USA, to becoming addicted to the drug.

The other example is from an earlier Ciba Foundation symposium on *The childhood environment and adult disease* (Bock & Whelan 1991), where there were several examples of effects that differed significantly depending on the stage of development. One example is that in middle life, being overweight is a substantial risk factor for coronary artery disease, whereas in the first year of life being underweight is a powerful predictor of coronary heart disease.

References

Bock GR, Whelan J (eds) 1991 The childhood environment and adult disease. Wiley, Chichester (Ciba Found Symp 156)

Katz I, Glucksberg S, Krauss R 1960 Need satisfaction and Edwards PPS scores in married couples. J Consult Psychol 24:205–208

Quinton D, Pickles AR, Maughan B, Rutter M 1993 Partners, peers and pathways: assortative pairing and continuities in conduct disorder. Dev Psychopathol 5:763–783

Robins LN 1986 The consequences of conduct disorder in girls. In: Olweus D, Block J, Radke-Yarrow M (eds) Development of antisocial and prosocial behavior: research, theories and issues. Academic Press, New York, p 385–414

Robins LN, Davis DH, Wish E 1977 Detecting predictors of rare events: demographic, family and personal deviance as predictors of stages in the progression toward narcotic addiction. In: Strauss JS, Babigan HM, Roff M (eds) The origins and course of psychopathology. Plenum, New York, p 379–406

Chronic problems in understanding tribal violence and warfare

Napoleon A. Chagnon

Department of Anthropology, University of California at Santa Barbara, Santa Barbara, CA 93016, USA

Abstract. This paper discusses problems confronting researchers whose work addresses the nature, causes and functions of violence and warfare in contemporary tribal societies and the interpretation of evidence on these topics from archaeological records. A major problem is the paucity of reliable ethnographic evidence describing conflicts, causes of conflicts and numbers of casualties suffered. There are few first-hand studies of warring tribesmen and little uniformity in data collection methods or specific topics covered by the studies. A second problem is the wide range of theoretical opinion on ultimate versus proximate causes of conflict and often polemic insistence that some causes cannot even be admitted into the explanatory framework, as illustrated by the debate between cultural materialists and evolutionary anthropologists. A third problem is the widespread belief that pre-colonial conflict and warfare was either rare or did not exist at all and that where contemporary tribesmen are found to be in lethal contests this has been provoked by contact with European colonial expansion. Finally, a new problem is emerging: ethnographic descriptions of violence in tribal societies are increasingly opposed by politically correct academics who argue that it is detrimental to the goals of advocates of native cultural survival. The paper concludes with a summary of some of the main features of Yanomamö violence and warfare, based on the author's field research and publications up to 1990, and introduces new data and theoretical issues that are emerging from his most recent field studies since 1990.

1996 Genetics of criminal and antisocial behaviour. Wiley, Chichester (Ciba Foundation Symposium 194) p 202–236

Let me begin with a discussion of what I mean by 'primitive' society, that kind of society to which my comments here are intended to apply.

The phrases 'primitive society' or 'primitive world' are generally taken to mean in anthropology societies whose social and political activities are almost exclusively organized around principles of kinship, marriage and descent. These three principles provide the internal social cohesion and integration of such societies—and embody most of the 'rules' and 'laws' about proper and improper behaviour. The primitive world is a kinship-organized and kinship-dominated world in which almost all the specialized institutions we are familiar with—courts, executives, judiciaries, armies, police, etc.—are absent as institutions. But the functions served by these institutions are 'embedded in' kinship groups, marriage-alliance groups and descent groups. There are leaders, but they are not dictators or presidents. They are usually men who have the largest number of kin in the group. There are 'rules' and 'customs', but they are not laws and, in the absence of courts, police and systems of justice, people can and often do 'take the law' into their own hands.

The primitive world includes all human societies for approximately the past 100 000 years, known only from archaeological data, and all pre-state societies that persisted into the 20th century but conducted their social and political affairs in complete or relatively complete isolation from state-organized societies. Cultural evolutionists, particularly in the USA, recognize and have defined various 'types' of primitive societies that range from less complex to more complex in terms of social organization, maximum size of permanent social group, and type of economy.[1] It is generally assumed that the smallest-scale, least-complex contemporary human societies—hunting and gathering peoples for example—more accurately represent the earliest human conditions found in early palaeolithic archaeological sites, and that larger-scale, more socially complex societies represent conditions that have developed more recently, such as the development of agriculture and the social, political and demographic revolutions this event provoked during the past 8000–10 000 years in various parts of the globe.

It is fundamental to the understanding of 'violence' and 'warfare' in the primitive world to keep in mind the type of society under discussion, for not all primitive societies have the same potential or capacity to engage in various types of conflict, either within the group or between politically distinct groups. Thus, the Bushmen of the Kalahari desert live in small groups that fluctuate in size from a dozen or so people to upwards of 50 people. Some Highland New Guinea societies and some African tribes number into the scores and hundreds of thousands, and members live in communities that may reach several hundred inhabitants. All are primitive societies, but not all are equal in kinds of, amounts of and capacities for lethal conflicts.

---

[1]Interested readers can consult any number of anthropology textbooks that define and discuss these evolutionary types and the high amount of variation found in them. Two useful introductions would be Fried (1967) and Service (1971).

The anthropological literature on warfare and violence in the primitive world is abundant and appears to be increasing, but the database on which it rests is small and is a very confusing and highly mixed bag, some characteristics of which I will discuss below.

First, the number of well-documented studies of tribal warfare by trained anthropologists who lived among the people at a time when they were still conducting warfare is very small—fewer than a dozen. Most of them come from Highland New Guinea and a few come from Lowland South America. Most 'sovereign' tribesmen[2] had long been pacified by the time anthropologists arrived to study them.[3] Thus, despite the increasing numbers of anthropological publications about primitive warfare, the database remains extremely small and opportunities to make field studies among yet-warring tribesmen have all but disappeared.

One consequence of the rather limited nature of the relevant database is the paucity of information on certain kinds of crucial topics, such as statistical information on rates of death due to violence, how people are related to each other expressed in some form of genealogical data, frequencies of conflict, native explanations for the conflicts, and data on long-term histories of previous conflicts between the same groups. These deficiencies are in part due to the fact that different anthropologists, because of differences in their training and in their specific interests, document different things. There is no agreed-upon set of topics, making it quite possible for two anthropologists trained at different universities to study the same warring tribe and produce results with very limited overlap—one of them might prefer a quantitative approach and count, weigh and measure lots of things, whereas the other may prefer a qualitative approach and focus on collecting verbal accounts of battles, skirmishes, etc.

A second problem in the study of primitive warfare stems in part from one of the items mentioned above—differences in training of anthropologists and the epistemological consequences. There is a wide range of theoretical opinion in the anthropological literature on primitive warfare. Some anthropologists argue, on first principles, that the subject matter of anthropology is 'cultures' or 'institutions' and not people with motives, attitudes, and actions—much less

---

[2]By 'sovereign', I mean tribesmen whose politics and warfare are not controlled by or affected by larger, more complex societies such as nation states. These would, however, include many societies where some items from the outside world have managed to find their way into otherwise isolated and remote areas. Thus, almost all the Highland New Guinea societies are heavily dependent on the cultivation of sweet potatoes, a crop introduced into Melanesia from the Americas after 1492.

[3]A useful, recently published bibliography of studies of primitive warfare is Ferguson (1988).

so as evolved organisms with biological histories, behavioural patterns, psychological mechanisms and ultimate goals that have been shaped by the process of evolution by natural selection in the long-term environments of history. In this paradigm, the actions of individuals and their strivings are considered to be irrelevant to the study of warfare and aggression in the primitive world: what individuals do, they do for the group or their culture, nor for themselves.

For example, one of the prominent and widely accepted approaches to the study of primitive warfare in the USA is found in many works of Marvin Harris (1974, 1977, 1979, 1984). His view is essentially that the material conditions of human existence can alone explain how and why cultures are constructed the way they are and what functions cultural institutions serve to make life more secure and 'adaptive' for people. His view is emphatically materialist, but ironically he argues that it is also evolutionary. But for him and his followers, it is culture that evolves and adapts, as if it were an organism, and the process of evolution deals almost exclusively with survival—principally of cultures and institutions, secondarily of the people who have them. Individuals and their evolved characteristics are 'factored out' of the cultural equation, a sociocentric dictum that goes back to the work of French sociologist, Emile Durkheim (1895), who argued to the effect that anytime a social fact is reduced to and explained in terms of a 'psychological' fact (and presumably a biological fact), you can be sure the explanation is false. This perspective has been adopted by the cultural materialist approach, largely because of the efforts of Leslie A. White (1949) and, later, Marvin Harris himself (1979).

Thus, warfare and other forms of violence in the primitive world exist because of shortages of material resources and can be adequately explained in exclusively resource-shortage terms. But the argument is logically redundant: people fight only over scarce material resources, shortages of which are evidenced by the fact that they are fighting. A. P. Vayda, one of the US scholars associated with the development of the materialist approach to the study of primitive warfare in the 1960s and early-1970s, later reflected on some of the mistakes, omissions and commissions in this approach: he admitted that he and others simply assumed that all or most primitive peoples were living at or near carrying capacity (Vayda 1989). Many groups, however, are probably just entering the ecological niches they occupy and are probably nowhere near reaching carrying capacity. The Yanomamö fall into this category (Chagnon 1990), as apparently do many other tribal groups, especially in the Amazon basin where fighting has historically been very common and intense but population densities very low. Unless there is clear and well-documented evidence for shortages of material resources, it is prudent to look for other reasons that are widely known to cause conflicts among humans.

Although there are many useful and valuable elements in the materialist approach, its major defect is that it refuses to (and is largely opposed to) considering human striving, especially reproductive competition, as causes of conflict, violence and fighting in the primitive world (Harris 1984, Chagnon 1990). A second important defect is the assumption that cultures as 'homeostatic' (self-adjusting, self-correcting) systems are analogous to, if not homologous to, living organisms and therefore the theory of evolution by natural selection can be fruitfully applied to both. But cultures do not 'reproduce' as organisms do, and some of the most important understandings in biology are left entirely out of the materialist theory of evolution: human conflicts frequently grow out of reproductive competition and sexual jealousy, and the theory of evolution by natural selection is a theory about the reproductive survival of individuals, not about the survival of groups or cultures. The materialists dismiss and often denigrate reproductive sources of conflict, as one of them put it in a criticism of some of my work, as 'libidinal speculation' (Ross 1978, Ross & Ross 1980).[4]

A third problem in the study of violence and warfare in the primitive world is the assumption that it is not an important topic because violence and warfare are rare events in the primitive world. Given the extremely few ethnographic studies of primitive warfare, this view is plausible, if not statistically defensible: there are far more ethnographies about non-warring people than there are about warring people. But this view stems more from a general philosophical, if not moralistic, preference for a Romantic view of the primitive world (typified by Jean-Jacques Rousseau's paradigm of the 'noble savage'), and especially the palaeolithic past about which we know very little except from archaeology. Thus, many anthropologists play down or dismiss as erroneous reports of violence and warfare in tribal societies, even when the accounts are well documented and the observations are repeated and independently verified by others. There is a moral premium associated with denying that violence can occur among primitive peoples living in their 'natural' state, which is assumed to be tranquil and largely free of conflict.

Several kinds of scientific difficulties result from this.

---

[4]At the School for American Research Conference on 1986, out of which came a volume entitled *The anthropology of war* (Haas 1990), I presented a paper discussing the somatic and reproductive aspects of conflict among the Yanomamö Indians. The discussant of my presentation was one of Marvin Harris's students, R. Brian Ferguson, a disciple of the materialist approach and opponent of biological approaches to human conflict. He began with a statement to the effect, 'I don't understand why you sociobiologists want to bring sex and reproduction into this. After all, when you have enough to eat, reproduction is more or less automatic.' See Ferguson (1989), Chagnon (1989a).

Professional rebuke. First, those anthropologists who produce ethnographic accounts of violence and warfare based on their observations are frequently criticized and accused of misanthropic malice (e.g. Carneiro da Cunha 1989) or of subscribing to an arbitrary Hobbesian view (Ross 1980). They are usually accused of either exaggerating the amount of violence that occurs, or of simply inventing it (Albert 1989; cf. Chagnon 1989b). There is a subtle system of professional censure that rewards people who deny that violence is common in the primitive world or who soundly criticize others who report on details of it in the societies they have studied (Chagnon 1989c).

Warfare is introduced by westerners. Second, there is a premium attached to explaining the undeniable occurrence of violence and warfare as either being an extremely rare thing in the anthropological literature—the occasional quirk or pathology—or by arguing that the natives who are engaged in it had it inflicted on them from the outside, capitalists from industrialized countries being a commonly cited source. This is based on the assumption, above, that primitive man in the state of nature is cooperative, non-violent and altruistic.

An amusing caricature of this view was captured in the popular film 'The Gods Must Be Crazy'. The happy, conflict-free Bushmen were going about their hunting and gathering business in the Kalahari desert, following their ancient ways of cooperation and amity. Then a plane flies overhead one day and the pilot sucks down the last gulp of his Coca-Cola and thoughtlessly discards the bottle out of the window. The Bushmen find it, are puzzled by this strange new materialist, capitalistic item, and begin arguing and fighting over it. The squabbling and discontent grow to intolerable levels and people are getting hurt in their struggles to possess this item. They then decide they liked the pre-Coke bottle days when nobody fought over anything. One of them is designated to take the Coke bottle to edge of the earth and toss it over. Peace and tranquillity are restored.

More serious attempts to make the same kind of argument are now beginning to appear as it becomes increasingly fashionable and politically more correct to explain away violence and warfare in native societies as something that post-dates colonialism and the undesirable effects of capitalism on native cultures. For example, R. Brian Ferguson has attempted to explain my data on Yanomamö warfare in essentially similar terms in several recent publications (Ferguson 1992, 1995), and has a book-length study of Yanomamö warfare in press. If you substitute the words 'machete' or 'steel tool' for 'Coke bottle', you get an academic version of 'The Gods Must Be Crazy' theory of primitive warfare.

Ideas of Indians are preferable to real Indians. The third (and newest) difficulty posing problems for the scientific study of violence and warfare in the primitive world is the rapidly growing intellectual movement (in at least the US academic community) known as post-modernism, deconstructionism, interpretivism and several other names. This is a complex movement with several distinct roots, a prominent one being the anti-scientific, and anti-intellectual works of Derrida and Foucault in literary studies. In overall philosophical and political tone, it tends to be associated with the rhetoric of the political left. Indeed, the entire ensemble of ideas has been given the name 'the academic left' in a widely cited recent book on the topic (Gross & Levitt 1994). This movement is having extraordinary impact on the American academic and educational communities. It involves 'deconstruction' of previously held theories and views, including well-established theoretical views and evidence in the hard sciences, and substitutes sometimes arbitrary and implausible alternatives. It tends to be highly 'feminist' and accords many previous ideas, discoveries and inventions assumed to have been made by (mostly white) men to women or to men and women from non-white populations and cultures. It argues that there is no such thing as an objective, real world and that alleged observations on the world are simply arbitrary constructs determined by the cultural views of the purportedly objective observer: facts are simply the distorted ideas of the observer of a non-existent real world. Since they are just arbitrary ideas, and the world is not real, then anybody's idea about the world is as good as anybody else's. Those who purport to be objective scientists constitute a conspiracy of white males from capitalistic countries whose hidden agenda is to maintain the academic status quo, where white men have all the privileges and rewards and suppress minority groups and women. Although this might sound preposterous, there are a number of recent, highly detailed studies and analyses of these trends (Gross & Levitt 1994, Carroll 1995).

More specifically, these ideas have become firmly established in many academic disciplines, including anthropology, and tend to be used to repudiate alternative, more empirical 'scientific' approaches. Cultures are no longer cultures, but texts. The role of the anthropologist is to 'interpret' the text with literary techniques, ideally using language and concepts so vague, imprecise and muddled that only the elect among the proponents purport to understand them. There is in fact an explicitly stated and admired goal: the more obtuse and unintelligible an interpretation is, the better it is. Cultures become constructs—an idea or set of ideas proffered by one of the interpreters, who fully realize the arbitrariness of their own constructs. They generously extend and attribute to others the same courtesy—their views are equally arbitrary and also freely invented. Since there is no objective real world, there is little need for anthropological field work, especially in places that are hard to get to and uncomfortable to live in. One can now simply 'invent' a culture in the comfort of one's office, and go about interpreting it.[5]

---

[5]These assertions might seem preposterous, but they are documented and discussed in D'Andrade (1995).

Given some of the previously mentioned epistemological threads in anthropology, these new intellectual trends are leading to a view that real people and the real things they do are just arbitrary constructs. If you want to construct an Indian, make him what you want him to be and let him do what you want him to do. And, if it is politically more correct and morally desirable to construct a Rousseauesque savage, that is the thing to do. And, in fact, that is now what appears to be happening.

In the case of the Yanomamö, who are now very much threatened by the invasion of illegal gold miners and are also highly visible in the academic as well as the public world, significant numbers of 'survival' groups have appeared, which claim to speak for the Yanomamö and to save them. They appear in general to operate on the assumption that this can be most readily accomplished by creating an ideal and highly desirable picture of a Yanomamö, regardless of how widely that image deviates from what real Yanomamö are like. Since there is considerable competition among these well-intentioned survival groups, they appear to be vying with each other to create the most highly polished view of an ideal, blemish-free Yanomamö and to identify and denounce all evildoers and the evils they do who are harming them, inventing evildoing where need be because the competition may scoop them on this or invent a better, more noxious evil. Needless to say, the ideal Yanomamö don't engage in warfare or violence and those who say they do are evildoers, probably in league with known evildoers such as miners, whose evildoing is so apparent and obvious to everyone that it doesn't have to be invented.

Summary

The history of anthropology (with its built-in aversion to both biological models and the consideration of human striving as relevant to understanding conflict), the preference for a Rousseauesque view of the primitive world within which warfare and violence are seen as rare, or pathological, or introduced by outsiders, and the growing intellectual, politically correct trends that deny the very existence of an objective real world and arbitrarily invent constructs of it, all contribute to the difficulty of studying violence and warfare in the primitive world. Since the amount of high-quality data on violence and warfare in sovereign tribes is small to begin with, and tribesmen everywhere are either being decimated or incorporated into more complex political systems, it is unlikely that much new, useful anthropological information can be collected in field studies in the future. Even where they can be done, opposition to such studies by the academic left is intense and adds to the likelihood that in the few places such studies are possible, they will not be conducted.

Data on palaeolithic and tribal violence

There are three possible sources of data on violence in the primitive world: palaeontological, archaeological and enthnographic. Let me make a few comments about each.

Palaeontological data

The study of violence and warfare in human history should take into consideration evidence from the fossil record. Several problems immediately come to attention when the palaeontological record is considered.[6]

For the earliest fossil forms there is the question of the degree to which their behaviour might have been representative of the behaviour of *Homo sapiens*. Palaeontologists classify most of the fossil antecedents to *H. sapiens* into different genera. Very little can be said about the social organization of and amount of violence—or its causes—in these fossil hominoids. Nevertheless, a few comments are in order.

There has been no recent publication discussing the evidence for violence based on a comprehensive survey of fossil hominoids. White and Toth are currently engaged in such a survey, but have not yet published their results.[7]

Over 30 years ago Robert Ardrey (1961) popularized the research and arguments of Raymond Dart, who discovered and did extensive forensic studies on South African 'ape-men' fossils now known collectively as the Australopithicenes. They lived some two million years ago. Both Dart and Ardrey attempted to create a picture of 'killer apes' regularly engaged in violent contests that involved high rates of within-group or between-group lethal conflict, based on Dart's interpretation of traumas found on crania and other bones of these fossil forms. Most palaeontologists and physical anthropologists reject their views on the grounds that most of the evidence for violence found on the bones could be explained more easily as post-mortem modifications caused by carnivores and scavengers. There is, however, one element of truth in Ardrey's otherwise discounted, but very popular book: there was extreme opposition among anthropologists to the view that violence occurred in our past, and that opposition was not entirely explainable by the nature of the physical evidence.

---

[6]It would, of course, be useful to discuss the occurrence of violence among non-human primates, which is beyond the scope of this paper. See, however, the fascinating paper by Manson & Wrangham (1991), which argues that chimpanzees engage in intergroup 'exported lethal violence' that has striking similarities to human warfare.
[7]My summary here is based very heavily on personal information provided to me by T. White, to whom I am grateful.

A similar conclusion must be drawn about *H. habilis*—there are few fossils, but the damage to them could have been caused by carnivores.

Although it is possible to interpret cranial damage in fossils of *H. erectus* (*Choukotien*) as evidence of cannibalism, other interpretations are possible and palaeontologists tend to be sceptical that cannibalism is the only explanation. Moreover, the original fossil skulls have been lost and the existing casts of them are insufficiently precise for more technical studies.

Neanderthal fossils are more abundant and, accordingly, possible evidence for violence is likewise more abundant. At the moment, White and Toth are having difficulties obtaining access to a number of specimens found in France, but what evidence exists indicates that there is a good possibility that cannibalism occurred among them, especially in the (unpublished) study of fossils from Karapina and a site in Vindija, tens of thousands of years earlier. In general, there is considerable evidence of trauma to post-cranial parts of Neanderthal fossils in larger collections, but how this relates to interpersonal of intergroup violence is still an open question.

Interestingly, the anthropological polarity between a Rousseauesque view of natural man and a Hobbesian view is also expressed in the study of hominoid fossils—Dart's 'killer ape' hypothesis is more Hobbesian than the Leaky/Isaac 'gentle food sharer' view, but like the origin of this hypothetical polarity, there is not a great deal of empirical evidence to support either view.

Archaeological data

The 'deep' fossil record provides little evidence for intergroup or within-group violence, in part because the sample of fossils is so small.

The archaeological record is richer and there is more evidence in it for violence and warfare in now-extinct populations.

Lawrence Keely, an archaeologist at the University of Illinois at Chicago Circle, has recently published a comprehensive review of the archaeological data on possible warfare in pre-state societies (Keely 1995). In general, he concludes that pre-state warfare was frequent, brutal, destructive, entailed very high rates of lethal casualties, and appears to have generally been associated with economic gain for the victors. He directly challenges anthropological arguments of the kind I called 'The Gods Must Be Crazy', i.e. that where warfare is found in pre-state societies, it must have been introduced from the outside—by people in state-organized societies. He argues that the above-mentioned features of warfare in the archaeological record appeared long before contact between tribes in the primitive world and nearby civilizations that were organized into political states, and, in fact, these warfare patterns developed long before any civilizations or state societies even existed.

He somewhat jokingly refers to his position, based on his interpretation of the archaeological record, as distinctly Hobbesian (personal communication).

In general, he characterizes the probable tactics in most cases as being those commonly found in guerrilla warfare in modern times—sneak attacks intended to wreak severe and intentionally mortal damage on the opponents, but conducted with limited means (stone tools, clubs, bows and arrows, etc.). He also finds a strong correlation in the physical remains of archaeological sites of very intense patterns of warfare being associated with what he considers to be one or more highly aggressive groups whose populations are undergoing rapid growth and whose communities are expanding militarily into adjacent areas and eliminating less aggressive groups on their periphery, appropriating their territories. However, he found very little evidence that population density itself was correlated with warfare intensity, which is also true in the Amazon basin where I have worked. He argues that trade and intergroup marriage appear not to have the effect of dampening or reducing the intensity of warfare between groups.

The bulk of his book is dedicated to debunking the commonly found anthropological arguments that primitive warfare is 'ritualized', non-destructive and involves few casualties in contrast to less ritualized, more destructive and high-casualty warfare erroneously assumed only to be associated with state-level societies.

A few specific archaeological sites are instructive.

The Crow Creek massacre, c. 1325.   One of the most dramatic examples of pre-state warfare among tribesmen in the Americas is the famous Crow Creek site in South Dakota, where the bodies of nearly 500 people were found, hastily buried in a ditch near their village, the largest pre-contact massacre site in North America. The residents of a relatively large community of farming people were apparently attacked by an overwhelming force of enemies and slaughtered in a single confrontation. Many of the victims had been decapitated, scalped and mutilated in other ways by their assailants—such as having their hands cut off with stone tools. Although portions of the site had been excavated in the 1950s, it was not until 1978 that the macabre mass burial was discovered when one member in a group of archaeologists touring the site to inspect for erosion damage noticed human bone fragments protruding from a bank. A few weeks later a looter also discovered the bone deposit and inflicted serious damage to the site, presumably digging for arrowheads and other artefacts. Steps were immediately taken to secure the site and excavate it. In 1981 a preliminary but rather comprehensive site report was published (US Army Corps of Engineers 1981). The site dates from the archaeological horizon in the Plains known as the Initial Coalescent period, which took form around 900 AD and lasted to about 1400 AD as aboriginal cultivators moved northward into the Dakotas from Kansas, Nebraska and Oklahoma, and blended with the already established Initial Middle Missouri cultures found there. It was apparently a time of intensive and extensive warfare—large, fortified communities were typical of this period. Descendants of the Crow Creek inhabitants are thought to be the historic and contemporary Arikara Indians of North Dakota, unrelated to the Dakota (Sioux) who moved into this area in the 17th century.

Demographic analysis of the skeletal remains indicates that young women aged between 12 and 19 years are relatively scarce, as are young children of both sexes. They were presumably carried off by the attackers. Hand and foot bones are scarce. Closer inspection reveals that the hands and feet of many victims had been cut or hacked off with stone tools, presumably for trophies. Most of the crania show clear marks of scalping and many bodies had been dismembered and butchered.

Forensic examinations of the skeletal remains also revealed that the population was poorly nourished and had lived under suboptimal dietary circumstances characterized by chronic vitamin and protein deficiencies, prompting some of the excavators to suggest that this incident was triggered by overpopulation and increasing pressure on arable land and other resources (Zimmerman & Whitten 1980).

Sanauktuk site (NgTn-1).   The archaeological explanation of preference for causes of prehistoric violence appears to be resource shortages that provoke intergroup conflicts, as in the Crow Creek instance above where there is some supporting evidence for this argument. However, there are also reports of opportunistic massacres and homicides in the recent archaeological record that imply that killings took place for motives other than resource shortages or resource competition.

One of the recently reported cases of this is a massacre site in the Canadian Arctic. Melbye & Fairgrieve (1994) have recently described their analysis of the remains of some 35 Inuit individuals (women, children and elderly people; apparent victims of a sudden raid by a group of neighbouring Amerindians). Ethnohistorical evidence suggests that the attackers were members of the Eastern Kutchin tribe. Melbye & Fairgrieve's (1994, p 74) discussion of this site in the context of a larger pattern of violence in the Arctic area is concise and informative:

'Contact between Amerindian and Inuit often involved violence, including murder, torture, mutilation and cannibalism. While men seem to be the primary perpetrators (probably as an extension of hunting parties), the victims included all ages and both sexes. The purpose is less clear, but there is no indication of competition for hunting resources, captives or material gain. Rather there appears to be endemic animosity—at least in some places in the early historic period. The violence is expressed not just in the death of the enemy; there is deliberate torture before death. Further, death does not appear to end the process. Instead, we see the continued mutilation of the

bodies after death, and some rituals probably involving sympathetic magic, probably including cannibalism.'
The specific site on which they report appears to have been a hunting camp occupied mainly by women, children and older people. The men appear to have been away hunting beluga whales. The essentially defenceless victims were apparently discovered by a Kutchin hunting party and massacred and then desecrated.

An especially interesting feature of Melbye & Fairgrieve's (1994) report is their seeming caution to describe their findings as clear-cut evidence of brutal violence, including cannibalism, in this ethnographic region. The reason is the apparent tendency among their colleagues to avoid describing similar evidence from other sites as representing prehistoric violence, or to insist on and demand stringent or even unreasonable criteria for concluding that things such as cannibalism took place prior to contact with outsiders.

The art of palaeolithic warfare.   Perhaps one of the most interesting comments on the archaeological evidence for pre-state warfare is a recent (1994) article by Paul Taçon and Christopher Chippendale in the *Cambridge Archaeological Journal* (summarized in *Science News* by B. Bower, vol 147, p 4). They have examined and studied some 650 aboriginal Australian cave paintings that date from between 10 000 BP to the ethnographic present. They classify aboriginal warfare in Australia into three phases, based largely on weapons used, numbers of participants depicted, and presumed 'intensity' of warfare as implied by the scenes. The third and most recent phase, beginning about 3000 years ago, implies larger battles, more frequent depiction in paintings of conflict and of figures of humans who have been wounded or are dying—with spears in their bodies.

In an interview with one of the authors, Bower (1994) reports: 'Warfare is often seen as a side effect of sedentary farming and then of urban societies... But organized conflict is decidedly a characteristic of mobile hunter-gatherers and *Homo sapiens* in general.' Joan Vastokas, an anthropologist at Trent University (Ontario) has a comment accompanying their published report: 'Conflict, aggression, warfare, and militarism... are not unique to "developed" civilizations ... Only the technology of warfare varies in scale and style from spears and boomerangs to fighter planes and nuclear warheads.' (Bower 1994, p 4).

Keely's book echoes one of the assertions made by Robert Ardrey over 30 years earlier, but Keely is on much more substantial, empirical ground: there is a clear tendency in anthropology and archaeology to underplay the existence of violence and warfare in the ethnographic and archaeological record. Anthropologists in general appear to not 'like' warfare and are 'opposed' to it on apparently emotional, philosophical or moral grounds. But that is hardly reason in science to dismiss evidence or deny that it exists. A surgeon who makes his living excising carcinomas is not, by so doing, advocating the spread of cancer. It appears to me that many anthropologists who deny, downplay, or claim that documented warfare in the primitive was introduced by state-organized societies are assuming that unless they do, they are somehow or other advocating the spread of violence and warfare.

The ethnographic record and the Yanomamö

As stated at the beginning of this paper, the number of field studies of primitive warfare by trained anthropologists who were there when the natives were free, sovereign and still fighting are few in number and difficult to compare. Moreover, they were done by anthropologists who had very different kinds of anthropological training and who, for their own reasons, had different interests. Most of these studies were done after World War II and during a time when anthropological theory was more inclined toward the view that human conflict could and should be reduced to conflicts over scarce material resources—land, water, cattle and, more recently, high-quality animal protein (Harris 1974).

Despite these differences in training, theoretical views and personal research preferences, whenever anthropologists did collect data on things such as rates of male mortality due to violence, they all tended to report similar statistics. These statistics show that mortality rates among adult males due to violence in tribes that were still at war when they were studied are very high—ranging from about 20 to 30% of adult male deaths.

In some studies the anthropologists were able to obtain only relatively small numbers in their samples, i.e. both the 'universe' consisting of all male deaths and the numbers of those due to violence were small. Converting these data to mortality rates due to violence per 100 000 deaths in order to make comparisons with other societies, especially large societies such as industrialized nations or modern cities, involves statistical difficulties. Missing a few deaths in a small population might cause a big change in calculated rates of violent deaths per 100 000 deaths for that population—which may never have had 100 000 people in it in its entire history, counting all the long-since deceased members as well as the currently living ones. Given these difficulties and problems, the gross pattern is nevertheless clear. In 1987 an American anthropologist (Knauft 1987) provided an estimate that allowed for such gross cross-cultural comparisons. Figure 1 is taken from his figures.

These figures clearly show that death due to violence was very common in the primitive societies where warfare was still being conducted at the time anthropologists were studying them, and it accounts for a very large fraction of all deaths among adult males.

Violent, lethal behaviour is not an unusual event or 'pathology', social or otherwise, but it appears to have been commonplace in the past, as Keely's survey argues, and is underrepresented in the contemporary ethnographic

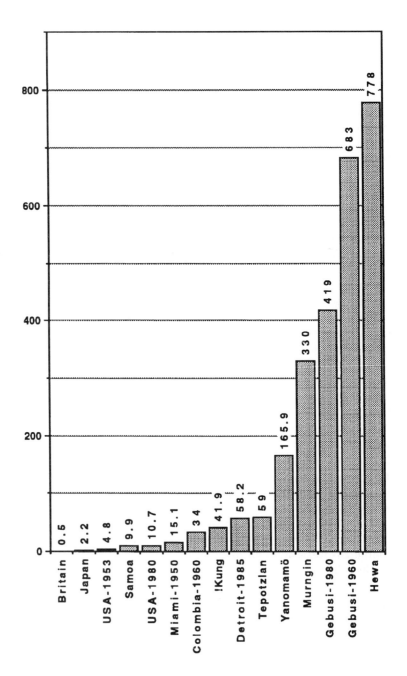

literature largely because anthropologists got to the peoples they studied long after they were decimated and pacified. It is interesting to point out that one of the most widely read ethnographic descriptions of a primitive society was a charming book by Elizabeth Marshall Thomas on the Bushmen of the Kalahari, entitled *The harmless people* (Thomas 1959). But when anthropologist Richard Lee, who studied them for many years, subsequently published statistical data on rates of male deaths due to violence, they turned out to have rates almost the same as those found in Detroit, Michigan, considered to be one of the more violent of large cities in the USA (Lee 1993 [1984]). But as Fig. 1 indicates, estimated rates of violent deaths per 100 000 deaths in other tribal populations such as the Yanomamö, Murngin, Gebusi and Hewa are much higher. The rates among the Yanomamö, if we can take Knauft's calculations based on my data as comparable to how he calculated rates for other societies, are actually quite low for the warring primitive world.

Yanomamö violence and social organization

I believe I am entitled to say, without pretence, that my 30 year study of the Yanomamö is generally regarded in the academic community as one of the more important studies of warfare in the primitive world and of how warfare, kinship behaviour, social organization, demography, economics and ecology are interrelated.

I want to summarize a few important aspects of their warfare and violence because I believe it is highly representative of one commonly found type of society in the primitive world—neolithic horticulturists who have recently made a transition from hunting and gathering to food production. Although food production appeared only in the past 9000–10 000 years in human history and laid the basis for the rapid growth and expansion of the human population all over the globe, many social, behavioural and demographic aspects of low-intensity horticultural populations resemble those found in most hunting–gathering societies. For example, the Yanomamö have what is known as an Iroquois kinship terminology with Dravidian kinship classifications of cousins and an emphasis on descent-reckoning through the male line. This system is also widely found among many hunters and gatherers, especially among aboriginal Australian societies. For some purposes, how the Yanomamö conduct their social activities can therefore be compared with how it is done in many hunting–gathering societies—whether they exist today or existed in the past. By contrast, some hunting–gathering societies, especially those found on the north-west coast of North America, lived in environments of such material

FIG. 1. Rates of homicide in selected cultures. (Based on Knauft 1987, p 464.)

abundance and dependability that their social organization became as complex as that found in relatively sophisticated, sedentary agricultural societies, and their local groups became quite large and very sedentary, yet they were 'hunters and gatherers'.

Before turning to Yanomamö warfare, violence and social organization, I want to make a few comments about definitional matters.

Theoretical problems regarding the nature of primitive war

Most social scientists interested in warfare cross-culturally tend to have a Clausewitzian view of warfare which is, in my estimation, somewhat ethnocentric or at least Eurocentric. In that view, wars are conducted by politically distinct, territorially defined entities, usually nation states. Warfare, as Clausewitz argued, was the 'extension of politics by other means' and, like most of us in modern industrial nations, he regarded 'politics' as something done by formally structured entities such as governments, with judiciary, executive, legislative etc. branches, each one of which having specific functions, duties and privileges. War was to advance the political goals of states. War involved armies of men, separated from their families, free to go on enduring campaigns unfettered by day-to-day parental obligations.

However, wars in the Clausewitzian view are actually more specific to centralized nation states that have specialized 'governmental' structures. According to a number of leading contemporary military theorists, war à la Clausewitz is technically specific to a very short period in western European history (Keegan 1993, Van Creveld 1991). The Clausewitz model of warfare is generally assumed to be the most appropriate model in anthropology for the study of all warfare and has led, in my estimation, to a number of pitfalls and confusions. In many regards, what anthropologists study in tribal societies would not technically qualify as 'warfare' in the Clausewitzian sense, but occasionally has enough resemblance to what he had in mind that the data are somewhat forced into a Clausewitzian model—and some of them fit very poorly. Almost none of the some 60 large, serious, lethal conflicts in the world today fit the Clausewitz model (Kaplan 1994, Gurr & Harff 1994).

One of the most serious sources of confusion is the assumption that, in the primitive world, wars start between territorially defined entities that are politically independent of each other. It is only when 'armed conflicts' emerge between politically distinct, territorially separated communities that anthropologists look at it as 'warfare' and begin to search for the 'causes' of the warfare—as if the conflicts started then and only then. This assumption is, however, consistent with the post-Durkheimian anthropological and sociological view that anthropology is the study of groups, institutions and cultural practices, not the study of people. The flaw in the combination of these two paradigms—the Clausewitz view of war and the view that it is groups, customs, societies etc. that are the proper subject matter of social science—is that it renders impossible the identification and comprehension of the multiplicity of events and personal incidents that normally lie behind most of the 'wars' between villages of tribesmen in the primitive world. It leads to sometimes ridiculous and empirically indefensible conclusions about the 'causes' of war in the primitive world. Wars in the primitive world have deep roots, usually involve repetitive conflicts between individuals who know each other and have axes to grind for personal reasons, and are not necessarily 'waged' by the members of the village they happen to be living in (Chagnon 1988, 1990). In short, much of the fighting in 'primitive war' is very personal, contenders often know each other well, and have crossed swords in the past—repeatedly in many cases. There are, of course, exceptions and I will mention a few below.

I have argued (Chagnon 1988, 1990) that much or most 'primitive war' in societies such as the Yanomamö should be considered as just one kind of conflict of interest between individuals and groups of individuals and that these larger conflicts grow out of a sequence of previous conflicts of interest among smaller groups of individuals, often traceable back to single conflicts between specific individuals. There are many reasons why individuals may be in conflict with each other in societies such as the Yanomamö, but one of the most common reasons has to do with male–male competition for females. Once started, conflicting males may take any affront, real or imagined, as sufficient cause for a fight, usually a formal, non-lethal duel like a club fight. It might be a verbal insult, refusal to share food, a fleeting glance at someone's wife. But the most common explanation the Yanomamö give when I ask about most fights and wars is that 'it started over women'. A specific fight might have started over a banana, but the fighters most likely had fought in the past over some woman.

Yanomamö conflicts and escalations of conflicts

I have demonstrated in previous publications that the Yanomamö population is growing at a relatively high rate and that villages can achieve a size of only some 250–300 people before they fission into two or more new villages. The reason is that as villages become larger, more and more fighting occurs because more and more people are increasingly less related to each other by kinship or tied to each other by marriage alliances. Strangers come into the village, women from other, distant villages are abducted and their offspring have fewer kin in the group, etc. There appears to be a maximum size to which their villages can grow due to inherent limitations of kinship obligations, marriage alliance patterns and descent group solidarity as cohesion-producing mechanisms (Chagnon 1982). This has probably been true for our ancestors and many other kinship-organized societies, i.e. my hunch is that what the Yanomamö do and cannot do is probably representative of what happens or happened in other similarly organized primitive societies elsewhere in time and space.

However, because people in neighbouring villages usually have old grievances and are prone to take advantage of enemies if the risks are low and the potential benefits high, large villages tend in general to coerce and intimidate small villages, usually to obtain women from them either through agreed marriages or simply by taking them by force. Thus, there is considerable advantage in keeping one's village large to avert or reduce the predictable coercive actions of larger neighbours. But because large villages eventually fission and the resulting smaller villages are more vulnerable, the members of all villages seem to be aware that eventually they will be coerced by larger groups. This seems to set limits on the degree to which they can take advantage of momentarily weaker neighbours—as does the fact that most villages are allied to other villages and that even a small village can put up a good fight if its allies help them. In addition, and probably in full awareness of these possibilities, members of larger villages may fission to reduce the amount of frequency of fighting within the village, but relocate themselves at a distance small enough so that they can come to each other's aid should a distant group be tempted to take military advantage of either one of them. They have a specific word for fissioning into two groups and relocating themselves close together—to live *he borarawä* (side-by-side). When you see two Yanomamö villages from the air, located far away from any other villages but situated close together, it would be reasonable to assume they have predictable, active and feared enemies who would attack either one of them should they move far apart.

Like many other primitive societies, the Yanomamö can settle personal grievances and conflicts with physical contests that are sub-lethal and have clearly understood 'rules' and conventions. The least violent conflicts are chest-pounding duels in which individuals strike each other on the pectoral muscles, one man from each faction taking his turn. These occasionally get out of hand when one of the groups has more or better fighters, and the 'losing' team wants to escalate the fight to something more serious, like side-pounding or club fighting. Chest-pounding and its variant, side-slapping from a kneeling position, usually occur between members of different villages and are often provoked by accusations of cowardice, sexual improprieties, stinginess, or theft of garden produce. Some individuals break the rules by concealing rocks in their hands, thus being able to deliver a more devastating blow. Men occasionally get killed in these fights—the blows can be powerful enough to cause internal bleeding of ruptured blood vessels or ruptured kidneys. If someone dies, the groups usually become mortal enemies and subsequently raid each other with the intent to kill.

Club fighting most often occurs within villages, especially large villages, and most often results from illicit sexual trysts that are discovered. However, members of one village sometimes challenge opponents in other villages to such a duel. The 'ideal' rules are that one man exposes his head and allows his opponent to strike him as hard as he can on the top of his head with a long, wiry pole, usually some six to eight feet long. He then gets to deliver as many blows back to his opponent as he received. The blows invariably cause bloodshed, and once the blood starts flowing, free-for-alls often follow and everyone starts clubbing opponents on any part of the body they can hit— bashing skulls and sometimes breaking arms and shoulders. An escalated version of this is to fight with very heavy, previously prepared palmwood staves called *himo* that are sharpened on the edges and can cut flesh and crush bones like a broadsword could. Risk of death is higher in both club fights and *himo* fights than in chest-pounding or side-slapping duels. Deaths in such fights lead to retaliatory revenge raids and warfare.

Raids are conducted by members of one village against members of other villages and the intent is to kill someone and escape without injury or mortal loss of any of the members of the raiding party. They are almost always sneak attacks in which the raiders hide outside the village of the enemy and shoot the first man that ventures out. Although they often hope to dispatch a particular hated man, they usually end up killing the first one that emerges—lest by letting him pass he will detect them and sound an alarm. Many raids end in failure and the raiders retreat without so much as shooting an arrow. On some raids they wait for hours for someone to come out, but the enemy is wary. They might shoot a volley of arrows over the roof of the village, hoping one of them will hit someone, and then flee. Sometimes they find that their enemy's village is deserted and go home. Sometimes they are detected before reaching the village and retreat. Sometimes someone in the raiding party has a bad dream that portends disaster, and they decide to abort the raid. Nevertheless, these desultory raids, over a long time, can lead to staggeringly high death rates, even though the number of victims per raid might be small.

As mentioned above, most raiding is conducted between groups whose members have known each other for many years and may even have spent the lion's share of their lives as members of the same village and are genetic relatives. Village fissions always result in new villages whose members are more closely related among themselves than they are to the kinsmen they separated from (Chagnon 1979), so killings between related groups usually involve men killing distantly related relatives. In fact, they will avoid shooting a man in an 'enemy' village if they recognize him and realize that he is a close relative, and some men refuse to go on raids against groups that include many close relatives; such men suffer no censure for their decisions. It is for this reason that it is a serious distortion of reality to argue that 'wars' can be understood as lethal conflicts between politically distinct, territorially defined groups. It is more meaningful to say that these lethal conflicts are between groups of genetically related contestants who are more closely related among themselves than they are to the group they are fighting. Thus, for some analytical purposes, lethal conflicts in the primitive world can be usefully compared to specific kinds of homicides in modern nations. The same pattern is true for within-group club fights (Chagnon & Bugos 1979, Asch & Chagnon 1975). In an analysis of victim–offender relatedness, Daly & Wilson (1988) showed a similar pattern for homicides cross-culturally, and in an unpublished paper given at a Human Behaviour and Evolution Society meeting in Ann Arbor in 1989 I demonstrated a similar pattern for intervillage killings among the Yanomamö: raiders were more closely related among themselves than they were to their victims, even though their victims were often blood relatives.

Let me also point out some things that are definitely not true about Yanomamö warfare, but have crept into the literature as alleged 'interpretations' of what I have published about their violence and warfare. First, intervillage raids are almost never conducted with the explicit intent of capturing women. Their 'wars' are not initiated or intended to capture females from enemies, although if they find a woman at a safe distance from the enemy village and dragging her back with them will not cause much additional risk, they may 'capture' her. Although abduction of females is common among the Yanomamö, most abductions take place right at home—when visitors from distant villages come in small numbers and bring their wives and daughters with them. If the risks are small the benefits high, they might retain the females and send the men packing. If the victimized village is small and therefore militarily weak, the risks are small. Another, less frequent way to abduct females is to feign friendship with a group, invite them to a feast, and then treacherously turn on them, often with the help of third-party allies from other villages who have long-term grievances with the victims. This is called a *nomohori* (a treacherous trick). Visiting men are often killed in *nomohoris*, and sometimes large numbers of women and girls are captured. This is a vile and despicable form of violence in Yanomamö eyes, but if they hate an enemy intensely enough, they will do it. The invariable result is a long-term period of raid and counter-raid, sometimes lasting decades. The compelling motive in these raids, as in most raids, is revenge for the deaths of lost kinsmen, but if possible, also to recover lost women. Some of the captured women escape and return home, but most of them remain among their captors for life, and in time they have children and grandchildren and may not even want to go home if given the chance. *Nomohoris* rarely occur between villages whose members are closely related.

Finally, some intervillage wars are started because of accusations of witchcraft and 'magical charms' thought to be blown on them by distant enemies that cause deaths, especially among children. This 'cause' of war, especially a new war between two groups whose members have had little or no previous contact, is not common in the area I have worked in where there are lots of other reasons for wars and raids, but it appears to be more common in other areas. In general, accusations of harmful magic in the area I work in are directed at groups with whom one already has other, long-term grievances: known enemies who have also killed some of your kin are usually also accused of practising harmful magic.

New data

The overall picture that emerges from my 30 year study of the Yanomamö is that their population has been growing at a high rate for upwards of 200 years, possibly as a consequence of the introduction of plantains and bananas via diffusion from other Amazonian groups who ultimately obtained them from European colonists after 1492.[8] The Yanomamö believe they have cultivated these crops since the beginning of time, along with a number of other highly productive native root crops such as manioc, xanthosoma and mapuey. Maize is also cultivated in small amounts but may have formerly been more important as a staple. The result of the population growth has been the constant growing, fissioning and dispersal of villages outwards in all directions from the rugged highland area known as the Parima mountains separating southern Venezuela from Brazil (Chagnon 1966, 1974). In some areas, particularly low-lying, well-drained large valleys, their villages were able to grow particularly large—upwards of 250–350 people. Here, warfare appears to be more intense and chronic than it is in other areas such as the more rugged highland areas. Most of my field studies until 1990 were done in the lowland areas. Outside of the lowland areas, and also on the periphery of the expanding front, villages tend to be smaller, ranging in size from about 40 to 60 people (Chagnon 1968).[9]

Warfare in these low-lying areas has some fascinating characteristics that I have only begun to explore in the past five years after I was able to go into these and adjacent hilly regions by helicopter and see from the air some of the geographical and ecological features that are not obvious from the ground or accurately represented on available maps of this region. I have published some of my new sociodemographic and ecological findings (Chagnon 1991, 1992) and will summarize the main features here.

(1) Warfare in the low-lying areas is more intense than in adjacent foothills and mountainous zones, although the inhabitants of those regions recently lived in the lowlands. While I am still collecting relevant field data, the picture

---

[8]It is also interesting that the Highland New Guinea societies, among which some of the best studies of primitive war were conducted, are heavily dependent on cultivated sweet potatoes, introduced after the discovery of the Americas and brought there from the Americas.

[9]Villages in the south-western periphery are an exception—they also tend to be large, probably because they have recently come from the low-lying areas nearby.

TABLE 1 Abducted women and unokais (men who have killed people) in eight recently studied highland villages in the Siapa/Shanishani drainages

Village (highland location)	Population	% Abducted females	% Unokai males
71 (foothill)	43	33.3	36.4
64 (foothill)	99	14.5	27.6
72 (foothill)	28	0.0	57.1
69 (mountain)	53	14.3	7.7
59 (mountain)	71	0.0	21.4
57 (mountain)	81	15.0	15.4
68 (mountain)	54	14.3	0.0
67 (mountain)	70	0.0	12.5
Total	499	—	—
Average	62	11.7	21.2

Averages for abducted females and for unokais were determined by dividing the actual numbers of cases by the total number of females and males of the appropriate age categories.

that is emerging is that populations in the lowlands are continuing to grow and fission, but the ability of newly fissioned villages to remain in the lowlands is limited by space and other reasons. Some villages are forced out, usually the smaller ones. These tend to relocate in the more defensible foothills and their members periodically attempt to relocate to the lowlands when their villages grow sufficiently large to compete effectively with the larger villages already there.

Some of the smaller, less viable villages are pushed further into the mountains and locate at higher elevations where resources are presumably less abundant and more energetically costly to produce or acquire. For example, many species of useful plants and animals are not even found there, such as caiman or tapir. Gardening is extremely difficult on the steep slopes and energetically very costly in comparison with lowland cultivation.

(2) Some villages that are expelled from one large lowland area find other, adjacent, large lowland areas that are unoccupied and colonize them. The process appears to be repeated in these areas, and the smaller villages are forced into more rugged terrain at higher elevations.

(3) Tables 1 and 2 present some of the sociodemographic contrasts between lowland, foothill and highland villages. In general, the lowland villages are the more bellicose as revealed by the higher percentages of *unokais* (men who have killed people) and higher percentages of abducted women in their villages. The abducted women most often are taken from smaller, weaker villages that are

TABLE 2 Comparison of male marriages in eight highland and lowland villages (all males > 20 years of age)

Variable	Lowland	Percentage	Highland	Percentage
Males > 20 years	223	24	123	25
No. polygynous	33	15	10	8
No. unmarried	24	11	28	23
No. monogamous	150	67	80	65
No. polyandrous	17	8	5	4
Total married	200	90	95	77

The total population in the lowland and highland villages is 931 and 499, respectively. Average village sizes for lowland and highland villages: 116 and 62, respectively. *Total married* is the sum of all polygynous, monogamous and polyandrous marriages. Percentages for types of marriage were calculated by dividing the number of cases in each category by the number of males aged > 20 years for each cluster of villages.

now found in the foothills or highlands. Abducted women found in the latter villages almost never come from the larger, more bellicose villages in the lowlands. Again, larger fractions of the men in the lowland villages are married and rates of polygyny are higher there.

These several geographical, ecological and sociodemographic variables suggest the following geographical and ecological models (shown in Figs 2 and 3) and political strategies for the essentially triangular area defined by the Mavaca, Orinoco and Siapa rivers.

The political strategy appears to be to try to remain in the lowlands, an area that appears to be more desirable. But to remain there, villages have to grow large and remain large in order to compete militarily with neighbours. As villages grow in size, more fighting and conflict occurs within the village because villages become genealogically and socially more heterogeneous: formerly abducted women have offspring in the village, and unrelated or distantly related people from nearby villages migrate into the village. The Yanomamö will sometimes give as the explanation for a fission something like: 'We were too many in the village and were fighting all the time with each other. We got sick and tired of all the fighting and decided to split into two groups.' Eventually, the large villages fission to reduce conflict, but they attempt to remain in the same area and remain allied. Thus, they must claim and defend areas much larger than those required for subsistence reasons alone. They appear to do so in order to have unoccupied safe havens to retreat into when military pressures from their enemies and combined, allied villages of their enemies become particularly intense. When villages they have forced into the foothills or mountains attempt to move back into their unoccupied safe havens, the larger villages tend to react belligerently to them and harass them. This

226

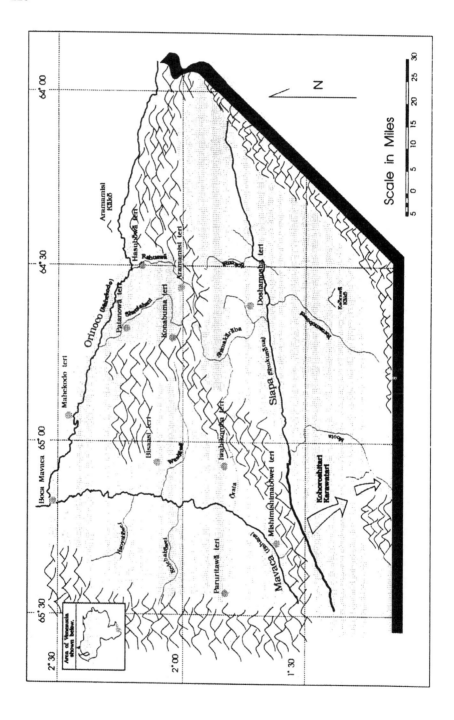

often takes the form of coercing them out of women should they tolerate their presence there at all, and the only way the smaller villages can remain there is to make peace with their larger neighbours and try to cultivate friendships and alliances with them. They may even be willing to tolerate the loss of a few women if that is the cost of occupying a more attractive lowland address. But each unchallenged act of coercion tends to lead to increased coercion: the strong exploit the weak if the costs are low and the benefits high. Eventually, members of the smaller group grow weary of the coercion and react, sometimes violently, and are forced out of the area again. A common example is when a group of men from the smaller village come to visit the larger village to demonstrate friendship and the men in the larger village forcibly appropriate all their women and send the men packing. A less common tactic is to invite the smaller village to a feast and then kill as many men as possible and take the women—the *nomohori* described above.

Why the lowland areas appear to be more desirable remains a problem that can only be settled with additional field research on the anthropology, demography, ecology and geography of both the lowland and highland areas, some of which I am planning to do in the immediate future.

Some plausible hypotheses suggest themselves. First, the energetic costs of gardening, hunting, fetching water and collecting firewood are extremely high in the foothills and mountainous areas compared with the lowland areas. Second, some useful and desirable plans and animals occur only in the lowlands or occur there in greater abundance, are more predictable and are easier to exploit. As elevation increases, species abundance and diversity tends to decrease. Third, not all low-lying areas are equally desirable—some are too low or too poorly drained to make it prudent to make high-cost gardens in them: an unanticipated season of unusually large amounts of rain will ruin a garden and lead to privation. I know the experiences of a number of Yanomamö groups whose members unwisely chose to make their villages and gardens in areas that were too low, and had to abandon them when they got flooded out. Not only were they bitter because of the enormous waste of energy and time, but also because they were aware that they would have to depend on the largesse of erstwhile allies whose aid would invariably be tendered for a price: some of their women or sexual access to them.

The most fascinating problem as I see it is the relationship between access to material resources (useful plants and animals) and the higher intensity of

---

FIG. 2. Schematic map of the triangular area defined by the Mavaca, Orinoco and Siapa rivers in southern Venezuela (redrawn from Chagnon 1992, p 84). The rivers are accurately shown but the mountainous regions are schematically approximated from radar maps of this region. If a North–South line were drawn through the middle of this map and the profile represented in schematic terms, the result would be approximately that shown in Fig. 3.

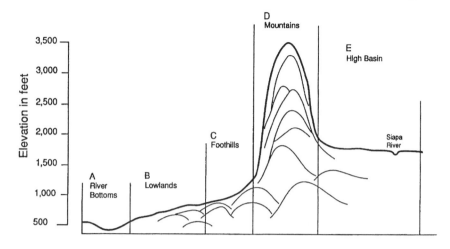

FIG. 3. Model of the geographical/ecological niches in the 'MOS triangle'. The elevations shown on this map are accurate, but the terrain has been schematically represented. The apparently more-desirable low-lying areas are those shown as *Region B, Lowlands*. The *River Bottoms* of region *A* are frequently and unpredictably inundated during the rainy season. Region *B* is generally well-drained and low-lying. Region *C* represents the foothill zone where defeated groups from region *B* take refuge and from which they try to return to region *B*. Some are forced into region *D*, the high and mountainous elevations, and become refugees. Some groups cross over into the Siapa river basin (*Region E*), a very high valley that is poorly known and basically unexplored.

warfare in the lowland areas. It is not a simple one in the sense that their warfare can be reduced exclusively to competition over scarce material resources, a debate of long standing between Marvin Harris and I. Resources of all kinds appear to be more abundant in the lowlands, but the Yanomamö there claim and defend far larger areas than they need for purely subsistence reasons. They appear to do so largely for reasons of military security—to have safe havens into which they can quickly move if they must. Large, militarily strong groups almost always return to areas they previously occupied when the military pressures abate in those areas. They would be less able to do so if someone else moved into them. By contrast, resources of all kinds appear to be less abundant and less easily obtainable in the higher regions, yet the frequency of fighting and conflicts there appears to be lower and the conflicts appear to be less deadly. Ironically, shortages of material resources are more associated with lower levels of violence than vice versa, and as regards 'protein deficiency', the more belligerent of peoples turn out to have higher levels of protein consumption than the less belligerent ones (Chagnon & Hames 1979).

A common-sense argument might simply be that people proximately strive for lifestyles that are relatively affluent, relatively easy to achieve at low cost in calories or time spent at the drudgery of subsistence, predictable over reasonable periods of time, with minimal risk or threat from predatory neighbours and maximum security to be able to lead the good life, however locally and historically defined. This makes maximizing local security through actual or threatened belligerence towards neighbours almost a predictable tactic or condition to achieve more basic proximate elements in the good or more desired lifestyle. The costs for that require that some men must fight and die, usually young men. There are basically just two kinds of reasons why they would take mortal risks. One is that by failing to do so they and their kin are vulnerable to the lethal predations of neighbours—it is a matter of defence and simple survival. The other is the possibility for some kind of gain or reward, and the most obvious of these is the esteem and admiration of peers and the possibly associated higher reproductive consequences where high-risk belligerence on behalf of kin is admired and rewarded with increased reproductive opportunities, either directly by taking women from weaker groups, or indirectly by being a more desirable mate for the daughters of co-villagers. Over time, the social or cultural rewards that lead to biological success (Irons 1979) become less obviously related to reproductive striving and eventually become 'tokens' like wealth, power, political office etc. that, in turn, are often and easily converted into reproductive differentials by the prominent and culturally successful (Betzig 1986).

Conclusions

The objective study of warfare in the primitive world is handicapped for several reasons. First, there is a paucity of data based on first-hand observation made by trained anthropologists at the time they studied warring tribesmen. Second, advocates of cultural materialist theories of primitive warfare often repudiate and denigrate alternative approaches and try to politicize them if they include arguments from biological theory. The history of anthropology reflects a general bias towards denying or down-playing the very existence of pre-state violence in the primitive world or to attribute it to the effects of contact with more complex societies. Third, the wide variation in training of anthropologists from different schools of thought and the personal research interests they have, make it difficult to compare their field research results. Fourth, recent political and anti-scientific intellectual trends in anthropology seem to inflict professional scorn on and repudiate those who study primitive warfare from a positivistic approach, and advocate a 'reconstructed' view of tribesmen that is decidedly Rousseauesque in overall tone. Some of the latter trends now interfere in attempts by others to collect additional data in the few places left on earth where such data can be gathered.

Lethal conflict among humans is just one kind of conflict. Not all lethal conflicts can be meaningfully equated with war, even when different groups are involved. These conflicts start, generally, from conflicts among individuals, and escalate into more serious and larger-scale confrontations involving larger numbers of contestants. The 'causes' of the final, larger-scale conflicts in primitive societies should be sought in the sequences of events that lie behind the escalations of minor conflicts into larger ones.

Lethal conflict is common in sexually selected species, including humans, and arises over competition for both material resources and reproductive resources.

Lethal conflict among humans is not a pathology unless we are willing to define as pathological the striving of humans for the somatic and reproductive resources necessary for reproductive survival. If so, then life itself is a pathology. Striving for such resources does not automatically result in lethal violence and most human groups have developed less-deadly means for resolving conflicts. But, where the costs are low and the potential gains high, then the use of coercion and violence are predictable and expected strategies for acquiring the resources of others. In the primitive world, costs, risks and benefits appear to be strongly associated with differences in size of potentially competitive groups, and larger groups are at an advantage because they are militarily more able to win any given conflict with smaller groups. Humans and other social species appear to be social because competitive ability is enhanced by cooperation within groups (Alexander 1974, 1979; cf. Axelrod & Hamilton 1981, Axelrod & Dion 1988). There has probably always been, in human history, a premium associated with the ability to maximize the size of local groups *vis-à-vis* neighbouring groups for security reasons and to be more effective in competition with them.

References

Albert B 1989 Yanomami 'violence': inclusive fitness or ethnographer's representation? Curr Anthropol 30:637–640
Ardrey R 1961 African genesis. Dell, New York
Asch T, Chagnon NA 1975 The ax fight (16 mm documentary film). Documentary Educational Resources, Watertown, MA
Alexander RD 1974 The evolution of social behavior. Annu Rev Ecol Syst 5:325–383
Alexander RD 1979 Darwinism and human affairs. Pitman, London
Axelrod R, Hamilton WD 1981 The evolution of cooperation. Science 211:1390–1396
Axelrod R, Dion D 1988 The further evolution of cooperation. Science 242:1385–1390
Betzig L 1986 Despotism and differential reproduction: a Darwinian view of history. Aldine de Gruyter, Hawthorne, New York
Bower B 1994 Seeds of warfare precede agriculture. Sci News 147:4
Carneiro da Cunha MM 1989 To the editor. Anthropol Newslet p 3
Carroll J 1995 Evolution and literary theory. University of Missouri Press, St Louis, MO

Chagnon NA 1966 Yanomamo warfare, social organization and marriage alliances. PhD thesis, University of Michigan, East Lansing, MI

Chagnon NA 1968 The culture–ecology of shifting (pioneering) cultivation among the Yanomamo indians. Proc VIII Int Congr Anthropol Ethnol Sci, vol 3, p 249–255 Tokyo and Kyoto

Chagnon NA 1974 Studying the Yanomamö. Holt, Rinehart and Winston, New York

Chagnon NA 1979 Mate competition, favoring close kin and village fissioning among the Yanomamo Indians. In: Chagnon NA, Irons W (eds) Evolutionary biology and human social behavior: an anthropological perspective. Duxbury Press, North Scituate, MA, p 86–131

Chagnon NA 1982 Sociodemographic attributes of nepotism in tribal populations: man the rule breaker. In: Current problems in sociobiology. King's College Sociobiology Group Staff (eds) Cambridge University Press, Cambridge, p 291–318

Chagnon NA 1988 Life histories, blood revenge, and warfare in a tribal population. Science 239:985–992

Chagnon NA 1989a Response to Ferguson. Am Ethnol 16:565–570

Chagnon NA 1989b On Yanomamö violence: reply to Albert. Curr Anthropol 31:49–53

Chagnon NA 1989c Yanomamö survival. Science 244:11

Chagnon NA 1990 Reproductive and somatic conflicts of interest in the genesis of violence and warfare among tribesmen. In: Haas J (ed) The anthropology of war. Cambridge University Press, Cambridge, p 77–104

Chagnon NA 1991 GIS, GPS, political history and geo-demography of the Aramamisi Yanomamö expansion. In: Behrens CA, Sever T (eds) Applications of space-age technology in anthropology. NASA Science and Technology Laboratory, John C. Stennis Space Center, Mississippi, MO, p 35–62

Chagnon NA 1992 Yanomamö: the last days of Eden, 4th edn. Harcourt, Brace, Jovanovich, New York

Chagnon NA, Bugos P 1979 Kin selection and conflict: an analysis of a Yanomamo ax fight. In: Chagnon NA, Irons W (eds) Evolutionary biology and human social behavior: an anthropological perspective. Duxbury Press, North Scituate, MA, p 213–228

Chagnon NA, Hames R 1979 Protein deficiency and tribal warfare in Amazonia: new data. Science 203:910–913

Daly M, Wilson MI 1988 Homicide. Aldine de Gruyter, Hawthorne, NY

D'Andrade R 1995 Moral models in anthropology. Curr Anthropol 36:399–408

Durkheim E 1895 Rules of the sociological method. The Free Press, Glencoe, IL (1962 edn)

Ferguson RB 1988 The anthropology of war: a bibliography. Guggenheim Foundation, New York

Ferguson RB 1989 Do Yanomamö killers have more kids? Am Ethnol 16:564–565

Ferguson RB 1992 A savage encounter: western contact and the Yanomami war complex. In: Ferguson RB, Whitehead NL (eds) War in the tribal zone. School Am Res Press, Santa Fe, NM, p 199–227

Ferguson RB 1995 Yanomami warfare: a political history. School Am Res Press, Santa Fe, NM

Fried M 1967 The evolution of political society. McGraw-Hill, New York

Gross PR, Levitt N 1994 Higher superstitions: the academic left and its quarrels with science. Johns Hopkins University Press, Baltimore, MD

Gurr TR, Harff B 1994 Ethnic conflict in world politics. Westview Press, Boulder, CO

Haas J (ed) 1990 The anthropology of war. Cambridge University Press, Cambridge

Harris M 1974 Cows, pigs, wars, and witches: the riddles of culture. Random House, New York

Harris M 1977 Cannibals and kings: the origins of cultures. Random House, New York

Harris M 1979 Cultural materialism: the struggle for a science of culture. Random House, New York

Harris M 1984 A cultural materialist theory of band and village warfare: the Yanomamö test. In: Ferguson RB (ed) Warfare, culture and environment. Academic Press, Orlando, FL, p 111–140

Irons W 1979 Cultural and biological success. In: Chagnon NA, Irons W (eds) Evolutionary biology and human social behavior: an anthropological perspective. Duxbury Press, North Scituate, MA, p 257–272

Kaplan RD 1994 The coming anarchy. Atl Mon 243:44

Keegan J 1993 A history of warfare. Knopf, New York

Keely L 1995 War before civilization. Oxford University Press, Oxford

Knauft BM 1987 Reconsidering violence in simple human societies. Curr Anthropol 28:457–500

Lee R 1993 (1984) The Dobe Jul'hoansi, 2nd edn. Harcourt Brace College Publishers, New York

Manson J, Wrangham R 1991 Intergroup aggression in chimpanzees and humans: violence and sociality in human evolution. Curr Anthropol 32:369–428

Melbye J, Fairgrieve SI 1994 A massacre and possible cannibalism in the Canadian Arctic: new evidence from the Saunaktuk site (NgTn-1). Arct Anthropol 31:57–77

Ross E 1978 Food taboos, diet and hunting strategy: the adaptation to animals in Amazon cultural ecology. Curr Anthropol 19:1–36

Ross J 1980 Ecology and the problem of tribe: a critique of the Hobbesian model of preindustrial warfare. In: Ross E (ed) Beyond the myths of culture: essays in cultural materialism. Academic Press, New York, p 33–60

Ross E, Bennett Ross J 1980 Amazon warfare. Science 207:590–591

Service E 1971 Primitive social organization: an evolutionary perspective, 2nd edn. Random House, New York

Taçon P, Chippendale C 1994 Australia's ancient warriors: changing depictions of fighting in the rock art of Arnhem Land, NT. Camb Archaeol J 4:211–248

Thomas EM 1959 The harmless people, 2nd edn. Vintage Books, New York

US Army Corps of Engineers 1981 The Crow Creek site (39BF11) massacre: a preliminary report. US Army Corps of Engineers, Omaha, NE

Van Creveld M 1991 The transformation of war. The Free Press, New York

Vayda AP 1989 Explaining why Marings fought. J Anthropol Res 45:159–177

White LA 1949 The science of culture. Farrar, Straus, and Cudahy, New York

Zimmerman LJ, Whitten RG 1980 Prehistoric bones tell a grim tale of Indian v. Indian. Smithsonian 11:100–107

DISCUSSION

Unfortunately, Napoleon Chagnon was unable to attend the symposium. In his absence, discussion comments were fielded by Martin Daly.

Hinde: I presume that war was included in this conference because of its relationship to aggression. I would like to make the point that aggression doesn't cause war, but wars cause aggression. In industrial societies, war is an institution—people fight not because they are aggressive, but because it's their duty to fight. As an institution, war has numerous roles for soldiers, generals, clinicians, doctors, transport workers and so on. People do what they have to do because of the rights and duties associated with the particular role that they occupy. We've been trying to collect evidence from different academic disciplines as to the nature of the forces that support war as an institution. These include the words we use in everyday speech, religion, propaganda and nationalism, parades and ceremonies, economics, historical factors and so on (Hinde & Watson 1994). I had thought that this might be a big difference between tribal societies and industrial societies, but what we've heard today shows that it is not so great: there is both individual aggression and a degree of institutionalization in this tribal aggression, as these ceremonies demonstrate.

Daly: This so-called primitive warfare in the Yanomamö has a lot more in common with what we think of as interpersonal individualized violence than with contemporary mass warfare (Chagnon 1988). There are often individualized grievances in these wars, and individuals are often the targets. Typically, few die in an intervillage raid. It's very likely that individuals target other individuals. There's ethnography to that effect in New Guinea, as well. Although people are acting collectively in these wars, this is not psychologically akin to the business of being sent off to fight for Queen and country. It has a strong element of knowing who you're fighting and knowing why. In this context, the boundaries between individualized interpersonal violence and warfare get kind of fuzzy.

Hinde: Part of my point is that it's culturally accepted that the way to get your own back on someone is to bash him over the head with a staff, rather than to adopt some other method of negotiation.

Lyons: In our Vietnam veteran twin studies we looked at genetic influences on individual differences in the number and variety of combat experiences. For example, we inquired whether or not the subject had ever been in an ambush, had ever been in a fire fight, or had served as a tunnel rat. We found that combat experiences were genetically influenced. Winning a medal in combat had a strong genetic influence and no family environmental influence. Being wounded also had a genetic influence. I talked this over with a friend of mine who had both a silver star and a purple heart, because to me this seemed sort of counterintuitive. He said it made perfect sense to him: every day on a tour of duty one made decisions. He gave the example of walking 'point'—that is, 200 yards ahead of the rest of your platoon. Some people routinely volunteered to do this, whereas other people managed always to avoid it. Although having a crazy commanding officer who volunteered your unit for suicide missions had absolutely nothing to do with you, almost every day there was some decision to be made that reflected the characteristics of the individual. We picked this up in our data.

Glover: You mentioned the different levels of violent conflict the Yanomamö resort to. Is there anything known about what determines whether people accept defeat at one level of violence rather than escalating to another level, where they might win?

Daly: Napoleon has assessed the average relatedness between men engaging in slap fights versus club fights versus axe fights: minor fights are or can be among relatives, but the more dangerous kinds of conflict tend to occur between more distantly related people (Chagnon & Bugos 1979).

Glover: Do higher levels of conflict arise out of escalation from lower levels, or do conflicts sometimes start off at the higher levels?

Daly: My understanding is that they do escalate.

Goldman: You made a comparison between so-called modern societies, with their particular governance and leadership structures, with these other societies. What is the leadership pattern in Yanomamö villages, and how does it affect these social behaviours? For example, do leaders assign a conflict to a particular level of conflict resolution, which may include a violent encounter?

Daly: There are headmen in these villages. Napoleon has mainly described this with respect to the lowland relatively-high-warfare situation. There are dramatic leadership style differences among headmen. There are those whom everyone fears, and there are those whom everybody respects: it's not exactly the same thing. His contention is that you don't get to be a headman without showing some courage, perhaps implying that you will not shrink from violence if need be, but you don't have to have terrorized people to become a headman. One way that a man can be a headman even though he hasn't necessarily done much violence is to expose himself to danger in the service of the village. But it seems clear from the descriptions of these intravillage conflicts that there's no sort of presiding judicial authority. There's a famous anthropological film that Napoleon shot, called 'The Ax Fight', in which there's a dispute within a village (Asch & Chagnon 1975). Men are yelling at each other, and there's a lot of chest-bumping and arguing. People go and get some weapons, blows are exchanged, and one guy incurs a serious injury. It looks pretty chaotic to the naive viewer. Certainly, there's a lot of independent initiative. Part of what Napoleon was interested in analysing was who lines up with whom, given it's a village where there are all sorts of conflicts and kinship links. This implies that there isn't a clear notion of what one has to do in this context. Nevertheless, it is rule-bound in the sense that people know what sort of a fight they're engaged in: someone who escalates the conflict by bringing in the wrong kind of weapons has made a dire move.

Bouchard: I recall when James Neel (1970) wrote his *Science* paper many years ago, he said: 'our field impression is that the polygynous Indians, especially the headmen, tend to be more intelligent than the non-polygynous. They also tend to have more surviving offspring. Polygyny in these tribes thus appears to provide an effective device for certain types of natural selection. Would that we had quantitative results to support that statement!'

Daly: In his first book (Chagnon 1968), there's a chapter about his friend Kaobawä, who is the most mild-mannered, non-violent leader of a major village. This guy managed this by being a terrific political, moral and rhetorical force. The most violent leaders probably get selected against, smart or not. Those who 'equilibrate' might live longer. But the main selective component has to do with the luck of the draw on how many kinsmen you have to help you.

Bartlett: If war raids are a way of settling grievances about women, are they also the context in which women are abducted? Or does this largely happen in other situations, such as from garden areas?

Daly: Wars are a context in which women are sometimes abducted but, as Napoleon Chagnon argues, most wars are started with the express purpose of revenge. That is, they are extensions of conflicts that started earlier over any number of causes, but led to at least one killing.

Rutter: At what level of generalization do you think these findings can be extrapolated to our own societies? What are the implications for violence in western societies?

Daly: I think the principle implication is that the capacity for violence (and the capacity to use it when the situation demands) is certainly not a pathology. It's probably an organized attribute of human nature as a result of selective consequence in pre-state societies, in which men who were capable in violent situations did well. Therefore we've got to think in terms of an evolved capacity for modulated violence. The cases where people who have immigrated after defeat from the lowlands to the highlands, and adopted a different lifestyle, illustrate that even within the individual lifespan of a person raised in a society in which there's strong social valuation of violent capacity, when the situation demands, people are well capable of laying off violence.

Mednick: In western societies we have studied individuals who have impulsive, uncontrolled violence, which is related to alcohol. It's possible this sort of person exists in tribal societies. How would they be viewed in this context? Would they be seen as deviants?

Daly: Possibly. In talking about headmanship, Napoleon has contrasted his friend Kaobawä (Chagnon 1968, 1992) with more violent individuals who have gained some power and prestige by terrorizing people. Möawä, a now dead headman who was more prone to violence than others, is described in a chapter of Chagnon (1974). He did poorly and his kin all but rejoiced when he died—he was a pain in the ass to them as well. Presumably, behaviour still has to be under control if someone is going to gain and retain headmanship. As regards drug use, the Yanomamö do use hallucinogenic drugs. They dance social displays of fierceness in drug-induced states, but I don't think they go on raids drugged-up.

Rowe: Disputes over women are very common causes of violence. In *The autobiography of an L.A. gang member* (Shakur 1993), it's striking that when

'Monster' Kody is thinking about whether to display violence, if there are women from his own neighbourhood present he will decide to stay and make a stand, even if there are many opposing gang members and just one of him. If there are no women present he'll just slide off. The Yanomamö also fight over women. When the Yanomamö make their serious raids, they use tactics like surprise attacks at dawn; it's not a fair fight. The same is seen in inner-city violence.

Daly: That's an interesting point about 'unfair' surprise attacks as opposed to more 'ritual' forms of limited warfare, because the sort of ritualized 'warfare' that has been described in the Dani and other New Guinea tribes, where two groups line up against each other and few get killed, seems to be somewhat rule-bound and restrained. Napoleon Chagnon argues that some archaeological sites provide evidence of opportunistic massacres, as opposed to the more constrained tit-for-tat stuff. He also discusses *nomohori*, where members of one village will feign friendship with another in order to lure them to their demise. Although this sort of violent ploy is looked down on by the Yanomamö, they will sometimes use it to settle long-standing grievances if they hate their enemies enough.

Hinde: On the question of impulsive aggression, the interesting thing is that it's not condoned in industrialized warfare; it's very rare, and when you get it (in places like the My Lai massacre in Vietnam), it's induced by long-term fear. It's very rare in modern warfare.

References

Asch T, Chagnon NA 1975 The ax fight (16 mm documentary film). Documentary Educational Resources, Watertown, MA
Chagnon NA 1968 Yanomamö: the fierce people. Holt, Rinehart, and Winston, NY
Chagnon NA 1974 Studying the Yanomamö. Holt, Rinehart, and Winston, NY
Chagnon NA 1988 Life histories, blood revenge, and warfare in a tribal population. Science 239:985–992
Chagnon NA 1992 Yanomamö: the last days of Eden, 4th edn. Harcourt, Brace, Jovanovich, NY
Chagnon NA, Bugos P 1979 Kin selection and conflict: an analysis of a Yanomamö ax fight. In: Chagnon NA, Irons W (eds) Evolutionary biology and human social behavior: an anthropological perspective. Duxbury Press, North Scituate, MA, p 213–228
Hinde RA, Watson H (eds) 1994 War: a cruel necessity? Taurus, London
Neel JV 1970 Lessons from a primitive people. Science 170:815–818
Shakur S 1993 Monster: the autobiography of an L.A. gang member. Penguin, New York

The implications for responsibility of possible genetic factors in the explanation of violence

Jonathan Glover

New College, Oxford OX1 3BN, UK

Abstract. Genetic determinism is unlikely to be true of most human behaviour. The discovery of a genetically based disposition to violent behaviour would not automatically undermine a person's responsibility for such behaviour. The relevant question is not just whether the genetic disposition plays a causal role, but whether it is so strong as to be irresistible. This requires complex evaluation of different kinds of evidence. When genetic causes are combined with others, including environmental ones, the resulting picture of human behaviour may be a more determinist one than we are used to. Such a picture, if it came to be accepted, would not necessarily undermine responsibility. The everyday distinctions between what we can and cannot do would still survive. But understanding the full implications of such a picture would in some ways modify our attitudes and practices. Blame would take a different form, and retributive punishment might come to seem unacceptable.

1996 Genetics of criminal and antisocial behaviour. Wiley, Chichester (Ciba Foundation Symposium 194) p 237–247

The conceptual framework within which we think about blame, punishment and responsibility for actions was in place long before the advent of modern science. I want to talk first within that traditional moral and legal framework, and then to talk about the extent to which scientific advances might lead us towards a more deterministic picture of human behaviour. This has possible implications for the revision of our traditional framework.

I assume that the vast majority of scientists believe that genetic determinism is a rather extreme thesis and rather implausible for explaining the great range of human behaviour. But there is a much more plausible wider view which could also be called determinism, which is simply that genes together with other factors, such as neurodevelopmental and environmental ones, determine what we do. On this view, if we knew enough about genetics and neurobiology, and we knew the genetic make-up of an individual and about his or her environment, in principle a full causal explanation of behaviour would be possible. A God-like scientist who had all this information would in principle be able to predict what that person would do. The theoretical possibility of the truth of determinism should make us rather more worried than we are. Determinism is an issue that is not faced. This is partly because we do not yet know it is true. It is partly because the build-up of evidence for it is incremental. It is partly because people tend to think in a rather confused way about what its implications are. There is a real question about how well our traditional conceptual scheme fits with the possible implications of determinism.

Thinking within the traditional concepts

Let us start inside the traditional conceptual scheme. The traditional moral framework used in modern thinking is one where we blame people for wrongdoing, we praise people for their virtues. It is also the context of talk about legal responsibility. This traditional moral framework lays great emphasis on the distinction between what we can and cannot do. When we make this distinction, we are contrasting two different kinds of explanation (which may dovetail together in some cases) of why, for instance, a person does something wrong. Sometimes the explanation is that the person does not want to do the right thing. Alternatively, the person may do wrong despite wanting to do the right thing, which, for one reason or another, they were unable to do. Some cases of addiction fit the second model. It is clear that some people truly desire to give up an addiction and are struggling to do so. But, however hard they try, they may be overwhelmed by the psychological forces resulting from the physical addiction. But other actions do not fit this model. If I park on a double-yellow line, it is not plausible for me to say I could not help doing this. If I had enough motive not to park there, I would not have done it. The reason I can be blamed for parking on a double-yellow line is that I had the ability to do something else, but I had the wrong motivation. When we blame people, essentially we are criticizing them for having the wrong motives. We do not criticize people in the same way for their lack of ability. So the key question in assessing someone's ability (when we ask whether he or she could have done otherwise) is: given different motives, would they have acted differently? In English law, the old test used to be: would the offender have committed the offence with a policeman standing at his or her elbow? Although that is much too crude a test, in principle it is on the right lines. Was it a lack of ability to behave otherwise, or was it simply inadequate motivation?

However, there are complications. First, the amount of free choice we have to behave is usually a matter of degree. It is not all-or-none. The other complication is that sometimes the lack of ability is at the level of motives. As a first approximation, I suggested that blame is appropriate where I do the wrong thing because I have the wrong pattern of motivation: where, if I had had a different motive, I would have acted differently. But this is too simple. Some cases of lack of ability involve the lack of ability to change one's own motives. To clarify this, philosophers have introduced the idea of second-order desires. First-order desires are simply the ones that influence my behaviour—I park on a double-yellow line because I am in a hurry. I want to be quick more than I want to keep the law. Second-order desires are relevant to cases where I cannot change my own motives, although I want to. We tend not to blame people morally where we feel they really *wanted* to be different, where they tried their hardest and failed. We think of this sort of case, which is typical of some kinds of addiction, as a case where the central motives of the person (those the person identifies with; the second-order desires) are praiseworthy and admirable desires. Such people are victims of irresistible first-order desires and we tend not to blame them for that. But of course there are tremendous empirical difficulties in establishing whether somebody really is a victim of first-order desires in this sort of way.

The upshot of all this is that moral blame is essentially a matter of criticizing people's *character*, which is seen in terms of their central motives rather than their abilities.

Thinking about a genetic disposition to violence

In principle, a genetic predisposition to violence is not different from an environmentally caused predisposition, if we are thinking about blame. Any tendency to act in a certain way presumably has some sort of causal explanation. And at some point the causal explanation will be traced back to things that are not under a person's control. I did not choose my genes—but, equally, I did not choose my early environment. It is unclear that there is anything radically different between explanations where the causal story goes back to the genes and explanations where the causal story goes back to early environment.

When we think about a genetic disposition there are two possible ways we might think this is relevant to moral or legal responsibility. There are two kinds of questions we could ask.

One, which I consider to be a misguided question, is simply to ask: did the gene play a causal role? If we ask this, the answer (if there is a genetic predisposition) is obviously going to be 'yes'. But that looks as though we are letting the person off from responsibility merely because there is a causal explanation. If we are going to do that, we then need to ask what is special about that causal explanation rather than an environmental one.

A scientific approach searches for causal explanations of what human beings do. This kind of determinism is not a metaphysical dogma, but is a regulative ideal: we hope to get always closer to the determinist picture. This should be borne in mind when we are thinking about possible excuses from responsibility. We should be worried about letting someone off simply because there is a causal factor on the basis of which their behaviour is predictable. This policy has the consequence that, as we get closer to the determinist ideal, we get closer to a position where we all get let off for absolutely everything.

I suggest that the relevant question to ask about the genetic disposition is really a variant of the traditional question: was the genetic disposition so strong that I could not resist it? There we apply the usual sort of tests. The statistics about people with that genetic disposition are going to be relevant here. So if it turns out that everybody with that genetic disposition acts in a certain way, that is going to be good evidence that the chances are that the impulse to act that way is virtually irresistible. Of course there are environmental factors, so if one says there is a disposition which is irresistible, one does not mean it is irresistible all the time, but there are going to be certain contexts where it may be. We need to ask the question: is it plausible that someone could have struggled successfully against this? If it turns out that there are considerable variations in how successfully people try to resist, this raises a big doubt about this kind of behaviour being genetically determined. There may be a chance of other sorts of influence effectively being brought to bear. Perhaps if you give people a stronger motive to act in a certain way, they will turn out able to resist the impulse towards violence.

The key moral question is one about motives versus abilities. But in practice, these empirical questions are enormously difficult to answer one way or the other. This is familiar to psychiatrists giving evidence in court. Psychiatrists often have an understanding of the rather patchy nature of human abilities. Our abilities come and go, they vary a lot according to different contexts, and there may not be a black-and-white answer to the question of whether this person could have acted differently. We are talking about a rather grey area. But, despite the existence of this grey area, the traditional questions about motives and abilities are the right ones to ask. It is not an advance to sweep away the empirical difficulties by saying that any sort of causal explanation via genes automatically reduces or eliminates responsibility. (It is better to be roughly right than precisely wrong.)

The implications of a more determinist picture

Should this gradual swing towards determinism—the filling in of more and more of the causal picture behind what people do—in any way undermine our normal way of thinking about morality and blame?

When most people say they are free and should be held morally responsible, they probably assume that causal determinism does not apply to their actions. But, at first sight, if causal determination applies, things seem different. Determinism suggests that if we knew all the scientific laws that were relevant, and all the initial conditions in which they operated, in principle we would be able to predict behaviour. Consider the billiard balls often used to illustrate

Newtonian physics. We assume that billiard balls are subject to Newtonian laws. If someone asks, 'could the billiard ball have gone somewhere else, other than where it did?', the answer we would normally give is 'yes, but only if the conditions had been different'. But if someone asks, 'given all the circumstances exactly as they were, could the ball have gone anywhere else?' there is a perfectly clear sense in which the answer is 'no'. For the ball to have gone anywhere else would have falsified the laws of Newtonian physics. Since we believe the laws of Newtonian physics are true, we think that it could not have done anything else.

On the determinist picture of human behaviour, if we knew everything about ourselves and about the laws of science, we would be as predictable as the billiard balls. There are two conflicting interpretations of such a determinist picture of people. Great battles have been fought over this in philosophy since the early-17th century. There is what is known as 'hard' determinism and what is known as 'soft' determinism.

Hard determinism says that if everything in principle is predictable, then, as with the billiard balls, we cannot do anything except what we do do. If we cannot do anything different, then we cannot help our actions and so it is unfair to blame us for them. Blame may be socially useful in various ways— perhaps it is something we cannot in practice give up—but deep down it is unfair. The hard determinist position is that moral responsibility is an illusion, part of the pre-scientific picture that ought to be abandoned.

But there is a powerful rival in the form of soft determinism. On this second view, even if everything we do is in principle predictable, we can still retain all the traditional moral attitudes. There is a real sense in which even if causal determinism is true, my parking on a double-yellow line because it happens to be convenient is still something which I could have chosen not to do. Even in a determinist world, somebody doing something as a result of an overwhelming psychiatric compulsion of some sort is in a very different state. Soft determinists say that the fact that determinism may be true does not obliterate these distinctions. Hard determinists are operating with one sense of 'can', which is different from the sense of 'can' which soft determinists are operating with.

I am largely sympathetic to soft determinism. This is partly because it seems to me that these distinctions which we operate with are real distinctions. They do not get obliterated by the fact (if it is a fact) that everything is in principle causally predictable. It is also unlikely that we would enrich human life if we gave up the moral attitudes we normally have towards people. If we give up blame on the grounds that people cannot help doing what they do, we also have to give up things like gratitude, resentment and a whole range of ordinary interpersonal attitudes that characterize real human relationships. If we were to follow hard determinism, we would adopt in all our relationships the detached clinical attitude of a psychiatrist towards a patient, or a social worker towards a client. Life would be a great deal less satisfactory if we had only these rather detached relationships. Also, it is not at all clear that it would be possible to disengage from our deeply rooted normal human attitudes.

Having said that, although I want us to keep our traditional distinctions, I am a little bit worried about whether it is really possible to do so. I am inclined to think that, at one level at least, we are going to have to revise the way we think about things. If we come to believe in some sort of broadly determinist causal story which may mean that everything is predictable (and I know that many of you may think that this is wildly jumping the gun to the science of 200 years' time), our everyday thinking about human abilities may start to seem superficial. We will realize that there is a fine-structure story that can be given. Take an obvious case where I seem to be quite free, where, for instance, I am parking on the double-yellow line because I cannot be bothered to go and find a parking space. If determinism is true, the chances are that if you knew everything about my genes, environment and neurodevelopmental story, then you would find that anyone with exactly the same causal history would act in that way. And we can take the causal history back. Supposing I have what, for soft determinists, is the maximum amount of freedom (I am not acting under coercion or external pressure, nor am I an addict), and I behave badly to one of you in some way. You, being a fair-minded person, before you blame me, ask whether anyone forced me to do this. I say 'no'. You say 'well, did you have an overwhelming urge, which you now bitterly regret, to behave in this way?' I say 'no, I am actually rather proud of having done this' (I think of myself as some Nietzschean Übermensch, who delights in his independence from conventional bourgeois morality). At this point you may think that I really am a candidate for blame. But I may ask you to consider where my second-order desires came from. If determinism is true, there is some causal story that goes back beyond these higher-order desires. At some level, we get back to the point where the basic structure of the motives from which I start is determined by factors outside my control. These factors may be early environment, or genetics, or neurodevelopmental influences. So, in some sense, ultimately we are only partially responsible for our character. We can shape ourselves to a certain degree; we can decide we want to be one sort of person rather than another and work at that. But if one asks about what decides whether we have the desires to shape ourselves in this way, then we ultimately get back to factors beyond our control.

A revised view of blame

We may very well find we have to, and indeed want to, retain the idea of blame. But, when the implications of a more determinist view are understood, on this view, blame becomes more like aesthetic appraisal. As we start to understand more about the causal story, I believe we will be somewhat less inclined to think that when someone does something wrong it is in every way their fault.

We may still want to have blame. It is a useful means of social control, and if we gave it up we would have tremendous problems influencing people to behave better. But blame would become more like a kind of aesthetic appraisal of a person's character. It could still be very effective as a means of social control. Instead of blaming someone for the disgustingly awful thing he has done wrong, we might feel sorry for him having such a hideously ugly character.

The other implication is that not only do we have to have blame in a slightly new key, it also becomes problematic justifying retributive punishment. We can certainly justify having certain rules which say that if you were not free to do otherwise in the conventional sense, because of some psychiatric illness or something of this sort, then we will not punish you. There are very good consequentialist reasons for that, about people having freedom to predict the intervention of the legal system in their own lives. It is important that most of us feel pretty sure that the state is not going to start locking us up unless we have actually chosen to break the law. So there is a strong case for saying that we ought to restrict punishment to those who in the ordinary conventional sense did the crime and could help it. But if we believe that deep down people are not ultimately to blame for the fundamental character that they have, either because of genetic or environmental causal explanations, then I think it is hard to see that we can justify insisting that people *ought* to suffer for the crimes they have done, in cases where the punishment does no social good. There will be a tendency to move towards more consequentialist theories, rather than retributive theories, in thinking about the point of punishment.

DISCUSSION

Denno: I was curious about your emphasis on motive rather than intent. The law predominantly emphasizes intent.

Glover: Intention is absolutely central to our moral appraisal, just as it is to our legal appraisal. But very often, in morality, we want to go beyond intention. In law, motive is often rather hard to establish. Morally, motive is also hard to establish, but we're more prepared to be flexible. We often want to know not just 'did you intend to do it?' but also 'why did you intend to do it?' because that makes quite a difference to the moral appraisal. For instance, I can intend to park on a double-yellow line, but it may be because I'm rushing to visit a dying child in hospital. That's a very different motive from simply not wanting to pay for the meter.

Hinde: Does your viewpoint take care of football hooligans, because they are acting in accordance their second-order motives, which are simply discrepant with ours? Is our judgement that they're doing wrong purely an aesthetic one?

Glover: It's a moral judgement that they're doing wrong.

Hinde: It's a moral judgement by our standards, not by their standards.

Glover: This takes us into a very large separate issue. There is a debate about whether objectively valid moral standards exist, or whether there are only subjective moral standards which reflect the particular commitments and values of particular individuals or groups of people. I am sceptical about the idea of an objective moral law independent of us, so when I make a judgement about football thugs I regard myself as expressing values personal to myself. But in this case they are values which are fairly widely held by many people in our society. The majority view in our society is that football hooligans have a character which is blameworthy. The view is that, all the way down, they have this unpleasant motivational structure. We should certainly punish them on grounds of deterring other people from behaving in this way. But we are also, in a certain sense, entitled to blame them. In the view I put forward, blaming them is not saying 'deep down you could help this because you're metaphysically free', it's saying 'maybe deep down there is some causal explanation of why you're like this but, all the same, we think your character is extremely ugly, and it is helpful to the wider society if we make it clear that we think this way'.

Gottesman: What role, if any, do you have in your 'soft' determinism for the role of chance or stochastic processes, or good and bad luck?

Glover: In one sense, our genes and our early environment are a kind of good or bad luck. We didn't choose our genes. We didn't choose our parents. We didn't choose our schools. So there is a certain amount of what is sometimes called 'constitutive luck' in the moral appraisal of people. This goes against a very deep intuition that many people have. The idea in the traditional religious picture (for instance, of people being sent to heaven or hell) is that you're only judged on your morality, and that mustn't be a matter of luck. It must be all down to you. Great secular moralists, like Immanuel Kant, have also reflected the idea that moral praise and blame must be totally independent of luck. But that is part of what I regard as a prescientific worldview.

Sometimes people suggest a way in which chance might allow us to escape from determinism. There might be quantum effects which mean that, at least at the neurophysiological or neurochemical level, we can't make predictions about behaviour. I am doubtful about that escape for two reasons.

One reason is scepticism about the claim that quantum effects actually do affect gross physical objects very much. I don't, for instance, expect this table suddenly to zoom up and hit the ceiling because all the individual electrons are behaving that way. It is plausible to suppose that the statistical laws which operate in quantum theory are enough to generate a fairly steady predictability at the macro level.

The other worry I have about that sort approach is that even if it could be shown that some of our behaviour was unpredictable—that indeterminism held for human decisions—it doesn't seem to rescue freedom. The Scottish philosopher David Hume, at the end of the 18th century, made the point that this just imports an element of randomness, and randomness does not seem a paradigm case of free and responsible action. Imagine I tell you how I voted in an election. You ask why I voted that way. My response is that I weighed up a list of considerations and they seemed to me exactly evenly balanced, so I went into the polling booth and just found myself making a cross against this name. This seems to be what the phenomenology of random or indeterminist action would be like, and it is hard to see that as a version of free and responsible action. An element of randomness does not seem to be the same as an element of freedom.

Brunner: If we assume that we are never going to know everything that underlies a particular behaviour—and I think that is a reasonable supposition— then how should demonstrating one factor, major or minor, make any difference in our judgement of an individual case?

Glover: We are always making decisions, including decisions about praise and blame, with incomplete and imperfect information. I am reluctant to take the view that because we are always working with incomplete information, we shouldn't welcome any additions to the information that we have. To go back to the example of voting for one party rather than another, I can't actually predict what will happen if the Labour party replaces the Conservative party after the next election, because there are a whole lot of factors which I don't know about. But because I do not have perfect information, it seems to me to be a counsel of despair to say that I'll then vote in a way that is insensitive to any information at all. The same goes for judgements of people and their actions.

Bouchard: In your analysis, when you get to the point where you say that we have to make moral judgements and bring moral blame, I do not see how that does not get you back to the argument of many religious leaders. It is remarkable that the topic of religion hasn't come up in this symposium. We've talked about personality dispositions, but nobody has admitted (and I say this from a non-religious standpoint) that in the literature the evils people in this room are studying and trying to prevent—alcohol abuse, drug abuse, abuse of health etc.—are all better predicted by religiousness than any other known variable (Bergin 1983, Gorsuch 1988, Koenig et al 1990, Morse & Rabinowitz 1990). If you go out and measure religiousness in almost all contexts, highly religious people take better care of themselves, drink less, use abusive substances less, are violent against each other less etc. In fact, it is one of the most powerful variables in psychology. It seems to me that your model clearly reinforces this, and argues that one should take a blaming stance for controlling behaviour.

Glover: I'm not sure that blame is confined to religious people.

Bouchard: It's not, but they make much more cultural use of it.

Glover: Whether you think that religion has an effect of damping down violence as against increasing it, partly depends on whether you look at the micro or macro level. It sounds plausible at the micro level.

Rowe: Is the free-will choice always making the morally responsible one? Jerome Kagan (1994), in his book *Galen's prophecy*, argues for a physiological basis of the temperaments of inhibited and uninhibited children. His last chapter deals with the fact that this temperament theory is very damaging to our notion of free will. But all these examples of free will are when you're confronted with particular temptations that you succeed in resisting. If free will has a directionality to it, then it's a predictable kind of behaviour. I thought that when we exercised free will we had the ability to do anything, even make the choice that is bad: I don't get that feeling from the discussions I've read about it.

Glover: There is a lot of ambiguity in the phrase 'free will'. But if the claim is that more often than we realize we are overwhelmed by temptations, which for physiological reasons we cannot resist, I would like to look at the evidence very carefully. It is very hard to actually carry out the relevant tests.

Virkkunen: Free will is connected with one's ability to control oneself. An increasing number of biological (and possibly even genetic) findings are coming to show that impulsivity is at least partly biologically controlled. Impulsive people simply cannot control themselves enough. How much free will do they have?

Glover: You say these people are impulsive and they cannot control themselves in the same way that we can, but your evidence for that is not genetic evidence.

Virkkunen: At this moment it's more biological, concerned with brain serotonin turnover and receptor expression in the brain.

Glover: I would have thought it is actually behavioural evidence. Is it going to be that we find that everybody who has this particular biological marker, whatever it is, acts impulsively? If that's not so, then we want to know by what means some people do control their impulses, and some don't. It does seem that the question of whether someone can control their impulse is not going to be answered by biology, but by observing behaviour in different contexts.

Virkkunen: Did the males studied by Brunner et al (1993), with a monoamine oxidase A mutation, have free will?

Brunner: I don't think any genetic factor is going to be determining enough for you to say that a particular biological characteristic determines behaviour. So we're never going to be able to say that if a person has this genetic character, then their behaviour is inevitable.

Daly: That's simply the point that everything is multiply caused. Some variance in the manifestations of a condition doesn't really rescue you from the problem of determinism, it is simply that there are multiple interacting determinants.

Brunner: It would seem to me that if a person commits a crime, the best way of knowing their true motives would be by asking the person about them and perhaps simulating certain situations and asking them how they would react. Surely this will give you a more complete picture than knowing about isolated biological variables.

Goldman: Yes, I think the crucial issue, and one to which you have so rightly drawn attention, is how much the genetic information really will tell us about an individual's motivational structure. Near the end of Steinbeck's *East of Eden*, Adam whispers 'Timshel'—thou mayest, expressing the idea that an individual may choose between good and evil. Can or cannot an individual hear an injunction to moderate his/her behaviour? If you have a genetic finding that a person is predisposed to a certain criminal behaviour, it is an incomplete descriptor. Perhaps all behaviour is deterministic, but one element in the determinism is the ability, which varies from person to person, to respond to an injunction or rule.

Glover: I think there is a perfectly good sense in which we do choose. For instance, if someone has a genetic disposition to arson, one day they don't choose to set fire to a building and another day they do. The question is, how difficult is it for them to resist across a period? How much does the genetic disposition make it harder for them to behave normally?

Goldman: That's right, they're not setting fires on very many days, but if there is a 1% risk per day, the probability that a fire will be set becomes, over time, almost inevitable. However, it never becomes fully inevitable.

References

Bergin AE 1983 Religosity and mental health: a critical reevaluation and meta-analysis. Prof Psychol Res Pract 14:170–184

Brunner HG, Nelen M, Breakfield XO, Ropers HH, van Ost BA 1993 Abnormal behavior associated with a point mutation in the structural gene for monoamine oxidase A. Science 262:578–580

Gorsuch RL 1988 Psychology of religion. In: Rosensweig MR, Porter LW (eds) Annual review of psychology, p 201–221

Kagan J 1994 Galen's prophecy: temperament in human nature. Basic Books, New York

Koenig HG, Sigler IC, Meador KG, George LK 1990 Religious coping and personality in later life. J Gerontol Psychol Sci 45:113–115

Morse DR, Rabinowitz MA 1990 A unified theory of aging. Int J Psychosomatics 37: 5–24

Legal implications of genetics and crime research

Deborah W. Denno

Fordham University School of Law, 140 West 62nd Street, New York, NY 10023-7485, USA

Abstract. Two controversial topics dominate discussions of the legal implications of genetics and crime research: (1) the viability and politics of such research, which has sparked fervent debate in the USA; and (2) the current status of new or atypical criminal law defences, which would include a genetic-defect defence to criminal behaviour. This chapter begins by examining the scientifically discredited XYY chromosome syndrome defence, the major genetic-defect defence that defendants have attempted, albeit unsuccessfully. It then focuses on attorneys' efforts to test for evidence of genetic abnormality in the recent and highly publicized case involving convicted murderer Stephen Mobley, whose family history reveals four generations of violent, aggressive and behaviourally disordered men and women. Mobley is currently appealing his death sentence before the Georgia Supreme Court on the basis that the trial court denied his request both to have genetic testing performed and to have such testing allowed as evidence into court. This chapter concludes by emphasizing that the question is not whether genetic evidence will ever be admitted into court, but when and under what kinds of circumstances. No doubt, genetic evidence, and comparable kinds of biological evidence, will have a major impact on juries when such evidence is more fully accepted by the legal and scientific communities.

1996 Genetics of criminal and antisocial behaviour. Wiley, Chichester (Ciba Foundation Symposium 194) p 248–264

Two controversial topics dominate discussions of the legal implications of genetics and crime research: (1) the viability and politics of such research, which has sparked fervent debate in the USA (Denno 1988, Gottesman 1994, Nelkin & Tancredi 1994); and (2) the current status of new or atypical criminal law defences, which would include a genetic-defect defence to criminal behaviour (Curriden 1994, Dershowitz 1994). This chapter begins by examining the scientifically discredited XYY chromosome syndrome defence, the major genetic-defect defence that defendants have attempted, albeit unsuccessfully. It then focuses on attorneys' efforts to test for evidence of genetic abnormality in the recent and highly publicized case involving convicted murderer Stephen Mobley, whose family history reveals four generations of violent, aggressive and behaviourally disordered men and women. This chapter concludes by emphasizing that the question is not whether genetic evidence will ever be admitted into court, but when and under what kinds of circumstances. No doubt, genetic evidence, and comparable kinds of biological evidence, will have a major impact on juries when such evidence is more fully accepted by the legal and scientific communities.

The XYY chromosome syndrome defence

In general, the criminal law presumes that behaviour is a consequence of free will. Some research in the genetic and biological sciences suggests, however, that this presumption overlooks a variety of factors that may in part determine an individual's conduct. This schism between the criminal law and science reveals tensions between two perspectives of human behaviour: free will and determinism. Between the two, the criminal law has reached a compromise. It generally treats 'conduct as autonomous and willed, not because it is, but because it is desirable to proceed as if it were' (Packer 1968, p 74–75). Yet, it also recognizes elements of determinism by providing defences or mitigating factors.

In the USA, defendants have mostly failed at using genetic evidence to establish either a defence or a mitigating factor. The earliest and best known cases of a genetic-defect defence concerned the XYY chromosome syndrome. The XYY chromosome syndrome has been studied most extensively in relation to crime and violence because, initially, the extra Y chromosome suggested possible evidence of greater 'maleness' or aggression. Yet critiques of the methodologically questionable XYY studies raised serious doubts that XYY individuals were significantly predisposed to aggression or violence (Carey 1994, Denno 1988).

Partly for this reason, the XYY syndrome defence was not successful in the five major American cases that have attempted to use it. The defence was introduced in the USA in *People v. Farley* (1969, unpublished), the only American case in which a court allowed the defendant's evidence of an XYY abnormality to go to the jury. In *Farley*, the jury rejected the defendant's claim that the XYY syndrome precluded him from forming the necessary intent to commit murder and found him guilty as charged (Farrell 1969). Two cases thereafter did not even allow such evidence to reach the jury, concluding that the defendant's XYY status failed to meet the State's requirements for insanity (Denno 1988).

The major issue in the fourth case, *People v. Yukl* (1975), was not whether XYY chromosome syndrome evidence met New York's standard for insanity, but whether it was sufficiently scientific to meet the State's standard for admissibility into evidence. Yukl was charged with the murder of a young woman after just having been released from prison for a similar type of murder. The court denied his request that a chromosome test be conducted and offered as evidence at trial. Instead, the court proposed that an XYY defence 'should be possible only if one establishes with a high degree of medical certainty an etiological relationship between the defendant's mental capacity and the genetic syndrome' (*Yukl* 1975, p 319). A year later, the Washington Court of Appeals echoed *Yukl* in *State v. Roberts* (1976), which concluded that 'presently available medical evidence is unable to establish a reasonably certain causal connection between the XYY defect and criminal conduct'.

The XYY syndrome has also been introduced as evidence in other countries. In 1968, an Australian court in *Regina v. Hannell* (unpublished) acquitted by reason of insanity the XYY defendant for the murder of a 77-year-old widow. Although news accounts attributed the case's outcome to the defendant's XYY evidence, an analysis of the trial transcript revealed that his XYY status was mentioned only once and was not the grounds for his acquittal. Four days later a French court convicted Daniel Hugon for the strangulation-murder of a prostitute, yet provided him with a mitigated sentence of seven years based upon his XYY chromosome abnormality (Note 1969). That same year, however, a West German court appeared to discount Ernest Dieter Beck's XYY status by giving him the maximum sentence of life imprisonment for three murders (Skeen 1983).

In general, then, both the legal and scientific communities have not accepted a proposed link between XYY chromosome disorder and violence or aggression, a direction supported by the results of a large and methodologically sophisticated study (Witkin et al 1976). Moreover, researchers still report limited knowledge of the genetic, biological, sociological and psychological correlates of crime (Carey 1994, Monahan 1993, 1994), despite advances in some areas (Brunner et al 1993). At the same time, courts' standards for the admissibility of scientific evidence have grown more flexible. In *Daubert v. Merrell Dow Pharmaceuticals, Inc.* (1993), the United States Supreme Court displaced the prior *Frye v. United States* (1923) standard (requiring that a scientific technique be inadmissible in federal court unless it is 'generally accepted' as reliable in the scientific community), with the following standard adopted from the Federal Rules of Evidence: 'If scientific, technical, or other specialized knowledge will assist the trier of fact to understand the evidence or to determine a fact in issue, a witness qualified as an expert by knowledge, skill, experience, training, or education, may testify thereto in the form of an opinion or otherwise' (*Daubert* 1993, Monahan & Walker 1994, Nelkin 1994). Such flexibility has also been demonstrated in some states' criminal evidentiary standards, prompting in part the growth of some 'new' criminal law defences (Dershowitz 1994). The next part of this chapter considers these developments in light of the recent and highly publicized USA case involving convicted murderer Stephen Mobley and his attempts to acquire genetic testing.

Genetics and the Stephen Mobley case

On February 17, 1991, 25-year-old Stephen Mobley entered a Domino's Pizza store in Oakwood, Hall County, Georgia. After cleaning out the cash register, he shot the store's manager in the back of the neck. Mobley confessed to the crime nearly a month later (Brief for Appellant 1994, Brief for Appellee 1994, *Mobley v. State* 1993). At trial, Mobley's attorneys requested that they be allowed to present evidence that Mobley's crime could have been attributable to his genetic make-up. The attorneys emphasized that they were not using this potential genetic evidence as a defence to be introduced during the trial's guilt phase, but only as possible mitigating evidence to be introduced during the trial's penalty phase (Brief for Appellant 1994). Explanations that would not in themselves establish a defence might be mitigating circumstances that would justify a life sentence rather than the death penalty.

Mobley's request regarding the testing and admissibility of possible genetic evidence was based primarily upon his family history of four generations of violence. Joyce Ann Mobley Childers, the first cousin of Mobley's father, testified that violence, aggression and behavioural disorder dominate the Mobley family tree, including Mobley's uncles, aunts and grandfather (Fig. 1, derived from Childers' unpublished testimony at Mobley's Sentencing Hearing). At the same time, the family tree contains several highly successful businessmen such as Mobley's father, Steve, a self-made multimillionaire (Brief for Appellant 1994). According to Mobley's attorney, the Mobley men demonstrate 'a fine line between aggressive success and violent outrage' (Curriden 1994).

Stephen Mobley's past was characterized by an inability to control his impulses or to internalize any kind of value system (D. Summer, personal communication 1995). His father claims that Mobley's behavioural problems began very early in life and grew worse as he aged. Consequently, Mobley was sent to numerous institutions, none of which successfully treated him. A psychiatrist at one institution diagnosed Mobley at age 16 with conduct disorder, a diagnosis that would have been labelled antisocial personality disorder had he been six months older. During the penalty phase of Mobley's trial, the State introduced additional evidence of Mobley's violent and criminal behaviour, including other armed robberies, prior convictions for forgery and credit card theft, fighting and an alleged sexual assault against an inmate (Brief for Appellant 1994, Brief for Appellee 1994).

At trial, Mobley's attorney requested expert assistance and finances of $1000 in order to perform preliminary neurological testing to ascertain whether Mobley was suffering from an imbalance of any one of a variety of neurochemicals. In support of this request, Mobley introduced into evidence a recent study by Brunner et al (1993), which identified a large kindred in The Netherlands containing several males who evidenced a syndrome of borderline mental retardation and abnormal behaviour, including aggression and violence. Testing of these males revealed that this syndrome was associated with a 'complete and selective deficiency' of enzymic activity of monoamine oxidase A (MAOA). The researchers further identified a point mutation in a structural gene that regulated production of MAOA (Brunner et al 1993). Dr Xandra O. Breakefield, a co-author of the study, agreed to perform the necessary genetic analysis on Mobley for point mutations, if preliminary testing indicated that he evidenced a possible genetic mutation (Brief for Appellant). Other researchers have also volunteered to conduct tests to determine whether Mobley is suffering from abnormal levels of neurochemicals which may be associated with aggressive behaviour, such as serotonin, MAOA, noradrenaline and adrenaline (Brief for Appellant 1994, Virkkunen et al 1994a,b).

In response, the State noted first that Mobley could not be compared with members of The Netherlands family because, with a full-scale IQ of 104, he was not borderline mentally retarded. For this reason, there was no factual basis for expecting that he suffered from a deficiency of MAOA. Moreover, the State noted that Brunner et al (1993) acknowledged that '[t]he inhibition of MAOA has not been reported to cause aggressive behaviour in adult humans but deficiencies throughout life might have different consequences' (Brunner et al 1993, p 579). As a result, the Hall County Superior Court denied Mobley's request to have the tests performed or to be allowed as evidence into court, explaining that '[t]he theory of genetic connection...is not at a level of scientific acceptance that would justify its admission' (Curriden 1994). On February 20, 1994, a jury found Mobley guilty and sentenced him to death. His case is currently on appeal before the Georgia Supreme Court.

Future legal implications

Recent news articles on the Mobley case are one quick source indicating the possible legal implications of research on genetics and crime. In *The National Law Journal*, interviewed attorneys offered a range of opinions, although on one issue there was some consensus: '[T]he question is not if this kind of genetic testing is admissible as mitigating evidence in criminal trials, but when' (Curriden 1994). Indeed, although news accounts inaccurately characterize the

Mobley case as breaking 'new legal ground' in its attempt to introduce genetic evidence (Felsenthal 1994), what is new is the case's procedural posture. Contrary to those strategies followed in the XYY chromosome syndrome cases, Mobley's attorneys were not using the evidence to justify insanity or partial responsibility; they were using it to mitigate his sentence in an attempt to avoid the death penalty.

The Georgia Superior Court's refusal to allow such testing or evidence in Mobley's sentencing strays from courts' increasingly liberal acceptance of biological and psychological evidence to justify defences (Dershowitz 1994). During the 1980s, for example, a number of courts considered the results of positron emission tomography (PET) scans in their sentencing decisions, relying in part on the presumption that a biological predisposition could preclude free will (Nelkin & Tancredi 1994). It was not until 1992, however, that any court rendered admissible into trial testimony concerning the results of PET scans to determine a defendant's sanity (Anderson 1992). In *People v. Weinstein* (1992), a New York court concluded that an expert's in-court consideration of the results of a PET scan and skin conductance response tests—indicating the existence of both an arachnoid cyst and metabolic imbalances in the defendant's brain—was not unreasonable in making a diagnosis of insanity. However, the court emphasized that attorneys could not mention at trial 'certain theories relating to human behavior' because they were not generally accepted as valid. These included statements that either arachnoid cysts or reduced levels of glucose metabolism in the frontal lobes of the brain, directly cause violence (*People v. Weinstein* 1992). Regardless, the State agreed to negotiate a plea rather than go to trial, thereby reducing the initial charge from murder to manslaughter (Anderson 1992).

The plea bargain in *Weinstein* as well as the evidentiary block in *Mobley* illustrate legal actors' perceptions of the importance of genetic and biological evidence in court, irrespective of the constraints on attorneys' use of such evidence to support causal links to violence. Yet, a major question is: why do courts shun genetic evidence at the same time as they are becoming increasingly liberal in their admissibility of a broad range of other kinds of evidence?

The answer may depend on various factors. First, relative to other kinds of evidence, both genetic and biological evidence appears more precise, constricts the need for interpretation by various experts, and therefore more quickly and definitively resolves otherwise complicated disputes. It 'offers seemingly definitive answers at a time of frustration with the vagueness of other disciplines' (Nelkin 1994). Because such evidence can give an 'aura of truth', it consequently provides more power to technical experts and those who can pay for the new scientific techniques (Nelkin & Tancredi 1994).

Indeed, the potential significance of genetic evidence in particular is illustrated by Dreyfus & Nelkin's (1992) comparison of two similar California cases involving disbarment proceedings based upon the misappropriation of client funds which each petitioner attributed to substance abuse. Whereas one attorney was disbarred (*In re Ewaniszyk* 1990), the other was merely placed on probation (*Baker v. State Bar of California* 1990) apparently because he presented evidence of a 'genetic predisposition to alcoholism', which rendered his claim for mitigation more compelling. A woman's recent acquittal for the murder of her son based on the defence that she had Huntington's disease, a heritable and terminal brain disorder, may have been influenced in part by evidence that the disease is genetic (Ellis 1994).

A second factor concerns the common myth that genetic structure is static (Gottesman & Goldsmith 1994), prompting some lawyers to suggest that treatment or rehabilitation for a genetically abnormal offender is 'probably pointless', since rehabilitation is based on the presumption that behaviour can be modified (Taylor 1982). Yet, some scientists debunk a 'genes for crime' concept, emphasizing instead that genes act developmentally and probabilistically—potentially predisposing some individuals to behavioural tendencies or 'liability', such as impulsivity, which may increase the probability that they will engage in crime under certain circumstances (Carey 1994, Gottesman & Goldsmith 1994). These perspectives would suggest that a genetic abnormality could be compared to other sorts of biological, psychological or sociological factors, which have been admitted as evidence into court—including, for example, a wide range of syndromes (Denno 1994, Monahan & Walker 1994) and cognitive or environmental influences (Denno 1990).

Genetic evidence may also be treated differently for reasons based upon moral and ethical concerns. These include: (1) its historical association with past abuses by the Nazis during the Holocaust (Gottesman 1994); (2) its potential chilling of our notions of free will; (3) its stigmatizing effect, exemplified by past efforts to screen and follow genetically abnormal children (Nelkin & Tancredi 1994) or by current concerns with the preventive detention of those genetically predisposed to violence; and, more recently (4) its potential absolution of societal responsibility for the social and economic factors that could lead to crime if society finds a genetic-defect defence acceptable (Nelkin & Lindee 1995). Genetic evidence could also become a double-edged sword, leading a jury to conclude that a defendant should be penalized more, not less, because he is dangerous and incurable.

All of these factors must be considered in assessing the legal implications of genetics and crime research. If scientists continue to devise more sophisticated tests for measuring genetic and biological factors, and begin to show stronger links between those factors and human behaviour, courts and legislatures will have to confront how this evidence should comport with the various criminal law philosophies and notions of causation. For example, legal scholars may conclude either now or later that none of this research—genetic or otherwise—

has begun to approach a scientifically sufficient level of acceptability, even under the *Daubert* standard. The problem, then, may not be with what the burgeoning scientific research will show—rather, the vague and inconsistent ways the legal system may approach it.

Acknowledgements

I am most grateful to Bruce Green, John Monahan, Dorothy Nelkin and Daniel Summer for their comments on this chapter. Any mistakes or misjudgements are mine. I give special thanks to Robert Renzulli and Marni Roder for their superb research assistance. Chris Hale, Charles Taylor and the Office of the District Attorney, Northeastern Judicial Circuit contributed helpful comments and information, for which I am thankful. Fordham University School of Law provided generous research support.

References

Anderson C 1992 Brain scan deemed admissible at trial. N Y Law J 210:1

Brunner HG, Nelen M, Breakefield XO, Ropers HH, van Oost BA 1993 Abormal behavior associated with a point mutation in the structural gene for monoamine oxidase A. Science 262:578–580

Carey G 1994 Genetics and violence. In: Reiss AJ, Miczek KA, Roth JA (eds) Understanding and preventing violence: biobehavioral influences, vol 2. National Academy, Washington, DC, p 21–58

Curriden M 1994 His lawyer says it's in the killer's genes. Natl Law J 17:A12

Denno DW 1988 Human biology and criminal responsibility: free will or free ride? Univ Pennsylvania Law Rev 137:615–671

Denno DW 1990 Biology and violence: from birth to adulthood. Cambridge University Press, Cambridge

Denno DW 1994 Gender, crime, and the criminal law defenses. J Crim Law & Criminol 85:80–180

Dershowitz AM 1994 The abuse excuse and other cop-outs, sob stories, and evasions of responsibility. Little Brown, Boston, MA

Dreyfus RC, Nelkin D 1992 The jurisprudence of genetics. Vanderbilt Law Rev 45:313–348

Ellis R 1994 'She's not a cold-blooded killer': unique defense frees mom convicted of killing son. Atlanta J & Constitution 127:1

Farrell PT 1969 The XYY syndrome in criminal law: an introduction. St John's Law Rev 44:217–219

Felsenthal E 1994 Man's genes made him kill, his lawyers claim. Wall Street J 224:B1, B5

Gottesman II 1994 Schizophrenia epigenesis: past, present, and future. Acta Psychiatr Scand 90 (suppl 384):26–33

Gottesman II, Goldsmith HH 1994 Developmental psychopathology of antisocial behavior: inserting genes into its ontogenesis and epigenesis. In: Nelson CA (ed) Threats to optimal development: integrating biological, psychological, and social risk factors. Lawrence Erlbaum, Hillsdale, NJ, p 69–104

Monahan J 1993 Causes of violence. In: United States Sentencing Commission (ed) Drugs and violence. US Government Printing Office, Washington, DC, p 77–85

Monahan J 1994 People with mental disorder and people who offend: collecting valid data. Crim Behav Ment Health 4:68–73

Monahan J, Walker L 1994 Social science in law: cases and materials, 3rd edn. Foundation Press, New York

Nelkin D 1994 After *Daubert*: the relevance and reliability of genetic information. Cardozo Law Rev 15:2119–2128

Nelkin D, Lindee S 1995 The DNA mystique: the gene as a cultural icon. W. H. Freeman, New York

Nelkin D, Tancredi L 1994 Dangerous diagnostics: the social power of biological information, 2nd edn. University of Chicago Press, Chicago, IL

Note 1969 The XYY chromosome defense. Georgetown Law J 57:892–922

Packer H 1968 The limits of the criminal sanction 74–75. Stanford University Press, Stanford, CA

Skeen D 1983 The genetically defective offender. William Mitchell Law Rev 9:217–265

Taylor LE 1982 Genetically influenced antisocial conduct and the criminal justice system. Cleveland State Law Rev 31:61–75

Virkkunen M, Rawlings R, Tokola R et al 1994a CSF biochemistries, glucose metabolism, and diurnal activity rhythms in alcoholic, violent offenders, fire setters, and healthy volunteers. Arch Gen Psychiatry 51:20–27

Virkunnen M, Kallio E, Rawlings R et al 1994b Personality profiles and state aggressiveness in Finnish alcoholic, violent offenders, fire setters, and healthy volunteers. Arch Gen Psychiatry 51:28–33

Witkin HA, Mednick SA, Schulsinger F et al 1976 Criminality in XYY and XXY men. Science 193:547–555

Cases

Baker v. State Bar of California, 781 P.2d 1344 (Cal. 1990)

Daubert v. Merrell Dow Pharmaceuticals, Inc., 113 S.Ct. 2786 (1993)

Frye v. United States, 293 F. 1013 (D.C. Cir. 1923)

In re Ewaniszyk, 788 P.2d 690 (Cal. 1990)

Mobley v. State, 426 S.E.2d 150 (Ga. 1993)

People v. Yukl, 372 N.Y.S.2d 313 (Sup. Ct. 1975)

People v. Weinstein, 591 N.Y.S.2d 715 (Sup. Ct. 1992)

State v. Roberts, 544 P.2d 754 (Wash. App. 1976)

DISCUSSION

Carey: Aside from the legal implications of introducing this kind of evidence, I just wanted to point out that this pedigree (Fig. 1) is entirely inconsistent with X-linkage. The affected locus would have to pass from Ralph (a man), through Steve (a man), to Stephen. From this alone, it's highly improbable that the MAOA locus is going to have any involvement in this type of disorder.

Denno: Let me say several things in response to your comment. First, Mobley's attorneys were using the MAOA deficiency research as a vehicle for suggesting that Stephen Mobley may have some genetic or neurochemical disorder. That disorder could be either a MAOA deficiency or, just as significantly, some other kind of deficiency comparably associated with aggressive behaviour. This is why Mobley's attorneys suggested that a wide range of testing be conducted on him, including tests to determine whether he was suffering from abnormal levels of neurochemicals found to be associated with aggression, such as serotonin, noradrenaline and adrenaline. Second, although a number of experts signed affidavits indicating their willingness to conduct such testing, no genetics expert has, as yet, even looked at Stephen Mobley. The court wouldn't allow it. Therefore, Mobley's attorneys could only offer what preliminary evidence they had. A part of that evidence was Joyce Ann Childers Mobley's testimony about the family. Third, even Joyce Ann's testimony is only preliminary. She did not provide a full family tree. Although I tried repeatedly to contact her, she was not to be found. Given the considerable publicity and legal controversy in this case—apart from simply the genetics issue—I thought it best not to pursue the matter further.

Waldman: It seems that the conceptualizations of criminality and its causes, in both legal and philosophical contexts, are similar to most contemporary conceptualizations of mental disorder, in having both a scientific and a value component to them. It is unlikely that we are ever going to be able to reduce our conceptualization of criminal behaviour and what to do about it to simply a scientific component. No matter how much we learn on the scientific side, there's always going to be this value component coming in.

Denno: I agree with you, but at what point do we declare that a person didn't really intend to engage in criminal behaviour?

Waldman: The point of my comment is that there's never going to be an answer to that question that is exclusively scientifically based; there's always going to be this value component.

Denno: My impression of these scientific defences is that the science is the least relevant; the defences are much more value based. The *Daubert* standard requires that the scientific evidence be reliable. Once the evidence is admitted, thereafter it's a value preference on the part of the jury as to whether they think, for instance, that premenstrual syndrome should reduce a defendant's offence from murder to manslaughter.

Rutter: Surely, the role of science is to provide good evidence on the level of probability for any given outcome associated with any specified risk variable. In principle, the determination of that probability is reasonably straightforward and, with at least some risk variables, sound evidence is already available. Necessarily, of course, the likelihood has to be expressed in probabilistic terms, because that is the way that biology works. From a scientific point of view, there are three main issues, all of which have implications for the way in which the evidence is used in court. Let me take 'being male' in order to illustrate the point. The increase in *relative* risk for crime is very high (Rutter & Giller 1983). Males are seven times more likely than females to be convicted of some crime. However, and this is the second point, the *absolute* risk is quite low. Only about one in five males are convicted. Which is the more relevant statistic? Of course, both are needed in order to obtain a proper picture. The third issue concerns the *mechanism* by which the increase in risk works. With respect to 'maleness', we do not know. However, the courts may be more likely to regard premenstrual tension or mental retardation as an extenuating feature than being male. Presumably, that is because the first two are viewed as more biologically intrinsic, but is that really the case?

The further issue that the court has to consider is what level of probability is needed in order to infer reduced responsibility of some type. It doesn't seem to me that it would make much sense to set any threshold above which the increase in risk would be legally acceptable. That is partly because any threshold would necessarily be extremely arbitrary, partly because if crime arises through the operation of multiple causal risk factors even fairly low absolute probabilities may be important if they are associated with a large increase in relative risk, and partly because the inference on responsibility probably should be based at least as much on the mechanism by which the risk operates.

Denno: I think a probabilistic model is very appealing, but scientifically it's hard to deal with.

Rutter: Why?

Denno: We've established that we have some difficulty finding probabilities. A number of people at this conference have attempted to quantify the genetic components of various behaviours but, for example, we aren't always able to measure their probabilistic contributions relative to other factors. For example, we don't know the probabilistic contribution of genetics as compared with poverty, because scientists rarely have an opportunity to examine genetics and poverty together.

Glover: I would like to make a general point about giving weight to genetic factors as opposed to environmental factors such as poverty. It can be illustrated by looking at the debate over genetic and environmental influences on IQ. People often assume that there's some answer to the question: what proportion of IQ comes from the genes and what proportion from the environment? But, in principle, there is no fixed answer to this. The proportion due to genes is going to depend on how variable the environment is. If, in the ideal case, you gave everybody an identical environment, you could assume that 100% of the variation would be non-environmental. There isn't a fixed answer to that question independent of the degree of variation in the environment.

If, in a particular context, the genetic predisposition is weak, this does not relieve us of all worries about determinism. If, in that context, a genetic predisposition only gives a 10% chance of committing a crime, then the question is whether the remaining 90% is explained environmentally or not. If it's to be explained environmentally, then you end up with complete determinism—it's just a more complex, multifactorial form of determinism. If, on the other hand, you believe in 'free will' in the traditional sense of 'no causal predictability', then you will presumably insert an element of randomness.

There is no precise level of probability of committing a crime where we can say that responsibility is diminished. It's obviously ridiculous to say that 10% probability is too little, but 11% probability is OK. However, this doesn't mean we shouldn't try to draw a rough and ready line. This applies to many questions of social policy; for instance, speed limits. There's no magic about 30 mph or 55 mph, as against 29 or 54 mph; we've got to get a boundary which is roughly right. The important thing is that it's better to be roughly right than precisely wrong. If we refuse to draw a boundary because any boundary is arbitrary, it is like saying we won't have any speed limits at all, because any speed limit is arbitrary.

Denno: Where would you draw the 'roughly right' cut-off point?

Glover: I'm genuinely not sure about that, because I would need to find out what happened in the individual cases where people did commit the crime. My question would be: how difficult was it for them to resist? I would want to talk a lot to them, I'd want to see what had happened on other occasions when they had a different structure of incentives, and so on. It's a very complex issue, and the idea of just plucking a number out the air is much too simple.

Denno: You were saying we should strive for this notion of probability. In one sense, if we know somebody's past offence history, we can predict with, for instance, an 80% likelihood that they're going to commit another offence if they've committed five before it. Is that sufficient?

Glover: No, I don't think it is, because one wants to know the causal story behind it. For instance, when Stalin worked closely with someone, it was more than 50% probable that they would end up being shot. I don't think that means Stalin was absolved from responsibility: one wants to know how he would have responded given a different incentive structure. If he had believed he had anything to lose by eliminating his colleagues, I think one would find a very different pattern of response. It's not mere statistical prediction, it's the kind of causal story that's behind it.

Denno: You say we should look at probabilities, but what you're really doing is looking at probabilities in a very moral- and value-laden frame.

Glover: I said we should look at probabilities, but they're probabilities that are relevant to the test: how hard was it for this person to resist?

Taylor: It is useful to question why all this information is needed in court. In England, the position is very different from the USA in terms of what happens in the various stages of a criminal hearing: in most cases, these kinds of issues are not aired during the trial phase. In relation to murder charges, the issue of responsibility might still be raised here because there is a mandatory consequence for being found guilty of murder. If the facts of the killing are proved, one of the excuses that may reduce the conviction to manslaughter and allow for flexibility in sentencing is that of diminished responsibility. In almost all other cases any pertinent evidence would be presented where, once the facts of an incident are established, it matters most—in the sentencing phase of the hearing, to assist the court with disposal. Where there is a mental disorder, any evidence about that disorder can be taken in mitigation at that point, and also in conjunction with what can or should be done for that person with mental disorder. An offer of treatment can be made, and, if relevant in the light of an explicit risk assessment, recommendations can be advanced as to how that treatment might best be offered—perhaps in security, or perhaps there may be adequate safeguards in the community. In any event, emphasis can be placed on balancing the competing needs of the sick offender and society.

I also wanted to raise the point that the presentation dealt almost exclusively with a single case. While single cases may provide precedents for a class of similar cases, it is as—if not more—important to consider statute. It seems to me that the law is never very responsive to evidence in that respect. This links back to something Jonathan Glover said earlier about second-order decisions; he said that we tend not to blame people for the inability to change their motivation. In fact, in both the USA and the UK, there is a strong tendency to do just that. Behaviours like substance abuse or sexual deviancy and the related offences are predominantly health problems, but one of the most fundamental difficulties in treating either is the sufferer's motivation for change. In fact, society, in the face of the shaky motivation of many, prefers to take a very moral view, and in turn apply the criminal justice system rather than the health system. Consequently, the majority of people with substance abuse or sexual deviancy problems go through the criminal justice system without touching the health system. Indeed, for England and Wales, the relevant mental health law—the Mental Health Act 1983—explicitly excludes the possibility of detaining in hospital for treatment people with a diagnosis in these areas as their sole mental health problem. I am not necessarily advocating compulsory treatment here, but commenting on society's different treatment of these disorders. Do you have any comments on the apparent dissonance between the presented evidence that there are genetic influences on these disorders, that we are probably correct to construe them as diseases, and the law? The statute is against the notion that these are health issues.

Denno: Personally, I would like them to be health issues, particularly substance abuse. In the USA, some legislators are starting to view drug abuse as more of a health issue, if only because drug offenders are taking much of the prison space. Legislators are increasingly saying that perhaps these people should be treated more and punished less.

Waldman: It seems to me at best rather humorous to say that because a particular criminal act has a heritability of 60%, we should send a person to receive health care rather than a prison sentence. These issues start to move very quickly out of the realm of science into the realm of values.

Rutter: Perhaps even more fundamentally, moving from proportion of population variance explained to individual risk is a hazardous enterprise, because the former has nothing directly to do with individual risk as the Down's syndrome example given earlier (p 132) illustrated.

Denno: Don't we have to rely on values, because we have so little else to go by?

Waldman: My point is that even if we do have the science in some ever more complete ways, it's just not going to get rid of the role of values in making such policy decisions.

Rowe: I disagree. To the extent that biological influences are found on criminal behaviour, it might change the view of the public as to the relative value to be placed on therapeutic as opposed to prison-type intervention. It's quite clear that the public has the free-will model of crime; for that reason they believe that the appropriate response to criminal behaviour is imprisonment. Suppose, for example, that an effective therapy were developed for various criminal behaviours. One of the factors against the therapeutic model being applied to crime is that the present therapies are very ineffective, as your recidivism figures indicate. If there were an effective intervention and a dissemination of knowledge to the general public that some criminals are biologically different from other people, those two factors together might lead to a therapeutic approach for a large population of those who formerly were just imprisoned.

Taylor: You are implying that if only we could educate the public, then there could be a different approach. I would like to believe this—it seems like a good way forward—but, unfortunately, there's a lot of evidence that this is not happening. For instance, with substance abuse, the case has been argued that genetic influences are powerful factors in its development. The use of only certain substances is designated criminal in the justice approach—it is very arbitrary. There is growing evidence that treatment is more effective than the moral–punitive response, and yet national preferences and apparently vote-winning promises in political campaigns are for more punitive approaches.

Bouchard: But just making the claim that putting people in jail comprises not doing anything is a powerful value judgement.

Taylor: On the most important point—that is, that treatment is more effective than imprisonment—there is good evidence favouring treatment (e.g. Sowers & Daley 1993). That is not merely a value judgement.

Bouchard: That is still a value judgement, and it doesn't depend on what the facts are. One can legitimately make the value judgement that criminals should be put in jail and argue that this is an appropriate activity or response. Such a person could argue that it is indeed 'doing something'. You and I may not agree with this person because we hold different values.

Glover: Inevitably, we're talking about values. I don't regard values as something we shouldn't discuss or that is embarrassing to mention. We're trying to see what the social implications should be of an increasing understanding of scientific explanations of various kinds of criminality. It's quite plausible to suppose that, as we gain a better understanding, we will indeed move over more from a punitive model to a treatment model. In my view, with some qualifications, this is largely desirable. It will come about partly because we'll shift to a more deterministic mode of thinking, but partly because the treatment mode will be manifestly more effective than locking people up in places where they just learn how to commit crimes from other prisoners. But if we are to move over to a treatment model, we need to think very carefully about some of the civil liberty implications. Although it's desirable not to have vindictive retributive punishment, there are also risks in putting someone into the hands of social workers and psychiatrists with infinite power to decide whether the person is still ill and needs further therapy. One needs to think very clearly about what the limitations of power should be in the treatment model.

Rutter: Following Barbara Wootton's lead some 40 years ago, many commentators have argued that the severity of the crime is an important consideration in deciding whether society has the right to intervene therapeutically, as well as punitively (see Morris et al 1980). The 'need for treatment' has sometimes been used to justify very considerable restrictions in liberty that seem out of proportion to the offence. The compulsory imposition of treatment needs to be decided on the basis of both the justification to intervene because of the seriousness of the offence and the evidence that treatment is likely to be effective. Thus, it would clearly be unacceptable to require several years of compulsory in-patient care for stealing a milk bottle from someone's doorstep, even if it could be shown that the treatment was 100% effective. The need to consider society's right to intervene is an important issue.

Daly: As far as treatment models are concerned, I think the issue of civil liberties is more serious than is being acknowledged. The medical model for the treatment of diseases is that they are clearly contrary to the diseased individual's interests, and in alleviating them you're doing that individual a service. It's far from clear to me that interventions against people who have committed self-interested acts that violate the interests of other people, are doing those individuals any service. It's too easy to define antisocial behaviour as behaviour that violates the interests of those who are holding the gun. It's too easy to define a defence that requires therapy from the perspective of the person whose interests are violated, and to intervene in ways that are contrary to the interests of the person being treated.

Rutter: Jonathan Glover, I'm puzzled that people haven't challenged you more about the issue of determinism. I don't understand why it is assumed that a scientific approach has to be deterministic, because biology doesn't work like that. It is probabilistic. For example, if you think of brain development, the migration of each neuron is not genetically programmed. Rather, a self-correcting system is set up in which there is migration and then selective pruning. There are many other similar examples. Biology works in terms of self-adaptation and self-correcting systems. It seems to me that a strictly deterministic view of biology is inconsistent with the evidence.

Glover: I'm not sure I agree, although it's true that when we're talking biologically, characteristically we're talking in terms of probabilities rather than 100% certainties.

Rutter: Surely it is more than that? Of course, to an important extent, probabilities rather than certainties reflect our ignorance. There are numerous examples in which causal explanations come to replace the invocation of 'chance' once we understand how the causal processes operate. Moreover, proving chance (i.e. a negative) is never really possible. Nevertheless, it seems to me that chance is a real phenomenon and, furthermore, one that constitutes an important element in how biological systems operate (see Goodman 1991). For example, it appears that which X chromosome is inactivated is randomly determined. Similarly, in Kartagener's syndrome, whether the viscera are in the usual place or right-to-left inverted seems random. It is not just that we do not know how it occurs, but also that the occurrence is 50:50, which suggests chance. A reluctance to accept complete determination derives, so far as I'm concerned, from my understanding of biological systems and not only from our ignorance about causal mechanisms. We should always strive to take our knowledge of causal mechanisms to both a more detailed and a deeper level, but I doubt that this could, even in theory, lead to complete determinism.

Glover: But it is a 'chance' process at *that* level of explanation. Is it then plausible to say that there is simply no causal explanation at all? In principle, you can't prove the absence of causal explanation. Scientists have characteristically been able to go down to lower levels of explanation, where things which seem merely chance at a higher level turn out to have some explanation at a lower level. Isn't it a bit dogmatic to say that we're not going to find a causal explanation? The scientific attitude is one of open-mindedness coupled with a kind of methodological determinism—that's to say, scientists never give up looking for causes.

Cairns: I think two issues are on the board today. One is the issue of moral judgement and our moral reasoning, and the other is the factors that may account for behaviour.

One of the counterintuitive findings in modern psychological research has been that moral judgements are virtually independent of moral behaviours. The assessments of moral reasoning and moral behaviour are really two different domains. Each has their lawful characteristics, but there's only modest linkage between the two.

Second, I'm terribly concerned about divorcing behaviour from biology. If we conceptualize behaviour outside of a biological framework, we're simply missing the boat. It's not a one-way direction from genes to actions: there's plenty of evidence to indicate that the behaviour changes the biology of individuals in significant ways, both in the immediate proximal factor as well as in the long term. If we lose sight of this basic phenomenon and its implications, we are going to be caught in the same intellectual cul-de-sacs that common sense has wrought us. Presumably, our job is to bring out new information and new paradigms.

References

Goodman R 1991 Growing together and growing apart: the non-genetic forces on children in the same family. In: McGuffin P, Murray R (eds) The new genetics of mental illness. Butterworth-Heinemann, Oxford, p 212–224

Morris A, Giller H, Szwed E, Geach H 1980 Justice for children. Macmillan, London

Rutter M, Giller H 1983 Juvenile delinquency: trends and perspectives. Penguin, Harmondsworth, Middlesex

Sowers WE, Daley DC 1993 Compulsory treatment of substance use disorders. Crim Behav & Ment Health 3:403–415

Concluding remarks

Sir Michael Rutter

Department of Child Psychiatry, Institute of Psychiatry, De Crespigny Park, London SE5 8AF, UK

During the course of this symposium, we have seen something of the range of research strategies that are being employed to investigate the role of genetic factors on individual differences in liabilities to engage in antisocial behaviour. It is clear that this field of research is active and productive, with some very interesting and important findings that carry promise that over the next decade we may gain a much improved understanding of the factors involved in the genesis of antisocial behaviour. Equally, it is apparent that researchers in this arena are constructively self-critical, with a deep awareness of the methodological hazards to be avoided, the inconsistencies across studies to be explained, and the marked limitations in the inferences that can be drawn from the findings so far. Nevertheless, it is evident that genetic factors do play a significant role in antisocial behaviour and that their investigation is likely to be useful, with respect to both theory and practice.

Despite that conclusion, it is obvious that the assumption in some media reports that researchers are involved in a search for the 'gene for crime' is seriously mistaken. Equally, the assumption by some critics of genetic research that genetic studies are predicated on a notion that there is a single homogeneous entity characterized by antisocial behaviour could not be more wrong. Not only does genetic research test for heterogeneity, but also genetic findings have been particularly informative on the nature of some important sources of heterogeneity. Thus, twin studies data indicate that genetic factors are probably particularly important in those varieties of antisocial behaviour associated with early-onset, pervasive hyperactivity. Conversely, it is likely that they are least influential in the case of adolescent-onset delinquency that has not been preceded by hyperactivity. At first sight, it might seem paradoxical that twin studies also show a stronger genetic effect with adult crime than juvenile delinquency. The paradox, however, is apparent rather than real because the varieties of childhood antisocial behaviour most likely to persist into adult life are those associated with early-onset hyperactivity (Farrington et al 1990). The findings from adoption studies indicate—perhaps surprisingly, and certainly counter to prevailing views in the general public—that the genetic component in violent crime is less than that in petty property crime. Adoptee data also point to the need to differentiate criminality associated with alcohol abuse from that unassociated with alcohol problems. The finding of a possible link between some forms of violent crime and schizophrenia indicates a further source of heterogeneity to be explored. The Dutch kindred data serve to remind us, too, that occasionally (but probably rarely) aggression may derive from an inherited medical disorder. The XYY chromosomal anomaly, although *not* leading to violent behaviour as first thought, also is associated with behavioural features that increase the likelihood of antisocial acts, although it does not cause them directly (Ratcliffe 1994).

The concept of a 'gene for crime' is mistaken, however, for reasons other than the heterogeneity of antisocial behaviour. Genes do not, and cannot, code for socially defined behaviours. Also, they do not lead people directly to commit criminal acts. That is, there may be an increased (in some instances greatly increased) propensity to aggression or antisocial behaviour, but whether or not the affected individual actually commits some criminal act will also be dependent on environmental predisposing factors and situational circumstances at the time. That will be the case to a far greater extent with multifactorially determined traits, as applies to all but a tiny fraction of antisocial behaviour.

The real interest, and value, of genetic findings does *not* lie in quantification of the genetic component but rather in understanding *how* the risk is mediated and *how* genetic factors combine with environmental influences to predispose to antisocial behaviour. This critically important question is being tackled both at the behavioural level and the neurochemical level. Thus, investigators are testing whether the risks are mediated through hyperactivity, impulsivity, sensation-seeking, reduced anxiety in stressful circumstances, predisposition to substance abuse (alcohol or illicit drugs), or aggressivity. The mere listing of these postulated attributes or personality features serves as an important reminder that the risks for antisocial behaviour may derive from characteristics that are not in themselves necessarily negative or harmful. A degree of risk-taking might be considered a useful element in creative research (!), and a diminished autonomic and behavioural response to stress may be protective against emotional disorders (see e.g. Kagan 1995). Thus, if future research should succeed in identifying genes associated with an increased liability to antisocial behaviour, it does *not* follow that society would want to eliminate those genes. Rather, the need may be to develop better means of channelling the trait appropriately to foster adaptive, instead of antisocial, outcomes.

Neurochemical mediation is being explored primarily in relation to the dopamine and serotonin systems. In this symposium, we have heard about both human and animal studies, each of which has its own particular strengths. The animal work gains from the possibility of greater experimental control, and the human work from greater ecological validity. The evidence is convincing that serotonin plays a role in predisposition to violent behaviour but the same evidence indicates that the vulnerability is not for antisocial behaviour as such, but rather for risk-taking behaviour that includes suicidal as well as antisocial acts.

The symposium noted the value of combining different quantitative genetic research designs: twin, adoptee, blended family and offspring of twins. Each has particular strengths and specific limitations. Fortunately, the patterns of strengths and limitations are not the same across designs; accordingly, if each produces much the same answer, there can be considerable confidence in the conclusions (Rutter et al 1990). Nevertheless, it is necessary that genetic research critically examines the key assumptions of the different designs; regrettably, this has not always happened. There is a need, for example, to consider the effects of biological differences between monochorionic and dichorionic monozygotic twin pairs (see e.g. Bouchard & Propping 1993), the effects of assortative mating (see e.g. Quinton et al 1993), the effects of secular trends (see e.g. Rutter & Smith 1995), intergenerational associations, and concerns about the selective placement of adoptees. Our discussions highlighted the potential value of looking at discrepancies in findings across different designs—not to find any hypothetical 'true' value for heritability, but rather because the discrepancies may serve to provide a focus on possible genetic and environmental mediating mechanisms. We noted the particular value of longitudinal designs for testing causal hypotheses about the factors responsible for changes in an individual's behaviour over time (see Rutter 1994a), and the importance of across-twin, across-trait analyses to investigate the relationships among different risk variables for antisocial behaviour (see e.g. Silberg et al 1995).

The past decade has made overt the huge potential of molecular genetic research. The discovery of microsatellite markers and the development of automated methods of genomic research have, together, opened the way for the study of multifactorially determined complex traits or disorders, as is well illustrated by the findings with respect to diabetes (Goodfellow & Schmitt 1994). Nevertheless, if the expected fruits of molecular genetic research are to be realized, it will be more important than ever to pay careful attention to the delineation of phenotypes, to consider genetic heterogeneity, to cross-validate findings in different samples, and to combine linkage, allelic and association strategies (see Rutter 1994b, Lander & Schork 1994). There is undoubted value in the study of unusual families, such as the Dutch kindred, but equally (as Han Brunner pointed out) the need to avoid the danger of rushing to premature conclusions on their meaning. Traditionally, the main method has been to start with a phenotype and then to use molecular genetic methods to test for linkage with genetic markers of one sort or another. David Goldman reminded us that it may be equally useful (in some circumstances more useful) to approach the question the other way round through what he termed direct gene analysis—namely, studying the behavioural consequences of candidate genes with known effects on neurochemistry.

Prompted particularly by Stephen Maxson's paper, we noted the value of animal studies because they may suggest candidate genes worth examining in humans, because they may allow the testing of hypotheses deriving from human research, and because they provide a means of examining the route from gene to gene product to behaviour through the use of animal models. The limitations of animal models were noted with respect to the lack of genetic or behavioural isomorphism across species, the problems of extrapolating from pathological extremes to variations within the normal range, and the difficulties involved in inferring gene action from gene knockout. We need to be aware of these issues and to take steps to deal with them appropriately; but the problems do not prevent animal studies from being highly informative, if they are used in the right way with proper attention to both conceptual and methodological issues.

The research findings clearly point to the role of serotonin systems in violence, but we noted some important apparent contradictions and inconsistencies across studies. For example, genetic factors seem to play an important role in the serotonin system (see e.g. Goldman et al 1995, Virkkunen et al 1995, this volume), yet genetic influences seem weak in the liability to violent behaviour (see e.g. Bohman 1995, Brennan et al 1995, this volume). Why? Many studies indicate an association between *low* serotonin levels and aggression, yet in the Dutch kindred *high* serotonin levels were characteristic of the affected individuals showing marked aggressivity. Why? Of course, too, it is important that we avoid the wrong-headed assumption that neurochemical changes necessarily *cause* behavioural change. The interplay between hormones and behaviour is two-way. Changes in social circumstance or in behaviour may lead to hormonal alterations, as well as the other way round (Rutter 1986).

In our discussions of genetic effects, we have been aware throughout that, for the most part, genetic research focuses on individual differences in liability. That is a most important causal question but it is far from the only one (see e.g. Rutter & Smith 1995). Thus, other research designs are needed to investigate the marked rise in crime that has occurred in most western countries over the past half century, or the huge differences between the USA and Europe in the rate of homicide, or the differences in crime rates among ethnic groups, or sex differences in rates and patterns of antisocial behaviour. Genetic research may be informative on those questions, but there is a real danger of making misleading and erroneous generalizations from within-group findings to between-group explanations. Another facet of the causal question concerns the situational factors involved in translating an underlying liability to antisocial behaviour into the committing of actual antisocial acts (see Clarke 1985). Equally, there is a need to consider the effects of person–environment correlations and interactions (see e.g. Wachs & Plomin 1991, Plomin 1994, Rutter et al 1995). People act in ways that serve to select and shape environments and part of the genetic influence may lie in these effects.

It is not sufficient, however, to consider the interplay between individuals and their environments in individual terms. That may be adequate with respect to, say, some forms of stealing, but clearly it is *not* adequate with respect to aggression or other forms of antisocial behaviour involving an interaction between two or more individuals. Dyadic and polyadic effects need to be studied. This has been well recognized by many investigators studying human behaviour but, as Stephen Maxson's paper demonstrated, the same issues apply to interactions between mice! The importance of situational effects on antisocial behaviour is generally accepted, but our understanding of how these work is decidedly limited. Improved ways of conceptualizing, measuring and classifying situations are much needed.

Martin Daly drew our attention to the value of an evolutionary perspective on antisocial behaviour; for example, with regard to the relative likelihood of violence to kin and non-kin. Our discussion of these issues served as a useful reminder that evolutionary considerations may be very valuable in understanding behaviour, even when, for one reason or another, evolutionary forces have only a quite limited opportunity to continue to operate in industrialized human societies.

The evidence from cultural anthropology reinforced a concern evident throughout the symposium; namely, that we should beware of equating violence with disorder, or psychopathology, or abnormality of any kind. Whether we like it or not, a propensity to violence in predisposing circumstances is part of the human condition. Equally, the level of violence in any social group is much influenced by social circumstances and by opportunity. The issue of continuities and discontinuities between normality and disorder brought us back to another theme that has been pervasive throughout our discussions. The behavioural traits that carry an increased risk for crime may not only be normally distributed but also may not be inherently negative. Many human characteristics carry with them both a negative and a positive potential. As I have noted, the presence of a risk factor does not necessarily mean that we should seek to remove that characteristic from the population. Often, we should instead consider how to actuate the potential for a good outcome.

All of us, in our research, are acutely aware of the ethical and moral issues inherent in the study of antisocial behaviour. Nevertheless, it may well be that we are least agreed on how best to deal with the morality component. Thus, there is the major difficulty of knowing how to invoke the concept of free will. All of us, in our daily life, act as if we and others have a choice in how we behave and hence are in some meaningful way responsible for our actions. So far as I am concerned, this is inherent in the probabilistic ways that biological systems operate (see e.g. Crick 1988). Accordingly, I was surprised by some people's claim that causal factors could operate in more deterministic ways than seem to me to be plausible. Nevertheless, although we may not be agreed on the details, we are all aware that, in considering societal responses to antisocial behaviour, moral issues are inescapable and need to be taken very seriously.

Finally, in our discussion we considered legal implications. Yet again, we noted the need to deal with risks in probabilistic terms, together with the danger of moving from population statistics to individual risks. Thus, a person may have a *relative* risk for antisocial behaviour that is greatly above population norms, but still have an *absolute* risk that means that serious crime is more likely *not* to occur than to take place. Undoubtedly, that poses a problem for the courts in deciding when biological (or for that matter psychosocial) factors should serve as extenuating features, either requiring a reduced sentence (because criminal intent was less) or a therapeutic rather than a retributive or punitive response (because the crime derived from psychopathology of some kind). We acknowledged that an informed appreciation of biological risks may well influence public values. On the whole, this appears to constitute a potential for good. But, it is crucial to consider civil-liberty issues and to strike a careful balance between the health/welfare perspective and individual rights.

Although none of us would wish to claim that our discussions have solved the problems that I set out in my introduction, the issues have been clarified to a worthwhile extent. I have learned a great deal from both the empirical findings and concepts that have been presented; probably, that applies to all of us. Altogether, it has been a most interesting and informative few days and I am confident that our future research will profit from the new perspective gained from the interdisciplinary interchanges that have taken place.

References

Bohman M 1995 Predisposition to criminality: Swedish adoption studies in retrospect. In: Genetics of criminal and antisocial behaviour. Wiley, Chichester (Ciba Found Symp 194) p 99–114

Bouchard TJ Jr, Propping P (eds) 1993 Twins as a tool of behavioral genetics. Wiley, Chichester

Brennan PA, Mednick SA, Jacobsen B 1995 Assessing the role of genetics in crime using adoption cohorts. In: Genetics of criminal and antisocial behaviour. Wiley, Chichester (Ciba Found Symp 194) p 115–128

Clark RVG 1985 Jack Tizard memorial lecture: delinquency, environment and intervention. J Child Psychol Psychiatry Allied Discip 26:505–523

Crick F 1988 What mad pursuit: a personal view of scientific discovery. Basic Books, New York

Farrington DP, Loeber R, Van Kammen WB 1990 Long-term criminal outcomes of hyperactivity–impulsivity–attention deficit and conduct problems in childhood. In: Robins LN, Rutter M (eds) Straight and devious pathways from childhood to adulthood. Cambridge University Press, Cambridge, p 62–81

Goldman D, Lappalainen J, Ozaki N 1995 Direct analysis of candidate genes in impulsive behaviours. In: Genetics of criminal and antisocial behaviour. Wiley, Chichester (Ciba Found Symp 194) p 139–154

Goodfellow PN, Schmitt K 1994 From the simple to the complex. Nature 371:104–105

Kagan J 1995 Temperamental contributions to the development of social behavior. In: Magnusson D (ed) The life-span development of individuals: behavioral, neurobiological and psychosocial perspectives. Cambridge University Press, New York, in press

Lander ES, Schork NJ 1994 Genetic dissection of complex traits. Science 265:2037–2048

Plomin R 1994 Genetics and experience: the developmental interplay between nature and nurture. Sage, Newbury Park, CA

Quinton D, Pickles AR, Maughan B, Rutter M 1993 Partners, peers and pathways: assortative pairing and continuities in conduct disorder. Dev Psychopathol 5:763–783

Ratcliffe SG 1994 The psychosocial and psychiatric consequences of sex chromosomal abnormalities in children based on population studies. In: Poutska F (ed) Basic approaches to genetic and molecular biological developmental psychiatry. Quintessenz, Berlin, p 99–122

Rutter M 1986 Meyerian psychobiology, personality development, and the role of life experiences. Am J Psychiatry 143:9

Rutter M 1994a Beyond longitudinal data: causes, consequences, changes, and continuity. J Consult Clin Psychol 62:928–940

Rutter M 1994b Psychiatric genetics: research challenges and pathways forward. Am J Med Genet 54:185–198

Rutter M, Smith DJ 1995 Psychosocial disorders in young people: time trends and their causes. Wiley, Chichester

Rutter M, Bolton P, Harrington R, Le Couteur A, Macdonald H, Simonoff E 1990 Genetic factors in child psychiatric disorders I. A review of research strategies. J Child Psychol Psychiatry Allied Discip 31:3–37

Rutter M, Champion L, Quinton D, Maughan B, Pickles A 1995 Understanding individual differences in environmental risk exposure. In: Moen P, Elder G, Luscher K (eds) Examining lives in context: perspective on the ecology of human development. American Psychological Association, Washington, DC

Silberg J, Rutter M, Meyer J et al 1995 Comorbidity among symptoms of hyperactivity and conduct problems in male and female juvenile twins. J Child Psychol Psychiatry Allied Discip, in press

Virkkunen M, Goldman D, Linnoila M 1995 Serotonin in alcoholic violent offenders. In: Genetics of criminal and antisocial behaviour. Wiley, Chichester (Ciba Found Symp 194) p 168–182

Wachs TD, Plomin R 1991 Conceptualization and measurement of organism–environment interaction. APA, Washington, DC

Index of contributors

Non-participating co-authors are indicated by asterisks. Entries in bold type indicate papers; other entries refer to discussion contributions.

Indexes compiled by Liza Weinkove

273

Subject index